PRAISE FOR *UND*

At last—a book that thoroughly challenges the myth that movements for reproductive rights and freedoms have been a mainly white, middle-class women's domain. Through meticulous documentation of African American, Asian and Pacific Islander American, Latina, and Native American women's activism since the 1960s to achieve sexual and reproductive justice for all, *Undivided Rights* sets the record straight about the broad meanings and antiracist, anticolonial roots of struggles to achieve reproductive justice in the United States. This book is a must read for everyone interested in the intersections of gender, race, and class; the dynamics of contemporary social movements; and the power of women of color to change history.

—Rosalind Pollack Petchesky
Global Prescriptions: Gendering Health and Human Rights

Undivided Rights goes a long way toward breathing new life into the "our bodies, our choice" mantra. By examining reproductive rights issues through women of color's eyes, the authors force a conversation that focuses not merely on one's sex but also on one's race, class, and social status, therefore radically obliterating the notion that reproductive justice issues are colorless, ageless, and classless. This is a necessary book that will help guide the reproductive rights movement into the twenty-first century.

—Dawn Lundy Martin
The Fire This Time: Young Activists and the New Feminism

Give *Undivided Rights* your undivided attention! This excellent book is a valuable gift to activists, scholars, and others interested in the powerful, vibrant, and inclusive reproductive justice organizing by women of color over the past quarter century in the United States. The authors reveal a history too rarely told of African American, Latina, Native American, and Asian and Pacific Islander American women developing theory, organizations, and public policy agendas that encompass the diversity of women's reproductive health needs and the mighty potential of an inclusive vision of reproductive rights.

—Sandra Morgen
Into Our Own Hands: The Women's Health Movement in the US, 1969-1990

Undivided Rights provides powerful, provocative stories of grassroots organizing and community health among contemporary women of color.

—Vicki L. Ruiz
From Out of the Shadows: Mexican Women in Twentieth-Century America

Undivided Rights is feminist political history at its finest. Its case studies bring alive the powerful story of how women of color organizing has transformed the reproductive rights movement by courageously challenging both population control and anti-abortion forces. In analyzing the political experiences of the past, *Undivided Rights* provides a rich legacy of strategies for the present and future. Clearly written and persuasively argued, it will appeal to a broad audience of activists, students, scholars, and anyone interested in the history of race and reproduction and progressive feminist organizing in the United States.

—Betsy Hartmann
Reproductive Rights and Wrongs: The Global Politics of Population Control

Does "reproductive choice" mean something different for women of color than white women? In *Undivided Rights*, Silliman, Fried, Ross, and Gutiérrez unequivocally answer the question by deconstructing the dichotomy of "pro-choice"/"pro-life" and usher us into the realities of women of color, where reproductive rights are inseparable from issues of class, race, sexuality, ability, and nationality, and the struggle for individual rights transforms into collective movements for comprehensive justice. Foregrounding the work in four communities of color . . . the authors not only document the histories of women's organizing and resistance but also challenge the myth of minority women's apathy and follower mentality. *Undivided Rights* is incisively analytical, affirming of women of color, and yet charts the possibility of interracial collaboration as well as redefining "reproductive rights" for all. Truly inspirational!

—Shamita Das Dasgupta
A Patchwork Shawl: Chronicles of South Asian Women in America

Undivided Rights is an important addition to both the history of reproductive rights and the current movement. By documenting the contributions and struggles of women of color, *Undivided Rights* highlights rarely heard perspectives and facets of women's ongoing fight for justice. These strong voices speak to the movement and to the greater society. The authors' own activism enriches the narrative and analysis. A must read for anyone interested in women's lives.

—Laura Kaplan
The Story of Jane: The Legendary Underground Feminist Abortion Service

UNDIVIDED RIGHTS

Women of Color
Organize for
Reproductive Justice

JAEL SILLIMAN

MARLENE GERBER FRIED

LORETTA ROSS

ELENA R. GUTIÉRREZ

Haymarket Books
Chicago, Illinois

First published by South End Press in Cambridge, Massachusetts.

This edition published in 2016 by
Haymarket Books
P.O. Box 180165
Chicago, IL 60618
773-583-7884
www.haymarketbooks.org
info@haymarketbooks.org

ISBN: 978-1-60846-617-7

Trade distribution:
In the US, Consortium Book Sales and Distribution, www.cbsd.com
In Canada, Publishers Group Canada, www.pgcbooks.ca
In the UK, Turnaround Publisher Services, www.turnaround-uk.com
All other countries, Publishers Group Worldwide, www.pgw.com

This book was published with the generous support of Lannan Foundation
and Wallace Action Fund.

Printed in Canada by union labor.

Library of Congress Cataloging-in-Publication data is available.

10 9 8 7 6 5 4 3 2 1

RECYCLED
Paper made from
recycled material
FSC
www.fsc.org   FSC® C103567

Contents

Preface to the Second Edition

In 2004, when *Undivided Rights: Women of Color Organizing for Reproductive Justice* was first published, the vibrant history of women of color organizing around reproductive issues was largely unknown to the general public and scarcely recognized in academic research. Even many within the reproductive rights, choice, and health movements were just beginning to realize the breadth of organizing in communities of color in resistance to reproductive oppression. The organizations profiled in the book were engaging in reproductive justice organizing but without self-consciously using the term. The SisterSong conference, held in Atlanta in November 2003, revived the concept of reproductive justice.[1] A year later, a large contingent marched under the banner "Women of Color for Reproductive Justice" in the spring 2004 March for Women's Lives in Washington, DC.

These events and the release of *Undivided Rights* heralded the increasing role and power of women of color in the US reproductive rights movement. The book signaled an important shift occurring among those who identified with reproductive justice: a transformation from viewing women of color primarily as *objects* of reproductive control[2] to focusing on their *agency* in determining their reproductive lives. Furthermore, it underscored the potential and ability of the reproductive justice movement and its multiple constituencies to produce new theories, new knowledge, and new forms of activism.

We decided to feature "reproductive justice" in the title of the book because it was clear from our research that this framework had the potential to be an empowering theme for women of color. The activists we spoke to voiced agreement about the need for an alternative to the limiting notion of "choice"—one that would represent the full range of their organizing, all of which was necessary in order for women in their communities to have greater control of all aspects of their reproductive health and lives. Reproductive justice is broad in its scope and fore-grounds the needs of low-income people and communities, especially those of color, who face individual, community, and structural challenges to securing their reproductive health, human rights, and well being.

Reproductive justice is a *theory*, a *practice*, and a *strategy* that can provide a common language and broader unity in movements for women's health and rights. It defines the complicated, intersectional injuries endured and enables the re-envisioning of collective futures. The power and elasticity of reproductive justice is derived from its ability to provide a grounded theory that holds the complex and changing ways that women of color define themselves.

Three of the groups profiled (NLHO [National Latina Health Organization], NAWHO [National Asian Women's Health Organization], and AAWE/BWRJ [African American Women Evolving / Black Women for Reproductive Justice]) no longer exist, but the roles that each played as leaders in this movement are essential to the historical record.[3] Today there are many new organizations founded and led by women of color, as well as allied groups that proudly count themselves as part of the reproductive justice movement and use this intersectional, human rights–based framework.[4]

Some mainstream groups that have historically been at the center of the pro-choice movement now also use the concept of reproductive justice. However, we recognize that using a particular terminology does not in itself necessarily transform an organization or a movement. In our estimation, changing priorities beyond issues of choice and access to abortion and contraception has been a more challenging process, as have efforts to introduce reproductive justice to the media and to the general public. News reports and discussions about reproductive politics continue to focus on threats to abortion rights. For example, the anti-abortion battle to defund and destroy Planned Parenthood has taken center stage in 2015. While such attacks genuinely threaten all women's reproductive rights and health, other issues that are also central to the lives, health, and well-being of low-income people of color and their families and communities are being eclipsed.

The wide-angle approach of the reproductive justice movement has enriched the political landscape by bringing in new constituencies and allies and deepened our understanding of how reproductive rights and freedom are linked to other human rights and social justice issues.

Reproductive justice efforts in their manifold expressions have multiplied since the publication of *Undivided Rights*. Here we include a snapshot of some of the major accomplishments of the reproductive justice movement since 2004.[5]

- **March for Women's Lives:** In 2004, the leaders of reproductive justice organizations (including the Black Women's Health Imperative and the National Latina Institute for Reproductive Health) were a catalytic force in renaming the March for Freedom of Choice the March for Women's Lives. This was important, as it better represented the intersectionality of the experiences of most women. This wider framing of the issue, along with the naming of Loretta Ross as codirector of the march, and the inclusion of more women of color in the organizing, resulted in increased participation of women of color and activists from many social justice organizations across the nation. It was one of the largest protest marches in the history of the United States.

- **Vision Papers on Reproductive Justice:** In 2005, Forward Together (formerly Asian Pacific Islanders for Reproductive Health) published "A New Vision for Advancing Our Movement for Reproductive Health, Reproductive Rights and Reproductive Justice." The report provided a more developed analysis of the reproductive justice framework from an organizing perspective by separating reproductive health, rights, and justice into three distinct but complementary parts of the movement. The report has become a valuable training tool. The paper was selected as one of the key documents in the Reproductive Justice Virtual Library. In 2006, the Center for American Progress (CAP) and the Women's Health Leadership Network, which was comprised primarily of women of color leaders and reproductive justice organizations, published "More Than a Choice," an early effort to introduce reproductive justice concepts to mainstream organizations. While these two pieces are themselves significantly influential, they also signaled an increasing emergence of reports, research, and policy analysis from reproductive justice organizations that are widely used by reproductive activists and beyond.

- **Polling of Latino Community on Reproductive Health:** Opinion research led by the National Latina Institute for Reproductive

Health and the Reproductive Health Technologies Project (NLIRH) conducted between 2006 and 2011 provided groundbreaking public opinion research on abortion and how to talk about the issue with a range of communities. The research, which oversampled Black, Latino, and younger respondents, informed major shifts in the field and successful state and federal advocacy, as well as the research, messaging, and outreach of PPFA (Planned Parenthood Federation of America). It included the largest-ever comprehensive bilingual poll of Latinos' attitudes on abortion, which demonstrated that they are much more supportive of abortion than popularly believed.

- **Race- and Sex-Selective Abortion Bans:** The National Asian Pacific American Women's Forum (NAPAWF) has been on the front lines of the race- and sex-selective abortion ban debate since 2009. Its work shows how issues of abortion play out in different communities and the ways that legislation that purports to counter sexism and racism is in fact being used to undermine women's rights. NAPAWF continues to provide in-depth and critical analysis of the impact of these bills on women of color and their potential to divide progressive movements and further chip away at *Roe v. Wade*.

- **"Personhood" in Colorado:** The Colorado Organization for Latina Opportunity and Reproductive Rights (COLOR) has helped to lead several successful efforts to defeat "personhood" amendments in Colorado. COLOR's work has been focused at the coalition and community level on educating, advocating for, and organizing communities to recognize the dangers of, and to vote against, this type of legislation.

- **Racist Billboard Abortion Campaigns:** In early 2010, billboards stating "Black Children Are an Endangered Species" and "The Most Dangerous Place for an African American Is in the Womb" were erected in Georgia, Illinois, Missouri, Florida, Texas, California, Tennessee, and many other states, attacking the dignity of Black women and Latinas who have abortions. Reproductive justice organizations led efforts nationally to raise awareness of these attacks and successfully removed these billboards from their communities. SisterSong formed the Trust Black Women Partnership to combat future attacks and also released the policy report "Race, Gender and Abortion: How Reproductive Justice Activists Won in Georgia," which detailed how women of color and their allies defeated legislation that sought to expand abortion restrictions by linking race and gender to abortion.

- **Louisiana's "Crime Against Nature" Law (CANL):** In March 2012, Women with a Vision led a statewide effort that resulted in Louisiana's CANL being declared unconstitutional. This victory made it possible for hundreds of individuals who were over-criminalized due to race, sexual orientation, or gender to have "crime against nature" by solicitation (CANS) convictions removed from their records. Because of its bold work, Women with a Vision's office, where they provide much-needed services, was firebombed after this victory.

- **Early Access to Abortion:** In 2013, Black Women for Wellness and California Latinas for Reproductive Justice leadership, as part of a California statewide coalition, helped pass one of the most far-reaching and progressive pieces of abortion rights legislation in the country, AB 154. The groundbreaking research done by SisterSong, Black Women for Wellness, the Black Women's Health Imperative, New Voices Pittsburgh, and SPARK Reproductive Justice NOW, in partnership with the Communications Consortium Media Center, on "African-American attitudes on abortion, contraception and teen sexual health," provided valuable data to help persuade Black legislators and associations to support the legislation.

- **Albuquerque 20-Week Abortion Ban:** Young Women United and Strong Families New Mexico were crucial in helping to defeat an Albuquerque ballot measure seeking to ban abortions after twenty weeks. In this case, the leadership of women of color changed the abortion debate, shifting it away from pro-choice language and creating messages based on deeply held community values. The victory also sent a strong message to anti-abortion groups that sought to use Albuquerque as a test site for future initiatives across the country.

- **Responding to Environmental Violence:** The Native Youth Sexual Health Network has been instrumental in continuing to respond to the impacts of extractive industries on the sexual and reproductive health of Indigenous women, youth, and their communities. The network's media arts justice campaigns, including "Connected to Body, Connected to Land" and "Our Bodies Are Not Terra Nullius," have sparked a number of community-based initiatives to make the connections between violence to the land and violence to our bodies.

- **Medicaid Expansion for LGBTQ Communities:** SPARK Reproductive Justice NOW released four fact sheets and an infographic. These include expert legal analysis provided by the National Center for Lesbian Rights that outlines the benefits of the Affordable Care Act and the impact of Medicaid expansion in Georgia for Black women and the Black LGBTQ community. The Sylvia Rivera Law Project (along with the Legal Aid Society and Willkie Farr & Gallagher LLP) filed a federal class action lawsuit against the New York State Department of Health on behalf of two transwomen who were denied medically necessary health-care coverage. In both states, organizations led by people of color are working against discriminatory and transphobic Medicaid exclusion within marginalized communities.

- **Standing Our Ground: Raising Our Voices Against Reproductive Oppression, Violence Against Women, and Mass Incarceration:** SisterSong Women of Color for Reproductive Justice played a leadership role in rallying support in defense of Marissa Alexander, an African American woman prosecuted for defending herself against her abusive husband.

- **Organizing against the Criminalization of Pregnant Women of Color:** NAPAWF, along with National Advocates for Pregnant Women (NAPW), are leading the effort to have the sentences of Purvi Patel and Bei Bei Shwei reduced or removed. Patel and Shwei, both Asian American, are the first to be charged under Indiana's feticide law.

In all these instances, women of color–led organizations showed how racism impacts the reproductive rights and health of their respective communities. They conducted research, advocacy, and organizing, and their work highlights the systematic gendered and racist workings of the criminal justice system. Racial justice is a key aspect of reproductive justice. Reproductive justice activists are actively engaged in the Black Lives Matter movement and the struggle for immigrant rights. The Black Lives Matter movement has brought greater visibility and mobilized resistance to racism and white supremacy, even as the underlying structures in society continue to support them. Similarly, the escalation of attacks on access to abortion and contraception has been a catalyst for political action. Accelerating anti-Black and anti-abortion violence are not unrelated. Both are examples of rogue vigilantes using deadly terror for social control. Reproductive justice activists demand the right to use abortion and birth control, as well as the right to parent their children in safe and healthy environments, free from violence by individuals or the state. Unequal citizenship intersects with racist brutality, undermining the basic right of all children to be safe.

The reproductive justice approach has changed policy priorities around abortion access and other issues. Reproductive justice organizations and their allies have created a strong coalition to restore public funding for abortion, including rescinding the Hyde Amendment. These efforts have led to the Equal Access to Abortion Coverage in Health Insurance (EACH Woman) Act, introduced by Congresswoman Barbara Lee (CA-13) in 2015. This proposed legislation will ensure coverage for the full range of pregnancy-related care, including abortion. Reproductive justice activists are working on initiatives to enable women to obtain the support they need to have and raise children. This includes campaigns to end shackling during prison births, to raise the minimum wage, to expand government funding for child care, and other efforts to ensure the dignity and well being of women, children, and trans* people. Their organizing has not only built a strong and dynamic reproductive justice movement, it has also brought awareness and new generations of activists into these struggles.

This impressive growth of reproductive justice praxis has been a catalyst for academic inquiry and furthered the development of reproductive justice theory by activists and academics.[6] Scholars and researchers have been drawn to the field.[7] They are developing curricula at the graduate level in various fields including legal, medical, and public health education. In 2015, the first undergraduate certificate in Reproductive Health Rights and Justice was introduced at the Five Colleges Consortium in Western Massachusetts.[8] In cyberspace the reproductive justice movement is spreading awareness in blogs such as *RH Reality Check*, *Feministing*, and *Echoing Ida*.

We are honored to have played a role in expanding the reach of the reproductive justice movement. The pathbreaking work of the eight documented organizations continues to inspire activism and touch people's lives. That *Undivided Rights* is still enthusiastically received by both activists and scholars is a testament to the strength of the reproductive justice framework, the movement, and those engaged in this struggle. It is mentioned as one of the texts most frequently cited in Google searches of "reproductive justice,"[9] and its continued usage in a variety of educational contexts has demanded this reprint. Perhaps most significant for us, activists of color and their allies have appreciated the book for making the breadth and depth of their work visible.[10] Bringing together their own words, founding documents, and recollections allowed us to show how their reproductive struggles, activism, and agendas not only offered an alternative to the mainstream pro-choice movement but prioritized community-based organizing as an effective way to achieve policy change.

We hope to introduce a new generation of scholars and activists to this history by reissuing *Undivided Rights*. In reinforcing the reproductive justice movement's origins in the experiences of communities of color, its insistence on intersectional understandings of reproductive politics, and its connection to the global human rights movement *Undivided Rights* continues to guide and inspire activism.

January 20, 2016

Notes

1   The term was originally coined by twelve African American women meeting in Chicago in 1994 at a larger pro-choice conference, which was organized by the Illinois Pro-Choice Alliance and the Ms. Foundation for Women. At the time, the Clinton administration's plan for heath care reform avoided the issue of reproductive health care, especially abortion, as they attempted to placate Republican opponents. The African American women met to discuss this plan, concluding that if health care reform did not loudly prioritize women's reproductive health needs, they could not support it. Further, they objected to how the administration's proposals isolated reproductive rights issues from other social justice issues. The proposals on the table did not make connections between the decision to become a mother—or not—and related issues such as economics, immigration, and incarceration. Finally, the women collectively questioned the primacy of abortion, though not its necessity. Placing *themselves* at the center of the analysis, they made the case that while abortion was a crucial resource, women of color also needed health care, education, jobs, childcare, and the right to motherhood. Taking this position was a powerful example of how placing oneself in the center of the lens led to discovering new ways of describing reality. These fresh perspectives—so different from the endless and debilitating debates that focused exclusively on abortion—radically shifted their thinking and launched the concept of reproductive justice, conjoining reproductive rights and social justice. Reproductive justice is not difficult to define or remember. It has three primary values: 1) the right *not* to have a child; 2) the right to *have* a child; and 3) the right to *parent* children in safe and healthy environments. In addition, reproductive justice demands sexual autonomy and gender freedom for every human being.

2   Objectified by family planners, elected officials, demographers, and eugenicists.

3   All these groups faced severe fund-raising challenges to sustain them.

4   Several long-standing groups have changed their names to reflect the broader mission encompassed by reproductive justice including Choice USA is now URGE (United for Reproductive and Gender Equity); Law Students for Reproductive Choice is now LSRJ; APIRH is now Forward Together; and SisterSong is now SisterSong Reproductive Justice Collective.

5   Several of the examples are drawn from the open letter to PPFA authored by Monica Simpson, executive director of SisterSong, and cosigned by thirty-eight organizations that support reproductive justice. The controversy contested the lack of attention paid to the critical work of women of color in a *New York Times* interview with Planned Parenthood staffers. The article focused on PPFA's decision to discard the terms "pro-choice/pro-life" while neglecting to mention the origins of the reproductive justice framework or its impact in changing the trajectory of reproductive politics in the United States.

6   *Undivided Rights* was an example of activists and academicians working together.

7   A recent overview of this growth of literature can be found in Zakiya Luna and Kristen Luker, "Reproductive Justice," *Annual Review of Law*

and Social Science, vol. 9 (November 2013): 327–52. Most of these documents are accessible at the Reproductive Justice Virtual Library, https ://www.law.berkeley.edu/centers/center-on-reproductive-rights-and-justice /crrj-reproductive-justice-virtual-library/.

8 The Five College consortium consists of Amherst, Hampshire, Mount Holyoke, Smith, and the University of Massachusetts.

9 Luna and Luker, "Reproductive Justice."

10 *Undivided Rights* was also a catalyst for archivists at the Sophia Smith Collection (SSC), Smith College, to work with Loretta Ross in order to bring the oral histories of many reproductive justice activists to the Voices of Feminism Collection at the SSC, www.smith.edu/library/libs/ssc/vof/vof-intro.html.

Preface to the 2004 Edition and Acknowledgments

W<small>E</small> are not dispassionate observers of our subject—from the outset this book was conceived of as a political project. We set out to "lift up" the voices and the achievements of women of color who are transforming the struggle for sexual and reproductive health and rights into a movement for reproductive justice. We culled vital lessons from their experiences of working to develop a more holistic and inclusive movement vision and suggestions on ways to better work together across differences.

Each one of us has been engaged with and committed to the work women of color have been doing to realize reproductive rights. Our activism has shaped the writing and analysis we developed in this book. As a multiracial team of women, we valued our very different movement histories as well as our varied frames of reference. Co-authorship meant debating and critiquing each other's writing and analysis and rethinking some of our own assumptions and perspectives. It required each of us to learn histories with which we were less familiar. As co-authors we deeply engaged with one another's analysis, bringing several lenses at once to understand the complex terrain in which women of color operate. Writing this together has been a profound learning and bonding experience.

Since how we understand the world and seek to shape it is determined by our pasts and visions of the future, we briefly sketch where each of us has worked over the years.

Jael Silliman has been an activist both in the US and international women's health and reproductive rights movements. She was a program officer at the Jessie Smith Noyes Foundation, an early supporter

1

of organizations of women of color. She was an associate professor of women's studies at the University of Iowa, where she wrote about social movements, women's health, and reproductive rights. She is currently the program officer for reproductive rights in the Human Rights Unit at the Ford Foundation. Her most recent book is *Policing the National Body: Race, Gender, and Criminalization*, co-edited with Anannya Bhattacharjee. She is from India and is an immigrant to the US.

Marlene Gerber Fried came to reproductive rights after her involvement in the civil rights, women's liberation, and anti-war movements of the 1960s. Since the late 1970s, her focus has been domestic and international abortion and reproductive rights. She works with student activists in her role as director of the Civil Liberties and Public Policy Program at Hampshire College, where she is also a professor of philosophy. Marlene is the founding president of the National Network of Abortion Funds, a co-founder and board member of the Abortion Access Project, and serves on the international board of the Women's Global Network for Reproductive Rights. She edited *From Abortion to Reproductive Freedom: Transforming a Movement.*

Loretta Ross has a 25-year history in the women's movement, both in ending violence against women and promoting reproductive rights in the United States and internationally. She was active in the black Nationalist and civil rights movements. She has written extensively on African American women and abortion, and organized two national conferences on reproductive rights for women of color in 1987 and 2003, respectively. Loretta is a co-founder of the SisterSong Women of Color Reproductive Health Collective, the founder and executive director of the National Center for Human Rights Education, and is on the board of SisterLove, a women's HIV/AIDS organization. Most recently, she was national co-director of the March for Women's Lives, April 2004, Washington, DC.

Elena Gutiérrez has researched issues in Latina reproductive health for 15 years. She is currently an assistant professor of gender and women's studies and Latin American and Latino studies at the University of Illinois at Chicago. She is completing another book, *Fertile Matters: The Politics of Mexican-Origin Women's Reproduction*, which is forthcoming from the University of Texas Press. She has worked closely with several women's health organizations and is the past board president of ACCESS/Women's Health Rights Collective.

While we are ultimately responsible for what we have written, this ambitious project could not have been undertaken without the support and inspiration of the many people who commit each day of their lives to advance women's human rights. We thank the leaders, boards, and staff of each of the organizations featured. They spent time with us in interviews; shared their organizational resources, reports, and files; suggested people with whom we should speak to develop a more comprehensive understanding of their work; and reviewed and commented on drafts, working with us to get the organizational histories and details right. It has been our privilege to document their activities. We hope that through this book the essential work that they are doing in their communities will be better known and appreciated. Our scholarship on the activism of women of color in the reproductive health movement is just a beginning. The people we have interviewed, the organizations we feature, and the many others we could not include deserve further research and documentation as they are pioneers in this broad and vibrant movement.

We thank the Open Society Institute, who selected our proposal under the Individual Fellows Program and also gave us a publishing support grant. This financial support enabled us to conduct the research and writing for this book and allowed South End Press to expand its outreach and publicity. We thank the women's studies department of the University of Iowa, the Civil Liberties and Public Policy Program at Hampshire College, the National Center for Human Rights Education, and the gender and women's studies and Latin American and Latino studies departments at the University of Illinois at Chicago for the institutional support they provided to carry this work forward.

In these harsh political times, we especially appreciated working with South End Press and its commitment to radical social change. We thank Loie Hayes and Jill Petty for their dedication to our book. We deeply value the many contributions of our main editor, Joey Fox, who believed in the book's importance. She worked with us through several drafts, always with great patience, thoughtfulness, and sensitivity. We also thank, in association with South End Press, Elizabeth Terzakis, Jess Lin, and Chris Hu for their relentless attention to detail.

We are indebted to Susan Harris for her early edits and Stephanie Poggi for her detailed read of a previous draft; both were critical in sharpening our thinking and focus. Jill Moffett of the University of Iowa assisted us through many stages of the writing and editing process and helped us with footnotes and bibliographies several times over. Others who assisted us in research, citation, and formatting include Katharina Mendoza, Karin Krslovic, Shell Feijo, Lauren Rice, Fiona Young, Cynthia Estep, Erin Howe, M. J. Maccardini, Liz Brown, Ariella Rotramel, Elizabeth Garcia, and Marisol Salgado.

So many women committed to reproductive rights and health also gave generously of their time and expertise. We especially thank Margaret Hempel, Sarah Littlecrow-Russell, Shira Saperstein, Andy Smith, and Sherry Wilson, who read, commented, and made suggestions to strengthen our research and analysis.

As it is for all writers, it is our families and friends who have nurtured and supported us through the always time consuming and often laborious process of writing a book. Each of us has special friends and family members that we wish to acknowledge, for they have helped us through anxious moments and seen us through long hours of research and writing.

Jael gives heart-felt thanks to her daughters Shikha and Maya, her parents Flower and David, and her friends in Calcutta, Iowa City, and New York City. They saw her through very difficult personal circumstances during which this book was written.

Marlene could not have written this book nor sustained herself as an activist without the personal and political support of her friends and family; her colleagues at the Civil Liberties and Public Policy Program—Betsy Hartmann, Amy Crysel, Eesha Pandit, Ryn Gluckman, Rosalind Pollan, and former staff member Mina Trudeau; the board and staff of the National Network of Abortion Funds and the many other activists she has worked with over the years who have been sources of strength and inspiration; and her husband Bill, who gave love, emotional support, and editorial help during what sometimes seemed like an endless process.

This book also would not have been possible without a true partnership between community activists and women in academic institutions who are dedicated to documenting the history and contributions of women of color. In particular, Loretta would like to thank Stanlie James, who first encouraged her to write about black women's reproductive rights activism in 1990. Other activists and/or scholars who have helped include Luz Rodríguez, Elsa Rios, Dázon Dixon Diallo, Nkenge Toure, Patricia Rodney, Rickie Solinger, Vanessa Northington Gamble,

Faye Williams (of SisterSpace & Books), Joyce Follet, Isa Williams, Alice Cohan, and, of course, the staff at the National Center for Human Rights Education: Dionne Vann, Deanna West, Malika Redmond, Katie Gurley, Maria Foley, and former staffers Sarah Brownlee and Pam Hester. Loretta would like to dedicate this book to her mother, Lorene Deloris Ross, who told her daughter to "never let success go to your head, or failure go to your heart."

Elena would like to thank Mona Jhawar for encouraging her to become involved in this project and supporting her throughout. She is grateful to Phil Bowman and the Institute for Research on Race and Public Policy at the University of Illinois at Chicago (UIC) for a fellowship that allowed her the time to begin this project. She'd also like to thank her colleagues at UIC, friends in Chicago, and Gail London for reminding her why writing this history is important. Finally, she'd like to thank her family for always supporting her work, and her ancestors for leading the way. Elena dedicates this book to her students at UIC, for their joy, their dedication, and their inspiration.

1

Women of Color and Their Struggle for Reproductive Justice

"WE'RE sick and tired of being sick and tired!" With Fannie Lou Hamer's words as their rallying cry,[1] more than 1,500 African American women gathered at Spelman College in Atlanta for the first National Conference on Black Women's Health Issues in 1983: "They came with PhDs, MDs, welfare cards, in Mercedes and on crutches, from seven days to eighty years old—urban, rural, gay, straight—in desperate search for themselves."[2] The conference gave birth to the National Black Women's Health Project (NBWHP),[3] the first ever women of color reproductive justice organization and the foremother of the other organizations profiled in this book.

The histories of NBWHP and the other reproductive rights organizations formed by women of color in the 1980s and 90s are stories of activism, courage, and determination that challenge the common belief that communities who have suffered the most from restrictions on reproductive rights do not organize on their own behalf. This book retrieves part of that history by documenting the reproductive rights activism of eight women of color groups in the United States.

Accounts of the reproductive rights struggle in the US have typically focused on efforts to attain and defend the legal right to abortion, efforts led predominantly by white women. What little information is provided about women of color tends to center on the abuses they have suffered and represents only a partial history. Most of the reproductive health organizing done by women of color in the United States has been undocumented, unanalyzed, and unacknowledged. Turning

7

the tide of this limited scholarship, Dorothy Roberts, Linda Gordon, Rickie Solinger, Jennifer Nelson, and others have brought to light both the struggles of women of color to resist reproductive oppression and the roles they have played in the fight for reproductive justice.[4] Theirs and similar works have highlighted the external challenges confronting communities of color and constraining their reproduction—population control, sterilization abuse, unsafe contraceptives, welfare reform, the criminalization of women who use drugs and alcohol during pregnancy, and coercive and intrusive family planning programs and policies.[5]

However, Dorothy Roberts cautions us against seeing women of color as passive puppets.[6] Therefore, this book focuses on what women of color have done for themselves, rather than what has been done to them. We put the activism of women of color in the foreground. By adopting this approach we neither discount the devastating consequences of reproductive abuses, nor deny the impact of structural forces such as white supremacy, capitalism, and patriarchy. But these issues are the backdrop for the organizing and do not take center stage.

This book utilizes a series of organizational case studies to document how women of color have led the fight to control their own bodies and reproductive destinies and have organized to define and implement a reproductive justice agenda to address the needs of their communities. We selected groups that reflect a wide range of organizing strategies, issues, and challenges from four ethnic communities: African American, Native American/Indigenous, Latina, and Asian and Pacific Islander. To illustrate the range of organizing occurring within communities of color, we included two organizations from each—a national group, more well-known and often with a longer history of organizing, and an organization newer to the work and/or one that is grassroots-oriented. All of the groups varied in size, focus of programmatic activity, and budgets.

Included in this book are the National Black Women's Health Project (NBWHP), Washington, DC; African American Women Evolving (AAWE), Chicago, Illinois; the Native American Women's Health Education Resource Center (NAWHERC), Yankton Sioux Reservation, South Dakota; the Mother's Milk Project (MMP), Akwesasne, St. Regis Mohawk Reservation, New York; Asians and Pacific Islanders for Reproductive Health (APIRH),[7] Oakland, California; the National Asian Women's Health Organization (NAWHO), San Francisco, California; the National Latina Health Organization (NLHO), Oakland,

California; and the Colorado Organization for Latina Opportunity and Reproductive Rights (COLOR), Denver, Colorado.

In writing the chapters on the histories of activism, we drew on unpublished theses and dissertations and the limited published material about the activism of women of color. For the organizational histories, we relied on interviews, organizational publications, personal accounts—both published and unpublished—and our own experiences and familiarity with the groups. While we are aware that we bring our own lenses to the project, we have taken our direction from the people we interviewed and have tried to tell the histories from their vantage points. Sometimes there were divergent understandings and interpretations of events. When this occurred, we attempted to determine the most accurate and inclusive account. However, because we could not interview everyone who had been involved in creating these histories, we realize there may be information and perspectives that we have not included. It is our hope that future scholarship and writing will expand on this work. We do not focus on internal organizational or personal debates and struggles, which we know are present in all organizations, because we found they obscured rather than illuminated events.

The interviews were guided by a set of common questions. We were interested in the founders' decisions to start autonomous organizations and the problems their organizations faced, as well as the gains they made. We asked participants to define what reproductive rights meant, and whether they viewed their organizations as part of the reproductive rights movement. We wanted to know who had been supportive of their organizing and helpful in moving their agendas forward, and what types of support were provided. We asked questions about the obstacles to and opportunities for collaboration both with women of color and mainstream groups.

We also set out to document their methods of organizing and their most significant accomplishments, limitations, and challenges. We explored organizational goals and programs. Because access to and adequacy of resources are essential for organizing, we examined fundraising strategies. We asked about the impact of the groups in their communities, on public policy, and on the mainstream pro-choice movement.

These contemporary struggles for reproductive justice arise from a long history of oppression and resistance, beginning before 20th-century battles to legalize contraception and abortion. Thus, each pair of case studies is preceded by an introductory chapter that grounds the organizational histories in the larger history of the community.

After much debate on terminology, we decided to use the umbrella term "women of color" to describe the four primary ethnic groups in the United States.[8] Since the term was coined by women of color in 1977 at the National Women's Conference in Houston, Texas, it has become a viable organizing principle in the United States for women who are most disadvantaged by white supremacy. The identifying language and terms that the various reproductive rights movements have employed to describe their work has evolved, depending on historical and political contexts. After legalization, the movement to defend legal abortion termed itself "pro-choice." Women of color and white activists who advocated for abortion in a broader framework that emphasized opposition to population control rejected the pro-choice terminology as too narrow and instead used "reproductive rights," "reproductive freedom," and "reproductive health." However, the distinctions between these terms have been blurred in the current context. Most pro-choice groups now use the language of reproductive rights—though their agenda is still focused on abortion rights. Some women of color organizations are using "reproductive justice" to recognize that the control, regulation, and stigmatization of female fertility, bodies, and sexuality are connected to the regulation of communities that are themselves based on race, class, gender, sexuality, and nationality.[9] This analysis emphasizes the relationship of reproductive rights to human rights and economic justice. In the case studies we take our terminology from the activists we interviewed. "Reproductive rights" and "reproductive justice" are used interchangeably.

Our research has yielded a tremendous amount of information, as well as experiences, insights, and perspectives that are critical to understanding the past and to crafting future organizing strategies. The remainder of this chapter presents the predominant themes of the aggregated histories and case studies. Despite significant differences among the groups, there are important similarities among them as well. All are engaged in (1) redefining reproductive rights to include the needs of their communities; (2) leading the fight against population control and asserting an inextricable link between the right to have children and the right not to; (3) organizing along lines of racial and ethnic identity in order to create the spaces to confront internalized and external oppression, forge agendas, and engage with other movements; (4) promoting new understandings of political inclusion and movement building that bridge historic divisions and create new alliances.

Redefining Reproductive Rights

Women of color in the US negotiate their reproductive lives in a system that combines various interlocking forms of oppression. As activist, scholar, and co-author Loretta Ross puts it: "Our ability to control what happens to our bodies is constantly challenged by poverty, racism, environmental degradation, sexism, homophobia, and injustice in the United States."[10] The groups in this book created their own definitions of reproductive rights—definitions that are grounded in the experiences of their different communities and that link oppressions. It is because of these intersections that women of color advance a definition of reproductive rights beyond abortion. Their critique of "choice" does not deny women of color agency; rather, it shows the constraints within which women of color navigate their reproductive lives and organizing.

Early in the abortion rights struggle, before these organizations were created, women of color resisted the coercion that masqueraded as "choice." In a 1973 editorial that was supportive of the *Roe v. Wade* Supreme Court decision legalizing abortion, the National Council of Negro Women sounded this important cautionary note:

> The key words are "if she chooses." Bitter experience has taught the black woman that the administration of justice in this country is not color-blind. Black women on welfare have been forced to accept sterilization in exchange for a continuation of relief benefits and others have been sterilized without their knowledge or consent. A young pregnant woman recently arrested for civil rights activities in North Carolina was convicted and told that her punishment would be to have a forced abortion. We must be ever vigilant that what appears on the surface to be a step forward, does not in fact become yet another fetter or method of enslavement.[11]

Twenty-five years later, in her introduction to *Policing the National Body*, co-author Jael Silliman expands their critique:

> The mainstream movement, largely dominated by white women, is framed around choice: the choice to determine whether or not to have children, the choice to terminate a pregnancy, and the ability to make informed choices about contraceptive and reproductive technologies. This

conception of choice is rooted in the neoliberal tradition that locates individual rights at its core, and treats the individual's control over her body as central to liberty and freedom. This emphasis on individual choice, however, obscures the social context in which individuals make choices, and discounts the ways in which the state regulates populations, disciplines individual bodies, and exercises control over sexuality, gender, and reproduction.[12]

"Choice" implies a marketplace of options in which women's right to determine what happens to their bodies is legally protected, ignoring the fact that for women of color, economic and institutional constraints often restrict their "choices." For example, a woman who decides to have an abortion out of economic necessity does not experience her decision as a "choice." Native American activist Justine Smith writes, In the Native context, where women often find the only contraceptives available to them are dangerous, where they live in communities in which unemployment rates can run as high as 80 percent, and where their life expectancy can be as low as 47 years, reproductive "choice" defined so narrowly is a meaningless concept.[13]

All of the organizations in this book include abortion and contraception as part of a much wider set of concerns. Access to resources and services, economic rights, freedom from violence, and safe and healthy communities are all integral to their expanded vision. While each group draws on its unique history, their similar definitions of reproductive rights reflect significant commonalities of experience and overall socioeconomic status. These include disproportionate rates of poverty, lack of access to health care information and services, lack of insurance coverage, and limited access to contraceptive services. For example, 23 percent of African American women, 42 percent of Latinas, and 25 percent of Asian American women lack health insurance, compared with 13 percent of white women.[14] For women of color, reproductive and sexual health problems are not isolated from the socioeconomic inequalities in their lives.

A broader cultural understanding of reproductive rights encompasses the race, class, gender, and immigration experiences of each group, linking reproductive rights and access to health care. For example, all the groups argue that culturally competent providers are crucial to achieving access to reproductive health services.[15] In addition to health care providers knowing the language of the people they serve, cultural competency requires an understanding of and respect for the cultures, traditions, and practices of a community. Stereotypes and a lack of accurate knowledge about communities are barriers to interpreting women's needs. They are also obstacles which prevent women who need information and care from getting it.

The expanded definitions also incorporate the less obvious ways in which the fertility of women of color is undermined. For example, several of the groups include environmental issues in their definition of reproductive rights and in their advocacy. Asians and Pacific Islanders for Reproductive Health responded to the threats from environmental toxins in their neighborhood and constructed a very broad definition that explicitly encompasses the right to safe food and a clean environment.[16] The Native American Women's Health Education Resource Center definition, coming out of Native Americans' historical struggle for survival, includes sovereignty, the right to live and parent as Native Americans. By incorporating more issues into the concept of reproductive rights, these definitions provide a nuanced and critical analysis of reproductive choices, birth control, and family planning.

Fighting for the Right to Have—or Not Have—Children

Women of color have had no trouble distinguishing between population control—externally imposed fertility control policies—and voluntary birth control—women making their own decisions about fertility. For women of color, resisting population control while simultaneously claiming their right to bodily self-determination, including the right to contraception and abortion or the right to have children, is at the heart of their struggle for reproductive control.

Although there has never been an official policy to reduce the growth of the US population, controlling fertility has been a persistent feature of other domestic policies directed at men and women of color, sometimes attempting to increase their fertility, but most often aiming to limit it. For example, during the colonization of the United States, Native American women were intentionally given blankets infected with smallpox. Population control during slavery took the form of brutal and coercive efforts to increase African American women's reproduction, with slave owners using rape and forced marriages to achieve this end. However, since then, population control efforts have been intended to prevent women of color from having children. Eugenics laws, immigration restrictions, sterilization abuses, targeted family planning, and welfare reform have all been vehicles for population control.

Since the 19th century, all of these population control strategies have been employed using racist ideologies as justifications. For example, efforts to maintain white "racial purity" underlie private and publicly funded efforts to control the fertility of those deemed "unfit" and "defective," understood by policy-makers to mean poor or not white. The mid-20th century saw advocates for domestic and international population control promulgating alarmist time bomb theories with strong racist overtones and raising fears among whites of people of color overrunning the Western world. In 1970, President Nixon supported establishing federal family planning services by appealing to whites' fears about population explosions that would make governance of the world in general—and inner cities in particular—difficult. Nixon's policy advisors assembled statistics that pointed to a "bulge" in the number of black Americans between the ages of five and nine, claiming the cohort was 25 percent larger than ten years before.[17] Population alarmists warned that this group of youngsters soon entering their teens was "an age group with problems that can create social turbulence."[18]

Recognizing the relationship between numbers of people and political power,[19] white politicians favored "helping" racial minorities limit their fertility. Determined to lower population growth in African American and Latino communities, many pro-segregation Southern politicians—both Republicans and Democrats—who had formerly opposed family planning, suddenly favored it as a way of regulating the reproduction of these groups. Opposition to welfare and the commitment to reduce welfare rolls by supplying free birth control services to poor women were joined in a race- and class-directed social policy. In one of the more overt expressions of this position, Leander Perez, a Louisiana judge, revealed in 1965 the link between coercive birth control and racism: "The best way to hate a nigger is to hate him before he is born."[20]

In the 1980s and 90s, fertility control remained a centerpiece of the nation's welfare program and continued to undermine the rights of low-income women and women of color to have children. Federal welfare reform policies such as family caps, institutionalized in President Clinton's 1996 Personal Responsibility and Work Opportunity Reconciliation Act (PRWORA), deny additional benefits to women who have more children while receiving public assistance. Women of color in the economic justice and reproductive rights movements have criticized family caps and other aspects of welfare reform, such as marriage promotion and funding for abstinence-only sexual education. These policies punish women for being poor by attacking their fertility while not offering any substantive relief from structural poverty.[21]

Although rooted in racism, population control programs did at times, at least in part, meet the needs and desires of women of color for birth control, thus creating a complicated political dynamic. This was the case when Nixon's federally funded family planning and contraceptive program was created in the 1970s.[22] African American communities provided the majority of family planning clinic clients in the Deep South because, since slavery, controlling one's own fertility had been associated with upward mobility. Despite the racist motivations of some proponents of the family planning–birth control movement, anthropologist Martha Ward, who researched federal population policies, notes: "Family planning became synonymous with the civil rights of poor women to medical care."[23]

Nevertheless, attempts to use family planning clinics to limit the population growth of communities of color were so blatant that they aroused a strong response from Nationalist movements that came to the conclusion that birth control and abortion were genocide. African American and Chicana women supporting birth control and abortion rights as part of their civil rights activism continually faced opposition from Nationalists who felt that the best way to fight racism and xenophobia was to encourage black and Latino communities to expand their population base. Thus, while women of color frequently worked with mainstream and Nationalist civil rights organizations, they had to criticize these organizations when they supported positions hostile to reproductive freedom.[24] In 1970, Frances Beal, coordinator of the Black Women's Liberation Committee of the Student Non-Violent Coordinating Committee (SNCC), made clear her support for both reproductive rights and civil rights:

> We are not saying that black women should not practice birth control. Black women have the right and the responsibility to determine when it is [in] the interest of the struggle to have children or not to have them, and this right must not be relinquished to anyone. It is also her right and responsibility to determine when it is in her own best interests to have children, how many she will have and how far apart. The lack of the

availability of safe birth control methods, the forced sterilization practices, and the inability to obtain legal abortions are all symptoms of a decadent society that jeopardizes the health of black women (and thereby the entire black race) in its attempts to control the very life processes of human beings.[25]

Almost 20 years later, in 1989, activist and scholar Dorothy Roberts encountered the same issues when she spoke about threats to abortion rights at a neighborhood meeting, and a man in the audience took her to task: "He said that reproductive rights was a 'white woman's issue,' and advised me to stick to traditional civil rights concerns, such as affirmative action, voting rights, and criminal justice."[26]

However, women of color have refused to divide civil rights from reproductive rights. Rather, they have transformed the fight for both by creating an ever expanding comprehensive reproductive justice agenda. Their agenda includes fighting against two of the methods frequently employed by the racially motivated family planning apparatus that have undermined women of color's right to have children: coercive sterilization and invasive long-term birth control technologies.

In the 20th century, Native American, Mexican American,[27] African American, and Puerto Rican women and other women of color were denied the right to have children through systematic and widespread sterilization abuses[28] practiced by the US government and by private doctors (who were more often than not subsidized by the US government). Women of color responded by taking up the fight against sterilization abuse. Native American, African American, and Latina groups documented and publicized sterilization abuses in their communities in the 1960s and 70s, showing that women had been sterilized without their knowledge or consent. They demonstrated that women who spoke only Spanish were asked to sign consent forms in English, and sometimes pressured to do so during labor and childbirth. Native American women were given hysterectomies by Indian Health Service without their permission.

In the 1970s, a group of women, which included Dr. Helen Rodríguez-Trías, founded the Committee to End Sterilization Abuse (CESA) to stop this racist population control policy begun by the federal government in the 1940s—a policy that had resulted in the sterilization of over one-third of all women of childbearing age in Puerto Rico.[29] CESA helped to create the Advisory Committee on Sterilization, a coalition of groups that developed regulations to protect women using public hospitals in New York City.[30]

Native American and African American women were also active on this issue. Norma Jean Serena, of Creek-Shawnee ancestry, filed the first civil suit of its kind in 1973, addressing sterilization abuse as a civil rights violation.[31] In 1974, another successful lawsuit advanced by the National Welfare Rights Organization and the Southern Poverty Law Center demanded restitution for the involuntary sterilization of the Relf sisters. These 12- and 14-year-old African American sisters were sterilized in Alabama without their parents' knowledge or consent.[32] By 1978, the federal government was forced to establish guidelines regarding sterilization. These included required waiting periods and authorization forms in a language understood by the woman, to prevent women from being sterilized without their knowledge or informed consent.[33]

Despite these efforts, new forms of coercion have arisen. In the 1990s, the Committee on Women, Population, and the Environment (CWPE) initiated a campaign to raise awareness about and to challenge CRACK (Children Requiring a Caring Kommunity), now called Project Prevention, a privately funded organization that pays women who are addicted to drugs $200 to be sterilized or to use long-acting contraceptives. Although private, CRACK is in fact implementing the same racist agenda manifest in the government policies previously discussed, namely, preventing "undesirable" women, overwhelmingly women of color, from having children.[34] Such continuing reproductive abuses of women of color lead CWPE to argue that a meaningful reproductive health agenda must include explicit opposition to policies that are disproportionately directed at controlling the reproductive capacity of women of color. The rights to bodily and reproductive autonomy are fundamental human rights.

While the resistance of women of color to oppressive reproductive restrictions has been focused on the government and private population control organizations, they have also had to contend with those white pro-choice activists in the mainstream movements for contraception and abortion who have been unable see how what may be reproductive freedom for them is reproductive tyranny for others. The mainstream movements have not linked policies and practices dressed in the benign language of family planning and welfare reform to restrictions on reproductive freedom. Thus, they were not the allies of women of color and sometimes were even at odds with women of color struggling for racial, economic, and reproductive justice.

Activist and philosopher Angela Davis wrote about this failure to confront racism:

> Birth control—individual choice, safe contraceptive methods, as well as abortions when necessary—is a fundamental prerequisite for the emancipation of women. Since the right of birth control is obviously advantageous to women of all classes and races, it would appear that even vastly dissimilar women's groups would have attempted to unite around this issue. In reality, however, the birth control movement has seldom succeeded in uniting women of different social backgrounds, and rarely have the movement's leaders popularized the genuine concerns of working-class women. Moreover, arguments advanced by birth control advocates have sometimes been based on blatantly racist premises.[35]

The fact that these views generally went unchallenged—and were sometimes embraced or not even recognized as racist—by the mainstream movements meant that women of color who opposed population control could not rely on these movements to counter such policies.

Further, Davis notes that the priorities of women of color are different from those of white women because of their different experiences. Thus, the reproductive rights agendas are shaped by the dynamics of class and race. The failure of white women to address their internalized racism and classism, and to appreciate the power of race and class dynamics to influence activist agendas, has sometimes had disastrous political results—specifically when initiatives promoted by the mainstream movement have actually turned out to limit the reproductive rights of women of color and poor women.[36]

For example, in the 1970s, when the major pro-choice and feminist organizations did not join women of color in demanding sterilization guidelines it was because their experiences with sterilization were radically different. While women of color were targets for coercive sterilization, white middle-class women had trouble persuading doctors to perform voluntary sterilizations, and often had to obtain permission from medical committees to do so.[37] Pro-choice organizations perceived guidelines regulating sterilization as infringing on women's choices, not enhancing them. While the National Organization for Women (NOW) did not take a position on the issue, the National Abortion and

Reproductive Rights Action League (NARAL)[38] and other groups that had traditionally supported abortion rights, such as Planned Parenthood, Zero Population Growth, and the Association for Voluntary Surgical Contraception, opposed the sterilization regulations on the grounds that they deprived women of "freedom of choice." In general, mainstream white feminists believed the guidelines were unnecessary and paternalistic and interfered with the doctor-patient relationship.[39]

More recently, we have seen a similar divergence in views regarding hormonal contraception. Population groups and mainstream pro-choice organizations enthusiastically greeted the development of Norplant and Depo-Provera as an expansion of reproductive choice for women. Depo-Provera injections were promoted in their joint campaigns as "highly effective, long-acting...and [offering] privacy to the user since the woman has no need to keep contraceptive supplies at home."[40] Their endorsement came despite the risk that Depo-Provera causes menstrual cycle irregularities, principally amenorrhea (the absence of periods), and increases the risk of endometrial and breast cancer.[41]

In contrast, along with progressive women's health groups around the world, women of color have been more skeptical of provider-controlled hormonal methods of contraception whose side effects and risks were unclear.[42] For example, they have criticized Norplant (subdermal implants) and Depo-Provera (injectibles), the two methods most aggressively marketed to young African American, Latina, and Native American women. In 1991, NBWHP, NAWHERC, and NLHO issued warnings of the potential for Norplant abuses.[43] Their concerns were validated merely two days after the contraceptive implant was approved by the United States Food and Drug Administration, when the *Philadelphia Inquirer* newspaper published an editorial advocating its use "as a tool in the fight against black poverty."[44] Although the newspaper later apologized for its racist editorial, judges and state legislatures continued to advocate for the use of Norplant among disadvantaged women.

There was a similar although much less publicized division in 1988, when mainstream pro-choice groups developed a campaign to introduce mifepristone into the US. Also known as RU 486, mifepristone is taken orally and is a non-surgical option for ending a pregnancy up to 49 days after the beginning of the last menstrual period. These organizations were not concerned that mifepristone had not been sufficiently tested on women of color in the United States, nor was attention given to the fact that women of color were less likely to have access to the follow-up care that is necessary for safe usage. The major pro-choice groups were universally enthusiastic about the campaign. Any criticisms that there might be a problematic side to mifepristone tended to be discouraged or dismissed as playing into the hands of the anti-abortion movement. It seemed that once again, in the drive to expand choice, women of color and their particular concerns were being ignored.

Opposition to population control and support for voluntary birth control and abortion—as paired feminist values[45]—are central to the political agendas of the activist organizations in this book. It was in their own reproductive rights organizations that they could most consistently define their agendas—embracing demands for safe abortion and contraception, broadening the meaning of reproductive rights, and rejecting racist efforts to impose fertility control. As we will see in Chapter 2, they were supported by white women who were also disaffected by the narrow vision of choice.

Identity-Based Organizing

This book documents women of color creating their own organizations and agendas that prioritize race, ethnicity, and class along with gender. This approach speaks to Dorothy Roberts's statement that

> there is something drastically wrong with a conception of reproductive freedom that allows this wholesale exclusion of the most disadvantaged from its reach. We need a way of rethinking the meaning of liberty so that it protects all citizens equally. I propose that focusing on the connection between reproductive rights and racial equality is the place to start.[46]

Women of color understood that white women and men of color, even with the best of intentions, could not speak to the uniqueness of their issues or represent the authenticity of their experiences. Women of color needed to claim leadership for themselves. By establishing organizations that were racially and ethnically specific and separate from white organizations, women of color created the visions and gained the support necessary to raise the visibility of their reproductive health concerns in their communities and in the broader society. Placing race and class at the center of their reproductive freedom agenda has allowed many of the groups studied to recruit supporters from other social justice movements, such as the civil rights, immigrant rights, economic justice, and environmental justice movements. This has also led to building support bases in communities of color for reproductive health issues. By grounding their organizing in community-identified needs, women of color do not have to isolate or separate themselves from the day-to-day concerns of their communities.

Women of color are subjected to racist and sexist stereotypes which send messages that they should not be in charge of their own reproductive and sexual destinies. When women of color internalize these stereotypes, it is damaging psychologically and a barrier to their activism. Groups based on racial and gender identities help participants overcome important barriers to activism by combating their internalized oppression. Toni Bond, founder and executive director of African American Women Evolving, writes about the toll of internalized oppression:

> Many of us have so internalized [racial] oppression that it has transformed into a self-hatred and seeps into and impedes even our ability to work together collectively, resulting in organizational upheaval and our further disenfranchisement...So emotionally bruised are women of color from racist oppression and our internalization of that oppression that we have trouble letting our guards down to share personal stories about our experiences around health or any other issue.[47]

Eveline Shen, director of Asians and Pacific Islanders for Reproductive Health, echoes Bond's point when she talks about the need to confront stereotypes just to make activism possible. She says, "Asian women are supposed to be docile and obedient. This model is not compatible with fighting for women's rights."[48] For women of color, challenging these myths and stereotypes is part of the process of reclaiming their humanity and redefining their own identities.

Women from all four racial/ethnic groups have faced and challenged racial stereotyping. For African American women, the images of Mammy and Sapphire emphasize maternalism and promiscuity.[49] Asian women are also portrayed in contradictory ways, as concubines, prostitutes, or model minorities, deriving unfair advantage from affirmative action.[50] Racist descriptions represent the Native American woman as a willing squaw, an alcoholic, or "a brown lump of drudge."[51] Reservation Indians are said to "wallow in welfare, food stamps, free housing and medical care, affirmative action programs, and gargantuan federal cash payments."[52] Latinas are stereotyped as oversexed "hot tamales" or as illegal immigrants wanting to have babies in the United States so they can obtain citizenship and welfare benefits. Some social scientists describe Latinas as "ideally submissive, unworldly, and chaste" or "at the command of the husband who keeps her as he would a coveted thing, free from the contacts of the world, subject to his passions, ignorant of life."[53]

These myths and stereotypes are part of the larger system of oppression and play an important part in perpetuating it. Characterizing women of color as sexually promiscuous and too irresponsible to make their own reproductive decisions and be good mothers serves as the rationale for enacting and legitimizing discriminatory policies, programs, and laws. For example, the 1950s image of the lazy "welfare queen" was rejuvenated during the 1970s and 80s to fuel cutbacks in public assistance. President Reagan referred to a woman on welfare as a "pig at the trough."[54] Images of hyper-fertile Mexican women crossing the border to bear their children on United States soil so that their children could secure social benefits helped to pass restrictive legislation such as Proposition 187 in California, which denied undocumented immigrants educational and health benefits.[55] Continuing the assaults against Latinos, Harvard professor Samuel Huntington's new book, Who Are We? The Challenges to America's National Identity,[56] suggests that Hispanic immigrants are undermining the "greatness" of the United States by diluting our national identity as an "Anglo-Protestant" country, a diatribe offered by someone who has been a lifelong Democrat.

Reproductive rights organizing by women of color challenges both the stereotypes and the policies that undermine reproductive autonomy. Through activism, women of color assert the value and dignity of their lives, the lives of their children, and their roles as mothers.

Building an Inclusive Movement

The histories and case studies in this book demonstrate the depth and scope of organizing by women of color on a wide range of reproductive health issues—including abortion. Despite their efforts, activists in predominantly white organizations have asked: "Where are the women of color in the struggle for abortion rights?" The very question excludes women of color by erasing their historical involvement in the birth control and pro-choice movements. It assumes that because women of color are not in white organizations, they are not involved in the struggle. Further, it indicates how far we are from having a multiracial, multi-issue, cross-class movement for reproductive freedom. Finally, it raises larger questions about identity politics and creating an inclusive movement.

We believe that two false assumptions underlie this thinking: that identity politics were invented and are only practiced by non-white minority groups; and that race/ethnic-based organizing creates unnecessary divisions among groups. To the contrary, all social movements, whether organized for the rights of people of color or gay people or workers or whomever, use identity politics in the sense that they are working on behalf of their constituencies who share an identity. Heterosexual white people have not recognized themselves as an identity group because they assumed their identity to be the universal norm. Consequently, many white women organizing for reproductive rights they assume that their agenda includes all women.

We reject these assumptions. Instead, we think that the reproductive rights organizing by women of color provides an opportunity to explore the benefits and limits of identity politics as an organizing strategy for women of color, as well as to analyze its impact on the overall movement. The necessity for such organizing by women of color raises basic questions about inclusion: Who is being included in what? What are the terms of inclusion? What are the political goals of an inclusive movement? This book suggests that being included in the mainstream was not the primary goal of women of color who created reproductive rights organizations.

We think the responsibility for reforming and transforming the mainstream movement lies with the predominantly white leaders of that movement, who must recognize that inclusivity is the only path to successfully achieving reproductive rights and justice for all women. "Perhaps," as activist and abortion provider Brenda Joyner states, "the question is not really where are women of color in the abortion rights and reproductive rights movement. Rather, where is the primarily white middle-class movement in our struggles for freedom?"[57] As mainstream organizations grapple with these issues, they should ask how they can be allies as women of color take the lead in shaping a broader movement which encompasses all of their issues.

The activists we interviewed have a positive definition of inclusion. To them, inclusion means creating an agenda and ultimately a movement that reflects the broad set of needs and concerns which all women face. Their organizations offer forward-looking strategies for creating multi-issue groups and for building an inclusive and representative movement for reproductive health and sexual rights for all women. We have seen that strategies focused solely on defending abortion are limited. The success of the Right in mobilizing a vocal and active constituency to threaten reproductive rights calls for a broad grassroots strategy capable of reaching across social movements and linking health and reproductive rights to other social justice issues. Introducing new frames like reproductive justice enables more women to be included. This broader agenda has the potential to revitalize the reproductive rights movement.

Many women of color reproductive rights activists increasingly find the human rights framework, successfully used by anti-racist and anti-fascist movements worldwide, to be one of the best ways of articulating and advancing their rights. Linking civil, political, economic, sexual and social rights, it bridges the gap between having legal rights and lacking the economic resources to access those rights. Those women of color who embrace the existing global human rights framework do so in order to locate reproductive freedom within a broad movement for human rights. In 2000, the Institute for Women and Ethnic Studies in New Orleans put forth a Reproductive Health Bill of Rights:

> All people are born free and equal with dignity and rights as set forth in the Universal Declaration of Human Rights. Historically, women of color across nations, cultures, and different religious and ethnic groups have been subject to racist exploitation, discrimination, and abuse. Manipulative, coercive and punitive health policies and practices deprive women of color of their fundamental human rights and dignity.[58]

Like other US based organizations serving women of color, the SisterSong Women of Color Reproductive Health Collective uses the global human rights framework in its activism, recognizing that the United States lacks a sufficient legal framework to guarantee women of color safe and reliable access to health care.[59] In order to ensure appropriate treatment and access to health care and to address the issues of class, race and gender that affect women of color, a comprehensive human rights-based approach to organizing that accounts for difference is necessary.[60]

Although this is the global direction in which reproductive rights activism is moving, the mainstream movement in the US—except for its more progressive wing—has yet to adopt it. Its emphasis on individualism and civil and political rights neglects economic, social, sexual, and cultural rights that address group or collective needs. Activists are unfamiliar with the Universal Declaration of Human Rights and international treaties that protect women's reproductive rights. Their failure to adopt the human rights framework inadvertently abets the Conservative movement that fiercely opposes the US government's signing international treaties, such as the Convention on the Elimination of All Forms of Discrimination Against Women, which would make the United States accountable to international norms and standards.

The activists and organizations profiled in this book have given us a new vision for reproductive rights that incorporates the specific needs of their communities within a social justice and human rights framework. They are raising the visibility of reproductive health issues for their constituencies, advocating on their behalf, and developing the strong leadership and institutions capable of meeting those needs. In pursuit of reproductive justice, women of color are insisting on undivided rights.

NOTES

1   Fannie Lou Hamer originally said this during a speech at the 1964 Democratic National Convention in New Jersey, during which Lyndon B. Johnson was nominated as the Democratic candidate for president.

2   Byllye Avery, "A Question of Survival/A Conspiracy of Silence: Abortion and Women's Health," in *From Abortion to Reproductive Freedom: Transforming a Movement*, ed. Marlene Gerber Fried (Boston: South End Press, 1990), 78.

3   The National Black Women's Health Project was renamed Black Women's Health Imperative in 2003.

4   Angela Davis, Loretta Ross, Sally Torpy, Evelyn White, Linda Villarosa, Marlene Gerber Fried, Rosalind Petchesky, Jesse Rodríguez, and Martha Ward are among others who have written on this topic.

5   For additional documentation of the activities of women of color in the reproductive rights movement, see Linda Gordon's classic study, *Woman's Body, Woman's Right: A Social History of Birth Control in America*, rev. ed. (New York: Penguin Books, 1990); Rickie Solinger's *Beggars and Choosers: How the Politics of Choice Shapes Adoption, Abortion, and Welfare in the United States* (New York: Hill and Wang, 2001); Rosalind Petchesky's *Abortion and Woman's Choice: The State, Sexuality and Reproductive Freedom* (Boston: Northeastern University Press, 1990); Dorothy Roberts's work *Killing the Black Body* (New York: Pantheon Books, 1997); Rickie Solinger's *Wake Up Little Susie: Single Pregnancy and Race Before Roe v. Wade* (New York: Routledge, 1992); Evelyn C. White's *Black Women's Health Book: Speaking for Ourselves*, rev. ed. (Seattle: Seal Press, 1994); and Linda Villarosa's *Black Women's Guide to Physical Health and Emotional Well-Being* (New York: Harper Collins, 1994).

6   Roberts, *Killing the Black Body*, 7.

7   Asians and Pacific Islanders for Reproductive Health (APIRH) was renamed Asian Communities for Reproductive Justice (ACRJ) in May 2004. For consistency and clarity, this book refers to the organization as APIRH throughout, the name of the organization during the time of research and writing.

8   Women in other countries rarely identify themselves as "women of color" because of the various permutations of white supremacy around the globe. For example, many feminists in Great Britain who would be called women of color in the United States prefer to call themselves "black." They have embraced the term "black" to express their political solidarity with the struggle of people from Africa, Asia, the Caribbean, and the Middle East against racism and fascism. Conversely, the terms "black" and "white" in many Latin American countries denote class status as much as skin pigmentation. Chandra Mohanty and Adrien Katherine Wing describe pigment color as a sociopolitical designation for women of African, Caribbean, Asian, Latin American, and Indigenous descent. Despite the fact that they constitute a plurality of the world's people, women of color are most frequently on the bottom rung of society, whether in developed or developing countries. The concept goes far beyond mere color or racial designation and speaks instead to their consciously

chosen political relationship to each other in opposition to sexist, racist, and imperialist structures.

9   This definition of reproductive justice was created by Asian Communities for Reproductive Justice (formerly APIRH) in May 2004.

10   Loretta Ross et al., "Just Choices: Women of Color, Reproductive Health, and Human Rights," in *Policing the National Body*, ed. Jael Silliman and Anannya Bhattacharjee (Cambridge, MA: South End Press, 2002), 147.

11   *Black Woman's Voice* 2, no. 2 (Jan/Feb, 1973).

12   Jael Silliman, "Introduction," in *Policing*, x-xi.

13   Justine Smith quoted in Andrea Smith "Better Dead Than Pregnant: The Colonization of Native Women's Reproductive Health," in *Policing*, 141.

14   Center for Policy Alternatives, "Reproductive Health for Women of Color," 2002 Policy Summary, http://www.stateaction.org/issues/reprohealthwoc/reprohealthwoc.doc.

15   Some of the groups, for example COLOR and NAWHO, argue that cultural "competency" is not sufficient and instead insist that health providers be culturally *proficient*, with extensive knowledge of a woman's cultural and social experiences.

16   For example, the definition of reproductive health, as set forth by APIRH states, "If women are to have true reproductive freedom, then we must have the ability to protect and determine all aspects of our physical, emotional, and spiritual well-being. This means that we live in homes free from sexual and physical violence, live and work without fear of sexual harassment, have our environment at work and at home be safe and protected from corporate exploitation, are free from hatred due to sexual identity, value all forms of work and labor, earn equitable and livable wages, eat safe and affordable food, determine and gain access to comprehensive health care for ourselves and our families, have the support and commitment of the government and private institutions to have or not have a child and live in an environment that can support our choices. In addition, we should receive an education that honors and teaches the contributions of women, people of color, the working-class, the gay, lesbian, and transgender communities."

17   Thomas B. Littlewood, *The Politics of Population Control* (Notre Dame, IN: University of Notre Dame Press, 1977), 56.

18   Ibid.

19   Ibid., 3.

20   Martha C. Ward, *Poor Women, Powerful Men: America's Great Experiment in Family Planning* (Boulder, CO: Westview Press, 1986), 31.

21   COLOR, *The Impact of Welfare Reform on Latina Reproductive Health*, Policy Position Paper (Denver: COLOR, September 2003).

22   A series of legislative reforms set the stage for federal support for family planning. Under the Economic Opportunity Act of 1964, known as the War on Poverty and launched by President Johnson, federal funds were used to increase the number of people eligible for public assistance. The Office of Economic

Opportunity (OEO) was created to provide grants for public and private agencies for social programs to address poverty. When Congress passed the Voting Rights Act of 1965, which made it possible for more African Americans and Latinos to participate in the political process, some elected officials felt it was urgently necessary to minimize the impact and effectiveness of minority voters. The 1965 Immigration Reform Act, which removed the national-origins quotas on immigration, also added to the pressure to limit minority political strength. The first direct OEO grant for family planning services went to Corpus Christi, Texas in 1964 to target low-income Mexican American families. Despite some congressional opposition, OEO support for family planning grew rapidly under the Johnson administration. Even more importantly, in terms of available funding, the Social Security Act governing Aid for Families with Dependent Children (AFDC) was modified to require that at least 6 percent of all funds available for maternal and infant care be spent on family planning. Moreover, states were authorized to purchase services from nongovernmental providers, such as Planned Parenthood, which created open-ended funding by the federal government for family planning.

23   Ward, *Poor Women, Powerful Men*, xiii.

24   For example, in the late 1980s when leading civil rights organizations wanted to expand support for affirmative action in the Civil Rights Restoration Act legislation, they compromised with Catholic anti-abortion groups who wanted Catholic colleges and universities exempted from the provisions of the legislation that would have made it illegal to discriminate against women faculty and students who supported abortion rights. For more on this see Loretta Ross's article "Blacks and Fertility" in the magazine of the Congressional Black Caucus, *Point of View*, Winter 1988, 12.

25   Frances Beal, "Double Jeopardy: To Be Black and Female," in *The Black Woman*, ed. Toni Cade (New York: Signet, 1970) quoted in Jennifer Nelson, *Women of Color and the Reproductive Rights Movement* (New York: New York University Press, 2003), 80.

26   Roberts, *Killing the Black Body*, 5.

27   Elena R. Gutiérrez, "Policing Pregnant Pilgrims: Situating the Sterilization Abuse of Mexican Origin Women in Los Angeles County," in *Women, Health and Nation: Canada and the United States Post-WW II*, ed. Molly Ladd-Taylor et al. (Toronto: McGill-Queens University Press, 2003).

28   See chapter two of *Killing the Black Body* and Angela Davis's chapter "Women Under Attack: Victories, Backlash and the Fight for Reproductive Freedom," in her *Women, Race, and Class* (New York: Vintage Books, 1983).

29   Davis, *Women, Race, and Class*, 14.

30   Nelson, *Women of Color*, 140–143.

31   Sally Torpy, "Endangered Species: Native American Women's Struggle for Their Reproductive Rights and Racial Identity: 1970–1990" (master's thesis, University of Nebraska, 1998), 38.

32   Nelson, *Women of Color*, 66–67.

33   Suzanne Staggenborg, *The Pro-Choice Movement: Organization and Activism in the Abortion Conflict* (New York: Oxford University Press, 1991), 111; Roberts, *Killing the Black Body*, 95; Susan E. Davis and the Committee for Abortion Rights and Against Sterilization Abuse (CARASA), *Women Under Attack: Victories, Backlash and the Fight for Reproduction Freedom* (Boston: South End Press, 1988).

34   Judith A. M. Scully, "Killing the Black Community: A Commentary on the United States War on Drugs," in *Policing*, 55–80.

35   Davis, *Women, Race, and Class*, 204–206.

36   While in this book we focus on race and class, we acknowledge that sexual orientation, disability, and age also play critical roles in determining a woman's reproductive experience. It is important to note that historically the struggle for abortion rights had significant participation and leadership from lesbians who were not "out" in the organizations. Issues of sexual orientation did not become explicitly part of the pro-choice agenda until the late 1980s and still have not been fully incorporated into the pro-choice agenda. Neither the pro-choice nor the disability rights movement has consolidated around a position on "choice" and disability, and young people continue to struggle for recognition of their issues and for leadership in the mainstream movement.

37   Lucinda Cisler, "Unfinished Business: Birth Control and Women's Liberation," in *Sisterhood Is Powerful: An Anthology of Writings From the Women's Liberation Movement*, ed. Robin Morgan (New York: Vintage Books, 1970), 255–256.

38   NARAL has gone through three name incarnations. It was founded in 1969 as the National Association for the Repeal of Abortion Laws. With the legalization of abortion in 1973, it became the National Abortion and Reproductive Rights Action League. In 2003, it became NARAL Pro-Choice America. This book uses all three depending on which time period referenced.

39   Davis and CARASA, *Women Under Attack*, 29.

40   Robert Hatcher, ed., *Contraceptive Technology: International Edition* (Atlanta, GA: Printed Matter Inc., 1989), 301.

41   Ibid.

42   Women and Pharmaceuticals Project, Women's Health Action Foundation, and WEMOS, *Norplant: Under Her Skin* (Delft, The Netherlands: Eburon Press, 1993), 3.

43   Ibid., 108.

44   Asoka Bandarage, *Women, Population and Global Crisis* (London: Zed Books, 1997), 85.

45   This phrase was originally coined by Rosalind Petchesky in her groundbreaking book, *Abortion and Woman's Choice: The State, Sexuality and Reproductive Freedom* (Boston: Northeastern University Press, 1990).

46   Roberts, *Killing the Black Body*, 294.

47   Toni Bond, "Barriers Between Black Women and the Reproductive Rights Movement," *Political Environments* 8 (Winter/Spring 2001): 1–5.

48   Eveline Shen, interview by Marlene Gerber Fried, January 2001, APIRH office, Oakland, CA.

49   Deborah Gray White, *Too Heavy a Load: Black Women in Defense of Themselves, 1894–1994* (New York: W. W. Norton, 1999), 19.

50   Huping Ling, *Surviving on the Gold Mountain: A History of Chinese American Women and Their Lives* (New York: State University of New York Press, 1998), 167.

51   Shirley Hill Witt, "Native Women Today: Sexism and the Indian Woman," *Civil Rights Digest* 6 (Spring 1974): 29.

52   Center for Democratic Renewal, "Indian Issues and Anti-Indian Organizing," in *When Hate Groups Come to Town: A Handbook of Effective Community Responses* (Atlanta: CDR, 1992), 138.

53   Adaljiza Sosa Riddell, "Chicanas and El Movimiento," in *Chicana Feminist Thought: The Basic Historical Writings*, ed. Alma M. Garcia (New York: Routledge, 1997), 93.

54   Found in Solinger, *Beggars and Choosers*, 156; originally quoted in Johnnie Tillmon, "Welfare Is a Woman's Issue," *Liberation News Service*, February 26, 1972, reprinted in *America's Working Women*, ed. Rosalyn Baxandall, Linda Gordon, and Susan Reverby (New York: Random House, 1976), 357.

55   Elena R. Gutiérrez, "Policing 'Pregnant Pilgrims."

56   Samuel Huntington, *Who Are We? The Challenges to America's National Identity* (New York: Simon & Schuster, 2004).

57   Marlene Gerber Fried, ed., *From Abortion to Reproductive Freedom* (Boston: South End Press, 1990), x.

58   Institute of Women and Ethnic Studies, *Reproductive Health Bill of Rights*, 2nd ed. (New Orleans: Women of Color and the Emerging Reproductive Health Technologies Project, IWES, 2000).

59   SisterSong Women of Color Reproductive Health Collective, *A Reproductive Health Agenda for Women of Color* (New York: Casa Atabex Ache, 2001).

60   Loretta Ross et al., "The SisterSong Collective: Women of Color, Reproductive Health and Human Rights," in "Health of Women of Color," special issue, *American Journal of Health* 17 (2001): 85–100.

2

The Political Context for Women of Color Organizing

THIS chapter outlines the multiple political contexts within which women of color have organized for reproductive rights. The first section charts the rise of a fierce anti-abortion movement, its role in the re-grouping of the Right, and subsequent efforts to control women's reproduction. While these forces threatened the reproductive rights of all women, women of color were often special targets. The second section sketches the various responses by three sectors of the women's movement, including the mainstream pro-choice, reproductive rights, and women's health movements. We see how each movement's response to the attack on women's reproductive freedom was framed by the ability, or inability, to meaningfully incorporate class and race into its organizing. With the anti-abortion movement and white women's responses to it as backdrop, the third section places the strategies and actions of women of color—organizing on their own behalf—in the foreground.

The Anti-Abortion Movement and the New Right

In the US, the Catholic Church has always opposed the government's support of birth control. In 1966, to explicitly condemn government support of contraception, it formed the National Conference of Catholic Bishops after the Supreme Court legalized contraception for married couples.[1] However, it was *Roe v. Wade*, the landmark 1973 Supreme Court decision legalizing abortion, that galvanized religiously motivated opponents of reproductive freedom and abortion into a "Right to Life" political movement.[2] In November 1973, the first edition of the National Right to Life Committee's newsletter issued a call to action: "We must work for the passage of a constitutional Human Life Amendment," signaling the beginning of an orchestrated campaign to re-criminalize abortion.[3] Since *Roe*, abortion opponents have pursued multiple legal and illegal strategies—even employing deadly violence—to undermine abortion rights. The growing anti-abortion movement had important legislative successes in restricting abortion rights. Its first major victory came in 1977 when Congress passed the Hyde Amendment prohibiting Medicaid funding for abortion at the federal level. Most of the states followed suit.[4]

The anti-abortion movement was becoming a more powerful political force in the late 1970s as part of a larger conservative mobilization. Incensed by the loss of the Vietnam War, the success of the civil rights movement in dismantling segregation, and the gains of the women's and gay rights movements, conservatives wanted to win back the White House from Democratic president Jimmy Carter. In the 1980 presidential election, the Republican Party courted the emerging anti-abortion, anti-gay rights, and anti-Equal Rights Amendment constituencies that came to be known as the New Right.[5]

Weaving together anti-gay and anti-abortion strands into a perversely labeled pro-family agenda, Republicans called for a return to traditional sex roles and patriarchal family structures. With this as the centerpiece of a broader conservative agenda, they were successful in mobilizing evangelical and fundamentalist Christians and thereby revitalizing the Republican Party. Jerry Falwell founded the "Moral Majority" in 1979, proclaiming the organization to represent the real majority in America. This and other New Right organizations brought Christian fundamentalists and Catholics into a coalition that helped to elect Republican Ronald Reagan as president in 1980.[6] In turn, his election bolstered the anti-abortion movement and enabled conservative Republicans to rapidly mobilize a legal and political backlash against feminism and civil rights.

President Reagan appointed staunch anti-feminists in virtually every social policy-making position, and he moved quickly against abortion rights. In 1981, he supported a Human Life Amendment to the US Constitution that would legally recognize fetuses as persons and subordinate women's rights to fetal rights. When this effort proved too politically divisive,[7] even among opponents of abortion, Reagan's administration opted for federal legislation that would have bypassed the onerous constitutional amendment process. Though both efforts failed, they bolstered subsequent attempts to elevate the legal status of the fetus. At the state legislative level, abortion foes pushed for restrictive legislation to control the behaviors of pregnant women which they claimed were endangering the "unborn," such as the use of illegal drugs and alcohol consumption. By 1999, an estimated 200 women in more than 30 states had been prosecuted for "fetal abuse."[8] Women have even been subjected to court orders forcing them to have cesarean births, and in 2004, a woman in Utah who delayed her C-section for two weeks was accused of murder when one of her twins was stillborn.[9] Professor of politics Jean Shroedel argues that many of the post-*Roe v. Wade* abortion cases decided by the Supreme Court have shifted concern away from the woman toward the fetus.[10] The most high-profile and significant development thus far came in April 2004, when President Bush signed the Unborn Victim of Violence Act which, for the first time, accords legal status to the fetus throughout pregnancy.[11]

During the early 1980s, Operation Rescue and its affiliates around the country mobilized thousands of eager participants in a strategy of civil disobedience.[12] Anti-abortion activists staged prayer vigils and sit-ins and blockaded entrances at family planning clinics. The success of Operation Rescue's tactics was evident in 1988 during the Democratic National Convention in Atlanta, when anti-abortion movement groups targeted local clinics in an effort to shut them down. Over 1,000 protesters were arrested, and thousands more were involved in the actions. While the clinics remained open during the "Siege of Atlanta," abortion providers were under daily attack, and the women who worked at the clinics, as well as the women who sought their services, had to cross a blockade of protesters.[13]

For this work, Operation Rescue claimed the mantle of the civil rights movement,[14] provoking the response of 14 veterans of the civil rights movement who issued a statement, "Civil Rights and Reproductive Rights," at a 1989 press conference, expressing their resentment at the theft of civil rights imagery:

> The adoption of the tactic of civil disobedience is their right, but the appropriation of the moral imperative of the civil rights movement is all wrong. The civil rights struggle sought to extend constitutional rights to all Americans and have those rights enforced. Today's anti-abortionists, quite to the contrary, are attempting, in the Operation Rescue protests,

to deny American women their constitutional right to freedom of choice. They want the constitution rewritten.[15]

Women of color were not taken in by the poorly disguised anti-abortion-as-civil-rights rhetoric. For the most part, they knew that the waves of primarily white (male) protesters were not seeking to save their babies, and that their real targets were young white women—who happened to be obtaining more than 70 percent of the abortions in the United States at that time.[16] Dázon Dixon Diallo, who worked at the Feminist Women's Health Center in Atlanta, described a client's resistance to the protestors' messages:

> The [young, black] client I was protecting seemed to handle the pleas to "save her baby from these murderers" very well—she realized that these people just didn't understand or care about her. But when a young-looking, blonde and blue-eyed man screamed charges at her that the Rev. Martin Luther King Jr. would "turn over in his grave for what she was doing" and that she was "contributing to the genocide of African Americans," she broke. She stopped, stared him in his eyes with tears in hers, then quietly and coolly said, "You're a white boy, and you don't give a damn thing about me, who I am, or what I do."[17]

Despite intense organizing, only a small number of people of color joined the anti-abortion movement. However, those who did, such as Dr. Mildred Jefferson, were vocal and prominently displayed. Jefferson was the first prominent woman of color to speak out publicly against abortion; she served as chairperson of the board of the National Right to Life Committee and she provided congressional testimony in 1974 in favor of a constitutional amendment that would protect fetal life. A few African American women who had experienced sterilization abuse were also recruited by the anti-abortion movement and gained national attention when they formed Blacks for Life. In 2003, sociologist Louis Prisock found it difficult to determine the number of African American anti-choice organizations, but he reports indications that their numbers are rising.[18]

Not all opponents of abortion embraced nonviolence. During this same period of time, anti-abortion terrorism developed,[19] and throughout the 1980s and 90s there was an escalation of violence against abortion clinics and clinic personnel, especially abortion providers. The tactics they used were borrowed from the far Right white supremacist movement and included bombings, arson, and kidnappings. By 1990, 80 percent of clinics had experienced some serious form of violence or harassment. Throughout the 1990s, these threats and attacks became routine. To date, there have been seven murders at abortion clinics, and clinics must now devote considerable portions of their budgets to security.

Violence and harassment have contributed to decreasing abortion access. These tactics are part of a long-term anti-choice strategy whose ultimate goal is outlawing abortion entirely. Legislation and judicial actions are also key to this strategy. Consequently, the anti-abortion battle in the courts has raged continuously since *Roe* with mixed success. In 1981 the Supreme Court upheld the Hyde Amendment.[20] Then, in 1989, with the decision in *Webster v. Reproductive Health Services*, the Court upheld the right of states to restrict abortion in a range of ways that had previously been deemed inconsistent with Roe.[21] In his dissent, Justice Blackmun, author of the *Roe* decision, articulated the fear that *Webster* augured the end of abortion rights:

> Thus, "not with a bang, but a whimper," the plurality discards a landmark case of the last generation, and casts into darkness the hopes and visions of every woman in this country who had come to believe that the Constitution guaranteed her the right to exercise some control over her unique ability to bear children...For today, at least, the law of abortion stands undisturbed. For today, the women of this Nation still retain the liberty to control their destinies. But the signs are evident and very ominous, and a chill wind blows.[22]

Following closely behind *Webster*, in 1990 the Supreme Court upheld restrictions on minors' rights to abortion in *Hodgson v. Minnesota*, which seriously curtailed abortion rights for young women under 18 years old. Again in 1992, in *Planned Parenthood v. Casey*, the Court further chipped away at abortion rights.[23] The assault on abortion rights abated somewhat at the federal level after Clinton's election in 1992 but reignited under the 2000 Bush administration. Meanwhile, state-level attacks have been persistent for over 25 years. The net result has been significant erosion in access to abortion, which has the most adverse impact on low-income women, young women, and women of color.

Responses to the Anti-Abortion Movement

Stopping Water with a Rake

Three parts of the feminist movement—the pro-choice, reproductive rights, and women's health movements—responded with significantly different approaches to the anti-abortion movement and the rise of the New Right. This section offers a glimpse into the differences and gives insight into the questions of inclusion raised in the first chapter. Although women of color were active in all three movements, the majority was primarily white and middle class. This section also details the evolution of and need for race- and ethnic-based organizing by women of color.

The Mainstream Pro-Choice Movement

While the legalization of abortion mobilized opponents, it demobilized the majority of pro-choice advocates. Because the ability to find and finance abortion services was not a problem for middle-class white feminists, it appeared to them that with *Roe*, the battle for abortion rights had been won. Thus in 1977, when Congress passed the Hyde Amendment prohibiting federal funding for abortions, the leading women's organizations that had rallied for *Roe* did not marshal a large-scale response. This issue was of primary importance to women of color, who are disproportionately low-income. Thus, this was a divisive and watershed moment for the pro-choice movement. It could have confronted the overt white supremacy of the Right's agenda and its own internal racism, had it made overturning Hyde and fighting for public funding a priority. By not doing so, it seemed to women of color that the pro-choice movement was not concerned with their rights.

As we have seen, between *Roe* and Reagan, a full-blown and multi-faceted war on abortion rights had been launched in the courts and in the streets. Finally, with the looming threat of an anti-abortion constitutional amendment, a visible pro-choice movement re-emerged in 1981. However, the pro-choice response was defensive and its mission narrow. Pro-choice activists framed their politics in terms of choice and privacy, instead of using the language of women's rights and autonomy. "Abortion" itself was replaced by the more neutral appeal to defend the "legal right to choose." Their focus was on creating a winnable strategy to defend the legal right to abortion, not to secure access.

Journalist William Saletan argues that mainstream pro-choice groups made a considered decision to recast their demands in an effort to broaden their base. Believing that most voters did not care about women's rights, they framed the issue in terms of intrusions by big government, a fundamentally conservative approach. In 1984, working with political strategists whose experience was in electoral politics in the Democratic Party, National Abortion Reproductive Rights Action League (NARAL), Planned Parenthood, and others conducted a national poll to determine what messages would be effective with conservative voters and could drive a wedge into the conservative opposition. They found that many voters, hostile to welfare and taxes, opposed both banning and paying for abortions. There was a clear racial divide: Blacks were in favor of funding, albeit by a narrow margin, while whites were overwhelmingly opposed.[24] Saletan starkly articulates the possible courses of action: "Confronted by this latent coalition of pro-life, anti-government, anti-tax, anti-welfare, and anti-black voters, abortion rights activists had two choices. They could declare war against all of these constituencies in the name of a broad liberal agenda. Or they could divide the coalition and isolate pro-lifers by seducing the other constituencies."[25] To woo voters who routinely opposed government interference in social issues,[26] they chose the latter and put a libertarian spin on it. Abortion restrictions were criticized as encroachments by big government on tradition, family, and property.

This approach was partially successful, at least temporarily. It split the opposition by bringing pro-family, anti-government voters into the pro-choice electoral coalition. However, adopting privacy as the rubric for long-term pro-choice organizing backfired politically. It undercut demands for public access to abortion that had characterized the feminist struggle for legalization in the 1960s and 70s.[27] It also played into the hands of conservatives who were denouncing "big government," thus reinforcing the federal government's position, under the 1977 Hyde Amendment, that it had no obligation to pay for women's private decisions to have abortions. Saletan argues that the pro-choice movement created a "mutant version of abortion rights as a viable alternative to the feminist, egalitarian version originally envisioned by pro-choice activists."[28] He further notes that the limited definition of abortion rights made it possible to be pro-choice *and* to accept restrictions such as parental involvement laws and bans on public funding of abortion.

It is important to acknowledge that within the mainstream, there were other dissenting voices. For example, the American Civil Liberties Union (ACLU) and the National Organization for Women (NOW) consistently kept a feminist women's rights approach that incorporated a breadth of issues and strategies.[29] NOW also believed in the importance of large, visible mobilizations. For example, on April 9, 1986, NOW organized the first national march for abortion rights, the March to Save Women's Lives. Exceeding the organizers' expectations, more than 600,000 demonstrators participated in what was at that time the largest women's march in US history. This was also a turning point in the age composition of the pro-choice movement—half the participants were young women who came of age in a country where abortion had always been legal. As we shall see later in the chapter, NOW, along with a handful of other organizations, made efforts—with varying degrees of success—to reach out to women of color. The organization was also an early opponent of welfare reform.

However, the broader and more radical approach did not prevail. Instead, the narrowly gauged conservative strategies and messages came to dominate the mainstream pro-choice movement. It did not address access to abortion or the larger context of reproductive health care and left out a central element of the reproductive rights agenda of women of color: the right to have children. While this framing brought moderate and conservative voters to abortion rights,[30] it was at the expense of dividing feminists, alienating poor women, women of color, more radical white activists, and those from the holistic women's health movement.[31]

We think that this strategy was a mistake in the long run, and that it was predicated on a misreading of the organizing tactics employed by the opposition. The Right created single-issue organizations for tactical purposes, but never lost sight of its multi-issue agenda. Thus it could achieve an important degree of unified action despite internal tensions on specific issues. In this way, people with strong feelings about a specific issue were brought into a broader conservative movement.

In contrast, the single-issue approach of the pro-choice movement did not create a broader politics or lead to building an enduring progressive coalition. Instead, activists with a broader perspective were driven away and created their own organizations outside the mainstream pro-choice groups. Some moved from choice to reproductive rights; others focused on access to and information about reproductive health services;

and women of color began mobilizing for a new reproductive rights agenda. The following sections explore these various approaches.

The Reproductive Rights Movement

The pro-choice movement's failure to mount significant opposition to the Hyde Amendment and its refusal to join women of color in connecting sterilization abuse to abortion rights mobilized white abortion rights advocates who had broader politics and different political roots. Activists who came from the progressive movements of the 1960s—civil rights, the New Left, the anti-war and the women's liberation movements—insisted on keeping abortion rights within a feminist framework, which emphasized sexual freedom and highlighted how race and class shape reproductive choice. These activists criticized the mainstream pro-choice movement for being too middle-class focused, for lacking an emphasis on access, and for being too defensive and conservative. They were also critical of the preoccupation with electoral politics. They formed grassroots groups and feminist clinics, articulated broader messages, and promoted radical and direct-action strategies. Their goal was to mobilize the large numbers of people who would not be attracted to the mainstream's politics.

One of the first and largest organizations to embrace a reproductive rights agenda was the Committee for Abortion Rights and Against Sterilization Abuse (CARASA). The organization was formed in 1977 by women who had been involved in the civil rights and anti-Vietnam War movements in the 1960s and 70s. CARASA distinguished itself from the major national organizations, specifically NARAL and Planned Parenthood, whose abortion rights efforts were focused primarily on lobbying, legislative work, direct mail, and education through the media. CARASA saw a need for other forms of activism: "While this work is necessary at the present time, exclusively focusing on it ignores the importance of grassroots organizing and education—going directly into neighborhoods, workplaces, schools, churches and the streets, where the Right-to-Life Movement has organized, in order to create a truly popular movement for reproductive freedom and not just a lobby of experts."[32] CARASA saw the mainstream pro-choice organizations as narrow at best and, at worst, as taking positions that undermined the reproductive freedom of many women. In this regard, they specifically cited hostility to regulations regarding sterilization abuse and the use of population control arguments for abortion rights. Following the lead of women of color, CARASA placed opposition to sterilization abuse on a par with support for abortion rights.

In 1979, CARASA co-founded the Reproductive Rights National Network (R2N2), an umbrella organization for national and grassroots groups that situated abortion rights within a broader social justice and anti-racist context. R2N2's membership was varied; affiliates included feminist health clinics, women's caucuses of national Left organizations, and unaffiliated local activist organizations. They defined themselves as reproductive rights activists to distinguish their perspective from the single-issue politics of the pro-choice movement. R2N2 also espoused the critique of population control and "choice" that had been articulated by women of color. It emphasized access to abortion services and funds, arguing that without access, abortion rights would not be realized for low-income women and women of color.

R2N2 was an eager ally for the newly emerging women of color reproductive rights organizations. However, while R2N2 saw the link between women's oppression and ending racism, it was not always successful in putting its politics into practice, nor was it equipped to deal with racism within its organizations. Thus, in 1981, national R2N2 split and ultimately dissolved over disputes about whether to make fighting racism within the organization its top priority. There was a painful struggle which pitted opposition to the anti-abortion offensives against internal anti-racist work. This polarization itself is evidence of the inability of many white women to overcome the racial divide. As activists and scholars of color have noted, at that time even the more radical wings of the women's movement did not consistently or meaningfully integrate race, class, and gender oppression into their agendas.

The Women's Health Movement

While there was some overlap in membership and in politics, the women's health movement developed outside and alongside the pro-choice and reproductive rights movements. Beginning in 1969, when abortion was still illegal in most states and reproductive health care was in the hands of the mostly male health care establishment, many feminists mobilized "to wrest back some control over their sexuality, their reproductive lives, and their health from their doctors, and particularly their obstetrician gynecologists."[33] This was a largely decentralized movement of grassroots organizations. Historian Sandra Morgen's description of its beginnings captures this well: "In different sites, through different means, across the country, women began to take their health care into their own hands."[34] Women's health activism took several forms, which included disseminating information, advocating new ways of providing services, promoting Self-Help, patient advocacy, community organizing and counseling services, providing safe illegal abortions, and in many communities, establishing feminist clinics.[35]

The post-*Roe* assault against abortion rights had a severe impact on women's clinics and health advocacy groups. Many had received financial support from federal or state programs. Thus the specific restrictions on abortion (such as the Hyde Amendment and similar laws at the state level), the overall cuts in social spending for programs and services for poor women, and the anti-abortion violence all took their toll. Organizations and clinics faced constant financial pressures. They were forced to lay off staff and cut programs. Ultimately, many had to close or were bought out by mainstream providers. Then, in the 1980s, HIV/AIDS brought new actors and issues, reinvigorating women's health activism.

Though the women's health movement was grounded in local grassroots activism, advocates sought to consolidate its influence on Capitol Hill. In 1975, the National Women's Health Lobby was founded in Washington, DC. Later renamed the National Women's Health Network (NWHN), the organization was established "to monitor Federal health agencies and ensure that the voice of a national women's health movement would be heard on Capitol Hill."[36] The network was a key player in the women's health movement in general and was particularly important to women of color, emphasizing organizational support for activists of color from the outset. When several women of color were brought onto the NWHN board at once, their presence and voting power were maximized. The diverse NWHN board membership also enabled the white women and women of color to learn from and support one another. Longtime network board member and program committee chair Judy Norsigian observed, "We developed relationships by making ourselves available for advice, counsel, and information. We provided ongoing support through these more informal yet sustained contacts. The idea was to be there when you were needed."[37] The network encouraged women of color to establish their own organizations.

The women's health movement developed a critique of mainstream health care, which incorporated racism and classism as well as sexism. This movement provided an important home and support network for women of color activists, many of whom worked in clinics or other feminist health advocacy organizations. However, like the reproductive rights movement, the women's health movement was a site of struggle around differences of race, ethnicity, class, and sexual orientation. In clinic settings these were not abstract debates, but intense disagreements, especially over specific issues such as mission, development and location of services, and hiring and firing.[38]

As we have seen, the politics of race and class permeated all three responses to the political threats posed by the rise of the New Right and the anti-abortion movement. These forces set the context within which women of color organized for reproductive rights.

Organizing by Women of Color

Although the National Black Women's Health Project (NBWHP), formed in 1984, was the first women of color reproductive health organization to be created and remained the only national women of color group until the late 1980s, many of the individuals and organizations of women of color featured in this study became active in pro-choice organizing in the 1970s and early 80s. They were alarmed by the thinly veiled white supremacist agenda of the New Right and the rise of the anti-abortion movement.

Women of color organizing for reproductive rights have always needed to respond simultaneously to state-imposed policies aimed at controlling their fertility and to social justice movements that neglected their reproductive health concerns. Loretta Ross sets out the various strategies used by women of color:

> Sometimes we work with predominantly white organizations that marginalize issues of race and class, and privilege abortion rights over other issues of reproductive justice...Some of us work with people of color organizations that marginalize gender and class issues, and where women's reproductive health issues are tangential to struggles against racism... Some women of color work with anti-poverty organizations that sometimes neglect race and gender issues altogether, assuming that class issues subsume concerns about reproductive health.[39]

This section outlines a few of the ways in which women of color organized for reproductive justice.

Working with Mainstream Pro-Choice Organizations

By the mid-1980s, several activist women of color had been recruited to positions of leadership in the large mainstream pro-choice groups. In 1978, Faye Wattleton became the first African American to head the Planned Parenthood Federation of America, a position she held for 14 years until 1992. Luz Alvarez Martínez joined the national NARAL board and called for greater representation of women of color in the organization. Emily Tynes was NARAL's first African American director of communications (1983–1988); Judy Logan-White and Faith Evans (an African American woman and man) created the Women of Color Partnership Program as part of the Religious Coalition for Abortion Rights (RCAR) in 1984.[40] Loretta Ross became the first director of Women of Color Programs at NOW (1985–1989), a post that had previously been called the "minority rights" staff position.

These activists were able to accomplish significant outreach to women of color through and in coalition with mainstream organizations. In 1986, women of color at RCAR, NOW, NARAL, and Planned Parenthood began organizing local and regional forums for women of color about reproductive rights.[41] These gatherings provided the opportunity for activists of color to meet together—often for the first time—to discuss how to move their reproductive health concerns to the national level.

On the heels of these synergy-building gatherings and one year after the historic 1986 NOW-sponsored pro-choice march, Loretta Ross organized the first National Conference on Women of Color and Reproductive Rights, held at Howard University. Despite the fact that women of color had been active and in the leadership of NOW from its inception, they were also skeptical of NOW.[42] Ross intended for the conference to build a bridge between women of color and NOW. She reached out to women of color she knew from other movements, including violence against women, teen pregnancy, and anti-poverty organizations, to involve them in reproductive rights activism. She states, "It was the first conference in history that brought women from the feminist, civil rights, and black Nationalist movements together to promote reproductive freedom."[43] Casting a wide net was necessary since, despite the fact that they were pro-choice, relatively few women of color activists would have responded to a narrow call.

In addition to Ross, this trailblazing conference was coordinated by women of color working at pro-choice organizations, including Planned Parenthood, NARAL, and RCAR, who were responding to the concerns of women of color who felt their perspectives and leadership were not adequately advanced by the pro-choice movement. As a result, at the conference of women of color, the white leaders of sponsoring organizations were not prominently featured. Of the more than 400 women of color who attended the conference, two-thirds were African Americans—with a sizable delegation from the NBWHP, by then a three-year old organization. Participants came together across identity groups to talk about the reproductive health issues in their different communities. Many of the women of color active in the movement today met for the first time at that conference, and went on to build long-term networks and relationships which spurred future activism.

The conference was a place for women of color to articulate their own agendas, and it demonstrated that they would mobilize for reproductive justice if race and class dimensions were prioritized. While the explicit purpose of the conference was to mobilize more women of color to participate in the pro-choice movement, the women who came also advanced a critique of that movement.[44]

Two years later, the impending Supreme Court decision in *Webster v. Reproductive Health Services* (1989) catalyzed other organizing activities by women of color. Seeking to limit the public provision of abortion services, *Webster* posed a severe threat to low-income women and women of color. A national conference called "In Defense of *Roe*" was organized in April of 1989 by the Women of Color Partnership Program of RCAR and Lynn Paltrow of the ACLU's Reproductive Freedom Project. Women of color, community organizers, and women of faith came together to strategize against the anticipated state-level attacks on *Roe v. Wade* that would follow *Webster*.

The meeting identified two priorities: a national reproductive rights organization for women of color and the development of local coalitions. It inspired women of color to engage in reproductive rights organizing across the country. For example, the meeting marked the first time that Asian and Pacific Islander women from different cultures came together to discuss reproductive rights issues. They wrote a collective statement stressing their diverse perspectives and common purpose: "This is a historic moment for us. Recognizing the tradition of family and community, including alternative lifestyles, we, as Asian Pacific American women, underscore the importance of a reproductive health agenda for our communities."[45]

Patricia Camp, state coordinator of the Illinois affiliate of the national RCAR, said, "Being able to make a movement of our own, which deals with reproductive health issues in our own way and from our own perspective is the most valuable service that this conference provided."[46] Inspired and angered by what she learned at the conference, Migdalia Rivera, consultant to the Hispanic Health Council of Hartford, Connecticut, took information about the potential impact of anti-choice public policies on poor Latinas back to her community and energized activists.[47]

The "In Defense of *Roe*" conference was planned to coincide with the second National March for Women's Lives organized by NOW. While more than 100 organizations of women of color had endorsed the first march, Sharon Parker of the National Institute for Women of Color described their actual presence as "drowning in a sea of white." In striking contrast to the 1986 march, in 1989 women of color took steps to make their presence highly visible. With Parker's assistance— further aided by the NBWHP sending 13 bus loads of women to the Washington, DC, march—a delegation of 5,000 women of color rallied behind one giant banner, "Women of Color for Reproductive Rights." Following the march, Reverend Yvonne Delk, director of the Office of Church in Society of the United Church of Christ, issued a call to action:

> We are women who have been and continue to be discriminated against in employment, locked into stereotyped roles, sexually exploited, politically subdivided, trivialized and domesticated by those who would deny us the right to control our bodies and our lives. What we say and do today has long reaching implications, not only for the women of color in this nation and for women of color throughout the globe, but it is our legacy to the generations of women who are yet unborn.[48]

In May 1989, one month after the *Webster* decision, Donna Brazile of the National Political Congress of Black Women and Loretta Ross of NOW organized African American Women for Reproductive Freedom, a new coalition of high-profile women. They published *We Remember:*

African American Women for Reproductive Freedom, written by Marcia Gillespie, then an editor of *Ms. Magazine*. The statement was a way to elevate African American women's voices in the public debate about abortion. Gillespie wrote:

> This freedom—to choose and to exercise our choices—is what we've fought and died for. Brought here in chains, worked like mules, bred like beasts, whipped one day, sold the next...Somebody said that we were less than human and not fit for freedom. Somebody said we were like children and could not be trusted to think for ourselves...Somebody said that black women could be raped, held in concubinage, forced to bear children year in and year out, but often not raise them. Oh yes, we have known how painful it is to be without choice in this land.[49]

We Remember was a profound articulation of the connection between reproductive justice and the struggle for racial justice. The *We Remember* campaign was overwhelmingly successful. In six brief months, more than 250,000 copies of the brochure were reprinted and distributed across the country, through mailings, at conferences, and at events organized by women of color. Faye Wattleton[50] of Planned Parenthood and Kate Michelman of NARAL provided the funding and agreed not to put their organizational logos on the brochure so that the focus would remain on women of color. The coalition's impassioned statement represented an important national collaboration between autonomous African American women's organizations that were not necessarily focused on abortion access and black women who worked in mainstream pro-choice organizations.

Women of Color Working for Social Justice Organizations

Historically, civil rights, environmental, and immigrant rights groups have not included reproductive rights in their agendas. Nevertheless, women of color participating in reproductive rights organizations have consistently looked for ways to work with groups that focus on economic and racial justice. Reproductive rights activists have joined in coalitions with the NAACP, Asian Pacific Environmental Network, American Indian Movement, and Mexican American Legal Defense Fund and drawn attention to reproductive rights in the context of these struggles.

In addition to bringing reproductive rights to social justice organizations, the search for allies has also led women of color to build coalitions that bring a wide range of groups to the service of reproductive justice. For example, the 1993 Campaign for Abortion and Reproductive Equity (CARE), organized by the NBWHP, brought over 300 civil rights, labor, and pro-choice organizations together in an effort to overturn the Hyde Amendment and restore federal Medicaid funding for abortion. While many of these groups were not interested in supporting abortion rights per se, they were concerned about equity and responded to the call to challenge discrimination and support racial and economic justice.[51]

Reproductive rights activists faced other challenges in trying to work with economic justice organizations. Although many of the organizations that work on poverty, homeless advocacy, and welfare reform are led by women of color, ironically, these groups have sometimes neglected race and gender issues. Because some groups are financially dependent on the Catholic Church, openly expressing their support for reproductive rights would jeopardize their funding.

Organizations and groups working on HIV/AIDS and violence against women have also been important allies for reproductive rights activists of color. Because problems such as HIV/AIDS and domestic violence are widespread in their communities, women of color have had more success recently in bringing these issues out in the open—after encountering initial silence and resistance. Through responding to the direct service needs of the communities, serving battered women and people with HIV/AIDS, they linked together advocacy and service delivery. Churches in particular have focused on helping women and children through direct services such as providing meals and shelter. Through these services, bridges were built between churches and other community institutions that had been reluctant to address feminist and gay and lesbian issues and advocates from these movements.

National Coalitions of Women of Color

Since the late 1980s, there have been four major national collaborations among women of color. Several of the founders of the eight organizations included in our case studies played leading roles in these efforts, met each other through these activities, and formed alliances that strengthened them as leaders. By 1992, there were national women of color organizations, but they were frustrated by their inability to be fully respected partners in the pro-choice movement. In order to have a greater impact on both the mainstream movement and US domestic policy, in 1992 six organizations launched the Women of Color Coalition for Reproductive Health Rights (WOCCRHR): Asians and Pacific Islanders for Choice, National Black Women's Health Project, National Latina Health Organization, Latina Roundtable on Health and Reproductive Rights, National Coalition of 100 Black Women, and Native American Women's Health and Education Resource Center. WOCCRHR represented the first effort to build a national women of color reproductive health coalition.

The most immediate challenge for WOCCRHR was to determine the role it would play in the third national March for Women's Lives organized by NOW in 1992, given that the women of color organizations had not been included in the planning. Despite excluding them from the leadership, march organizers expected women of color to mobilize their constituencies to attend. Ultimately WOCCRHR decided to support the 1992 NOW march, but published a statement objecting to the fact that they were not included in the organizing process. A memo from the NBWHP circulated with WOCCRHR's statement clearly states the problem:

> The NBWHP has joined with a number of women of color reproductive rights organizations to protest NOW's process (or lack of process) for the inclusion of women of color in the scheduled April 5 March for Reproductive Freedom...We do not want people to stay away, especially women of color. These issues affect us and we need to be seen and heard in support of reproductive freedom. However, we must also speak out regarding NOW's practices involving the lack of inclusion of all the women of color reproductive rights groups.[52]

The coalition's response was an unprecedented challenge from women of color to NOW and the other major pro-choice organizations regarding their politics of exclusion. NOW's practice in march planning had been to invite to the decision-making table only those people who were able to commit significant financial resources to organizing multi-million-dollar marches. This process ensured that women with power stayed in power and marginalized women of color.

Two years following NOW's third March for Women's Lives, the founders of WOCCRHR organized again in order to have an impact on the September 1994 United Nations International Conference on Population and Development (ICPD) in Cairo, Egypt. As part of the US delegation to the Cairo conference, WOCCRHR delegates and other women of color within the larger delegation, in a first joint effort, established the US Women of Color Delegation Project. The project members authored a "Statement on Poverty, Development, and Population Activities," which they presented at an ICPD workshop. The introduction outlines the reasons for their intervention:

> Much of what is known of US policies is developed mostly by white, upper and middle class Americans. This document reflects a people of color perspective on issues of population as they interact with institutional policies of racism, political oppression, and classism and gender bias to entrench poverty and "underdevelopment" within our society.[53]

The delegation's statement connected the lack of reproductive freedom for poor and marginalized women in the US, many of whom are women of color, with that of women in developing countries. It made clear that many women in the US did not enjoy reproductive rights.

Through these efforts, WOCCRHR brought the situation of women of color in the United States to the attention of the international community and created enduring friendships and alliances. Upon returning from Cairo, they decided to join ranks a third time to bring women of color to the United Nations Fourth World Conference on Women in Beijing, China in September 1995. The US Women of Color Beijing coalition provided information, leadership training, and strategic planning for women of color to participate effectively in the Beijing conference.

After the Cairo and Beijing conferences, the women in WOCCRHR found that funding was unavailable for them to continue their working relationships once they returned home. This was largely because funding for international "population" activities is separated from funding for domestic reproductive rights work within foundations. Nevertheless, their participation in these international events produced significant shifts in their thinking about how to frame the demand for reproductive freedom for women of color in the United States. By attending the conference, they connected their local and national struggles to the global movements against poverty and for women's rights. They returned home determined to forge ahead in building a national movement of women of color for reproductive health that would, for the first time, incorporate the global human rights framework into their activism.

The fourth coalition effort came in 1997 when the SisterSong Women of Color Reproductive Health Collective was formed.[54] The Collective included 16 organizations representing four communities of women of color: African American, Asian American and Pacific Islander, Latina, and Indigenous. SisterSong's original mission was advocacy for the reproductive and sexual health needs of women of color. Its strategy has been to mobilize at the grassroots level while also developing a public policy agenda.[55]

The groups involved in SisterSong address a wide range of reproductive health issues, including HIV/AIDS services, midwifery, services for incarcerated women, health screenings, abortion and contraceptive advocacy, clinical research, teen pregnancy programs, cancer screenings, drug and alcohol treatment programs, and programs for the treatment and prevention of sexually transmitted diseases. This inclusive range of programs illustrates the scope and depth of the organizing work on reproductive and sexual health issues done by women of color from Puerto Rico to Hawaii. SisterSong sponsored its first national conference on women of color and reproductive health and sexual rights issues in November 2003 at Spelman College in Atlanta. More than 600 people, mostly women of color, participated in this event, marking a new era of reproductive justice organizing by women of color. Most recently, the collective organized women of color to participate in the April 2004 March for Women's Lives under the banner "Women of Color for Reproductive Justice."

These coalitions have taken essential steps in building a movement of women of color for reproductive justice. The threats to reproductive rights and women's health continue unabated. As always, the effects from erosions in access to care and services fall disproportionately on women of color. It is our belief that the following eight case studies offer the visions and strategies we need to move forward on an inclusive reproductive agenda.

NOTES

1   In 1965, the Supreme Court decision in *Griswold* legalized contraception for married couples. See Pam Chamberlain and Jean Hardisty, "Reproducing Patriarchy: Reproductive Rights Under Siege," in *Defending Reproductive Rights: An Activist Resource Kit* (Somerville, MA: Political Research Associates, 2000), 3.

2   Marcy J. Wilder, "Law, Violence and Morality," in *Abortion Wars: A Half Century of Struggle, 1950–2000*, ed. Rickie Solinger (Berkeley: University of California Press, 1998), 79.

3   Ibid.

4   For more information on the Hyde Amendment see Rosalind Petchesky, *Abortion and Women's Choice: The State, Sexuality and Reproductive Freedom* (Boston: Northeastern University Press, 1990), 293–294, 297–299. For updated information about the ongoing impact of the Hyde Amendment, see *Justice Demands Abortion Funding: Mobilizing to Meet Women's Needs, Challenging Restrictions on Public Funding*, a report published by the National Network of Abortion Funds in April 2004.

5   Anita Bryant's *Save Our Children* campaign in Florida and the Briggs Amendment in California both occurred during the 1970s.

6   Petchesky, *Abortion and Women's Choice*, 261.

7   Chamberlain and Hardisty, "Reproducing Patriarchy," 4.

8   Lynn Paltrow, "Pregnant Drug Users, Fetal Persons, and the Threat to *Roe v. Wade*," *Albany Law Review* 62 (1999): 1000.

9   "Harm to Fetuses Becomes Issue in Utah and Elsewhere," *New York Times*, March 27, 2004. Ultimately the murder charge was dropped, but she was given 18 months of probation on a charge of child endangerment.

10   Jean Reith Schroedel, *Is the Fetus a Person? A Comparison of Policies across the Fifty States* (Ithaca, NY: Cornell University Press, 2000), 46. In addition, Schroedel documents the elevation of the fetus in legal cases involving third-party fetal killing/injury.

11   The Unborn Victims of Violence Act, also known as Laci and Conner's Law, is named for Laci Peterson, a woman who was murdered when she was eight months pregnant. Her husband is being tried for the murder. Public outrage over this case dovetailed with anti-abortion strategy to pass the UVVA. More than 30 states have similar laws. Attorney Lynn Paltrow, executive director of National Advocates for Pregnant Women, sees UVVA as a threat not just to abortion rights but also to women wanting to continue their pregnancies. In her article "Policing Pregnancy," she argues that "far from safeguarding pregnant women or children, the UVVA creates the legal foundation for policing pregnancy and punishing women who carry their pregnancies to term." Lynn Paltrow, "Policing Pregnancy," *Tompaine.com*, http://www.tompaine.com/scontent/10189.html.

12   In 1988–89, 32,000 people were arrested. About 12,000 people were arrested once and 5,750 people account for the remaining 20,000 arrests, as documented

by Ann Baker in her article "Pro-Choice Activism Springs From Many Sources," in *From Abortion to Reproductive Freedom: Transforming a Movement*, ed. Marlene Gerber Fried (Boston: South End Press, 1990), 179.

13   Patricia Baird-Windle and Eleanor J. Bader, *Targets of Hatred* (New York: Palgrave/St. Martin's Press, 2001), 112–113.

14   Operation Rescue did not invent the anti-abortion claim of being a civil rights movement; it had previously been used in the 1970s by John O'Keefe. Ironically, several of those who became active in the extremist wing of the anti-abortion movement met in jail in Atlanta. For more on this history, see James Risen and Judy L. Thomas, *Wrath of Angels: The American Abortion War* (New York: Basic Books, 1998).

15   "The Campaign Report" quoted in Baker "Pro-Choice Activism," 184.

16   Loretta Ross, Sherrilyn Ifill, and Sabrae Jenkins, "Emergency Memorandum to Women of Color," in *From Abortion to Reproductive Freedom*, 149.

17   Dázon Dixon, "Operation Oppress You: Women's Rights Under Siege," in *From Abortion to Reproductive Freedom*, 185–186.

18   Louis Prisock, "If You Love Children, Say So," *The Public Eye* 17, no. 3 (2003): 6.

19   These acts were not recognized as terrorism, nor was there a federal response until President Clinton's election in 1992.

20   *Harris v. McRae*, 448 US 297 (1981).

21   For example, *Webster* allows states to prohibit public facilities and public employees from performing or assisting in abortions which are not necessary to save the life of the pregnant woman, permits states to conduct tests to determine fetal viability on women seeking abortions who appear to be at least 20 weeks pregnant, and grants states the new power to ban an abortion if the fetus is viable.

22   *Webster v. Reproductive Health Services*, 109 S. Ct. 3040, 3077–3079 (1989), found in Rhonda Copelon, "From Privacy to Autonomy: The Conditions for Sexual and Reproductive Freedom," in *From Abortion to Reproductive Freedom*, 27.

23   In *Casey*, the Court replaced the strict judicial scrutiny which governs other "fundamental" rights with the weaker and vaguer undue burden standard. This opened the door to a wide range of federal and state criminal restrictions.

24   William Saletan, *Bearing Right: How Conservatives Won the Abortion War* (Berkeley: University of California Press, 2003), 15.

25   Ibid.

26   William Saletan, "Electoral Politics and Abortion: Narrowing the Message," in *Abortion Wars*, 118.

27   Ibid.

28   Ibid., 119.

29   Its origins were in DC policy circles. NOW was created in 1966 by women who had been delegates to a conference of Equal Employment Opportunity Commission state commissions. Two years after the Civil Rights Act was

passed, the EEOC seemed uninterested in enforcing the sex discrimination part of the act. When a resolution to do so was blocked from a vote, angry delegates, including Betty Friedan, Pauli Murray, Mary Eastwood, and Kathryn Clarenbach, founded NOW. While ending sex discrimination was the overarching goal of NOW, there were several political tensions within the organization, including friction between members who did not think it necessary to challenge the prevailing social and economic system to achieve that goal and others who believed that patriarchal capitalism would have to go. See Winifred D. Wandersee, *American Women in the 1970s: On the Move* (Boston: Twayne Publishers, 1988), 40.

30   Saletan, "Electoral Politics," 117.

31   It was a reminder of the racist, population-control skeletons in the pro-choice movement's closet. For example, Planned Parenthood, a key player in contemporary pro-choice politics, has historical ties to both eugenics and population control politics. The founders and most of the early activists of NARAL (originally National Abortion Rights Action League—now, NARAL Pro-Choice America) came from the world of family planning, but some were from the population control movement. Even though NARAL adopted a women's rights rather than a population control approach to abortion rights, the organization's roots in the population control movement were a red flag for women of color.

32   Susan E. Davis and the Committee for Abortion Rights and Against Sterilization Abuse (CARASA), *Women Under Attack: Victories, Backlash and the Fight for Reproduction Freedom* (Boston: South End Press, 1988), 59.

33   Sandra Morgen, *Into Our Own Hands* (New Jersey: Rutgers University Press, 2002), 3.

34   Ibid.

35   Ibid., 70. Morgen estimates there were 50 women-controlled clinics by 1976.

36   Ibid., 29. Morgen obtained this information from material published by the NWHN in 1976.

37   Judy Norsigian, phone interview by Jael Silliman, July 12, 2003.

38   Morgen, *Into Our Own Hands*, 225.

39   Loretta Ross et al., "Just Choices: Women of Color, Reproductive Health, and Human Rights," in *Policing the National Body*, ed. Jael Silliman and Anannya Bhattacharjee (Cambridge, MA: South End Press, 2002), 148.

40   Faith Evans was the first African American man who was not an abortion provider to become prominently involved in national organizing for reproductive rights. He had an unusual feminist consciousness derived from his status as a single father with six children. He joined RCAR in after working for years in the National Welfare Rights Organization. In 1993, RCAR broaden its mission and changed its name to the Religious Coalition for Reproductive Choice (RCRC).

41   Forums were held in Washington, DC, Philadelphia, PA, Chicago, IL, Atlanta, GA, Pierre, ND, and Hartford, CT.

42   Two African American women were heavily involved in the founding of NOW: Pauli Murray co-authored NOW's first statement of purpose, and Aileen Hernandez was NOW's second president. However, Hernandez resigned in 1979, telling black women that they should not join the organization until it confronted its own racism.

43   Loretta Ross, "African American Women and Abortion," in *Abortion Wars*, 193.

44   Participants had developed what Chlea Sandoval calls "oppositional consciousness." For more information, see Chlea Sandoval, *Methodology of the Oppressed* (Minneapolis: University of Minnesota Press, 2000), 42–45.

45   Women of Color Partnership Program, *Common Ground, Different Planes* (Washington, DC: Religious Coalition for Abortion Rights, August 1989), 13.

46   Patricia Camp, "An African American Woman's Perspective," *Common Ground*, 10.

47   Migdalia Rivera, "A Puerto Rican American Woman's Perspective," *Common Ground*, 10.

48   Yvonne Delk, "The Time Has Come to Stand Up," *Common Ground*," 5.

49   African American Women for Reproductive Freedom, *We Remember*, reprinted in *Our Bodies, Ourselves for the New Century*, ed. Boston Women's Health Book Collective (New York: Touchstone Press, 1998), 413–414.

50   Later that year, Faye Wattleton became the first woman to receive an award from the Congressional Black Caucus for her work on reproductive freedom.

51   In another instance, several groups that joined the major mainstream pro-choice groups in a broad-based coalition succeeded in blocking confirmation of Robert Bork's 1987 nomination to the Supreme Court and participated in similar, albeit unsuccessful, efforts to defeat Clarence Thomas's 1991 nomination to the Supreme Court, and again in 2001, to prevent confirmation of John Ashcroft as attorney general.

52   Cynthia Newbille-Marsh and Byllye A. Avery of NBWHP, Memorandum, March 31, 1992.

53   US Women of Color Coalition for Reproductive Health Rights, "Statement on Poverty, Development and Population Activities," prepared for the International Conference on Population and Development, Cairo, 1994, 2.

54   The collective evolved from roundtable discussions organized in 1997 and 1998 by the Latina Roundtable on Health and Reproductive Rights, led by Luz Rodríguez.

55   Loretta Ross et al., "The SisterSong Collective: Women of Color, Reproductive Health and Human Rights," in "Health of Women of Color," special issue, *American Journal of Health* 17 (2001): 79.

3

African American Women Seed a Movement

T HE reproductive history of African American women has been shaped by coercion, cruelty, and brutality.[1] Reproductive tyranny has taken many forms over time, including rape, forced marriages between slaves, the breakup of slave families, sterilization abuse and the promotion of long-acting contraceptives to control fertility, and current state welfare policies that seek to control black women's efforts to freely determine the number of children they will bear.

Twenty-first-century efforts to control black women's fertility are rooted in stereotypes of black women that were originally created and employed to help justify slavery. Slave women were classified as "breeders" rather than "mothers."[2] Angela Davis notes a South Carolina court ruling that stated that slaves had no legal claims whatsoever on their children, who could be sold away from their mothers at any age because "the young of slaves...stand on the same footing as animals."[3] Women slaves were branded as sexually promiscuous Jezebels procreating with abandon, mirroring the current stereotypes imposed on black mothers receiving welfare. At no time has value been placed on black women mothering their own children.[4]

Slavery ended in 1865, but the myths about black women's fertility, sexuality, and inability to appropriately mother persisted and gave way to other oppressive racist and misogynist ideologies. Throughout the 20th century, black women have been blamed for the social and economic problems of African American families. This accusation was first articulated in the 1920s. It resurfaced in the 1930s, during debates around the establishment of the first federal assistance program for mothers and children,[5] and recirculated in the 1960s through the belief that, in order to reduce the number of "undeserving poor" dependent on welfare, government had the right and responsibility to control black female fertility. From the 1965 Moynihan Report, "The Negro Family: The Case for National Action," to current policies that push marriage as the answer to poverty and a host of measures in between, the scapegoating of single black mothers has been a consistent feature of the debates on welfare and has been institutionalized in public policy.[6]

The history of racial discrimination against African Americans, including its impact on black women and their reproductive health, has been well documented.[7] African American spokespeople have long recognized that racism compromises African Americans' well-being. Poverty, as a central by-product of racism, serves as the driving force behind much of the disparity between black and white Americans. In 2000, 30 percent of all black Americans lived in poverty, and nearly 32 percent of all black women were poor.[8] The black poverty rate was three times greater than the white poverty rate in 2002.[9]

Poverty is only one manifestation of institutionalized racism. Racism also contributes, directly and indirectly, to disparities in physical health between African American and white populations. Black women are often employed in administrative support and service occupations in health care, food service, cleaning, and maintenance. These jobs tend to be low-wage and without health benefits, and women who hold them receive little or no preventive medical care. Black women's overall lack of adequate medical care reflects multiple issues: nonexistent or inadequate health insurance, a paucity of neighborhood health facilities, and racial discrimination in diagnoses and treatment.

Other indicators underscore the distinctly different health statuses of black and white women. Black infants are almost two and a half times as likely as white infants to die before age one. The 2001 mortality rate was 14 deaths per 1,000 live births for black infants and 5.7 per 1,000 for white infants,[10] a significant differential. HIV/AIDS is another serious reproductive health concern for many black women. In 1999, women represented 18 percent of all reported AIDS cases in the United States, and black women accounted for 61 percent of those cases.[11] As these differentials indicate, health disparities between black and white Americans persist. Furthermore, public policies like the "War on Drugs" disproportionately target women of color and undermine their rights and health status. Low-income women dependent on public facilities are disproportionately tested for drugs without their consent or knowledge during prenatal exams. Often, their newborns are also tested. If the tests are positive, they are arrested and charged with drug possession, child neglect, or distribution of drugs to a minor.[12] In South Carolina in 1989, all of the women arrested under these charges were black, with one exception—a white woman with a black boyfriend.[13]

But African American women have not just been victims of institutional racism in its many forms, they also have a rich and complex legacy of activism in the struggle to control their own bodies and reproductive lives. Contemporary leadership by African American women in the field of reproductive health and rights comes from a long history of their political organizing to challenge racism and poverty.

Resistance and Organizing

Slave women drew on African folk knowledge about contraception and abortion as forms of resistance to the oppressive conditions of slavery.[14] They were so successful that entire plantations of slaves failed to have children, frustrating slave owners' plans for profit. In an 1856 essay, Dr. E.M. Pendleton claimed that planters regularly complained of women who failed to have children. He believed that "blacks are possessed of a secret by which they destroy the foetus at an early age of gestation."[15]

After slavery officially ended, the African American women's club movement provided black women in the late 19th century with the opportunity to develop their political voices and speak out to "uplift their race."[16] The club movement was started in the 1890s by elite African American women to provide forums in which they could meet and speak on their own behalf about issues of "race leadership, negative stereotypes, women's suffrage and women's rights, and civil rights and civil liberties."[17] Women also carried out a range of educational and service projects in black communities through the clubs. By the 1916 convention of the National Association of Colored Women, there were 1,500 affiliate clubs.[18]

The women involved in this movement were keenly aware of their double oppression as women and as blacks. The ideology of racial uplift, developed by well-educated African Americans, responded to continuing racism and segregation, as well as to discrimination against women. Its creators believed that they were obligated to represent and "lift up" less privileged African Americans through moral rectitude and hard work. The issue of birth control was part of the "uplift" agenda, due to the belief that a woman could provide a better quality of life and education to her children if she could determine how many children she wished to have and rear. In her 1892 volume of essays, *A Voice from the South*, Anna Julia Cooper endorsed uplift ideology and the inseparability of race and gender for black women.[19]

Though birth control was illegal, in 1918 the Women's Political Association of Harlem responded to the call of birth control pioneer Margaret Sanger and was the first African American women's club to schedule lectures on birth control. Other clubs were quick to follow this lead. They demanded that Sanger's American Birth Control League (ABCL) place birth control clinics in African American communities so that African American women could control their fertility and "improve" their race.[20] National Association for the Advancement of Colored People (NAACP) co-founder W.E.B. DuBois wrote in 1919 that "the future [African American] woman...must have the right of motherhood at her own discretion."[21]

Some African American ministers held discussions about birth control in their churches and others, like the Reverend Adam Clayton Powell of the Abyssinian Baptist Church, who spoke at public meetings in 1932 in favor of family planning. Leading African American organizations such as the NAACP and the National Urban League, as well as the black press, promoted birth control as part of the agenda for uplifting the race.[22] The black press also championed the cause of black doctors who were arrested for performing illegal abortions and decried the mortality rates resulting from septic abortions.[23]

The broad-based African American support for family planning was challenged by Marcus Garvey's public opposition to birth control. Garvey, a black Nationalist, opposed the integrationist goals of the NAACP. He criticized proponents of racial uplift for their elitist ideology, for their practice of favoritism toward lighter-skinned blacks, and for being too accommodating to white supremacy. Garvey argued that birth control used by African Americans was a form of genocide. His organization, the Universal Negro Improvement Association, unanimously passed a resolution opposing birth control in 1934.[24] Many African American leaders, women and men alike, however, resisted Garvey's opposition, and stood firm in their support for birth control.[25]

By 1949, approximately 2.5 million African American women were organized in social and political clubs and organizations. Many of their organizations supported access to birth control and abortion while critiquing the eugenicist policies and programs often espoused by those organizations that supported birth control. Despite their fear and distrust of the proponents of birth control, black women sought access to contraception when and where clinics were available to them. The birth control methods available to them included abstinence, infrequency of coitus, the withdrawal method, spermicidal douching, diaphragms, rhythm, and underground abortions provided by doctors and midwives operating illegally when other methods failed.[26]

Birth Control for Some, Population Control for Others

Whereas African American women were generally supportive of birth control, they were aware of attempts to use it to assert white supremacy. The early feminists of the birth control movement, symbolized by Emma Goldman and Margaret Sanger, emphasized that reproductive control for all women, regardless of race and class, was essential if women were to control their lives. However, eugenicists were also proponents of birth control, and instead of promoting a woman's right to control her fertility, they seized upon birth control as a tool for promoting "better breeding." They thought that birth control could help to weed out society's "undesirables." While definitions of who was fit and unfit varied, blacks, alcoholics, the handicapped, and the poor generally fell within their purview of who should be eliminated. Loretta Ross notes that by 1919, the American Birth Control League began to rely heavily for legitimacy on the growing eugenics movement, which provided pseudoscientific and authoritative language that legitimated women's right to contraception.[27]

Despite the protests of African Americans, the eugenicists were successful in their efforts to promote the sterilization of the "unfit." The US became the first country to permit mass sterilization to "purify the race."[28] By the mid-1930s, 20,000 Americans, mostly African American and Native American, had been sterilized against their will and eugenics laws had been passed in over 20 states.[29] According to estimates, a total of over 70,000 persons were involuntarily sterilized under those statutes.[30] Ross comments on how the legacy of the ABCL, tainted by eugenicist philosophy and practice, continues to spawn distrust between white birth control advocates and people of color: "It is extremely likely that the racism of the birth control organizers, coupled with the geno-cidal assumptions of eugenics supporters, increased black distrust of the public health system and has fueled black opposition to family planning up to the present time."[31]

During World War II, eugenics philosophies and techniques were discredited by their association with and use in Nazi Germany, and sub-sequently white birth control advocates tried to distance themselves from the philosophy of white supremacy. In 1941, the ABCL was renamed the Planned Parenthood Federation of America. Planned Parenthood stressed the importance of birth control in social planning and estab-lished a Negro Advisory Council to strengthen its efforts to reach black populations.[32]

In the 1950s and 60s, the ideology of population control was again used by policy-makers in the US to justify disseminating birth con-trol internationally. They claimed that controlling the fertility of poor women, especially in the "developing" world, was necesary to avert pov-erty, prevent the spread of communism, and increase the ability of the United States to govern world affairs.[33] In the mid-1950s, the popula-tion control establishment also intervened in domestic policies to reduce the population growth rates of poor blacks in the US, especially in urban areas.

In the 1960s, the federal government funded family planning pro-grams to "eliminate poverty."[34] President Johnson relied on the popula-tion control movement, led by the Population Council, the Population Crisis Committee, Planned Parenthood, and the Ford Foundation to raise public consciousness about the "threat of overpopulation" through a steady flow of books, pamphlets, magazines, and newsletters.[35] The rhetoric of these organizations and concurrent policies and programs made some sections of the African American community feel that they were being specifically targeted for fertility control.[36] For example, a Mississippi state representative, David Glass, introduced a bill in 1958 mandating sterilization for any unmarried mother who gave birth to an illegitimate child. He justified the bill with the myth that, "the negro woman, because of child welfare assistance, [is] making it a business...of giving birth to illegitimate children...The purpose of my bill was to try to stop, or slow down, such traffic at its source."[37]

Black Women Lead

The civil rights movement brought attention to issues of race and inequality and mobilized African Americans and others to take action to reduce inequalities based on race. As the civil rights movement gained ground in the 1960s, proponents of family planning and birth control reframed their message to reflect the politics of the time. For many civil rights activists, access to family planning services became "synonymous with the civil right of poor women to medical care."[38] In addition, Martin Luther King Jr. and the NAACP reiterated their support for "dissemination of information and materials concerning family health and family planning to all who deserved it."[39] African American women also played pivotal roles in promoting their right to control their own bodies. Dr. Dorothy Brown, a surgeon from Tennessee, was one of the first state legislators to introduce a bill to legalize abortion in 1967, despite the fact that black Nationalist radicals and black Muslims had assailed family planning as a plot against black communities.[40]

Frances Beal, who headed the Black Women's Liberation Committee of the Student Non-Violent Coordinating Committee (SNCC), articulated the right of individual women in the struggle to decide whether or not to have children in 1970.[41] Her position was echoed by other women leaders in the civil rights movement, even when distrust of white motives to provide birth control to black populations reached a peak in the 1970s and despite the public rhetoric of many black Nationalist male leaders who attempted to close clinics.[42] Women often resisted these attempts, for example the National Welfare Rights Organization in Pittsburgh "declared they would not tolerate male expression of territorial rights over women's bodies."[43] Their declaration was supported by African American women across the country. Black women leaders like Shirley Chisholm and Toni Cade Bambara insisted that black women's liberation from welfare, poverty, and oppression would begin with their "seizing control of their bodies though contraception and legalized abortion."[44]

Despite opposition from black women leaders, the attacks launched by black Nationalists[45] resulted in a few mainstream African American organizations, such as the Urban League and the NAACP, reversing their positions on birth control. Marvin Davies, head of the Florida NAACP, stated: "Our women need to produce more babies, not less...and until we comprise 30 to 35 percent of the population, we won't really be able to affect the power structure in this country."[46] Despite these reversals it is important to note that many church members who supported birth control in the 1940s and 50s held on to their position even when birth control came under siege in many parts of the black community.[47]

During the 1960s and the early 1970s, black women were active in the women's rights and women's health movements, tailoring agendas to meet their community needs. Shirley Chisholm, Pauli Murray, Anna Arnold Hedgeman, and Aileen Hernandez were African American women involved in founding the predominantly white National Organization for Women (NOW) in 1966. Among others, Frances Beal and Toni Cade Bambara spoke in support of birth control, abortion, and sexuality when it was difficult to do so because of opposition from some portions of the black community. They combined their support for birth control and safe and legal abortion with their opposition to sterilization abuse. In so doing, they negotiated a space that at once distanced them from white feminists who prioritized legal abortion and birth control to the exclusion of other reproductive rights issues and those black Nationalists who declared all contraception and abortion genocidal. A number of black women, including Byllye Avery, founder of the National Black Women's Health Project (NBWHP), participated in organizations that referred women to abortion practitioners when the practice was still illegal.

Under the leadership of Dorothy Height, the National Council of Negro Women (NCNW) broadened its agenda in the 1970s to speak out more broadly on civil rights issues and worked to ensure that civil rights organizations understood women's issues as race issues.[48] The NCNW spoke out in support of birth control, took a pro-choice stance in the 1970s, and continues to this day to serve as a voice for African American women on a broad range of issues.

Black feminist thinking and organizing were crucial for reframing the issue of birth control and abortion in the black community. A variety of black feminist grassroots organizations sprang up in cities across the country in the early 1970s. Though many of these groups only lasted for a few years, their critique of the limitations and scope of both the black liberation and women's liberation movements laid the foundation upon which contemporary black women's reproductive rights activism is based. The Sisterhood of Black Single Mothers, founded in 1972 in New York by Safiya Bandele to help meet the survival needs of teenage mothers, built on the principles of both the feminist and the civil rights movements.[49] Three African American women—Faye Williams, Linda Leaks, and Mary Lisbon—formed the Black Women's Self-Help Collective of Washington, DC, in 1981. These activists were the first black women to popularize the use of cervical self-exam in the African American community.

In 1973, Margaret Sloan and Flo Kennedy formed the National Black Feminist Organization (NBFO) in New York. This group, which existed for only three years, carefully defined the terms under which it would support family planning and birth control. Its members organized against sterilization abuse and for abortion rights and pledged to address the availability of child care centers, unemployment, job training, domestic worker rights, black female addiction, welfare rights, and black women's health care. The group also supported the ratification of the Equal Rights Amendment and the rights of black lesbians. Members discussed issues of sexism that they were not able to address adequately in the broader women's movement or in the civil rights movement. The NBFO was not afraid to criticize black Nationalists for refusing to confront the sexism that it believed was destroying the black community from within. They reminded the black Nationalists that liberation for half the race was not liberation at all.[50]

Some members felt that NBFO was not incorporating issues of classism and heterosexism adequately and broke from the group to establish the Combahee River Collective in 1974. The collective set forth its manifesto—a rallying cry for black feminist activists—critiquing racism, sexism, poverty, and heterosexism and providing black feminists with ideological cohesion. Like the NBFO, the Combahee River Collective worked on issues of abortion rights, sterilization abuse, and health care.[51] Barbara Smith, one of the co-founders of the Combahee Collective, helped organize a forum in support of abortion rights in 1974 for black women in Boston. Collective members conducted workshops on college campuses and politicized hundreds of young black women. However, the activism and theoretical insights of these new black feminists were not widely accepted in the black community. The collective was criticized for placing the needs of women above the needs of the community, which was considered divisive. Black feminists challenged this characterization and insisted that they were an arm of the civil rights struggle. They consciously celebrated their links to a history of black protest and played a crucial role as they "lifted the veil and broke the silence on a variety of black women's issues."[52]

As these black feminist organizations developed their agendas, other black women, like Faye Wattleton, were working for change within mainstream organizations. Wattleton was the first African American president of Planned Parenthood, serving from 1978 to 1992, and the first woman to head the organization since Margaret Sanger founded it in 1916. Wattleton was a role model for many black women and played a crucial role in getting more black women to work at Planned Parenthood. For many years, Wattleton was the face of diversity within the mainstream pro-choice movement. "I felt that my being African American was a vital aspect of my leadership; that it provided insights and experiences that I am certain would have been missing if I had not been black,"[53] writes Wattleton in her account of her tenure as president of Planned Parenthood. "I believed that my ethnic identity gave me firsthand experience with those who suffered the most from the oppression of illegal birth control and abortion."[54]

Other African American women also rose to prominence in reproductive health professions. Jocelyn Elders, later appointed surgeon general under President Clinton, managed a statewide health department in Arkansas. Similarly, Joan Smith headed a statewide program in Louisiana. Their significant contributions notwithstanding, women like Wattleton, Elders, and Smith have sometimes been described as "leaders without a constituency"[55] because the majority of African American women distrusted the white pro-choice organizations. They perceived the organizations, even when they had visible black leadership, to be largely middle-class, racist, and irrelevant to the lives of African American women.[56]

The socioeconomic changes of the 1960s and 70s—the increased opportunities in education and employment for black women—enhanced the prospect of self-determined life choices for many middle-class and working-class black women.[57] By the early 1980s, significant numbers of black women were going to college, and the black middle class was growing. Increased numbers of professional black women, a long history of political and social organizing, the engagement of black feminists on issues of health and empowerment, and the existence of a few well-placed black women leaders who were outspoken on issues of family planning, provided fertile ground for the emergence of the NBWHP.

NOTES

1   Dorothy Roberts provides a detailed account of how and why black fertility was controlled during slavery. She shows how black procreation helped to sustain slavery and gave slave owners the economic rationale to control women's reproductive lives. Essentially, black women, by bearing children, reproduced the slave labor force. Black women were forced to bear children who belonged to the slave owner, and from the outset were marked "as objects whose decisions about reproduction should be subject to social regulation rather than to their own will." Dorothy Roberts, *Killing the Black Body* (New York: Pantheon Books, 1997), 22–55.

2   Angela Davis, *Women, Race, and Class* (New York: Vintage Books, 1983), 7.

3   Ibid.

4   Roberts, *Killing the Black Body*, 12–13.

5   Mimi Abramovitz, *Regulating the Lives of Women: Social Welfare Policy from Colonial Times to the Present* (Boston: South End Press, 1996), 318–319.

6   Roberts, *Killing the Black Body*, 18.

7   For books on the history of African American women, see Gerda Lerner, *Black Women in White America* (New York: Vintage Books, 1972); Paula Giddings, *When and Where I Enter: The Impact of Black Women on Race and Sex in America* (New York: Harper Collins, 1984); Kim Marie Vaz, ed., *Black Women in America* (Thousand Oaks, CA: SAGE Publications, 1995); Darlene Clark Hine and Kathleen Thompson, *A Shining Thread of Hope: The History of Black Women in America* (New York: Broadway Books, 1998); Angela Davis, *Women, Race, and Class* (New York: Vintage Books, 1983); Loretta Ross, "African American Women and Abortion," in *Abortion Wars: A Half Century of Struggle 1950–2000*, ed. Rickie Solinger (Berkeley: University of California Press, 1998); Loretta Ross, "African American Women and Abortion: A Neglected History," in *Journal of Health Care for the Poor and Underserved* 3, no. 2 (1992); and Deborah Gray White, *Too Heavy a Load: Black Women in Defense of Themselves 1894–1994* (New York: W. W. Norton, 1999).

8   US Bureau of the Census, 2000, http://www.census.gov/main/www/cen2000.html.

9   See the report authored by Dedrick Muhammad, Attieno Davis, Meizhu Lui, and Betsy Leondar-Wright, *The State of the Dream 2004: Enduring Disparities in Black and White* (Boston: United for a Fair Economy, 2004), 1.

10   Ibid.

11   Shannon L. Hader et al., "HIV Infection in Women in the United States: Status at the Millennium," *Journal of the American Medical Association* 285 (2002): 1186–1192.

12   Judith A. M. Scully, "Killing the Black Community: A Commentary on the United States War on Drugs," in *Policing the National Body*, ed. Jael Silliman and Anannya Bhattacharjee (Cambridge, MA: South End Press, 2002), 63.

13   Roberts, *Killing the Black Body*, 166.

14   John M. Riddle, *Eve's Herbs: A History of Contraception and Abortion in the West* (Cambridge, MA: Harvard University Press, 1997), 35–37. Riddle reports on an Ebers Egyptian Papyrus dated between 1550 and 1500 B.C. that recommends a recipe "to cause a woman to stop a pregnancy in the first, second or third period (trimester)." Also, the Kahun Papyrus of about 1900 B.C. contains several contraceptive recipes. See also Darlene Clark Hine and Kathleen Thompson, *A Shining Thread of Hope: The History of Black Women in America* (New York: Broadway Books, 1998), 14, 98–99.

15   Deborah Gray White, *Ar'nt I a Woman? Female Slaves in the Plantation South* (New York: W. W. Norton, 1985), 85.

16   Kevin K. Gaines, *Uplifting the Race: Black Leadership, Politics, and Culture in the Twentieth Century* (Chapel Hill: University of North Carolina Press, 1996), 136–137.

17   White, *Too Heavy a Load*, 16.

18   Ibid., 33.

19   Gaines, *Uplifting the Race*, 132–133.

20   Loretta Ross, "African American Women and Abortion," in *Abortion Wars*, 168.

21   Ross, "African American Women and Abortion: A Neglected History," 4.

22   Loretta Ross, "African American Women and Abortion," in *Abortion Wars*, 168–169.

23   Ross, "African American Women and Abortion: A Neglected History," 5.

24   Roberts, *Killing the Black Body*, 84.

25   Some women in Garvey's movement fought for an equal role in shaping black Nationalism, and a few women held important positions in his Universal Negro Improvement Association. Garvey, however, rejected the ideas put forth by the women's clubs that black women should shape the direction and thoughts of their age and become the leaders of the race. He equated manliness with militancy and called on black men to play this leadership role. White, *Too Heavy a Load*, 121.

26   Loretta Ross, "African American Women and Abortion," in *Abortion Wars*, 172.

27   Ibid., 171.

28   Ibid., 170.

29   Linda Gordon, *Woman's Body, Woman's Right: Birth Control in America*, rev. ed. (New York: Penguin Books, 1990), 260.

30   Roberts, *Killing the Black Body*, 89.

31   Loretta Ross, "African American Women and Abortion," in *Abortion Wars*, 172.

32   Gordon, *Woman's Body, Woman's Right*, 355.

33   Ibid., 342–349.

34   Thomas B. Littlewood, *The Politics of Population Control* (Notre Dame, IN: University of Notre Dame Press, 1977), 8–10.

35   Donald T. Critchlow, *Intended Consequences: Birth Control, Abortion, and the Federal Government in Modern America* (New York: Oxford University Press, 1999), 50–55.

36   Littlewood, *The Politics of Population Control*, 60.

37   Roberts, *Killing the Black Body*, 213–214.

38   Loretta Ross, "African American Women and Abortion," in *Abortion Wars*, 177.

39   Ibid.

40   Critchlow, *Intended Consequences*, 60.

41   Loretta Ross, "African American Women and Abortion," in *Abortion Wars*, 183.

42   Ibid.

43   Ibid., 182.

44   Toni Cade, "The Pill: Genocide or Liberation?," in *The Black Woman: An Anthology*, ed. Toni Cade (New York: Mentor Books, 1970), 162–169.

45   The Black Panthers were the only black Nationalist group to support free abortion and contraceptives on demand. Though this issue was controversial among the Panthers, many party women supported it.

46   Littlewood, *The Politics of Population Control*, 75.

47   Martha C. Ward, *Poor Women, Powerful Men: America's Great Experiment in Family Planning* (Boulder, CO: Westview Press, 1986), 93.

48   Ibid.

49   For more information on the Sisterhood of Black Single Mothers, see Barbara Omolade, *The Rising Song of African American Women* (Routledge Press: New York, 1994), 168.

50   For more on information on the National Black Feminist Organization, see White, *Too Heavy a Load*, 242–246.

51   "Combahee River Collective Statement" in *Home Girls: A Black Feminist Anthology*, ed. Barbara Smith (New York: Kitchen Table Press, 1983), 281.

52   Darlene Hine quoted in White, *Too Heavy a Load*, 256.

53   Faye Wattleton, *Life on the Line* (New York: Ballantine Books, 1996), 183.

54   Ibid., 188.

55   Loretta Ross, "African American Women and Abortion," in *Abortion Wars*, 187.

56   Ibid.

57   Petchesky, *Abortion and Woman's Choice*, 153.

4

Founding the National Black
Women's Health Project

A New Concept in Health

THE National Black Women's Health Project (NBWHP), founded in
1984, is the oldest of the organizations whose work we feature. The
project has played an important role in mobilizing African American
women on the issues of health and reproductive rights and in bringing their perspectives, voices, and concerns to national and international
attention. In the tradition of the black women's club movement and the
National Council of Negro Women (NCNW), the NBWHP has made
African American organizations understand that women's reproductive
health issues must be addressed in the African American community.
The NBWHP has also advocated within the pro-choice movement for
a broadening of its agenda on reproductive rights and health to include
the concerns of women of color.

The history of the NBWHP is a story of charismatic leadership coming at a time when there was a latent but unarticulated need among
African American activists to explore their sexual and reproductive
rights. The NBWHP evolved from a primarily grassroots organization
to one that is policy driven and policy focused, creating a movement of
women of color for reproductive rights defined broadly to express the
needs of the various communities that women of color represent.

The NBWHP also reflects some of the challenges that most women
of color groups face when they organize to advance their sexual and
reproductive rights. These include funding, the strains of doing both
grassroots and policy work, and the stress of being constantly called upon

to serve as the voice or the representative of the various communities of color or of women in color in general. The NBWHP, from very early on in its development, was pulled in several directions at one time, and the unrealistic demands placed on it were a very heavy burden to carry.

The Founders

Byllye Avery

Avery, the dynamic founder of the NBWHP, had no particular movement involvement—in either civil rights or feminism. Rather, a confluence of personal, social, and political forces shaped her life and readied her for envisioning and realizing a black women's health movement that has had an impact in the national and international health arena and on white women and other women of color.

Avery grew up in central Florida, where she witnessed segregation and the vast array of inequities that it spawned within her community. Upon graduation from historically black Talladega College in Alabama, Avery moved to Gainesville, Florida, where she worked in a children's mental health unit at a local hospital. Her experiences in health and politics, the effects of a rapidly escalating and unpopular war in Vietnam, the strident currents of cultural Nationalism, and the awakenings of a solid feminist movement shaped her political consciousness. Avery was drawn to the field of women's reproductive health at a time when black women were dying at an alarming rate from illegal back-alley and self-induced abortions. In the early 1970s, when abortion was illegal in Florida, Avery worked with a referral network in Gainesville that helped women travel to New York for abortions. Before her experience with the referral network, the idea of an abortion was alien to her: "I didn't know anything about abortions. In my life that word couldn't even be mentioned without having somebody look at you crazy."[1] She notes that while the issue of abortion was not openly discussed in the black community, illegal abortion was a fairly widespread practice among black women.

In 1974, the year after *Roe v. Wade* legalized abortion, Avery joined with Margaret Parrish, Judith Levy, Betsy Randall-David, and Joan Edelson to open the Gainesville Women's Health Center. While there were other black women on staff, she was the only black woman in the center's inner circle of founding members. The next year, Avery attended the first National Conference on Women and Health organized by the

Boston Women's Health Book Collective.[2] She was inspired by the work and ideals of the women's health activists she met and joined the board of directors of the newly formed National Women's Health Network (NWHN), a nonprofit health advocacy group that sought to give women a greater voice in the US health care system. Avery continued her work in Gainesville with women in her community while she participated on the NWHN board. These mutually reinforcing experiences were the basis for the landmark conference she organized in 1983 that led to the founding of the NBWHP in 1984.

Unlike women in the white feminist movement of the mid-1970s, NWHN members who had radical politics were extremely sensitive to issues of race and class. NWHN stressed strong personal relationships among its members, and from its inception paid attention to building bridges among different groups of women.[3] Feminist health activist Judy Norsigian, co-author of *Our Bodies, Ourselves*, emphasized the commitment of the NWHN to having a substantial presence of women of color on its board.[4] Avery was especially inspired by Dr. Helen Rodríguez-Trías and Dolores Huerta, who both served on the board with her. Avery's experiences with the women's health movement shaped the way in which she later was to imagine and develop the NBWHP, and years later the NWHN members would assist Avery with development and fundraising. This experiential base and the network's organizing and analytical perspective were important reference points from which she defined and directed her work on African American women's health.

Through her work at the Gainesville Feminist Women's Health Center, Avery made contact with Brenda Joyner, Debra David, and Dolores Nolan, all African American women abortion providers and activists in the Federation of Feminist Women's Health Centers (FFWHC). The FFWHC emphasized women's power and knowledge, and stressed the importance of community control of health care. Because members of the FFWHC were deeply committed to addressing issues of race, class, and gender, the federation was a hospitable space for women of color. The Gainesville Feminist Women's Health Center was in sync with the character, politics, and goals of the FFWHC and served as yet another force for instruction in Avery's life. The FFWHC's political stance and demonstrated capacity for activating their agenda not only politicized Avery but also radicalized her.

In 1977, the Hyde Amendment cut off Medicaid funding for abortions. Avery immediately became aware that this was a punitive measure against poor women. "Taking away Medicaid funding says to poor women, 'you can't have this—you don't deserve to have this.'"[5] She states: "For poor women abortion is a matter of survival: if I have this one more child, it etches away my margin of survival."[6] Around the same time, Avery noticed that a disproportionately high number of black women came to the center for abortions, but few black women participated in the OB/GYN care that the health center offered. She realized that black women had too many other worries to make their own health a priority. She worked with center staff to establish a new model of health care and services based on black and poor women's needs, to provide an environment where women could feel comfortable and take control of their own health. Through sweat equity and fundraising, the staff and their supporters renovated a clinic, transforming it into a beautifully furnished facility that offered "exquisite services" when it opened in 1974. In addition to providing abortions, the center provided well-woman gynecological services, such as pregnancy tests, and information about other reproductive health needs. The staff worked hard to make sure that the center's physicians were sensitive to the range of their clients' needs. The clients expressed their appreciation for the care and attention that they received, and the center rapidly became well-respected in the community and was not harassed for providing abortions. The "exquisite" model of care the Gainesville Women's Health Center provided stood in stark contrast to the institutional environment of most health care facilities of the 1970s.

Abortion remained an important reproductive rights issue for Avery and for the NWHN, but by the late 1970s women's health advocates started to look critically at birthing practices. New ideas about birthing, including a re-examination of the role of the midwife, gained ground. In 1978, in response to the requests of Gainesville center clients for assistance during their pregnancies and deliveries, Avery, along with Judith Levy, Margaret Parrish, and Nancy Redfern, opened Birthplace, an alternative birthing center managed by certified nurse midwives. By drawing attention to the important roles black midwives played in health care delivery, Avery hoped to get younger generations of black women interested in midwifery. Avery found this work exhilarating, but soon learned that few African American women used the alternative birthing services because their medical insurance did not cover out-of-hospital births. She realized she needed to make expanding access to health care a priority.

Through her work as a feminist health activist, Avery developed her awareness of the importance of ethnicity and class to women's health status. She says she began "to look at myself as a black woman. Before that time I had been looking at myself as a woman."[7] At the Gainesville center, Avery came to understand the need for a more holistic approach to health care for black women, one that went beyond the provision of services; one that would take into account the difficulties poor women face when they try to get health care and would also find ways to address the powerlessness that so many women experience.

Avery left Birthplace in 1980 to teach at a community college in Gainesville. There she noticed the high level of absenteeism among young women due to illness. She started to analyze the health status of black women at the college and found that they did not know very much about their general or reproductive health. She brought "these sisters together to talk about their lives. It was there that I started to understand the lives of black women and to realize that we lived in a conspiracy of silence."[8] Avery wanted to encourage black women everywhere to take an interest in their own health care. She knew that in order to reach them, she had to move to a place with a larger black population. She relocated to Atlanta in 1981.

In Atlanta, deeply aware of and concerned about the disparities in health between black and white women, Avery focused her energies on developing a national black women's health project within the National Women's Health Network. She decided that the first step would be to hold a national conference on black women's health issues. NWHN members encouraged Avery's work and supported her long-range goals. Pamela Freeman, her colleague on the NWHN board, a social worker and political activist, worked with her for over two years to plan the first black women's health conference.

The conference planning committee faced the challenge of developing a model of collective leadership in which everyone on the committee was equally responsible for all decisions. This model was chosen by the committee to deliberately counter the pervasive charismatic leadership model used in the civil rights movement, which invested power in a single dominant male figure. Using a model of collective leadership that was shaped by the consciousness-raising feminism of the 1960s and 70s, the women on the committee addressed their internalized racism, sexism, and homophobia. They were committed to organizing African American women in a way that would represent and respect the perspectives of women from all economic classes. One woman on the planning committee, Lillie Allen, would become a co-founder of the National Black Women's Health Project with Byllye Avery. The remarkable synergy between Avery's and Allen's visions laid the foundation for the national network.

Lillie Allen

Lillie Allen was a health educator and Rockefeller Fellow in Population at Morehouse School of Medicine in Atlanta in 1983.[9] Allen had also worked in teen pregnancy prevention programs in public housing communities in Atlanta in the early 1980s. As a Rockefeller Fellow in Population, she had been contracted to provide birth control education to young black women. In response, she developed a program based on art and dialogue in which young women used dance and self-expression to explore how they wanted their lives to be different. According to Allen, she wanted to

> build a group of young people looking at the issues of birth control, not just by looking at what [contraceptives] they can and don't use, but looking at birth control from a place of what they want in their lives. I wanted them to understand how to have a life. What are the things they must have in place to assure their vision? So if you don't want to have children, are you just talking about birth control? You have to first talk about your life and how you feel about your life and having a future, and what are the elements of that?[10]

Allen's approach to reproductive health education was based on her exploration of the effects of internalized racism, which she first recognized as an undergraduate student at the all-black Bethune-Cookman College for women in Florida. Allen, a child of migrant farmworkers, grew up in an all-black community with an internal color hierarchy, and at Bethune-Cookman she learned what it meant to be in an all-black educational institution and feel that she was not accepted because her skin was "too dark." She was critical of the school's leadership for doing little to challenge either the school's institutionalized color-based discrimination or the prejudice in the student body. "I questioned the leadership, which did not understand its disproportionate impact on the lives of very young women, but I had no analysis other than the hurt and the disappointment which were telling me you can't trust black women, you can't trust black folks."[11] Allen felt that she became less able to express and affirm herself because she could not trust the place "that I thought was mine"—a college founded by Mary MacLeod Bethune for black women. Later, while she was a graduate student earning her masters in public health at the predominantly white University of North Carolina at Chapel Hill, her interest in studying and exploring internalized racism and black women's leadership deepened through facing her own internalized oppression and led her to develop ways to work through it.

Allen became involved in Re-evaluation Counseling (RC). RC is a process of dialogue and active listening in which the participants work though difficult emotional issues so that they can effectively use their intelligence to address their problems. This intense process focuses on one person at a time, providing rare group and individual attention with which to "discharge" emotions.[12] It is popular partly because it makes some basic psychotherapy and self-disclosure techniques accessible to a large number of people in free support groups.

Allen saw that there were too few black people involved in the RC process. White RC participants had a problem with her insistence on talking about racism and its impact on her: "They wanted to talk about social change, but I couldn't ignore that I was the only black person in the room. They didn't want me to talk about that." She also found RC to be one-dimensional: "It is important to have your feelings, but the key question is what are you going to do with them? What are the actions you are going to take if you are interested in building a community of people?" She developed a self-disclosure process that she called "Black and Female," grounded in her own struggle with oppression: "I knew what [the process] could look like because I had gone through it myself, learning to act outside of my oppression, building a relationship with myself, and understanding how to maintain relationships with your own people first to understand what it means to be with people not coming from a place of oppression." With "Black and Female," Allen had successfully politicized RC and called it Self-Help.

Allen brought "Black and Female" to the black women's health conference planning committee because the members came from vastly different walks of life—women from public housing and women with PhDs. She felt that to create a successful conference, committee members would have to do the internal work of overcoming the class barriers that prevented them from hearing each other. Initially, the committee intended to include white women who had allied themselves with the National Women's Health Network. However, they finally decided that the black women on the committee needed to work through their own intra-racial tension without simultaneously having to deal with issues between black and white participants. The planners spent two years developing the conference while examining their relationships with each other. They were able to work together, "as lesbians, as straights, as married, or not married" in a way that none of them had ever experienced.

The leadership of Byllye Avery and Lillie Allen, along with the support of the other committee members and the National Women's Health Network, launched the founding conference of what ultimately became the National Black Women's Health Project.

The Birth of NBWHP

In 1983, the groundbreaking first National Conference on Black Women's Health Issues was held at Spelman College in Atlanta. Avery, Allen, and the planning committee had not foreseen how ripe the time would be for black women's health activism.[13] Each woman on the planning committee organized in her local community to encourage women to attend.[14] The committee also raised scholarship funds to bring black women from rural and urban communities all over the South to Atlanta. Directed toward low-income black women, Allen's "Black and Female: What Is the Reality?" was not made available to all conference participants initially. However, as word spread about the workshop, the planning committee was forced to relocate it to increasingly larger rooms to accommodate the participant demands. Loretta Ross described 500 women trying to crowd into a room as a "movement moment." "Black and Female" resonated deeply with conference participants. By the end of the conference, 1,500 of the 1,700 attendees had engaged in this process.

Throughout the conference, black women spoke candidly with one another about their health and the realities of being African American women. Participant Loretta Ross reflects that "what was particularly exciting about this opening conference was it brought poor black women and middle-class women, rural and urban women in dialogue that was enriching and exciting to both."[15] Allen's "Black and Female" evolved into what became known as the Self-Help process, one of NBWHP's legacies. By all accounts, the participants felt elated by the conference planners' vision, as it addressed black women's health issues from a holistic, deeply spiritual, and empowering perspective and sparked self-healing and social action. According to Allen, "What drew women to the project was the opportunity to work on themselves as part of the process of social change."[16]

Spontaneously, conference participants demanded the creation of an independent organization dedicated to black women's health. Attendees felt convinced that by working together, in sisterhood, they could improve black women's health and well-being. The conference planners were buoyed by the feeling that thousands of women were waiting for them to provide leadership. Thus, the National Black Women's Health Project was born. Avery and Allen set out to grow the budding organization. The rough division of labor between the two leaders had Avery developing the funding and structure of the organization and Allen providing "Black and Female" workshops at retreats around the country to keep potential members engaged in supporting the growth of the NBWHP. They established the first chapter in Philadelphia the same year.

Through her hands-on experience in the women's health movement, Avery had come to understand the connections between racism, powerlessness, and poor health. To improve the health and well-being of black women, Avery realized, the NBWHP would have to address the issues of racism, poverty, low self-esteem, and extreme stress that lay at the root of black women's health problems—from the beginning, these insights drove the NBWHP agenda. Allen's model of Self-Help shaped the work of the NBWHP in its formative stage. According to Avery: "Lillie Allen brought the understanding that we are dying inside. Unless we are able to go inside of ourselves and touch and breathe fire, breathe life into ourselves, then of course we can't be healthy."[17] Consequently, for the first ten years of the NBWHP, Self-Help was central to its mission.

The Early Role of Self-Help in NBWHP

Allen envisioned her process of "Black and Female" as not only vital to building the NBWHP, but also integral to the decision-making process and structure. From the time of her involvement as a planning committee member, Allen determined that the NBWHP would have to tackle the question of leadership in a different way, because leaders should embody the vision:

> You have to always be that which you say you are about. As a leader, if you don't check yourself, you are supposed to build a place in which you can be checked. The purpose is to make sure that you are living out that vision and you are consistent with that vision. Because I am responsible for bringing a process to a group of people, I'm also responsible for my lessons in that. I don't have the luxury of not being responsible for how people carry out the teachings I've provided. And that is the value of Self-Help, so that black women in leadership have a supportive process in which they can be authentic visionaries with integrity.[18]

At subsequent conferences and workshops, African American women continued to be attracted to the Self-Help model, which addressed their physical, spiritual, emotional, and psychological health needs. According to Sharon Gary-Smith, the NBWHP's first Self-Help group developer, Self-Help has provided many women with "a safe, validating environment for us to learn how to come together to share our stories, to be appreciated for the struggles we have participated in, to review our circumstances, and to make decisions designed to change our lives and our health circumstances."[19] Allen extended the model to multiracial work through a program called "Sisters and Allies." It worked with white and black activists to build trust to enable them to work together to build an inclusive movement. Allen's Self-Help work was also introduced to other women of color who adopted the process in their work.

Evolving an Organizational Structure

The NBWHP initially set up its headquarters in Atlanta in a beautiful Victorian mansion, dubbed the Mother House, which it purchased through a significant donation from an individual.[20] In addition to Avery, there were two other staff members.[21] The small staff was deeply committed to grassroots action but had little experience in creating the kind of organizational infrastructure that could harness the array of strategies, resources (human and material), and plans that emerged from the hugely successful founding conference. They consulted with nonprofit management experts and were substantively aided by volunteers who were anxious to move the fledgling organization forward. One of the first issues that arose was whether or not to include white members. After a great deal of debate, the women of NBWHP decided that progressive white women could be members. For white women, membership involved attending "Sisters and Allies" Self-Help workshops and providing financial support to keep the NBWHP going. The NBWHP was incorporated as a nonprofit organization in 1984. A year later, due to the development efforts of Avery and a planning committee, NBWHP had its first board of directors, with cochairs Julia Scott and Eleanor Hinton-Hoytt serving alongside other prestigious black women leaders, including Angela Davis. Both Avery and Allen were on the initial board.

The NBWHP sought to develop chapters across the country to implement its vision. In its first five years, it put into place a rudimentary chapter structure and a modest membership base. Each chapter was conceived as a community for women who value health and wellness. Members were supposed to meet with each other and women in the community to develop programs that promote wellness and relationships that stimulate a lifetime of personal and professional growth. Chapter activities allowed black women to network with one another and created opportunities for activism.

By the end of 1989, the NBWHP had chapters in 22 states and was the fastest growing black women's organization in the US. Despite this phenomenal growth, the chapter structure was fragile. There were no clear guidelines for chapter formation. Financial support for the chapters, logistical information, and training were never fully developed, making it difficult for chapters to sustain their activities. Avery had envisioned that the board, NBWHP staff, and members in chapters across the country would galvanize a national movement for black women's health. However, from the outset, NBWHP's work was primarily based in Atlanta and run by staff and volunteers.

Developing an Agenda and Implementing Programs

The NBWHP set out to assemble a constituency of poor and middle-class women and address their key health concerns. It wanted to take the "Empowerment and Wellness" message to the African American community and create an organization whose members were held together not only by their experiences of oppression, but also by an affirming organizational culture. It did this in a variety of ways. The organizational magazine, *Vital Signs*, was the first publication on health and reproductive rights from the perspective of African American women. Written by members, it offered a range of articles on health and healing, featured legislative updates and calls for action, and included news of the project and its members. NBWHP also developed a Self-Help training manual and other materials, such as a video, *On Becoming a Woman*, to help mothers and daughters talk about menstruation.

The central method for popularizing its message among black women across America was through a network of conferences and workshops. The conferences emphasized the development of connections and caring among members. For almost a decade, these conferences and "Black and Female" retreats attracted hundreds of black women. The conferences also attracted other women of color leaders who were looking to establish similar opportunities for women in their own communities. Two women who sought the NBWHP's guidance were Luz Alvarez Martínez, a Latina from San Francisco, and Charon Asetoyer, a Native American from South Dakota. Both used the NBWHP model in their own communities and became national voices on women's health. Consequently, NBWHP assumed the important role of mentoring other women of color organizations.

Spirituality and emotional support were key elements of NBWHP organizing. Although explicitly nondenominational, the NBWHP invested considerable energy in elaborating rituals and celebrations, such as pouring libations for the ancestors, a ritual enacted at conferences, retreats, and other gatherings. The song "Something Inside So Strong" was the project's anthem in its first decade. These cultural and spiritual practices validated the experiences of African American women, were uplifting, and brought women together across many divides. This environment offered many women their first opportunity to combine politics, health care, and spiritual wellness in the pursuit of better health for themselves and their families.

From its inception the project was keen to be part of the global movement for women's rights. Thus, it participated in the 1985 United Nations World Conference for Women in Nairobi, Kenya. Of the 20,000 women who participated in this first global conference on women in Africa, 1,100 were African American. The vision and activism of the global women's movement influenced the politics of the NBWHP, which was attentive to, and educated other African American women about, global concerns and challenges. The NBWHP drew on that interest in transnational organizing among black women to get African American voices heard on a broad range of women's health issues at the national and international level.[22]

In 1988, the NBWHP established the Center for Black Women's Wellness in the Mechanicsville section of Atlanta. This first health center developed by the organization embodied NBWHP's holistic vision of health care and dedicated itself to improving the quality of life for women in Mechanicsville's low-income and public housing communities. It provided coordinated health services, social services, referrals, education, and advocacy skill training. From its inception, the center used Lillie Allen's Self-Help model to organize small groups of women to discuss their concerns and work through their health issues. The center pioneered "Plain Talk," an innovative program for teenagers on pregnancy and related concerns. It continues to be one of the most successful programs to grow out of the NBWHP.

These diverse organizing and outreach efforts, however, were very labor-intensive and devoured the organization's financial and human resources.

Taking On Abortion and the Pro-Choice Movement

Abortion was a tricky issue for the NBWHP. While Avery and some women in the NBWHP were deeply dedicated to supporting abortion rights, others were more ambivalent or oppositional. Views ranged from perceiving abortion as a white woman's issue to seeing it as anti-Christian, to considering it genocidal. Initially, the NBWHP did not take a stand on abortion rights directly because of the issue's potential divisiveness. However, due to the concerted effort to roll back abortion rights, the NBWHP evolved a pro-choice position in concert with other key national black women's organizations.

Their support was first manifest in the 1986 March for Women's Lives organized by the National Organization for Women (NOW). The National Council of Negro Women, and the National Political Congress of Black Women, along with the NBWHP and more than 100 women of color organizations endorsed the march, demonstrating broad-based African American support for abortion rights. Subsequently, NBWHP participated in pro-choice marches and rallies in defense of *Roe v. Wade*, and in 1989, Avery was one of the women who signed *We Remember*, the first statement by black leaders who took a public pro-choice position.

Since the NBWHP was the most established organization among women of color working on health and reproductive rights, it was relied on to challenge racism in the predominantly white pro-choice movement and to open the door for women of color to speak out on reproductive health priorities. Women of color working in mainstream organizations, such as Sabrae Jenkins in the Religious Coalition for Abortion Rights (RCAR), looked to the NBWHP to help them make changes in their organizations and bring more attention to issues concerning women of color. There was also pressure from pro-choice organizations hoping that the NBWHP could galvanize a new constituency in support of reproductive rights and broaden the base of the pro-choice movement.

Over time, the NBWHP built an African American constituency that supported women's right to abortion and became a leader in the struggle for reproductive rights and justice. In response to the pending *Webster* decision and in an effort to expand support for reproductive rights in 1989, the NBWHP organized meetings to bring the perspectives of women of color to the mainstream movement and focused its efforts on building coalitions of women of color and partnerships with mainstream groups. The next year, the NBWHP sponsored the first national conference for African American women on reproductive rights, called Sisters in Session About Our Reproductive Health. It brought together most of the leading black women's and civil rights organizations to develop a reproductive rights agenda for African American women. Clearly, women of color had a crucial message to communicate and a role to play in demonstrating broad support for abortion rights. Thus, through the 1980s and into the 90s, the NBWHP was intensively engaged in negotiating its place and creating space for other women of color in the pro-choice movement.

The NBWHP provided new political leadership in support of reproductive rights and demonstrated that there is broad support in the African American community for improving reproductive health care and access to abortion. Establishing itself as a necessary participant in discussions of reproductive rights and health, and in many instances serving as the conscience of the pro-choice movement, the NBWHP worked with many mainstream groups on attending to issues that concern black women.[23] By defining the meaning of reproductive rights in the African

American community, it pushed mainstream groups to address issues that were not necessarily a priority for them.

New Directions in the 1990s

In retrospect, it is clear that in its first five years the NBWHP became overextended, which is not surprising given the many demands placed on it by its constituency, supporters, other women of color, donors, and the pro-choice movement. Expectations for the NBWHP, as *the* representative voice of black women on issues of reproductive rights and sometimes of all women of color, were extremely high and unrealistic. Thus, the NBWHP was always working on several levels at the same time without having the time or money required to develop the structures necessary to be optimally effective. Avery's vision and visibility kept the organization going at high speed. When she won a MacArthur "genius" award in 1989, Avery reframed her role in the NBWHP from hands-on director to president, and board member Julia Scott was named interim director. The change in Avery's engagement marked a turning point for the organization.

Between 1989 and 1994, the staff of the project expanded rapidly and the organization went through a period of financial and organizational turmoil.[24] Tensions arose when NBWHP staff and board members, including Avery and Allen, disagreed on the continued role of Self-Help. Allen felt that Self-Help was vital to building the NBWHP, and that it was a mistake for staff or board members to opt out of Self-Help support groups. Women who were unfamiliar with Self-Help or who chose not to practice it saw the "Black and Female" workshops as a way to attract women to the NBWHP but not as integral to maintaining the NBWHP's integrity or vision. Staff loyalties were torn between the two visionary leaders. The organizational tensions led to dissension over NBWHP's strategic focus—building grassroots Self-Help chapters across the country or influencing public policy. Although the NBWHP originally embraced both goals, some members felt it would be easier to raise funds for policy activities than for the more nebulous work of organizing Self-Help groups, which did not lend itself to easy measurement or have clear policy outcomes. In the midst of this "vision crisis," approximately one-half of the staff of ten members was laid off because of budgetary constraints.

In 1990, the entire staff and board were participating in conflict resolution. They determined that the Self-Help model was no longer central to NBWHP's mission. By year's end, Allen left NBWHP and founded Be Present, a training center to popularize the Self-Help process she had developed. The NBWHP, meanwhile, opened a Washington, DC, policy-based office with Julia Scott at its helm. The relationship between Allen, Avery, and the NBWHP continued to be strained.

One of the first projects of the Washington office was to set up the Public Policy and Education Program (PPEP). Headed by Scott, a board member with a long history of activism in the reproductive rights movement, PPEP was established to promote a broad range of public policies to improve black women's health and to ensure that black women could set their own agenda on reproductive rights. PPEP was also charged with developing educational resources for members, such as legislative updates, background information, analyses, and calls for action on health issues concerning black women, so that they could assert their political muscle. PPEP called attention to the reproductive rights concerns of the black community and articulated an African American perspective both to the public and to the reproductive health community. The establishment of the public policy office further shifted the focus from grassroots mobilization across socioeconomic groups to making NBWHP a player in mainstream politics and a voice for women of color in the pro-choice movement.

In 1991, Cynthia Newbille-Marsh was hired as the NBWHP executive director. It was a pivotal time in the project's evolution, as original board members and staff left due to financial pressures and personal tensions that made it difficult to carry out the level of activism that members and allies had come to expect. Based at the Mother House, she was charged with placing the project on a firm financial footing. She focused on developing fundraising and management plans. The institutional complexities, coupled with her lack of organizing experience and direct involvement in the women's health movement, were serious handicaps. Despite her numerous administrative and management skills, the organization's initial base of support eroded.

Innovation During Tough Times

Even in this precarious phase, the NBWHP continued to develop new initiatives. In 1992, the NBWHP launched its Walking for Wellness program, featuring Olympic champion Wilma Rudolph, to encourage African American women to improve their health through exercise. That same year it produced *It's OK to Peek*, a video on gynecological self-exam. A 1992 campaign on unsafe contraceptives focused on educating African American women about Norplant and Depo-Provera. In 1993, the NBWHP co-organized a coalition of women of color to work on both the 1994 International Conference on Population and Development (ICPD) in Cairo and the 1995 Fourth World Conference for Women in Beijing.

In the 1990s, the role of the NBWHP was enhanced by its involvement with President Clinton's pro-choice administration. As a key spokeswoman on African American health issues, Julia Scott was regularly called upon by the administration to give her input on health policies and regulation. She was among nine African Americans chosen to review the president's Health Care Task Force proposals in 1993. The NBWHP worked intensively on health care reform and endorsed the single-payer health care system. It committed its members, chapters, and Self-Help groups in an attempt to ensure that—at a minimum—state and federal legislation and policy decisions on health care reform would be responsive to the unique health needs of African American women and their families.

The signature public policy effort of the NBWHP was the 1993 National Campaign to End Discrimination in Federal Funding for Abortion Services. It led a broad-based coalition to repeal the Hyde Amendment. The initiative, called Campaign for Abortion and Reproductive Equity (CARE), demonstrated to the US Congress that African American women could no longer be ignored in the shaping of public policy.

The NBWHP brought reproductive rights concerns such as the Hyde Amendment and abuses associated with Norplant and Depo-Provera to national attention. However, it only marginally succeeded in broadening the mainstream agenda to include other issues of reproductive health, such as infant mortality, substance abuse during pregnancy, infertility, and sexually transmitted diseases, issues that were integral to NBWHP's definition of reproductive health.

In addition to its policy initiatives, NBWHP published *Body and Soul: A Black Women's Guide to Health and Well-Being*, edited by Linda Villarosa, in 1994. In 1998, it produced *Our Bodies, Our Voices, Our*

Choices, a black women's primer on reproductive health and rights. In 1999, Scott served as a delegate to the United Nations Commission on the Status of Women.

The Challenges of Foundation Support

Though PPEP was able to garner foundation support for its work, limited resources made it hard to support both the Washington office and the Mother House in Atlanta. Reproductive health funders were for the most part more willing to support the public policy office in DC than the grassroots mobilization work associated with the Atlanta office. Continuing financial difficulties and management problems led Avery and Scott to make the hard decision to shut down the Atlanta office and lay off the staff in 1996. Publicly, the NBWHP attributed the closing of the Atlanta office to a change in priorities. The closing led to disaffection among some members who perceived the grassroots mobilization and Self-Help work as the NBWHP's distinguishing feature. The absence of a space for black women to work on themselves and their health concerns left black women health advocates in a vacuum.

With the closing of the Atlanta office, the NBWHP was consolidated to a staff of three in Washington, DC, under the direction of Julia Scott, who replaced Cynthia Newbille-Marsh as executive director. Avery continued to serve as president and remained an important fundraiser and public face for the NBWHP. The board of directors was made much smaller, and the 1996 annual conference scheduled to be held in Jamaica was canceled. The NBWHP announced that instead of holding its annual meeting, it would find other ways to exchange information and strategies. *Vital Signs* was transformed into a smaller, glossier publication and made self-supporting through advertising. The magazine headlined key NBWHP events and was disseminated to members, legislators, and policy-makers. Once again, the NBWHP tried to put itself on firmer financial footing and to develop a communications strategy to reach members, donors, and policy-makers that did not involve the direct outreach that had been its hallmark. As the primary spokeswoman for the NBWHP on a day-to-day basis, Scott faced tremendous demands to represent black women on numerous initiatives brought by the pro-choice community and the federal government.

The NBWHP strived to develop the next generation of leaders by creating partnerships with historically black colleges and universities and looked for ways to use the internet more effectively as an outreach tool. Finally, the enormous staff and financial resources required to run membership and chapter activities continued to present a challenge. By the late 1990s, the NBWHP worked much more closely with several federal agencies, including the Federal Office of Population Affairs, the Office of Women's Health, and the Surgeon General's Office, and tried to develop an ongoing relationship with the Congressional Black Caucus.

Into the 21ˢᵗ Century

A new chapter began for the NBWHP at the turn of the century. Julia Scott resigned in 2001, and the board of directors selected Dr. Lorraine Cole to lead the organization, with Avery still serving as president. Once again, the change in leadership was accompanied by staff upheavals and severe budgetary crises. A significant number of staff was laid off as Cole worked to redirect the organization into its next phase. Cole's efforts to revamp the NBWHP have been criticized for both compromising and commodifying what was essentially a radical vision and practice. The most recent articulation of the NBWHP's goals involves establishing four national centers for education, health policy, research, and knowledge and leadership. Self-Help has been reintroduced and is seen as a "key to ensuring that our programs are conducted within a context of cultural understanding of the comfort of other black women."[25] The Education Center will "design, develop, coordinate, and implement programs to promote health as a way of life for black women and their families."[26] The Health Policy Center will coordinate the development of a health policy platform on a range of issues affecting black women's health and promote that agenda at the state and national level. The Research Center will conduct qualitative research on black women's health issues and act as a conduit for black women to participate in clinical trials research. The Knowledge and Leadership Center will "engage experts in the social, legislative, academic and health arenas to inform the health policy statements and agenda of the organization."[27] In 2003, the NBWHP changed its name to the Black Women's Health Imperative (BWHI), or "The Imperative."

Over the last 20 years, the NBWHP evolved from a collectivist, grassroots, radical feminist organization to an "inside the Beltway" organization with policy, research, and education as its primary functions. The organization is more bureaucratic and hierarchical than it was at its outset, but it is more financially secure. The DC office has a decidedly different flavor from the Mother House, and the constituency of the NBWHP has shifted, with policy-makers, health researchers, and professionals as its primary constituents. Today the BWHI is being developed as a think tank and resource for health information and not as a catalyst to spark the activism of poor black women.

Unresolved Challenges

The NBWHP never overcame the ongoing problems of supporting its chapters and ensuring their effectiveness. Most of the chapters barely functioned, and strong chapters, like the one in Los Angeles, effectively became autonomous organizations. Yet the NBWHP never formally abandoned the chapter framework. It has never been clear whether or not the chapters could rely on the national office for technical and financial resources, a situation that has often led to disillusionment and a sense of abandonment on the part of the chapter members. Although the chapter structure never quite developed as originally envisioned, the NBWHP inspired many black women's groups that practice Self-Help, such as the SisterLove Women's AIDS Project in Atlanta.

The issue of whom the NBWHP represents was also never resolved. Historically, NBWHP sought to represent the concerns and issues facing low-income women. The membership today, however, is primarily older, well-educated, and middle-class. The issues faced by this constituency are very different from those faced by poor women, and this discrepancy has made the development of a programmatic strategy difficult. The turn towards education, health, policy, research, and leadership training under the direction of Avery and Cole seems to consolidate the policy direction of the organization away from the needs of low-income women, although perspectives from the African American community that are more grassroots and diverse and less institutionalized than the BWHI are still urgently needed. Though Self-Help as a self-actualization strategy is not a central component of BWHI's mission, BWHI sees the Self-Help legacy as its significant contribution to the movement, but it remains unclear how Self-Help will be integrated into the new BWHI structure.

Much of the funding for NBWHP came from foundations and individual supporters of reproductive rights. Thus, it was always a struggle for the NBWHP to develop programs on a broader range of health issues. While it did obtain some government funds for its work on health disparities, most non-reproductive-related programs did not receive sufficient support. Projects that generated funds received the most emphasis, even when this did not match member priorities. Furthermore, the NBWHP raised more funds for the public policy office in DC than for the grassroots education and mobilizing done in Atlanta. The offices were not supposed to compete for funds, but many of the foundations supporting choice were the mainstay of the NBWHP's funding base and chose to fund only the policy office because they believed that advocacy work was key to advancing their own pro-choice agendas. This bias in foundation strategy, favoring policy and advocacy work over grassroots education, has shaped macro-level reproductive rights organizing and strengthened national organizations over movement-building strategies. The Atlanta office provided the grassroots support base for the DC office. Without Atlanta, DC became a policy office cut off from the support and fresh ideas of its constituency. This led to a shift from direct to virtual organizing and education, from outreach and empowering across class lines to reaching primarily middle-class black women.

The Significance of the NBWHP

An extremely important contribution of the NBWHP was its expansive definition of the meaning of reproductive freedom for African American women. While black feminists had defined this vision, the NBWHP brought it to the attention of the mainstream movement and public policy-makers, and it became a model for other women of color groups who subsequently organized around reproductive rights. The NBWHP notion of reproductive freedom was far broader than the more defensive and reactive mainstream pro-choice definition devised to protect the legality of abortion. For NBWHP, reproductive freedom included rights to comprehensive, age-appropriate information about sexuality and reproduction; choice of whether or not to have a child as well as help for infertile women to achieve pregnancy; good, affordable health care to assure safe pregnancy and delivery; and accessible health care. This holistic definition of reproductive rights not only underlined the right of women to decide whether or not to have children, it also embodied the idea that women have the right to the physical, emotional, spiritual, and economic means to parent children. This definition called for commensurate social support to make childbearing safe, as well as for control over one's own body.

The NBWHP blazed the path for other groups of women of color to carry out similar work in their own communities. It was inspirational to many other projects organized by women of color, such as the National Latina Health Organization and the National Asian Women's Health Organization, which were modeled on the NBWHP.

Since 1984, the NBWHP has tracked the health status of black women. At that time, calling attention to the unique problems of black women was a novel idea. There was no Office of Minority Health and no Woman's Health Initiative at the National Institutes of Health to address the inequities in the health status of black and white women. By drawing attention to these issues, the NBWHP provided the rationale and impetus for those federal agencies to take shape and helped frame their agendas for research, policy, and action. The work of the NBWHP provided greater understanding of the role of racism, ethnicity, and culture in the health care system. In addition, the NBWHP paved the way for including psychological well-being in discussions of health and placed this issue on the public agenda.[28] The NBWHP laid the foundation for increased legislative advocacy and developed a sustained relationship with black women legislators committed to, knowledgeable about, and willing to speak out on black women's health concerns.[29]

Whatever future direction the Black Women's Health Imperative takes, the National Black Women's Health Project has already left an impressive legacy. Other African American women's organizations, like African American Women Evolving (AAWE), which we turn to next, have built on its work. The visionary pioneers of the NBWHP—Avery and Allen—provided a space for African American women to explore their collective history, analyze their past, and identify their struggles and triumphs as they move to wellness.[30] They made wellness a positive goal. This inspirational vision, coupled with Self-Help as a tool to achieve that end and save the lives of African American women, launched a "spiritual revolution in America."[31]

NOTES

1   Byllye Avery, "A Question of Survival/A Conspiracy of Silence: Abortion and Black Women's Health," in *From Abortion to Reproductive Freedom: Transforming a Movement*, ed. Marlene Gerber Fried (Boston: South End Press, 1990), 75.

2   This was the feminist collective that wrote *Our Bodies, Ourselves*. The collective was dedicated to giving women the information they needed to make their own health decisions. It believed that asserting control over health care was an essential part of the struggle for liberation.

3   Judy Norsigian, telephone interview by Jael Silliman, 2002.

4   Ibid.

5   Avery, "A Question of Survival," 76.

6   Ibid.

7   Ibid., 77.

8   Ibid., 78.

9   Lillie Allen, interview by Loretta Ross, 2003.

10 Ibid.

11 Ibid.

12 "International Re-Evaluation Counseling Communities," http://www.rc.org.

13 Sandra Morgen, *Into Our Own Hands: The Women's Health Movement in the US, 1969–1990* (New Brunswick: NJ: Rutgers University Press, 2002), 45.

14 "Reflections on the Decade," *Vital Signs* 10 no. 3 (1994).

15 Loretta Ross, interview by Jael Silliman, 2002.

16 Allen interview.

17 Ibid.

18 Ibid.

19 Morgen, *Into Our Own Hands*, 53.

20 The Mother House was in the historic Auburn area of Atlanta. It was purchased through the work of chapters from Philadelphia to California and individual contributions from Diane Rowley, Byllye Avery, and Ama Saran. The down payment was provided by a local white donor.

21 NBWHP's first staff members were Shay Youngblood, a young writer, and Lillie Steadman, a senior citizen who came to work at the NBWHP through United Way. Both women remain active in the program.

22 Loretta Ross, "African American Women and Abortion," in *Abortion Wars: A Half Century of Struggle, 1950–2000*, ed. Rickie Solinger (Berkeley: University of California Press, 1998), 189.

23 The groups included Catholics for a Free Choice, the Center for Reproductive Law and Policy (now the Center for Reproductive Rights), the Allan Guttmacher Institute (especially the Washington, DC, office), the Religious Coalition for Reproductive Rights, the Center for Women's Policy Studies, the NOW Legal Defense and Education Fund, Planned Parenthood, and NARAL.

24 Julia Scott, telephone interview by Jael Silliman, 2002.

25 Byllye Avery, "Who Does the Work of Public Health," *American Journal of Public Health* 92, no. 4 (April 2002): 570–576.

26 Ibid.

27 Ibid.

28 Avery, interview by Jael Silliman, 2002.

29 These legislators include Maxine Waters, Cynthia McKinney, Carrie Meeks, Donna M. Christiansen, Eleanor Holmes Norton, and Barbara Lee. The Congressional Black Caucus co-sponsored a panel on women's health issues with Representative Sheila Jackson Lee for which the NBWHP can take considerable credit.

30 Morgen, *Into Our Own Hands*, 54.

31 Linda Villarosa, ed., *The Black Women's Guide to Physical Health and Emotional Well-Being* (New York: Harper Collins, 1994), 386.

5

African American Women Evolving

Aᴛʀɪᴄᴀɴ American Women Evolving (AAWE), established in Chicago in 1996, is one of the younger groups included in this volume. AAWE shares with the other groups a holistic vision of health. As current board chair La Donna Redmond says, AAWE is trying to "reconnect women's health and bodies with the rest of their lives."[1] AAWE is also trying to bring more women of color to the reproductive health movement, even though it is acutely aware of the barriers to inclusion. Unlike the other organizations in this book, AAWE was founded by people with long histories of involvement in the mainstream pro-choice movement. AAWE was the only group to be initiated within a predominantly white pro-choice organization. Toni Bond, AAWE's current CEO, continues to play a visible role in predominantly white mainstream abortion rights organizing. She is a good example of someone who simultaneously uses a variety of approaches to organizing, as described by co-author Loretta Ross in Chapter 2. AAWE's experience illustrates the possibilities and limitations of pursuing a woman of color-focused agenda in predominantly white groups.

Although there were several strong pro-choice groups in Chicago at the time AAWE was created, none addressed the varied reproductive health needs of black women. Pro-choice groups had not reached out to black women to find out about their particular reproductive health needs and concerns. AAWE did—through community dialogues, surveys, and conferences. Winnette Willis, one of AAWE's founding members, notes, "When you have the increases in AIDS [that we see in our community], high infant mortality rates, and a host of other health problems—something is seriously wrong."[2] By combining grassroots organizing and outreach with policy work, AAWE tackled the underlying causes of this health crisis. The mission touched a deep chord in former staff member L.T. Evans while she was interviewing for her position: "I cried in my interview when I realized how much I needed AAWE—women of all ages need this organization."[3]

Getting Started

AAWE's founders had been involved in the Chicago Abortion Fund (CAF) since 1994. Since 1985, CAF has provided thousands of low-income women in Illinois and surrounding states with the information, referrals, and direct financial assistance they needed to have safe, affordable abortions. While the leadership of CAF was primarily white, the organization had a long-standing commitment to diversity and building the leadership of women of color. Mary Morten, a well-known and respected African American activist, became CAF's board chair in 1994. Under her leadership CAF recruited Toni Bond, another well-respected African American woman activist, to be executive director in 1994. The two women worked together to increase CAF's visibility within the African American community. When Morten left two years later, Winnette Willis, another African American woman, replaced her as board chair.

At that time, women of color were also under-represented in the membership of pro-choice organizations. CAF's women of color leadership was unique in the larger Illinois pro-choice community. While there were a few women of color within the Planned Parenthood network, Bond was the only black woman leading a mainstream reproductive rights organization in Illinois, the only black executive director in the National Network of Abortion Funds (NNAF), and the first black woman on the NNAF board.

For both Bond and Willis, abortion access was a very personal issue. Willis had had an illegal abortion with the Jane Collective; Bond had had a legal abortion just after the Hyde Amendment was passed, and obtaining the necessary funding had been a real struggle for her family. The experiences of CAF's clients were close to their own, and they knew this was true for other women of color whom they wanted to engage in the movement. However, the racial dynamics within CAF were a barrier. Despite the fact that two African American women led CAF, Bond and Willis still saw it as an organization of white women that provided services to women of color. Most of the board members were white, and the majority of donors and supporters were white middle-to-upper-class women and men. Bond and Willis thought that some of the white women on the board were paternalistic in their approach to CAF's clients. Willis also thought that some of the white board members were not adept at communicating with or interpreting the behavior and needs of CAF's black clientele. As a result, the board's decisions regarding CAF's mission and the provision and delivery of services did not speak to some of the clients' reproductive health needs. The board had not addressed these issues. Hence there were unresolved tensions between white and black women in the organization.

Willis and Bond felt impelled to do something that would nurture and develop black leadership in the reproductive rights movement.[4] They contacted African American women who had been active in pro-choice organizations to see if they could be brought back to the movement.[5] They also drew on their personal connections to reach out to other women who were supportive of women's and social justice issues but who had not been active on the abortion issue. In all, 80 women were invited to an informal roundtable discussion about the struggles that women of color have faced in mainstream reproductive rights organizations. Among the women who responded were those who became, along with Willis and Bond, the founders of AAWE—Sharon Powell, Toylee Green, and Billie Woodard.

During the discussion, the women shared the problems they faced as black activists working in mainstream reproductive rights organizations. They spoke about battling just to be heard on the subject of what reproductive rights meant to women of color and the toll it had taken on them personally. Most felt their efforts to bring the perspectives of women of color to their organizations' agendas were unsuccessful. They expressed frustration that abortion was always at the forefront of mainstream groups' concerns, even when they said they wanted to broaden their agendas. Bond sums up the general feeling expressed in this way: "I spoke—but I was never heard. It is hard to feel like you belong, like this is your movement."[6] Even in organizations where black women had leadership positions, white members seemed unable to share power. Bond captures the common experience:

Black women are treated as invited guests in the reproductive rights movement—outsiders to someone else's event—despite the fact that issues of access to abortion services, forced and coercive sterilization, reproductive tract infections (RTIs), and infant and maternal mortality and morbidity impact us. When we do come to the meeting, it is always a constant challenge to keep other reproductive health concerns on the table with the issue of abortion. It all just makes us want to leave and never come back.[7]

These activists had also faced the challenge of resistance to reproductive rights organizing within their own community (see Chapter 1 for a fuller discussion). Bond remembers one incident when she was tabling for the Chicago Abortion Fund at a health fair held in a black church: "Some of the women there expressed sheer revulsion about my organization and issue. I live in my community. I understood how much I was risking by being involved."[8] Bond talked about the fact that even speaking about abortion is still taboo in a community where ministers give sermons condemning women who have abortions. She also echoed the critique of "choice" shared by other women of color (see Chapter 2 for a detailed discussion).

At the same time, roundtable participants reported that when they became involved in the anti-sexual violence and health movements, as well as in the substance abuse prevention community, they found to their dismay that they confronted the same lack of a holistic vision of health that had alienated them from the mainstream pro-choice groups. They cared deeply about the health of African American women, wanted to work in this area, but had not found a political home. Thus, they valued the space Bond and Willis had created. They could talk openly and gain affirmation for working on reproductive rights in spite of what seemed like roadblocks on all sides.

For Bond and Willis, the only agenda of the meeting was to bring African American women to the table and give them a greater stake in CAF's work. They had not anticipated that women coming to the meetings needed to tell their own stories. However, talking about the clients of CAF brought up the subjects of rape and incest and one by one participants talked about their experiences with sexual and domestic violence as well as access to health care in general:

The sharing of stories was very draining but we decided to meet again. If all of this was happening to us, it must be happening to others too. We knew we had to do something. We didn't feel helpless. Somehow we were empowered in our pain and felt we could make a difference. We also knew we had to do it for ourselves and in our own organization where we set the agenda instead of struggling to fit it into a pro-choice organization with a different focus. This was our version of Self-Help.[9]

At their next meeting, the group discussed how they might formulate a black women's health agenda. Several of them had been involved in attempts to organize a Chicago chapter of the National Black Women's Health Project (NBWHP). The first attempt failed in part because Chicago is a politically divided city, but also because NBWHP had not been able to address the particular needs of African American women in Chicago. A subsequent attempt had also been unsuccessful because the women rejected the NBWHP's Self-Help model as too therapy-based. The women decided that they did not want to ground their work in this way. "We were being told to work out of our pain. But we didn't want that. We needed to work out of our strength."[10] Without denying their own histories, they wanted to start from the point of survival.

The experience with NBWHP made these women wary of getting involved in a new initiative. They did not want be part of another failed attempt by African American women to organize for reproductive rights. Despite their apprehension, the group continued to meet, drawn together by their shared dedication to reproductive health and the possibility of developing a grassroots black women's health agenda. They deliberated about how they could raise reproductive health concerns in their communities. They agreed that any discussion of reproductive health and sexuality had to include discussion of the problems of substance abuse and violence, HIV/AIDS, and access to general and reproductive health care. At one meeting, Willis said she was "in awe of everyone here and our sharing around our personal and professional health."[11] Her sentiment resonated deeply. The women decided to use the acronym AAWE—African American Women Evolving—to refer to themselves. The name not only reflected the esteem in which they held one another but also established a central goal—to evolve into a force for social change.

AAWE's first public activity was a conference on black women's health in 1998, entitled "Black Women: Loving the Mind, Body and

Spirit."[12] The conference promotional materials declared: "This space is about us. The topics are relevant to us. This conference is for us."[13] By centering the needs of African American women in a way that had not been done before in Chicago, the conference attracted over 200 black women of all ages from different socioeconomic groups. It was a unique opportunity for black women to "share our wisdom, strength, personal and professional experience."[14]

Participants attended workshops on a wide array of topics, such as AIDS and other sexually transmitted diseases (STDs), menstruation, sexual assault, new contraceptives, traditional African healing methods, and internalized oppression. The issue of abortion, though not explicitly on the conference agenda, was discussed in various workshops. Conference presenters and resource people promoted a positive view of health. They provided pertinent information on ways to achieve mentally, physically, and emotionally healthy and balanced lives. At the "Doc Walk," health agencies and professionals provided services and information on diabetes and checked women's blood pressure. In collaboration with the Illinois Maternal and Child Health Coalition, AAWE conducted a survey in which conference attendees were interviewed about their preterm low-birth-weight babies and douching practices.

Because of tremendous community support AAWE was able to hold the conference with extremely limited resources.[15] Conference participants appreciated receiving the latest health information and having the opportunity to come together and bond with each other as black women. Special efforts were made to reach a cross-section of the community: no admission fee was charged, free meals and childcare were provided, and women from shelters and drug treatment facilities were invited to attend.

Through the time of the conference, AAWE had been a somewhat ad hoc organization existing under the aegis of CAF. CAF offered staff time, meeting space, and limited financial support to the group. The success of the conference confirmed that AAWE should become an independent organization rather than continue as a project of CAF. Conference evaluations underlined the need for a group that could generate broad discussions of sexuality and reproductive health in the black community. Comments included "Wow! All of these black women together"; "I came hungry for information and got it"; "There has never been an event like this in our community."[16] In the months after the conference,

AAWE was invited to organize workshops and presentations on women's health across Chicago. Just as a groundbreaking conference 15 years earlier had launched the National Black Women's Health Project, so "Black Women: Loving the Mind, Body and Spirit" launched African American Women Evolving.

While seeking to incorporate and function as a separate organization, AAWE continued to operate as a project of CAF until it could be successfully independent. As AAWE gained greater visibility, a few CAF board members felt that AAWE's agenda was draining staff time and resources from the core mission of assisting women in getting abortions. The CAF board disagreed about whether or not AAWE's work was the most effective use of CAF's resources. This led to a prolonged battle regarding the board members' relationships with CAF executive director Toni Bond and board chair Winnette Willis, who were both founders and major players in AAWE. The CAF board's conflict over Bond's relationship to AAWE placed Willis in a difficult position. She was forced to fend off conflict of interest charges levied at Bond regarding AAWE.

Upon review of Bond's tenure as executive director, the board found that increased services to communities of color had resulted in gains for CAF on several fronts. Raising CAF's visibility in those communities had garnered financial support from women of color. Further, by creating a national reputation for CAF through her participation on the National Network of Abortion Funds board and in other national and international activities, Bond had increased the number of volunteers, and overall support from foundations had grown. Ultimately, the majority of the CAF board was supportive of Bond, and thought that AAWE's work was an important CAF activity. The board urged AAWE to stay on as part of CAF as long as it wanted to do so.

CAF's support of AAWE came at some cost to the organization. The two board members who challenged Bond's direction resigned. Both had been major donors, contributing a substantial part of the budget. The sudden drop in CAF's funding led to significant financial difficulties and put pressure on the organization to increase its fundraising efforts. CAF surmounted this hurdle, and the financial crisis it experienced was relatively short-lived. The fact that CAF weathered this storm showed its commitment to diversity and recognition of the importance of leadership by African American women in the movement for reproductive freedom.

Building a Grassroots Organization

Since 1999, when AAWE formally separated from CAF, the groups have maintained a strong collaborative relationship. Despite the initial difficulties and some hard feelings in CAF, over the years the two organizations have enjoyed a collegial relationship, each supporting the work of the other.

Establishing the organization as an independent entity was not an easy process. Initially, AAWE operated out of board members' homes, and Bond used her own personal resources to maintain the organization. For the first year of its existence, AAWE did not have its own nonprofit status to solicit foundation grants. In July 1999, AAWE officially joined the National Network of Abortion Funds, incorporating under NNAF's group nonprofit tax exemption. Though it was difficult to initiate projects during this unsettled time, the group did organize a second conference in May 1999. Modeled on the first conference, this event brought together 150 women to discuss black women's health concerns.

Eventually, the fiscal sponsorship of NNAF allowed AAWE to raise funds for its activities. It received grants from the Ms. Foundation and the Jessie Smith Noyes Foundation.[17] In 2001, additional foundation support enabled Bond to leave her executive director position at CAF and devote herself full-time to AAWE as the organization's president and CEO.[18] Bond, who had until then continued to work for both CAF and AAWE, gave the CAF board notice of her intent to resign at the end of 2001. Though board members were saddened by Bond's decision, they were supportive of her need to move on after devoting seven years to CAF. Nitrice Johnson, also an AAWE board member, succeeded Bond as CAF executive director.

While the conferences were good vehicles for introducing women to health issues and to each other, AAWE was not committed to holding them every year. The members realized that this high-intensity work was hard to sustain and took substantial organizational resources. Instead, AAWE has hosted smaller community events that have provided women with the opportunity to work together on a continuing basis.

AAWE's Vision and Activities

Like the other organizations in this book that emphasize grassroots work, AAWE was committed to developing its agenda based on the needs of women in its community. AAWE has used a variety of methods to solicit feedback from the community about which issues it should address. From 2000 to 2001, AAWE developed and administered a reproductive health survey to 300 African American women in Illinois between the ages of 18 and 60. The findings of this survey called attention to the serious health problems that African American women face and demonstrated the need for better health services in black communities. The results pointed out that black women must become better educated about their bodies and reproductive health, that African American cultural beliefs need to be respected, and that it is important to dispel myths and stereotypes about black women's sexuality.[19] A summary of the data, "Differences in Dignity," was published and made available to the public.[20] Organizing and participating in conferences and workshops provided other opportunities for community input into AAWE's programming and activities. In this way AAWE developed a holistic view of health:

> AAWE believes women need information about methods of contraception and information about harmful side effects, preventing HIV/AIDS and other sexually transmitted diseases, understanding and learning how to chart the menstrual cycle, infertility, prenatal care, infant and maternal mortality, menopause, breast cancer, accessing safe abortion, exploring our sexuality, etc.[21]

AAWE has made holistic community health education a priority. This has guided decisions about which projects to advance and what materials to produce.

As part of AAWE's commitment to helping women build their organizational, advocacy, and other skills, AAWE opened the Center for Health and Wellness in 2001, thereby providing a place for African American women to access resources on reproductive and general health. The center's library has publications on subjects ranging from women's health and feminist theory to human rights and cultural competency.[22] Through the center, AAWE has offered workshops and training sessions, distributed condoms, and provided referral information for health care. AAWE has plans to hold workshops for medical providers to sensitize them to the needs and problems of African American women, so that ultimately community women will receive better care. AAWE has also produced brochures and kits on safe sex, HIV/AIDS, and other sexually transmitted infections (STIs), and taught women how to conduct cervical self-exams. In 2001, AAWE began training members with these tools so they could conduct peer education sessions for young and adult women on the same topics: safe sex, HIV/AIDS and other STIs, cervical self-exams, and contraception. Through all of its projects, AAWE is committed to developing the next generation of activists by conducting outreach primarily to young, college-age women.

Working with individuals and other organizations in the black community, AAWE initiated a series of dialogues on abortion and reproductive rights. AAWE organized an intergenerational dialogue to encourage more honest communication between mothers and daughters about menstruation, douching, sexuality, and other reproductive health issues. As one facilitator noted, there were few models for this type of discussion, as most of the women's mothers had not talked with them about these issues. AAWE's video, *Mothers and Daughters: Sharing the Knowledge*, and a companion discussion guide grew from this effort.

To raise awareness within the African American community about emergency contraception (EC), AAWE conducted a survey of 299 pharmacies in Chicago and nearby suburbs. Its goal was to find out how accessible EC was to women of color. Included in the assessment was whether or not the pharmacy carried EC, the quality of the information provided, and the manner in which the caller was treated. After the pharmacy survey was completed, AAWE's commitment to grassroots work was demonstrated when it called a meeting of community groups. It wanted to share its findings and develop a cohesive strategy for increasing access to EC. AAWE was adamant that the community should receive the information first in order to make decisions about how to frame the survey results before the press entered the debate. AAWE's approach is a departure from the tactics used by larger pro-choice organizations, which tend to be more concerned with using data to make a media splash rather than using it to empower a community. Ultimately AAWE did publish the results of the pharmacy survey with the feedback of the larger community shaping its response. AAWE highlighted the inadequacy of access to EC and made policy recommendations aimed at increasing its availability to women of color.

Providing direct assistance to women has also been an integral feature of AAWE's agenda. Consequently, its Reproductive Care Support Program provides financial assistance to obtain ultrasounds, critical post-abortion follow-up examinations, and contraception for uninsured women and for those whose insurance does not cover contraception. The program also makes available money for childcare costs and other expenses that women incur in the process of obtaining an abortion. While the program's primary focus is to provide financial assistance and support services to women in Chicago and Illinois, AAWE hopes to make it available to women in other states. AAWE does not want to replicate the work of groups that fund abortions for women who cannot afford to pay for them. Rather, it seeks to augment that work by providing reproductive care, culturally appropriate health information, and financial support so that women can have access to contraception and other reproductive health services that they are unable to afford.

AAWE recognizes the importance of policy and advocacy work, but does not separate policy efforts from grassroots activities. AAWE is committed to bringing the voices and concerns of community women to state, national, and international arenas and vice versa. Hence, it participates in local and national letter-writing and postcard campaigns, rallies, legislative briefings, voter education, and voter registration. It issues fact sheets and policy reports. In 2000, AAWE played a leadership role in NNAF's national Campaign for Access and Reproductive Equity (CARE), advised the National Abortion and Reproductive Rights Action League (NARAL) on its draft of federal and state legislation addressing the health needs of women of color, and is part of the Hospital Access Collaborative, an initiative to increase abortion access at hospitals. AAWE's Healthy Vagina Campaign (HVC) is another example of grassroots community-based education making an impact on policy and advocacy. HVC brings information to women and, based on survey findings described in "Differences in Dignity," seeks stricter review and regulation of companies that manufacture products to "sanitize" women's bodies.

Informing its grassroots constituency about national and international reproductive rights analyses and issues is key to this strategy of mobilizing community women to have their perspectives on reproductive health heard at the national level. AAWE's workshops on reproductive health and social justice include discussions and updates on topics such as welfare reform, the Beijing Platform of Action (developed by women's groups around the world who participated in the Fourth World Conference on Women held in Beijing in August 1995), the Convention on the Elimination of All Forms of Discrimination Against

Women (CEDAW—a treaty which most countries have signed but not the United States), and developments in new reproductive technologies.

While the development and implementation of AAWE's agenda has been directed by the community at large, its work has also benefited from its commitment to a board that reflects the range of women it serves. The board includes women from different socioeconomic backgrounds, as well as women with varying levels of experience in reproductive rights work and other social movements. It is made up of 14 members, who range in age from 20 to 50 years old. There has been some tension between older, seasoned activists and younger women newer to organizing; the younger activists have complained about not being heard and having their perspectives discounted, while the older women feel that their experience and past work are not always appreciated or respected. Despite these differences, the intergenerational board has made AAWE more representative and better able to respond to the community it serves.

The Contributions of AAWE

AAWE's history vividly illustrates some of the challenges African American women encounter from both the African American community and the mainstream reproductive rights movement. By simultaneously working at AAWE and serving in leadership positions in predominantly white organizations—Bond is the board chair of National Network of Abortion Funds and Nitrice Johnson is the executive director of CAF—AAWE members demonstrate their commitment to developing a movement that is inclusive of women from all races and classes. Although they have articulated a critique of the pro-choice movement, they remain committed to ongoing participation in it.

AAWE's leaders play an important role in bridging mainstream reproductive rights work with the perspectives and needs of women of color. While the interactions between AAWE and mainstream groups have not always been easy, their experience shows that white women in mainstream organizations can be good allies to organizations of women of color. Their experience with CAF also highlights the conflicts that must be resolved between women of color and mainstream reproductive rights activists and organizations in order to build a more inclusive movement. For example, most of the women at CAF believed in AAWE's mission and importance but at the same time, they had trouble letting AAWE

become autonomous. A few did not really understand the need to establish an organization exclusively of and for African American women.
Thus, CAF experienced AAWE's independence as a loss, even though
the majority of CAF members stood behind their commitment to developing African American leadership and were supportive of AAWE.

AAWE's founders had the vision, commitment, and professional
expertise to create an autonomous organization; however, their initial
lack of financial resources and access to funding reflects the inequities
of access between mainstream organizations that target the issue of
abortion access and women of color organizations that must address a
broader range of reproductive health issues. Resource inequities underline the important role that white women and mainstream organizations
can play as allies to women of color and their organizations. CAF and
then NNAF provided temporary institutional homes for AAWE and
helped develop funding connections.

AAWE has found the association with NNAF to be very positive and
mutually beneficial, both at the organizational and personal levels. Toni
Bond described NNAF's founding president and co-author Marlene
Gerber Fried, a white reproductive rights activist, as her mentor and ally.
Bond defined a mentor as a person who

> at the base level understands what it means to support someone—and
> has a basic level of compassion and humanity. An ally is someone who is
> able to extend [herself/himself] and take risks. An ally or mentor is not
> the only one who is giving something in the mentoring relationship—
> a good mentor also learns something through this interaction. An ally
> understands that being an ally is a learning process that enables her/him
> to stretch, learn, and see things in a different way.[23]

A genuine effort to equalize the power relationships between organizations and individuals is key to building successful inter- and intra-racial
and class partnerships. If the level of funding and organizational longevity continuously outweighs the other strengths and attributes that each
group offers, organizations of women of color will, by default, always
be junior partners in collaborative efforts. Even well-meaning dependence is a recipe for resentment. In the connections AAWE developed
with CAF and NNAF, significant working relationships were strengthened by the differences in age, race, and experience that characterized
each organization and by mutual acknowledgement that each brought

something critical to the partnership. Both CAF and NNAF have helped AAWE in gaining access to independent funding and making its voice an important one in policy circles. AAWE in turn has made them realize the importance of diversity and in so doing has enriched NNAF's and CAF's programs and outreach efforts.

While Willis and Bond continue to engage with white activists, there have been strategic differences of opinion among AAWE members about how much energy should be spent on such work. Some members think that keeping the white mainstream movement informed about the reproductive health needs and priorities of black women is vital. They point to pragmatic reasons to continue working in the white world even when they work primarily in communities of color. Willis explains, "[White society] is where the resources are—the entire grant-making structure—you have to deal with white institutions—it is dealing with the outside world. You need to be in both places."[24] On the other hand, board member La Donna Redmond counters this core AAWE vision by insisting that working in the black community is in itself a large enough task for AAWE. She feels that if AAWE focused its efforts on the black community, it could provide African American women with important services, and therefore should not spend time trying to get mainstream groups to become more inclusive.

Willis thinks that white groups can learn from black women on several fronts, such as how to reach more vulnerable women in their own communities. She knows that black women cannot organize poor white women. However, she believes that AAWE's work could serve as a model for reaching working-class and low-income white women on issues of reproductive health, since poor white women face many of the same problems as African American women. These problems include a lack of access to health services, the insensitivity of health care providers to the needs of ethnically diverse women, and inadequate information and options. Willis also sees AAWE's holistic approach as important for trying to reach a wide range of women across ideological divides. For example, even though AAWE is clearly a pro-choice organization, the group wants to reach out to women and men who do not support abortion rights.

Developing a plan to help black women in Chicago secure reproductive rights means addressing the economic, emotional, cultural, and spiritual issues that are at the core of all black women's reproductive health problems—including the founders' own. When the women who founded AAWE first came together, the emotional safety of the group helped them work on the challenges and concerns that are particular to African American women. Nitrice Johnson put it this way, "Ultimately those of us in AAWE see ourselves as doing this work for us—not for other women."[25] In the process of talking with each other, they healed old wounds and dealt with internalized oppression. AAWE and the NBWHP both illustrate that such work continues to be crucial to African American women because it enables them to connect with one another, to overcome barriers to activism, and to potentially build bridges across other social divides. Redmond sees working on internalized oppression as an ongoing task for activists, one that is essential for building healthy organizations.

The Legacies of the NBWHP and AAWE

There is a critical need to have several African American organizations working on reproductive rights to meet the distinct needs of varied constituencies within the African American community. AAWE has helped to address this need. The National Black Women's Health Project influenced the course of organizing for African American reproductive rights by its broad definition of reproductive rights; through the connections it made between Self-Help, health, and activism; and by the outreach it conducted through workshops and conferences. The NBWHP has shown that African American women are an important constituency who can have an impact on the national health agenda. Due to the efforts of the NBWHP and other groups of women of color, policy-makers, researchers, and the public now pay more attention to issues of race-based health disparities.

AAWE drew inspiration from the NBWHP, and AAWE members pay tribute to the NBWHP for bringing black women's reproductive health issues into focus. However, the NBWHP model did not address the organizational, logistical, and ideological needs of African American reproductive rights activists in Chicago. AAWE members wanted to involve women of different classes in their organization and outreach efforts. While the sharing of difficult histories was important in the creation of AAWE, its members were critical of the NBWHP's Self-Help model. They were concerned that it does not guarantee a safe space for all women, and that the Self-Help groups could cross the line, becoming therapy sessions without trained clinicians on hand. Bond thinks that despite the original intention of its founders, Self-Help sometimes lacked the emotional boundaries necessary for providing support while safeguarding individuals in the process. In light of its critique of Self-Help, AAWE developed its own approach to sharing their difficult histories, while acknowledging that Self-Help, as practiced by the NBWHP, has created important opportunities for women to share their experiences.

In its grassroots program and outreach, AAWE continues where the NBWHP left off when it shifted its focus to public policy work. AAWE's emphasis on outreach to black women across socioeconomic divides and its holistic reproductive health education is similar to NBWHP's during the first five years of its existence. As the NBWHP directed more to national issues and was less engaged in direct community organizing and outreach, it left a void in reproductive rights activism in the African American community. AAWE is attempting to fill that gap in the Chicago area.

Clearly, there is still an ongoing need for African American women to come together in safe spaces to articulate their needs, get the information they require regarding their health and rights, and work on specific issues in their communities. At present, despite their aims, AAWE's programs primarily reach educated black women who are struggling to achieve economic and professional security. The organization has not yet been able to systematically reach women with fewer resources. Its goal is ultimately to speak to a cross-section of black women, including those who are most vulnerable. AAWE's grassroots approach to education, policy, and advocacy complements the more national orientation of the NBWHP. AAWE's leadership brings significant new voices to the reproductive rights movement, in Chicago, nationally, and internationally.

NOTES

1 La Donna Redmond, interview by Jael Silliman, March 2002.

2 Winnette Willis, interview by Jael Silliman, March 2002.

3 L.T. Evans, interview by Marlene Gerber Fried, September 2002.

4 Toni Bond, interview by Jael Silliman, January 15, 2002.

5 Their contacts included women working with the Illinois chapter of the National Abortion Rights Action League, the Illinois Pro-Choice Alliance, and Chicago National Organization for Women.

6 Toni Bond, interview by Silliman.

7 Toni Bond, "Barriers Between Black Women and the Reproductive Rights Movement," *Political Environments* 8 (Winter/Spring 2001): 3.

8 Toni Bond, interview by Marlene Gerber Fried, September 2002.

9 Toni Bond, interview by Silliman.

10 Ibid.

11 Ibid.

12 Co-sponsoring the conference with AAWE was Tongues of Fire, a student group from Columbia College.

13 AAWE, Conference Brochure, 2000.

14 Ibid.

15 Many African American women who came were sponsored by state and local health agencies. Donated staff time from the Chicago Abortion Fund (CAF) and small grants from the Ms. Foundation and the Chicago Foundation for Women were also critical to the success of this first initiative.

16 AAWE, Conference Evaluations, 2000.

17 AAWE was also able to secure project funding from the Chicago Foundation for Women and the Crossroads Fund.

18 This funding came from the Public Welfare Foundation and the Chicago Community Trust.

19 In its 2000–2001 survey of 300 African American women, AAWE found that over half the respondents (52 percent) douched, with 37 percent douching, on the average, once per month. 23 percent douched more than once per month. They were at greater risk for HIV/AIDS, other reproductive tract infections and cervical cancer. Douching, which was practiced by over half the women surveyed, further increases the chances of contracting STDs.

20 AAWE, *Differences in Dignity: Race, Class, and the Reproductive Health of Black Women* (Chicago: AAWE, 2001).

21 From the AAWE mission statement, which is available at the website, http://www.AAWEonline.org

22 Files were bequeathed to AAWE by the now defunct Women's Health Education Project and provided the nucleus for a library.

23 Bond, interview by Silliman.

24 Willis interview.

25 Nitrice Johnson, interview by Marlene Gerber Fried, September, 2002.

6

Native American Women Resist Genocide and Organize for Reproductive Rights

"I T is because of a Native American woman's sex that she is hunted down and slaughtered, in fact, singled out, because she has the potential through childbirth to assure the continuance of the people."[1] The colonizers killed Native American women and children as part of a strategy to conquer, subdue, and destroy Indian nations and take control of their lands. Andrew Jackson recommended that after massacres, the troops should systematically kill Indian women and children to complete the extermination of Native peoples.[2] Thus, for Native American women the issues of cultural survival, land rights, and reproductive rights cannot be separated.

The US government justified the conquest of the Native peoples by calling its invasions a "civilizing mission." Indians were perceived as savages to be tamed and brought under Christian influences. This justification was also predicated upon the perceived "sexual perversity"[3] of Native peoples. Native women's sexuality was perceived as a threat to the political order,[4] making it necessary to control their fertility. Involuntary sterilization, the promotion of unsafe and long-acting contraceptives, and the denial of federal funding for abortion are part of a long history of attempts to destroy Native cultures and Native peoples.[5] Native American efforts to reassert sovereignty over their lands are inextricably tied to their efforts to reassert control over their reproduction.

Native nations hold more than 300 treaties with the United States that define land boundaries, rights to hunt and gather, rights to water and other resources, and the means by which Native people will be

111

remunerated for allowing the US to live on and use their land. Although the US has not abided by the treaties, they are legal documents, valid under international law, ratified by the US Congress, and recognized by Article VI, Section 2 of the US Constitution, which calls treaties the "supreme law of the land." Native American nations that have treaties are called "federally recognized." "Inherent sovereignty" is the fundamental right of indigenous nations to be self-governing entities with full and complete rights of self-determination. This sovereignty has existed "since time immemorial." It does not depend on, nor can it be terminated by, the US government, though the government has tried to do so by exercising a great deal of control over Indian nations.

For Native American activists, reproductive rights include the essential right to pass on their culture. Their struggle for reproductive rights is intimately connected to the struggle for cultural survival and control over their land base. This connection distinguishes reproductive rights activism in the Native American community: "Organized beyond the simple binary of 'pro-choice' v. 'pro-life' positions on abortion rights, Native activists attempt to address the underlying causes of Native women's reproductive un/freedom—colonialism, racism, economic exploitation, etc."[6] In their struggles, they have had to fight not just to be able to have children but to keep them in their custody.

Cultural Destruction

The Appropriation of Native Children

Native Americans attribute the "insidious erosion of identity, culture, spirituality, language, scientific and technical knowledge" to policies which sanctioned the removal of Native children to non-Native schools and families. These policies have created chaos and violence in Native women's lives.[7] Forcing Native children to attend boarding schools contributed to the destruction of Native cultures. Since the 1600s, Native youth have been sent to Western religious institutions where they were forced to worship as Christians and to abandon their traditions. In these schools students were punished for speaking Native languages. This form of schooling for Native children was formalized in 1878, when Congress set aside funds to erect schools that would be run by churches and missionaries. The explicit goal of this school policy was religious conversion and the cultural assimilation of indigenous peoples into Western culture by breaking the ties to Native religions, families, and communities. Despite many years of complaints by Native peoples, time spent at these schools was often accompanied by physical and sexual abuse. Only in 1987 did the Bureau of Indian Affairs finally make reporting sexual abuse in these schools mandatory.

The centuries-long policy of assimilation of Native children took its toll. In 1974, the Association of American Indian Affairs estimated that as a result of these policies between 25 and 35 percent of all Native children in certain states were adopted by non-Indian families or placed in non-Indian foster homes or institutional settings, while another 25 percent were "temporarily placed in government or church run boarding schools."[8] Some Native Americans contend that the forcible and systematic transfer of care of Native American children to non-Indians through the boarding school system and adoptions violated the 1948 Convention on Punishment and Prevention of Crimes of Genocide. It was not until the Indian Child Welfare Act (ICWA) of 1978 that the federal government finally renounced this century-old policy, and replaced jurisdiction over cases of foster care and adoption of Native children with tribal governments, with disputes to be heard in tribal courts.[9] Due to ICWA, Native children are increasingly adopted or placed in foster care with Native families. However, over the last ten years activists have been concerned about attempts to undermine ICWA and reverse this trend.

To stop the loss of culture that has ensued over the last two centuries, the establishment of Native schools has been a central concern for many activists. "There is no resource more vital to the continued existence and integrity of Indian tribes than their children."[10] While boarding schools still exist they are increasingly under the control of community boards.

The Termination Era Policies

A major push to extinguish Native American families, tribes, and cultures occurred in the 1950s, when federal policies were enacted to end treaty rights and decrease services to Native American populations. This period is commonly referred to as the "Termination Era," during which more than 100 tribes were cut off from federal funding and social and health services altogether. Another Termination Era policy was the federal government's "relocation program." This program encouraged Native Americans to leave their reservations by providing them with one-way tickets to cities.[11] The federal government was using the policies of the

Termination Era to "get out of the Indian business."[12] The impact of this action on Native Americans was devastating, causing further damage in Native families and communities. The splitting up of families contributed to intergenerational disconnectedness. The move to the cities, without the necessary support systems, led to unemployment and poverty among urban Indians.

Termination Era policies also changed the way in which health care was delivered and administered. In 1955, the Indian Health Service (IHS) was transferred from the Department of the Interior to the Department of Health, Education, and Welfare (later renamed the Department of Health and Human Services) as a first step toward terminating health care rights for Native Americans. However, the Public Health Service actually managed to improve the health of Native Americans living on reservations by introducing new sanitation programs and constructing clinics and hospitals,[13] and fortunately, termination as a policy ended without having "terminated" Native American health care rights.

Blood Claims and Assimilation

As part of its ongoing effort to take land away from Native Americans, the US government created a policy for determining Native status that was designed to reduce the number of people who could legitimately claim to be Native Americans. The federal government requires tribal governments to establish and enforce criteria for tribal membership based on a blood quantum. Generally, one-quarter Indian blood qualifies a person as Indian, although there is variation among tribes. Government interference with the definitions of tribal membership, coupled with population control policies, reduces the numbers of Native people enrolled as members of federally recognized tribes.

Native scholar Annette Jaimes explains that the rapid rate of assimilation among Native peoples is a contemporary threat to their cultural survival, pointing out that the loss of people's "claims" as Indians amounts to the "statistical extermination" of Native Americans.[14] Assimilated Native Americans will no longer be able to assert their identity and claims as Indians, which in turn reduces the Indian presence in government records. Since only Native Americans with official status have access to federally funded health care, loss of Indian status has health consequences as well.[15]

The process of assimilation and consequent land loss is intensified by the present rates of intermarriage and birth among Indians and non-Indians: the currently recognized Indian population with one-quarter or less Indian blood is expected to rise from 4 percent in 1980 to 59 percent in 2080.[16] This statistical absence is another dimension of the "present absence" syndrome that Kate Shanley describes as endemic in the American colonial imagination, and "reinforces at every turn the conviction that Native peoples are indeed vanishing and that the conquest of Native lands is justified."[17]

The issue of blood quantum remains highly charged and controversial both within and outside of Native American communities.[18] Native American scholar and activist Andrea Smith draws the connection between colonization and the desire to reduce Native American reproductive capacity. She asserts that the reproductive capacity of Native women impedes further colonization of Native lands, threatening "the continued success of colonization."[19] Since Indian lands contain the vast majority of raw materials needed for energy production, the long-term stability of domestic energy production hinges on the ability of the US government and corporations to freely extract those resources. Their ability to control those resources is strengthened when they can control Native women's reproductive capacity. Controlling Native women's fertility reduces Native American populations, directly weakening Native American control over their lands.

Environmental Racism

Survival of Native peoples is also threatened by environmental racism. Native American environmentalist Winona LaDuke refers to the current siting of hazardous wastes on Indian lands as "radioactive colonialism"—another mechanism used to weaken and subdue a people.[20] She calls the aggressive industrial interventions on the remaining Native lands a toxic invasion of Native America. "Three hundred and seventeen reservations in the United States are threatened by environmental hazards, ranging from toxic wastes to clear cuts."[21] She decries the 1,000 atomic explosions on Western Shoshone land that have occurred over the last 45 years, making the Western Shoshone the most bombed nation on earth.[22] In the early 1970s, when the second wave environmental movement was only just gaining ground,[23] Madonna Thunderhawk, a Native activist, recognized the connection between environment and reproduction when she examined the impact of water contamination on women's reproductive health. The adverse environmental impact of such nuclear and hazardous waste policies on health, particularly on reproductive health, have been clearly documented; for the last 30 years the impacts of environmental racism have been debilitating for indigenous peoples, and have mobilized many Native environmental justice advocates.[24]

Indians Organize for Cultural Survival

During the 1960s, Native Americans organized, demonstrated, protested, and died to protect their political, cultural, and legal rights. At a historic meeting in Chicago in 1961, 500 Indians representing 67 nations adopted a Declaration of Indian Purpose. In 1962, the National Indian Youth Council was formed, and its members demonstrated against the denial of Native American rights. The American Indian Movement (AIM), a militant Indian rights organization, was founded in Minneapolis in 1968.[25] In the late 1960s and early 70s, several other powerful national and international Native organizations emerged, such as United Native Americans Inc., International Indian Treaty Council (IITC),[26] and Women of All Red Nations (WARN).

These organizations wanted to unite Native peoples across tribal lines to promote the general welfare of Native peoples, to advocate for rights to health and land, and to establish legal rights of self-determination. Together, they launched campaigns against the Indian Health Service[27] and other governmental institutions related to Indian peoples. Several of these organizations focused on protecting the health of their communities and were particularly concerned about reproductive rights abuses.

The American Indian Movement's mission has been to preserve cultural identity.[28] In response to the cultural disintegration that occurred though the religious and boarding school system, AIM sought to provide Indian children with an alternative education. It organized community schools named "survival schools." These schools, some of which continue to exist, were dedicated to teaching Native culture, language, and politics; to nurturing self-esteem and pride; and to giving young people the strength, skills, and knowledge to work within their own nations. AIM worked closely with the IITC on this effort, because both groups wanted to promote Native sovereignty and culture. In the 1970s and 80s, AIM, IITC, and WARN published a joint newsletter, conducted conferences, and sent their members to speak at national and international meetings.

WARN, one of the first pan-Indian organizations to address reproductive health issues, was established in Rapid City, South Dakota, in September 1978. Many of WARN's founders were active in AIM, which was heavily male dominated. Some women members of AIM felt the need for a space of their own to work on issues they identified as critical to sovereignty and cultural survival that were not being addressed. An early WARN action was to bring women from over 30 Native nations to a conference in Rapid City to address a range of issues including sterilization abuse, the deteriorating health care system, adoption, the abuse of Native children in boarding schools and in foster care, and the destruction of Native lands. These areas remain the focus of Native American reproductive rights and health activism today.

Explicitly Nationalist in its political orientation, WARN held that Native women were oppressed first and foremost as Indians colonized by the United States. Lorelei DeCora, a founding member of WARN, stated: "Decolonization is the agenda, the whole agenda, and until it is accomplished, it is the only agenda that counts for American Indians."[29] Within WARN there was disagreement about the meaning of "feminism" and divisions over whether the organization should engage with the mainstream feminist movement.[30] Some members did not want to become involved with the women's liberation movement because "they would divide us among ourselves in such a way as to leave us colonized in the name of gender equity." They saw European American women as "standing on their land" and in that context "just another oppressor trying to hang on to what's ours."[31]

WARN defined and expressed feminism to make it consistent with Native American cultures.[32] They looked back to precolonial Indian societies for inspiration and Native American paradigms of gender equity. Native scholars like Paula Gunn Allen have noted that for the most part, Indian societies were not male dominated, and many tribes were matrilineal and matrilocal. Indian history provides numerous examples of women who were political, spiritual, and military leaders. Native American health activists look to the wisdom in Native cultures as they seek new models of health for their people.

Opposing Reproductive Abuses

Sterilization Abuse

The UN Convention on Genocide states that measures to prevent births within a group of people are acts of genocide. According to the IITC measures such as the

> sterilization of women are direct attacks on nationhood. Sterilization must continue as a birth control choice for women, but for Native people it should be seen in the context of national identity. If an Indian woman is a member of a 3000 member nation, sterilization has serious consequences for the survival of the people as a whole.[33]

Sterilization abuse has been a focus of health organizing by Native peoples and continues to be a source of concern. In the early 1900s and through the 20th century, Native women, as well as other people of color and poor white women, were systematically subjected to involuntary sterilization. In 1973, the first legal challenge to sterilization abuse among Native women was brought by Norma Jean Serena, a Native woman of Creek-Shawnee ancestry, whose civil suit addressed sterilization abuse as a civil rights issue.[34] Her case "exposed the American public to the reality of epidemic numbers of Native American children being taken from their families, coupled with an equally staggering number of sterilizations of Native American women of childbearing age during the 1970s."[35]

The publicity generated by this legal case led Constance Redbird Pinkerton Uri, a Choctaw-Cherokee physician and law student who worked with the IHS, to examine the issue of sterilization abuse more closely. Uri found that an alarming number of young, healthy Native women were being sterilized on reservations. She raised the issue of sterilization abuse with Senator James Abourezk, chair of the Senate Subcommittee on Indian Affairs. After interviewing tribal leaders and Indian women's groups, as well as examining IHS records, the subcommittee concluded that the sterilization abuse complaints being made warranted further investigation. The subsequent Government Accounting Office (GAO) report found that between 1973 and 1976, Native women had been coerced through misinformation or threats to undergo unnecessary and permanent sterilization in four different IHS areas.[36] The GAO report led to class action lawsuits and more Native American activism on this issue.

Many Native women have argued that the government's desire for control over Native American natural resources was the motivating factor for these state-instituted sterilization programs. Barbara Moore, a Dakota woman and dean at the Crow Dog's Indian Way School on the Rosebud Reservation in South Dakota, is one such woman. She carried out community education to alert people to this violation of Native reproductive rights, one which many Native Americans perceive to be a form of genocide. Native American women health advocates must still defend themselves and their people against efforts to control their population.

The Illegal Use of Depo-Provera

Andrea Smith contends that "while sterilization abuse in the US has ebbed since the 1970s, state control over reproductive freedom continues through the promotion of unsafe, long-acting hormonal contraceptives like Depo-Provera and Norplant for women of color, women on federal assistance and women with disabilities."[37] In the 1980s, the use of Depo-Provera as a contraceptive was banned because of a lack of adequate health and safety studies and questions about its long-term safety. Nevertheless, Depo-Provera injections were given to mentally impaired Native women in institutions to stop their menses for "hygienic" purposes. IHS physicians never obtained consent from these women, nor did they keep reliable records about the administration of Depo-Provera. In 1987, a Senate subcommittee investigation revealed that doctors from the Phoenix, Navajo Nation, and Oklahoma City–area offices of the IHS admitted to injecting approximately 50 women ranging from ages 15 to 50 with Depo-Provera. The IHS defended its use of Depo-Provera, citing its use in 40 other countries.

Activists from the women's health movement, including Norma Swenson from the Boston Women's Health Book Collective (BWHBC) and Sybil Shainwald of the National Women's Health Network (NWHN) represented Indian women in the Senate oversight hearings that were held to address this transgression. In the hearings, Swenson expressed the particular reproductive rights concerns of Native women very poignantly:

> After all, most women take contraception in order to preserve their fertility for future use, not to end it altogether. In the case of Native Americans, these considerations have an even more powerful dimension.

Native Americans are in constant danger of losing their population base altogether, due to poor health, economic conditions, and many other factors. They have every human right to know and to determine the risks of permanent infertility to their childbearing women and to future generations.[38]

Though there was no national Native organization representing Native women at the Senate hearings, individual Native women testified. The hearings resulted in new legislation that protected women against the abuses by requiring clearer forms for getting a woman's informed consent, restrictions on who could be injected, and a call for greater monitoring of physician use of long-term contraceptives.[39] As a result of these hearings, the IHS amended its protocols. Though Depo-Provera has been approved by the Food and Drug Administration (FDA), Native activists are continuing to monitor the use of Depo-Provera in their communities, as it is an unsuitable contraceptive for many women with pre-existing conditions such as high-blood pressure, obesity, or diabetes. Native health advocates also monitor and question the introduction of other dubious reproductive health technologies.

Abortion

In some Native communities, the issue of abortion is closely tied to cultural survival and the maintenance of traditional practices. In many traditional Native American cultures, choosing to abort a pregnancy was a woman's individual decision. A woman would seek assistance from tribal midwives and other knowledgeable members of women's societies who provided herbs, medicines, and techniques for ending an unwanted pregnancy.[40] Most traditional midwives have died or are now in their 80s or 90s. Knowledge of abortion methods and herbs is disappearing.[41] However, there has been a strong effort to reclaim Native midwifery. Native American health activists want to ensure that traditional Native practitioners and practices be preserved and included in the health care system.

Since the IHS is a part of the Public Health Service, it is a federally funded agency and must follow federal health policies, including the Hyde Amendment, which prohibits the use of federal funds for abortions. Under Hyde, the IHS provides abortion services only in three situations: to save the mother's life, when the pregnancy is the result of rape, or when the pregnancy is the result of incest. However, since

Medicaid is jointly funded by state and federal governments, states have the option of using Medicaid funds to pay for abortions under more liberal circumstances than dictated by the Hyde Amendment. This creates a situation of differential access, whereby a Native woman seeking health care from the IHS does not necessarily have the same access to abortion as a non-Native woman receiving Medicaid.

A survey of the IHS conducted by the Native American Women's Health Education Research Center (NAWHERC) in 2002 found that 85 percent of the IHS units surveyed were noncompliant with the official IHS abortion policy. The survey found that 62 percent of IHS facilities provide neither abortion services nor funding in cases of rape or when a woman's life was endangered by her pregnancy. Thus, Native women, who were rape victims or whose lives were endangered by a pregnancy, had to first find a clinic that performs abortions and had to pay for the service out of pocket. According to this same survey, only 5 percent of IHS clinics performed abortions at their facilities. IHS facilities also did not make mifepristone (RU 486) available, despite a statement by the chief medical officer of the IHS that they may do so.[42]

Highlighting a twist on how federal funding has been used as an effective tool against Native women's reproductive control, Andrea Smith notes that the Hyde Amendment discontinued federal funding for abortion services for many Native women, while federal funding for sterilization continued. Commenting on federal restrictions that do not allow the IHS to provide abortions unless the mother's life is in danger, Smith states:

> Abortion policies then become another strategy to coerce Native women to pursue sterilization or long-acting hormonal contraceptives to avoid the trauma of unwanted pregnancy...By increasing the pain and trauma associated with abortion, or by making it inaccessible, Native women feel even more pressure to agree to sterilizations or dangerous contraceptives to avoid the traumas of unwanted pregnancy.[43]

The Native American Women's Health Education Resource Center is currently engaged in an effort to show how IHS Service Units are not in compliance with the official IHS abortion policy, which results in Native women not receiving services to which they are legally entitled.

The State of Health and Health Services

As of June 2001, the reported cases of HIV/AIDS among Native women represented .3 percent of all cases among women in the US; Native women represent 18 percent of AIDS cases among Native Americans,[44] with some considerable variation between states with regard to the percentage of Native women with AIDS. For example, Native women in Minnesota represent 32 percent of the reported AIDS cases among Native Americans in that state.[45] A study in three Western states reported that the HIV rate among Native women in their third trimester was four to eight times higher than childbearing women of all other races.[46] However, the numbers may be much higher, as AIDS among Native Americans may be considerably under-reported. Numerous high-risk behaviors, such as early sexual activity, injection drug use, high rates of alcoholism, and lifetime trauma including domestic violence, place Native women at a high risk of infection.[47] HIV/AIDS has additional and unnecessarily grave consequences for the Native community because the substandard health care it receives leads to both a lack of monitoring and of treatment.

Beyond the dispiriting HIV/AIDS statistics, the general reproductive health care that Native women receive is seriously compromised. Native women with cervical cancer are often diagonesed later and have a lower rate of survival.[48] Health professionals estimate that the prevalence of reproductive tract infections (RTIs) may be as high as 65 percent among Native women.[49] The rates for one STD, chlamydia, are also 6 times higher among Native women than among white women in the United States.[50] Alcoholism, and drug, physical, and emotional abuse, all extensive among Native women, correlate to high-risk sexual behavior and thus are considered risk factors for RTIs.

Inadequate services threaten women's health and compromise their right to have healthy babies. Pregnancy is a high-risk experience for Native women, and they often do not receive appropriate medical care due to a lack of federally provided health services and few options for community-based care:

> The degradation of traditional health care has led to a loss of faith by the Native community in its ability to care for itself. American values have been grafted onto Native culture and have limited traditional learning.

Native American women's participation in self-initiated and self-controlled health care has been curtailed.[51]

The IHS infrastructure itself works to undermine Native Americans' health. Based on its division of the country into 12 service areas, the IHS provides health care to Native American Indians and Alaska Natives who belong to federally recognized tribes and live on or near reservations. Because there are few IHS facilities and vast geographic distances between them, it is extremely difficult for both rural and urban Indian women to obtain routine and reproductive (prenatal and postnatal) health care. For example, there are only two IHS facilities east of the Mississippi River and they are supposed to serve all the Native Americans from Maine to Florida. Furthermore, many of the existing facilities are underfunded and understaffed. Since October 1995, to supplement the failures of IHS, 34 Indian-operated health clinics or community service and referral centers have provided care for Native Americans who live in urban areas and lost eligibility for IHS care on their reservations as a result of moving to cities.[52]

Given this history of abuse, some Native Americans charge that IHS officials, by providing poor-quality health care, have contributed to the extermination of their people.[53] To counter this, tribes have managed to achieve some positive changes in the Indian health system. The Indian Self-Determination and Educational Assistance Act of 1975 allowed tribes to manage health programs in their communities that were previously managed by the IHS. As a result of this policy, tribes are asserting their rights to manage their health systems. Approximately half of the IHS budget is now managed by tribes, and there is growing evidence that, on average, they are better able to address the health problems of American Indians and Alaska Natives.

Yvette Roubideaux, an American Indian physician working in the IHS, argues that the underfunding of the service places a constant stress on the Indian health system. Whereas the IHS budget for 2002 was $2.8 billion, tribal leadership estimated a needs-based budget for Indian health care to be closer to $18 billion. This underfunding significantly contributes to continuing health disparities in Indian communities. In addition, bureaucratic abuse and neglect, high turnover of medical personnel, and geographic isolation contribute to the poor-quality health care given Native women. Thus, "any discussion of the health of

Native women must begin with a consideration of their fourth world context."[54] The cumulative effect of their fourth world status and the injustices Native Women have suffered constitutes considerable "historical trauma." This trauma is intergenerational and has been defined as "unresolved trauma and grief that continues to adversely affect the lives of survivors of such trauma."[55] This trauma further undermines Native health in general and Native women's health in particular.[56]

Compounding the lack of health care and services is abject poverty. More Native American women live in poverty than any other group in the United States. As many as 27 percent of American Indian individuals, including Alaska Natives, have reported incomes below the poverty line, but in the 26 percent of American Indian and Alaska Native households where the head of the family is a woman, 50 percent have incomes below the poverty line. It has been estimated that half of all Native children live in poverty.[57] High rates of unemployment have fostered welfare dependence and diets replete with government commodity foods that are high in fat and calories and lead to other health risks, like diabetes and obesity.

While Native American women have been fighting for reproductive sovereignty for centuries, it was in the late 1980s and 90s that several Native American women's groups organized to provide reproductive health education, training, and services to their communities. Their efforts can be placed in a historical framework where women, both mythical and real, have played central roles in the healing of their nations:

> Contemporarily, Native women's power is manifested in their roles as sacred life givers, teachers, socializers of children, healers, doctors, seers and warriors. With their status in these powerful roles, Native women have formed the core of indigenous resistance to colonization, and the health of their communities in many ways depends upon them.[58]

Continuing in the healing tradition are the Native American Women's Health Education Resource Center on the Yankton Sioux Reservation in Lake Andes, South Dakota, and the Mother's Milk Project in the Mohawk country of upstate New York. Their activism to restore the health of their respective communities offers paradigm-shifting examples of the true meaning of reproductive health, rights, and justice.

NOTES

1   Ines Hernandez-Avila quoted in Andrea Smith, "Better Dead Than Pregnant," in *Policing the National Body: Race, Gender and Criminalization*, ed. Jael Silliman and Anannya Bhattacharjee (Cambridge, MA: South End Press, 2002), 123–124.

2   David Stannard, *American Holocaust* (Oxford: Oxford University Press, 1992), 121.

3   One of the practices considered "perverse" by colonizers was that Native women could divorce their husbands.

4   Andrea Smith, "Sexual Violence and American Indian Genocide," *Journal of Religion and Abuse* 1, no. 2 (1999): 35–37.

5   Smith, "Better Dead Than Pregnant." Also, Stannard, in *American Holocaust*, points out that control over women's reproduction and the destruction of women and children are essential to the destruction of a people.

6   Smith, "Better Dead Than Pregnant," 141.

7   NAWHERC, *Moving Forward: The Native Women's Reproductive Rights Agenda* (Lake Andes, SD: NAWHERC, 2001), 11.

8   M. Annette Jaimes with Theresa Halsey, "American Indian Women," in *The State of Native America*, ed. M. Annette Jaimes (Boston: South End Press, 1992), 326.

9   For text of Indian Child Welfare Act, see http://www.nicwa.org/policy/law/icwa/ICWA.pdf.

10   *Indian Child Welfare Act of 1978*, US Code, secs 1901–1963.

11   Forced relocation also took place in the 1830–50 period, when tribes were relocated from east of the Mississippi River to Oklahoma. This relocation policy led to hostility toward Indians, and the later relocation led to greater unemployment and poverty.

12   Ann Metcalf, "Old Woes, Old Ways, New Dawn: Native American Women's Health Issues," in *Women's Health: Complexities and Differences*, ed. Sheryl Burt Ruzek et al. (Columbus: Ohio State University Press, 1997), 280.

13   Metcalf, "Old Woes," 279–280.

14   M. Annette Jaimes, "Federal Indian Identification Policy: A Usurpation of Indigenous Sovereignty in North America," in *The State of Native America*, ed. M. Annette Jaimes (Boston: South End Press, 1992), 137.

15   This policy of assimilation and subsequent loss of status works in the opposite direction to US government policies toward African Americans. During slavery, African Americans were segregated and a drop of African blood was tantamount to being considered a negro. Hypersensitivity to African blood enabled those of mixed blood to be considered negro and their labor expropriated.

16   Lenore A. Stiffman and Phil Lane Jr., "The Demography of Native North American: A Question of American Indian Survival," in *The State of Native America*, 41.

17   Smith, "Sexual Violence," 33.

18   Ward Churchill, in his book *A Little Matter of Genocide: Holocaust and Denial in the Americas, 1492 to the Present* (San Francisco: City Lights Books, 1997), draws chilling comparisons among the Reservation system, the blood quantum system, and Nazi policy.

19   Smith, "Better Dead Than Pregnant," 123.

20   Ward Churchill and Winona LaDuke, "Native North America: The Political Economy of Radioactive Colonialism," in *The State of Native America*, ed. M. Annette Jaimes (Boston: South End Press, 1992), 241–266.

21   Winona LaDuke, *All Our Relations: Native Struggles for Land and Life* (Cambridge, MA: South End Press, 1999), 2.

22   Ibid., 3.

23   The second wave environmental movement was launched in the early 1970s on the heels of the publication of Rachel Carson's book *Silent Spring* (New York: Fawcett Crest, 1962). Since that time, a growing environmental movement has galvanized a range of organizations and legislation to protect the environment. For a more detailed examination of this movement, see "Environmentalism's Second Wave," in Ramachandra Guha's *Environmentalism: A Global History* (New York: Longman, 2000), 63–97.

24   For more on this subject see LaDuke, *All Our Relations*.

25   Rebecca L. Robbins, "Self Determination and Subordination," in *The State of Native America*, 101.

26   The IITC was awarded non-governmental organization status in 1977 and works mainly through the United Nations. It was formed in Standing Rock, South Dakota, and is comprised of more than 5,000 representatives from 98 nations; it represents a coalition of indigenous peoples of North, Central, and South America, and the Pacific. Its mission is to gain sovereignty, self-determination, and the protection of rights, culture, and land. Its efforts include work in the United Nations and international forums to gain recognition of treaties and agreements between indigenous people and nations. In addition, the IITC opposes colonialism, works to build a network of support for indigenous people, and provides information on indigenous people's human rights and other issues. Through grassroots activism, IITC provides information dissemination, networking, coalition building, technical assistance, organizing, and facilitating of the effective participation of traditional peoples in local, national and international forums, events, and gatherings.

27   The Indian Health Service (IHS) had been administered by the Bureau of Indian Affairs (BIA) under the Department of Interior. In 1954, under the Transfer Act, IHS was transferred into the Public Health Service (PHS) under the Department of Health, Education, and Welfare (HEW). HEW was renamed in 1979 as the Department of Health and Human Services.

28   The American Indian Movement began in 1968 with the "Minneapolis AIM Patrol," which was created to address issues of police brutality. In 1972, AIM presented Congress with its 20-point manifesto, "Trail of Broken Treaties." The goal from the very beginning was self-determination, with an emphasis placed

on schools, housing, and employment. AIM continues to work in the areas of legal representation, education, reclaiming tribal lands, and self-determination.

29   Jaimes with Halsey, "American Indian Women," 315.

30   Ibid., 314.

31   Ibid.

32   For more information on the roots of feminism in indigenous cultures, see the pioneering work of Paula Gunn Allen.

33   International Indian Treaty Council, "A Question of Genocide," June 1997.

34   Sally Torpy, "Endangered Species: Native American Women's Struggle for their Reproductive Rights and Racial Identity, 1970–1990" (master's thesis, University of Nebraska, 1998), 38.

35   Ibid., 40.

36   Lin Krust and Charon Asetoyer, *A Study of the Use of Depo-Provera and Norplant by the Indian Health Services* (Lake Andes, SD: NAWHERC, July 1993), 11.

37   Smith, "Better Dead Than Pregnant," 131.

38   Torpy, "Endangered Species," 95.

39   Ibid., 94.

40   NAWHERC, *Moving Forward*, 37.

41   Ibid., 15.

42   NAWHERC, *Indigenous Women's Reproductive Rights: The Indian Health Service and Its Inconsistent Application of the Hyde Amendment* (Lake Andes, SD: NAWHERC, October 2002).

43   Smith, "Better Dead Than Pregnant," 139–140.

44   NAWHERC, *Inconsistent Application of the Hyde Amendment.*

45   Irene Vernon, "Violence, HIV/AIDS, and Native American Women in the Twenty-First Century," *American Indian Culture and Research Journal* 26, no. 2 (2002): 116–117.

46   Karina L. Walters and Jane M. Simoni, "Reconceptualizing Native Women's Health: An 'Indigenist' Stress-Coping Model," *American Journal of Public Health* 92, no. 4 (2002): 520–524.

47   Irene Vernon explores the intersections between domestic violence and HIV/ AIDS in "Violence, HIV/AIDS."

48   Loretta Ross, "Just Choices," in *Policing the National Body*, 161.

49   There are three known types of RTIs that are grouped by cause of infection: sexually transmitted diseases (STDs) are caused by bacterial or viral infections, endogenous infections result from an overgrowth of microorganisms (bacteria, yeast), and iatrogenic infections result from medical procedures. Ibid., 155–161.

50   NARAL, *The Reproductive Rights and Health of Women of Color* (Washington, DC: NARAL Foundation, 2000), 28

51   Ross, "Just Choices," 162.

52   Indian Health Service website: http://www.ihs.gov.

53   Torpy, "Endangered Species," 110.

54   Walters and Simoni, "Reconceptualizing Native American Women's Health," 520. In the article, the authors define "fourth world" by drawing on the work of J.D. O'Neil, in which the term refers to "situations in which a minority indigenous population exists in a nation wherein institutionalized power and privilege are held by a colonizing, subordinating majority." J.D. O'Neil, "The Politics of Health in the Fourth World: A Northern Canadian Example," *Human Organization* 45, no. 2 (1986): 119.

55   Vernon, "Violence, HIV/AIDS, and Native American Women," 123.

56   Ibid.

57   These statistics on poverty among Native Americans are taken from the Wilhelmina A. Leigh and Malinda A Lindquist, *Women of Color Health Data Book* (Bethesda, MD: Office of Research on Women's Health at the National Institute of Health, 1998), 3.

58   Walters and Simoni, "Reconceptualizing Native American Women's Health," 520.

7

The Mother's Milk Project

THE Mother's Milk Project underlines the centrality of women's bodies and birthing in Native American culture. A woman's body is seen as the first environment and is not separable from the external environment.[1] With this understanding, reproductive rights struggles are part of struggles for sovereignty and land. Degrading the health of mothers and their children is organically connected to the degradation of Native lands. Protesting against General Motors for leaving behind a Superfund site[2] that has "tainted the land, water and ultimately the bodies of the Mohawk people, their babies included"[3] is thus a reproductive rights struggle. For Native American women, environmental justice and reproductive rights struggles intertwine in the body of each woman.

A community of about 8,000 Mohawk lives in Akwesasne—"land where the partridge drums."[4] This 25-square-mile reservation, also known as the St. Regis Mohawk Reservation, is located along the St. Lawrence River (Kariatarowaneneh, or "majestic river," in Mohawk) and the international border between northern New York and Canada. Akwesasne is well watered, thickly forested, and had some of the largest runs of sturgeon, walleyed pike, and bass in northeastern North America until the opening of the St. Lawrence Seaway in the late 1950s. At that time industries came to the region because of cheap power and easy access to both the Atlantic Ocean and the American heartland. Many corporations, like Reynolds Metals, General Motors, and Alcoa, came for the rich raw material resources. They stripped the land, operated manufacturing plants that used polychlorinated biphenyls (PCBs), dumped thousands of pounds of PCBs into the St. Lawrence, and poured toxic substances from their unfiltered smokestacks into the air.[5] This industrial pollution has severely contaminated the land, air, and water and led to the discontinuation of a way of life for the Mohawk.

Akwesasne is also the home of Katsi Cook, a Mohawk woman and Native women's health activist. Katsi organized the Women's Health Dance Program and the Mother's Milk Project (MMP), two overlapping and related initiatives that promote Native sovereignty through Native women asserting control over the birthing process. Her projects are the focus of this chapter.

"I was born to a Mohawk woman from a reservation across the St. Lawrence River from Montreal, Kahawague, by the rapids,"[6] writes Katsi. Katsi describes growing up on the reservation as being "colonized"—her education in Christian schools undermining her connection to her own culture. As a young adult, Katsi began her personal process of decolonization as she rediscovered the customs and traditions of her people. A major turning point for Katsi was when, as a teenager, she attended her first traditional Women's Dance in Akwesasne. The structure and nature of the dance raised many questions for Katsi about women's roles and women's culture in her community. Most importantly, Katsi wanted to know why only women danced in this ritual. Katsi's first Women's Dance experience set her on a lifelong quest to realize who she was as a Native woman and to help other Native women make similar discoveries.

Katsi came to learn that Native women express their identity and connection to their culture through dance. Every aspect of the Long House women's dance she witnessed was invested with symbolic meaning. For example, in the shuffle, the dancers' feet never leave the ground, expressing the indivisible tie between women and Mother Earth. With their feet firmly on the ground, the women are reminded to live by the laws that govern this sacred relationship and of their responsibility to provide food, clothing, and shelter. Men do not participate in this particular dance but attend it to honor the women. In addition to being a tool for cultural education and social interaction, in Mohawk culture dance is recommended as a treatment for many ailments.[7] Thus, through traditional dance, women can heal themselves as well as find their identity and oneness with their culture and people. Katsi says, "Seeing traditional ways of thinking was a huge revolution for me as a colonized woman... [in] every part of my life."[8]

As a young woman, Katsi was familiar with the mainstream women's movement and some of its leading figures, among them Gloria Steinem and Betty Friedan. She was intrigued by these feminists and their assertion of greater power and visibility for women; the issues raised by second wave feminists informed the questions she asked about the women's dances. However, in larger part, she did not find their gendered critiques of society pertinent to her life. The discrimination faced by her people as indigenous people was her primary concern.

Katsi was more deeply influenced by the Red Power Movement's commitment to self-determination and freedom from oppression than by the growing feminist movement.[9] In 1977, leaders of the Iroquois nation, including John Mohawk and Jeannie and Audrey Shenandoah, gathered to define for indigenous people of North America the meaning of sovereignty. Their definition included control over six key areas of life: land base, jurisprudence, education, psycho-religious life (including language restoration), and control over both production (the productive resources of the community) and reproduction. Katsi selected from the mainstream feminist movement what was useful to her and applied it in her efforts to address how Native women could simultaneously address issues of Native women's oppression and Native sovereignty.

Midwifery and Native Sovereignty: Rebirthing the Nation

As the daughter of a midwife, Katsi understood the role and tradition of the midwife as the key intersection of feminism and sovereignty and a space for critical activism that could affect both individuals and society. Committed to principles of Native sovereignty, Katsi believed that traditional midwives had an essential role to play in the rebirthing of the Nation. For Native Americans to control the destiny of their people, Native women had to be in charge of birth and death, "the most joyful and most terrifying moments in life...Without taking control over our lives, starting with the birthing process, we would simply be wards of the state."[10]

Thus, Katsi set forth to study midwifery in the Women's Health Training Program at the University of New Mexico and graduated in 1978 as a health specialist. She also attended a Planned Parenthood program that trained women specialists to run reproductive service clinics in underserved areas. As a fourth generation traditional *Kanienkehaka*[11] midwife, Katsi incorporates traditions passed down through her lineage—especially from her grandmother, a noted Mohawk midwife—into her practice.

Mohawk midwifery, says Katsi, involves more than just helping women through labor. She speaks of the deep connection between childbirth and the land:

> Everything we know in midwifery we learned from the corn. All our knowledge comes from the corn, and inside of each kernel of corn is many generations of knowledge. Part of my training as an aboriginal traditional Mohawk midwife was to raise fields of our original corn. The songs, the ceremonies that go with the growing of corn in the field also have to do with the gestation of the human baby, and so the corn plays a big part in the birth process also, and is also a good-quality protein when mixed with beans for the mother to eat.[12]

From her elders, Katsi learned that the mother is the first environment every human being experiences. A baby inside a woman's body sees through the mother's eyes and hears through the mother's ears:

> At the time of the child's birth it is greeted by its family and is identified with the events that occur in the natural world at the time of its emergence from its mother's womb. At the breasts of women, the generations are nourished. From the bodies of women flows the relationship of those generations both to society and to the natural world. In this way the earth is our mother, grandma says. In this way, we as women are earth.[13]

According to the Mohawk, women need to be reawakened to the power that is inherent in the transformative birth process. Katsi talks about the excitement of seeing how a young woman working with her midwife can learn how to become self-determining. She explains that learning to make responsible decisions about their fertility enables women to make other important decisions in their lives and ultimately to become decision makers in their community.

Fundamentally, Katsi's work on birthing and women's health is also based on the belief that Native women must become whole again; as colonized women, they must find their cultural roots. For Katsi, these cultural roots include various Native traditions and conceptions of self and community. She believes that the relationship of trust and respect between a woman and her midwife empowers the woman to ask questions and obtain the information she needs to make real choices about her health and life. Furthermore, for a Native woman, making the right decisions for herself means that she also makes them for her people, because there is no strong separation between the individual and the society. People trust and respect women and the decisions that they must make, knowing that what is best for a woman is also best for her community. Thus, the concepts of society and self, when infused with honor and respect, are mutually reinforcing rather than dichotomous. Native women do not have to choose between Native sovereignty and self-determination; they are one and the same.

Working With Women of All Red Nations

After completing her training in New Mexico, Katsi followed the Mohawk tradition of practicing healing in other Native communities before returning to her own people.[14] In 1978, she went to the Dakotas, a center of American Indian Movement (AIM) activism, where she attended the founding meeting of Women of All Red Nations (WARN) in Rapid City. WARN women felt they could organize more effectively in a traditional sex-segregated social environment, which they saw as a political equivalent of traditional Native women's societies. WARN was committed to ensuring sovereign nation status for Native peoples and asserting control over their own affairs, without the interference of the US government. WARN believed that by embracing traditional culture, the ravages of colonialism could be remedied. As Phyllis Young, a co-founder of WARN, explains:

> What we're about is drawing on our traditions, regaining our strength as women in the ways handed down to us by our grandmothers and their grandmothers before them. Our creation of an Indian women's organization is not a criticism or division from our men...Only in this way can we organize ourselves as Indian women to meet our responsibilities, to be fully supportive of the men, to work in tandem with them as partners in a common struggle for the liberation of our people and our land...So, instead of dividing away from the men, what we are doing is building strength and unity in a traditional way.[15]

For WARN, struggles for Native sovereignty against the violation of treaty rights included opposition to sterilization abuse, the loss of children to extra-tribal adoption, the theft of Native lands, and the incarceration of Indians as political prisoners. WARN publicized the issue of sterilization abuse among Native women. While Katsi recognized the importance of sterilization abuse, she was also concerned about the issues underlying Native women's powerlessness.

Katsi saw that the lack of knowledge about their bodies led to a lack of control over their reproductive health. In New Mexico, she witnessed the banning of community-based and traditional Native American approaches to health and health care. The devaluation of Native approaches by white society caused Native communities to lose faith in their ability to take care of themselves.[16] For example, in the year that Katsi did her clinical training among the Navajo people she saw the terrible scars women bore from unnecessary cesarean sections that suited the convenience of the providers. She was dismayed to see how little women knew about their own health and, consequently, how powerless they were to challenge such practices. She became convinced that Native American activists had to go beyond taking the federal government to task for the abuses it perpetrated. In Katsi's view, for real change to occur, Native women needed to take responsibility for the birthing process. Community-controlled health care was essential if Native women were going to reassert political control over their lives

Reclaiming Health Through Culture

WARN members were impressed and inspired by Katsi's knowledge of midwifery and her commitment to the principles of Native sovereignty. They asked her to set up a clinic at the Red Schoolhouse in Minnesota to teach midwifery, investigate sterilization practices, and pioneer culturally appropriate health care, so that Native women would not be vulnerable to the abuses of inadequate and manipulative government health programs. Hence, the Women's Dance Health Program (DHP), initiated in 1979 as a project of the WARN Youth Program and based in Minneapolis/St. Paul, was dedicated to placing health care back in Native hands. Under Katsi's leadership, the program trained women to assist in birthing the traditional way. Once the women were trained, they became members of a Birthing Crew.

Native children, Katsi said, were "taught to be submissive, empty and have no identity."[17] The DHP worked with other regional organizations to implement healing practices for the sexual and mental health of children who had been educated in boarding schools. When Katsi left Minneapolis, the project was adopted by the Oneida of Wisconsin. Since 1980, other Native women dedicated to reproductive health care issues have focused their efforts on regaining knowledge of traditional practices and reclaiming traditional midwifery. Several Native American groups now work to promote reproductive health in their communities, providing culturally appropriate health education and services that give people knowledge so they can make their own choices about their health.

Organizing in Akwesasne

When Katsi returned to Akwesasne in 1980, the Native sovereignty movement was strong: 23 Iroquois leaders were under indictment for their political militancy, and a US military encampment had been set up at Akwesasne to contain the political situation. The Akwesasne Freedom School, founded by Mohawk parents in 1979 to ensure the survival of their language and culture, demonstrated the commitment of the community to the principles of sovereignty. Akwesasne was also located in close proximity to a General Motors site that posed a serious environmental threat to the Mohawk. In this political context, Katsi introduced the DHP in Akwesasne.[18]

One of the first initiatives of the DHP was to train a Birthing Crew at Akwesasne. Crew members set out to "organize the families and the women to recover birth as the way to keep our people strong, to give our children a sense of community."[19] To build trust among community members, the crew offered prenatal classes and examinations, individual case counseling, and home births. Katsi reports:

> Birthing takes place primarily in our homes, often with children and relatives present. In this situation we find ourselves not building a long list of "clients" or "patients," but creating a web of family relationships which serves to further our goals in the natural course of community life.[20]

Providing midwifery services was the nucleus around which other Akwesasne community health programs grew. Katsi's programs at Akwesasne provide one-on-one woman-based health education—a goal of many other contemporary Native women's health programs. The DHP created a safe space that fosters trust between caregiver and patient—an essential part of providing Native women with the opportunity to make informed health decisions and, in doing so, realize their reproductive rights.[21]

A Ms. Foundation grant enabled the DHP to recruit more women to its well-trained Birthing Crew, to provide community health education, and to make resources on family health available to the community. As Katsi explains:

> Education is the most important work of the Women's Dance Health Project at Akwesasne. We now have available two basic kits for Birthing Crew use. One is an educational kit for midwifery skills and "patient education." This kit includes a pelvic model complete with fetus, cord, and placenta to demonstrate position, lie, and attitude of the fetus. It includes such items as the maternity center's birth atlas and disposable plastic speculums for demonstration of the pelvic exam—particularly useful for mothers who have never visualized a cervix…[The] videotapes, *1000 Births* and *Common Complications of Labor and Delivery*, are especially useful. Slides, charts, and information packets make up the remainder of the kit. It is in a portable trunk, and can be carried or loaned to workshops or conferences quite easily.
>
> The birthing kit includes all the equipment and supplies necessary for prenatal, birthing, and post-partum care. Because of the expense of critical items and the need for adaptability and versatility in rural areas (and in some cases even the deep woods!), the birthing kit has been put together with an eye towards portability and professional quality, and in keeping our birthing up to standards.[22]

Katsi served as project director for the DHP from 1983 to 1989. In 1989, Beverly Cook, a licensed nurse and former director of the Akwesasne emergency team, was hired on a part-time basis to serve as a liaison between the program and tribal organizations. Beverly facilitated a series of workshops and training sessions for the Birthing Crew and assisted with prenatal, birthing, and postpartum care. Other women, such as Priscilla Thompson and Niddie Thompson Cook from the Birthing Crew, trained for and also became involved in other aspects of the program.

Birthing Crew members included clan mothers who attended the home births of their relatives. Mothers brought their daughters and daughters-in-law for prenatal care or counseling. Teenagers who had taken the fertility awareness classes offered by the DHP were also involved in the program's activities. This high level of community engagement was an indicator of the need for health care and education. To develop this work further, group members organized conferences and training activities for health care providers in the region. A few doctors and practitioners also led trainings and workshops on the reservations. Dr. Nic Drouet and his wife Françoise, a French couple who visited Akwesasne, even supplied much-needed medical equipment to the Dance Health Program.

The Birthing Crew communicated with tribal programs and service organizations in the area to improve the quality of services they offered. They discussed their perspectives on Indian health issues with staff from the IHS. They reached out to other lay midwives and alternative birthing organizations in New York State through their participation in health conferences and networked with other Native women's groups and health projects. At the Awasis Atoskewin (caring for children) conference in Regina, Saskatchewan, Katsi acquainted hospital staff and program directors with traditional Native values regarding maternal and infant health care. These conferences provided her with an opportunity to share this traditional knowledge with urban Iroquois women.

National and International Networking

In 1980, Katsi was invited to join the board of the National Women's Health Network (NWHN). She notes:

> It mattered a great deal to have respect and be given a seat at predominantly non-Native meetings—the NWHN was a wonderful time for me. [It] trained the community agent to see the bigger picture. Those women were wonderful. They invited me to speak at conferences about midwifery and helped me to work through our [Native American] pain.[23]

Through the NWHN, Katsi was introduced to both the national and the international women's health movements. For example, she learned about the work that Byllye Avery was doing on midwifery at the Birthing Center and became acquainted with important information and materials that enriched her own work. She feels this exposure to broader issues was invaluable: "I began to learn about community movements outside the tribe, which is very important as tribes have a different process."[24] She was also able to advocate on behalf of other Native women and to share her contacts and information. Katsi stayed on the network's board for only a year, as she was a young mother and found it hard to find the time to participate. However, in this short period, she made important friends, like Judy Norsigian and Norma Swenson from the Boston Women's Health Book Collective, who have remained allies over the years.

Katsi also speaks of the important role that Wilma Mankiller played in encouraging her and other Native women to speak out about their concerns. Mankiller's pioneering work on tribal development projects brought her national recognition. She was a member of the boards of many prestigious national social justice and women's organizations and used her position to amplify the voices and work of Native activists.[25] By the early 1980s, Katsi was often called upon as a spokesperson for Native American women in the women's health movement. During this time she also got involved in international campaigns, such as the Nestlé boycott.[26] Through this activism, she built an international network on birthing, midwifery, and Native women's health issues.

The Akwesasne Mother's Milk Project

Though much of Katsi's early work focused on midwifery, she was very interested in working with Native women on other issues related to their health. In the early 1980s, the community women with whom she interacted through her Birthing Crew work and the Nestlé boycott raised questions regarding the safety of breastfeeding. While the Nestlé boycott reinforced the health and cultural value of breastfeeding, corporate environmental devastation forced them to re-evaluate their decision in a scientific context. Mohawk women suspected that local industries were producing toxic chemicals that were released into the water, air, soil, and food chain, contaminating their breast milk and possibly causing birth defects. Katsi said:

> The fact is that women are the first environment [in which babies live]... We accumulate toxic chemicals like PCBs, DDT, Mirex, HCBs, etcetera, dumped into the waters by various industries. They are stored in our body fat and are excreted through breast milk. What that means is that through our own breast milk, our sacred natural links to our babies, [our babies] stand the chance of getting concentrated dosages [of these chemicals].[27]

Katsi and other women at Akwesasne were determined to understand the actual risks posed by this high level of pollution. In 1985, the Mother's Milk Project (MMP) was created to "understand and characterize how toxic contaminants have moved through the local food chain, including mother's milk."[28] Katsi approached scientists to investigate the toxicity of breast milk. The MMP also conducted its own community-based research that focused on analyzing organo-chlorines in mother's milk, fetal cord blood, and maternal and infant urine.

They invited scientists from the New York State Department of Health and the State University of New York School of Public Health to provide chemical analysis of breast milk samples. However, Katsi found that members of the MMP did not have the knowledge they needed to interpret the results that the scientists presented to them. To address the lack of scientific literacy among Mohawk women, the MMP trained about 125 Mohawk women to be health researchers and advocates. Since some of these women were also participants in the study, they became "researchers of their own reality."[29]

The MMP, together with members of the Tribes Environmental Office, conducted a bioaccumulative analysis of the entire food chain at Akwesasne, from fish to wildlife to breast milk. Katsi raised funds from General Motors, one of the contaminators, for this research project. The project studied new mothers each year for several years with a total of 50 new mothers participating in the study. The study documented a 200 percent greater concentration of PCBs in the breast milk of those women who consumed fish from the St. Lawrence River compared to the general population. This research showed how PCBs, fluorides, and hexachlorobenzene (HCB), all toxins dumped by local industries into the St. Lawrence River and into the air, made their way, through the food chain, into the bodies of local women, infants, and children. These toxins posed particular risks for women, since "PCBs mimic the reproductive hormone estrogen which is responsible for many of the physiological changes in a woman's body in puberty, menstruation, reproduction, and menopause."[30] Elevated levels of PCBs can trigger earlier puberty and menopause, each having a series of negative health impacts that are under-researched and not understood.

From Research to Action

The MMP published a newsletter, *First Environments*, to inform the community of the research process and its findings and issued advisories on prenatal and infant nutrition in a toxic environment to safeguard community health. When the studies indicated high levels of contaminants in some community wells, the MMP alerted families and pregnant women to this danger and recommended actions they could take to ameliorate the problem. For example, they asserted that Native children are at greater risk from *not* being breastfed than from environmental contaminants, and worked to re-establish breastfeeding in the community by launching a breastfeeding promotion campaign. The MMP advised pregnant and nursing mothers to eliminate consumption of fish from contaminated waters, and to avoid excessive weight reduction during pregnancy and postpartum, since weight loss may mobilize the chemicals stored in fat tissues.[31]

As a result of these warnings and recommendations, Mohawk women stopped eating fish so they could protect their children from PCBs and still continue to breastfeed. However, Mohawk women were angered by the lifestyle changes they had to make to protect the health of their children. Katsi speaks for the local women when she states:

> Our traditional lifestyle has been completely disrupted, and we have been forced to protect our future generations. We feel anger at not being able to eat the fish. Although we are relieved that our responsible choices at the present protect our babies, this does not preclude the corporate responsibility of General Motors and other local industries to clean up the site.[32]

She explains the impact on Mohawk women's day-to-day activities: "We feel anger about not being able to ... grow our gardens and practice our cultural ties to the earth. Our whole cycle of life has been affected."[33]

To strengthen community responses to issues of pollution, the MMP collaborates with the Akwesasne Task Force on the Environment (ATFE), which is made up of tribal and Mohawk council officials, the traditional Long House, and concerned members of the community. By sharing skills, research, contacts, and resources with the ATFE, the MMP has increased community awareness of the links between environmental degradation and health. The Mother's Milk Project has enhanced the self-esteem of Mohawk women and their families by giving them the information they need to fight critical environmental challenges. It has helped develop a network of environmental and health organizations that work to clean up the environment and compensate the victims.

The research gathered about breast milk also provided a great deal of information on other health issues of concern to Mohawk women. For example, the data indicated that the rate of induced abortion had increased considerably among Mohawk women. Katsi interpreted this as a result of more women being in the workforce and having greater access to health information, which enabled Mohawk women to exercise greater control over their fertility. The statistics also indicated a high level of thyroid disease in menopausal women. The MMP has been able to use such information to improve health awareness and education in

Akwesasne. It continues to help with birthing, conducts on-site research, and provides environmental-health education.

The MMP collaborated with the Inuit of Canada and Alaska to protect aboriginal midwifery and share environmental health information. For example, when the Inuit of northern Ontario became aware of the presence of PCBs in the food chain, deposited on their land as a by-product of the American government's highway construction and in the operation of Distant Early Warning stations during the Cold War,[34] Inuit midwives shared the statistics on this subject with the Mother's Milk Project. Through its extensive networks in the Native community in the US and Canada, the MMP helped establish the Six Nations Birthing Center, which was funded by the Ministry of Health in Ontario. Commenting on their success, she states:

> In Ontario last year, 37 Mohawk and Seneca, Oneida, Onondaga, Tuscarora, and Cayuga babies were born into the hands of their own people, on their own land, using our traditions and culture, and taking back the responsibility of life. The door of life and the door of death are the same door, and when you lose the knowledge of how to be born, you lose the knowledge of how to die.[35]

The MMP worked with the Inuit of northern Quebec when they decided to restore the power of birth to their communities. Previously they had a 20 percent cesarean rate. Under the government's evacuation policy, these women were flown out to cities in the south to have their babies alone, disrupting their families and depriving them of community support. Since 1985, they have had four practicing Inuit midwives and have reduced the cesarean rate in the village to 6 percent, with 95 percent of the births now conducted in their own language.[36]

Much of the work to promote aboriginal midwifery is done by Katsi herself. She initiated "Native Midwives," through which she works with aboriginal midwives across the United States and Canada, often serving as a trainer and a speaker at conferences, and developing educational and policy materials. She has also helped aboriginal women work with public health advocates to raise sufficient funds for research on traditional midwifery practices. Katsi has helped to establish aboriginal midwifery as a profession. She is currently working with the Aboriginal Nurses Association of Canada on a sexual and reproductive health issues guide for aboriginal communities.

The primary goal of the Mother's Milk Project is to create a society in which women are healthy. Holistic midwifery addresses all the factors that shape a mother and her baby's health and well-being: "whether it is [General Motors] contamination or the mental health of the mother, all must be cared for if the baby is to be healthy."[37] MMP strengthens the social bonds of the community. As Katsi says: "One home birth will impact 30 people."[38] Katsi still hopes to see the development of a midwifery center in Akwesasne.

Linking Reproductive Health, Environmental Health, and Cultural Survival

Their work on reproductive health led MMP staff members to become environmental health activists. The contamination of their environment had both an immediate and long-term impact on the Mohawks' ability to practice their culture. For the Mohawk people, fish are a symbol of fertility and were traditionally fed to young women who wished to conceive healthy children. Mohawk mothers had to give up eating fish in order to protect their children and to continue breastfeeding. The absence of this excellent, low-cost protein has affected the ability of families to feed themselves. Thus, for Native American women, the right to a non-toxic environment is also a basic reproductive right.

The MMP also demonstrated that the reproductive health of the Native community is closely tied to issues of environmental contamination and cultural survival. Because Native people have close ties to and depend on their land for survival, Native women are distinctly aware of the connection between reproductive rights and environmental justice. The Mother's Milk Project continues to monitor the environment and press for a meaningful cleanup of the hazardous waste sites of local industries. They have been engaged in a lengthy battle with General Motors, Alcoa, General Electric, and Reynolds, some of the companies responsible for hazardous waste dumping in their area. The project's goal is to restore the environment so that people are able to eat fish and wildlife and resume traditional lifestyles. As a result of these efforts, some financial settlements have been made on behalf of Native people.

The Mother's Milk Project is an example of how work on reproductive health can be made central to the life and cultural survival of communities. Katsi's life goal is to labor as an aboriginal midwife in the fields of social change of the Haudenosaunee and First Nations communities for the respect and empowerment of Onkwehon,...to restore the power of birth to the hands of women, and to work for the protection of the Seven Generations whose faces are yet coming towards us out of the mother earth.[39]

Contributions of the MMP

The Mohawk belief that a woman is the first environment makes the strong connection between women's health, the health of the entire community, and environmental justice. This holistic way of thinking is now gaining ground among medical and scientific professionals and is a significant conceptual contribution of the MMP and a model for activism that could be adopted by other communities.

The Dance Health Program and the MMP have helped restore competent, culturally appropriate midwifery services and women's health care to Mohawk women and their families. The revival of Native midwifery in Akwesasne has increased the support for it from health professionals and the Canadian government. There is a wider acknowledgment of the importance of midwifery in Native health care than there was in the past. Katsi's work has also had a significant impact on the Indian world. Today, Native reproductive health activists are aware that for Native women to control their reproductive health and future, midwifery is essential. By addressing health care in a holistic fashion, the Mohawk have created a template that other groups can use to build more comprehensive and culturally specific reproductive health programs. The MMP has also made the public more aware of the role of PCBs in the environment and led the Environmental Protection Agency (EPA) to initiate a health study at Akwesasne, a Superfund site.

Initially sparked by the "mothers' questions" in the 1980s, the MMP evolved into a remarkable model of community activism. Combining the knowledge and expertise of health research scientists, members of the community, and health care providers, the MMP initiated the first such study ever undertaken at a Superfund site. Mohawk women have been empowered by their participation in the research process. Not only has this participation deepened community understanding of environmental problems, it has also been a step towards greater health realization. By underlining the importance of Native women conducting their own research, Katsi has helped create opportunities for them in the fields of health sciences and education. There are now more than 20 Mohawk women involved in various aspects of research at Akwesasne, and several Native women, including one from Akwesasne, have pursued careers in science.

The partnership between the Mother's Milk Project and the Akwesasne Task Force on the Environment serves as a model in the Native American community for community control over research. The two groups have developed their own tribal Institutional Research Boards to ensure that their communities are made aware of, educated about, and involved in research. Researchers, including epidemiologists and physicians, who wish to study aspects of a community must first sign a contract which restricts them from entering the community without a member of the community accompanying them and stipulates that community members—not the researcher—own all the information obtained in the study. Anything that is published has to be approved by a community review board. Community members, rather than outsiders, are subcontracted by the researchers to conduct the work.[40]

The advocacy, research, and direct service programs of the MMP address many different community needs simultaneously. This is similar to the work of most of the other women of color groups we examined. The multi-issue agenda developed by the Mother's Milk Project serves as an important lesson for the mainstream reproductive rights movement: breaking away from single-issue politics empowers a movement to draw connections between several issues and in the process can galvanize new constituencies and new sources of funding to support reproductive rights and health.

Women's funds, notably the Ms. Foundation and the Ruth Mott Foundation, were of critical importance to the success of the work done at Akwesasne. Katsi's participation in the National Women's Health Network was also crucial, since it exposed her to the efforts of other women's groups. Her experience showed her how important it was to have Native American women in positions of influence in order to promote Native American concerns.

Instead of building one large organization to carry out all the projects her community needed, Katsi's work grew organically from the community and culture of which she is a part. As a leader, she empowered hundreds of Mohawk and other aboriginal women to develop important skills and to take political action for Native reproductive health.

NOTES

1   The term "first environment" was coined by Katsi Cook because a woman's body is the first environment that a fetus encounters.

2   In response to growing concern over health and environmental risks posed by hazardous waste sites, Congress passed the Comprehensive Environmental Response, Compensation, and Liability Act (CERCLA, also known as "Superfund") in 1980 to fund the cleanup of these sites.

The Superfund program is administered by the US Environmental Protection Agency in cooperation with individual states and tribal governments. The law created a revolving trust fund called the Superfund. This large pot of money is used by the EPA and other agencies to clean up hazardous waste sites.

The trust fund is used primarily when those companies or people responsible for the contamination at Superfund sites cannot be found or cannot perform the cleanup or pay for the cleanup work. To make sure that those responsible clean up or pay for the cleanup as much as possible, the EPA Superfund enforcement program identifies the companies or people responsible for contamination at a site and negotiates with them to do the cleanup. If the EPA pays for some or all of the entire cleanup at a site and then finds the people responsible, the EPA can recover from them the money it spent. ("Superfund," Environmental Protection Agency, http://www.epa.gov/compliance/cleanup/superfund/index.html).

3   Winona LaDuke, *All Our Relations: Native Struggles for Land and Life* (Boston: South End Press, 1999), 12.

4   The Mohawk, or Six Nations people, are part of the Iroquois Nation, who originated the concepts of constitutional government and representative democracy. The name of their land means "land where the partridge drums." This comes from the sound that young male ruffled grouse make during courtship rituals in the spring.

5   PCBs are environmentally hazardous toxins that enter the food chain through the ingestion of contaminated fish.

6   Katsi Cook, "Into Our Hands," *Yes! A Journal of Positive Futures* 13 (Spring 2000). This article can be located at http://63.135.115.158/article.asp?ID=325.

7   In addition to general health, these dances are connected to reproductive health and can be prescribed for healing treatment after an induced abortion.

8   Katsi Cook, telephone interview by Jael Silliman, June 16, 2002.

9   Red Power came out of the National Congress of American Indians in 1967. Though the Red Power movement did not explicitly address sterilization abuse, it encouraged the incorporation of self-determination over reproductive rights.

10   Cook, interview by Silliman, June 16, 2002.

11   Katsi Cook wrote "In the Mohawk language, a midwife is 'one who helps them with their first breath or one who scoops them from the water.'" Cook,

"Women are the First Environment," *Native Americas* 14, no. 3 (Fall 1997): 58–59.

12   Neil Harvey and Jeff Wessman, "An Interview With Katsi Cook," *Talking Leaves* 10, no. 1 (Spring/Summer 2000).

13   Cook, "Women are the First Environment," 58.

14   Cook explained that in Mohawk culture it is necessary for a person to go away and be a leader before one is recognized as a leader in one's own home. Cook, interview by Silliman, June 16, 2002.

15   Phyllis Young's November 1978 statement at Manderson, South Dakota quoted in M. Annette Jaimes with Theresa Halsey, "American Indian Women at the Center of Indigenous Resistace in Contemporary North America," in *The State of Native America*, ed. M. Annette Jaimes (Boston: South End Press, 1992), 329.

16   This continues to be a concern of Native women and was articulated by Native American women in the SisterSong Collective.

17   Cook, interview by Silliman, June 16, 2002.

18   The program, no longer under the auspices of WARN, received initial support for its operations in Akwesasne from the Ms. Foundation. The Ms. Foundation not only provided financial support but also connected the group members with other women's health groups working on midwifery.

19   Harvey and Wessman, "An Interview."

20   "Akwesasne Community Health Project Report" (unpublished grant report, 1983).

21   The Native American caucaus in the SisterSong Collective reasserts that this is critical to Native American health in the contemporary context.

22   "Akwesasne Community Health Project Report."

23   Cook, interview by Silliman, June 16, 2002.

24   Ibid.

25   For more on Mankiller, see Wilma Mankiller and Michael Wallis, *Mankiller: A Chief and Her People* (New York: St. Martin's Press, 1993).

26   The Nestlé boycott began in 1973 and continued until 1984. It was initially sparked by Oxfam and Christian Aid, who charged that the Swiss company was dissuading mothers (particularly in the third world) from breastfeeding their infants through aggressive promotion of infant formula. The boycott united activists, medical professionals, foreign aid workers, and the general public. For more about the boycott, see John Dobbing, ed., *Infant Feeding: Anatomy of a Controversy: 1973–1984* (London: Springer-Verlag, 1988).

27   Quoted in LaDuke, *All Our Relations*, 18–19.

28   Ibid., 19.

29   Cook, interview by Silliman, June 16, 2002.

30   Cook, "Women Are the First Environment," 58.

31   These recommendations were made in 1983 under the auspices of the Dance Health Program—before the Mother's Milk Project was established specifically

for this purpose. "Akwesasne Breastmilk Monitoring Program" (unpublished report, 1983), 2.

32 LaDuke, *All Our Relations*, 20.

33 Cook, "Women Are the First Environment," 59.

34 Leanne Simpson, "Listening to Our Ancestors: Rebuilding Aboriginal Nations in the Face of Environmental Destruction," Snowchange.org, Northern Indigenous Views on Climate Change and Ecology at http://www.snowchange.org/views/indigenous/leanne_list_en.html.

The Snowchange Project is a multi-year education-oriented project to document indigenous observations of climate change in the northern regions, coordinated by Tampere Polytechnic's Department of Environmental Management and Engineering in Tampere, Finland.

35 Katsi Cook, "Into Our Hands."

36 Ibid.

37 LaDuke, *All Our Relations*, 22.

38 Ibid.

39 From Katsi Cook's curriculum vitae, May 2001.

40 Nilak Butler in NAWHERC, *Moving Forward: The Native Women's Reproductive Rights Agenda*, SisterSong Native Women's Reproductive Health and Rights Roundtable (Lake Andes, SD: NAWHERC, 2001), 25.

8

Native American Women's Health Education Resource Center

THE Native American Women's Health Education Resource Center (NAWHERC) demonstrates a whole life approach to reproductive rights; for NAWHERC, reproductive rights are integral to all other Native health and political struggles. A comprehensive understanding of health guides the organization as it conducts direct service, research, public policy, and advocacy to improve Native women's health. Being rooted in the Yankton Sioux reservation gives the center an authentic voice with which to effectively advocate for Native peoples at the local, national, and international level. For the past 16 years, the center has been dedicated to ensuring the reproductive rights, health, and well-being of Native American women and children in the broader context of the Native struggle for cultural and community survival.

NAWHERC begins with the story of the dedicated leadership of Charon Asetoyer, a tireless voice for Native women's health concerns in the national and international women's health and reproductive rights movements. Prior to founding NAWHERC, Asetoyer, a Comanche from Oklahoma, worked for the American Indian Health Clinic and sat on the board of the American Indian Center in San Francisco. She also served as the director of the Health Program for Women of All Red Nations (WARN) for the Yankton Sioux, Cheyenne River, and Standing Rock Reservations. Asetoyer's perspective and activism were deeply influenced by the philosophy of the American Indian Movement (AIM); she believed that indigenous rights, sovereignty, and nationhood were closely tied to community health issues and that a community needed to be healthy to ensure its political rights.

While studying criminal justice at the University of South Dakota, Asetoyer met her future husband, Clarence Rockboy. After she completed her degree in 1985, the couple decided to live on Rockboy's Yankton Sioux Reservation (Ihanktonwan). Once on the reservation, Asetoyer began to work locally on women's health by identifying several unmet health needs. Together, Asetoyer and Rockboy founded the Native American Community Board (NACB). In 1988, three years after NACB started working in the community, it purchased a building and incorporated the Native American Women's Health Education Resource Center.

The center was established to raise awareness of Native women's rights over their bodies and their lives. While representatives from the center speak nationally and internationally about reproductive rights issues in the Native American community and work in coalition with other Native American groups and organizations of women of color, the center is firmly rooted regionally. It is specifically committed to improving the health of Native American women living in the Aberdeen area, which, as defined by the Bureau of Indian Affairs (BIA), consists of North Dakota, South Dakota, Iowa, and Nebraska, where 54.5 percent of the Native American population live below the poverty line, almost four times the US all-race rate of 13.1 percent.[1]

The Historical Context of NAWHERC

NAWHERC places its struggle to attain reproductive rights in a historical perspective. According to NAWHERC, before colonization, Native women enjoyed freedom, participated in decision making, and exercised control over their reproductive functions. Generally, across tribes and nations, women's power over their own bodies was culturally implicit, in the sense that their bodily autonomy was "institutionalized." Native American lawyer and health activist Sarah Littlecrow-Russell explains that the concept of institutionalized liberation is hard for many white feminists to comprehend, because they have never had this authority or control over their own bodies. Instead, white feminists understand their reproductive capacities within the context of institutionalized oppression.[2] The resource center describes life before the Europeans in the North Central Plains in the following way:

The aboriginal people of the North Central Plains lived in not only a democracy, but also a matrilineal society when Pierre Radisson, the first white person, visited the village in 1654. The Native women enjoyed a life unknown to white women in Europe, being free to own their own homes, participate in decisions about their government, and have control of their bodies.

In the ensuing years, the people were herded into reservations and today live in hostage status, suffering every deprivation and loss of freedom. Our children were forcibly taken from their families...the insidious erosion of identity, culture, spirituality, language, scientific and technical knowledge and power created the chaos and violence in which we, as women, struggle to survive and live a decent life.

With knowledge and appreciation of our history, we fully realize our status in today's society, as we state our rights and aspirations as Native women.[3]

Retrieving, nurturing, and affirming Native culture and spirituality is central to NAWHERC's philosophical and political orientation. This orientation grounds the center's work, which includes providing direct services, conducting research, organizing advocacy programs, and forging coalitions with other Native American women in the framework of cultural renewal and Native sovereignty. The center has worked closely with other groups of women of color, promoting an understanding of the reproductive rights concerns of Native women and lobbying for reproductive rights in indigenous communities worldwide.

Fetal Alcohol Syndrome

Due to the high rate of fetal alcohol syndrome (FAS) among babies on the Yankton Sioux reservation and among children born to Native American women in general, the first issue that NAWHERC tackled was FAS. The rate of alcoholism in Native men and women is higher than in any other ethnic group in the US. At the time NAWHERC began grappling with FAS in the community, statistics showed that among Native Americans and Alaska Natives, mortality rates due to alcoholism for women aged 25 to 34 were nearly 21 per 100,000, compared with 2 per 100,000 for women of all races. Native women between the ages of 35 and 44 had a mortality rate of 47 per 100,000, nearly 10 times the rate of women of all races.[4] Native Americans often yield to alcohol and drugs to cope with prior victimization from incest, rape, and other forms of sexual assault. Annette Jaimes describes the collective and individual hopelessness engulfing Native America as a "colonially induced despair" that has given rise to a host of socially disruptive behaviors, with alcoholism—and concomitantly FAS—chief among them.[5]

NAWHERC crafted its approach to slowing FAS in the community within a reproductive rights framework. The center explicitly opposed the "right-wing approaches" to reducing the incidence of FAS that entailed preventing Native women from having children. The center challenged the widely held notion that the sterilization of Native women was an appropriate response to FAS. New reproductive technologies such as Depo-Provera and Norplant were also gaining popular support as a solution to FAS by those who did not want to deal with the root causes of high rates of addiction among Native women. Instead of addressing why Native women were delivering babies with FAS, the government's approach was to control their reproduction.

The national attitudes toward drug and alcohol addiction have tended to ignore the structural issues fueling it. Furthermore, rather than dealing with addiction as a public health issue, it has been criminalized and characterized as an individual failure. These attitudes, coupled with institutional racism, isolation, and a lack of resources have had an adverse impact on Native American communities. Minimal efforts have been made to address the real issues that could affect prevention. Asetoyer and her colleagues have pointed to the lack of treatment—and the lack of culturally appropriate care when treatment was offered—for those women who are already pregnant and are alcohol- and drug-dependent. Native American women who are substance abusers are rarely hospitalized and rarely receive detoxification or counseling for their addictions. Instead, they are often jailed or deprived of their parental rights.[6] The center's work on FAS led to research on a wide range of other health issues, including the underlying causes of alcoholism and drug addiction. NAWHERC's understanding of the real causes of FAS, and their critique of the responses to it, motivated them to strive to make health policies and services appropriate and responsive to the cultural needs of Native women.[7]

Redefining Reproductive Rights

In 1990, NAWHERC organized "Empowerment Through Dialogue." This historic three-day gathering brought more than 30 Native women, representing over 10 nations from the Northern Plains to Pierre, South Dakota.[8] Many wanted to address the social, cultural, economic, and community concerns that affected their daily lives and go beyond a narrow focus on abortion and contraception. They created "The Agenda for Native Women's Reproductive Rights,"[9] informed by Native American history and ancestral teachings in which "all matters pertaining to us as indigenous women, including reproductive rights issues, were, are, and always will be the business of women."[10] At the Pierre meeting, women redefined reproductive rights to include: age-, culture-, and gender-appropriate information and education for all family members about sexuality and reproduction; affordable health care, including safe childbirth within Native communities; and access to safe, free, and/or affordable abortions, regardless of a woman's age, with confidentiality and free pre- and post-abortion counseling. They called for active involvement in the development and implementation of policies concerning reproductive rights issues, including, but not limited to, pharmaceuticals and technology. They saw domestic violence, sexual assault, and HIV/AIDS as reproductive rights issues.

They also determined that reproductive rights work should include programs to reduce infant mortality and high-risk pregnancy and to meet the nutritional needs of women and families. Culturally specific, comprehensive, chemical-dependence-oriented prenatal programs— including, but not limited to, prevention of fetal alcohol syndrome and its effects—were an integral part of their reproductive rights agenda, as was putting an end to coerced sterilization. They underlined the importance of cultural and spiritual development, culturally-oriented health care, the right to live as Native women, and Native determination of tribal members. Support for women with disabilities, as well as the right to parent in a non-sexist and non-racist environment, were also part of their far reaching reproductive rights agenda. The programs and outreach activities of the center are built around this set of principles proclaimed at Pierre.

This agenda still guides Native women's thinking and activism. In January 2000, 10 years after the first meeting, 37 women representing over 10 tribes met again to set guidelines for implementation of the reproductive health and rights agenda for Native American organizations and other concerned groups. These women stressed that reproductive health and rights continue to be major concerns for Native peoples.

The Mission of the Resource Center

The center's goal is to meet the reproductive rights and health needs of women in the Aberdeen community by offering a range of services and educational programs. It conducts primary research on the health status of women in its own community to advocate on their behalf and to address the health concerns of other Native women. To carry out this mission, it has established partnerships with both local and regional (South Dakota, North Dakota, Minnesota, Nebraska, and Iowa) agencies and organizations. The center also works with local Native women's societies and with progressive Native women in the area.[11]

The resource center collaborates with national and international women's organizations and groups, like the Indigenous Women's Network, that share their efforts to advance the rights of indigenous women. It brings Native women's concerns to mainstream reproductive rights and health groups through published reports and advocacy in the broader reproductive rights community, participation in conferences and meetings, and in coalitions with other women of color. Through its work with women of color groups (such as the National Black Women's Health Project, the National Latina Health Organization, and the Women of Color Coalition for Reproductive Health Rights) and their mostly white counterparts (such as the National Women's Health Network and the Boston Women's Health Book Collective), NAWHERC established a national and international presence. The center is truly distinctive in its ability to work at all of these levels while remaining firmly grounded in the Yankton Sioux Reservation community.

Community-Based Research and Reporting

To anchor its research in the community, NAWHERC uses the roundtable process, a traditional Native American approach to information sharing and processing.[12] In many ways, it incorporates some of the concepts of Self-Help as utilized by the Latina and African American women's organizations in this book. The philosophical basis of the roundtable is a belief that participants can demystify problems and find appropriate solutions to challenges facing the community. The roundtable provides a safe space for individual participants to discuss issues such as domestic violence, rape, and drug, alcohol, and sexual abuse. Participants are encouraged to verbalize their personal, social, and historical realities and to identify crucial issues relating to the specific topic being addressed.

This space enables participants to deal with internalized oppression and reinforces the traditional systems of women's societies where women come together to address their problems.[13] Furthermore, the format acknowledges that all community members are experts through their life experiences and have the necessary information and solutions to address their concerns.

Through speaking and sharing, partnerships are forged, creative abilities sparked, and women work to solve problems for themselves, their families, and their communities. They share knowledge of traditional teachings so that they may be integrated into their analysis and solutions. A facilitator who is charged with providing direction, support, and encouragement often leads these discussions. The facilitator is encouraged to work creatively with the group and is not expected to conform to a particular preset format. Typically, the participants generate a set of recommendations collectively. The roundtable process is an example of consensus decision making based on traditional principles that fosters women's leadership in the Native American community.

In the 1990s, the center conducted three Dakota Roundtables on reproductive rights. These meetings brought together Native women from the Aberdeen area to look at specific issues utilizing the roundtable process. The first Dakota Roundtable discussion, in 1993, focused on problems faced by children in the community and paid a great deal of attention to the high rates of mortality for infants and young children. The Second Dakota Roundtable, in 1994, elicited their perspectives on key concerns facing women. They identified their reproductive health as a key concern. The Third Roundtable, in 1996, brought mature and young women together to address issues faced by Native teenage mothers and their experiences of pregnancy.

NAWHERC scrupulously documents and publishes the words of the speakers anonymously so that they "will inspire local, regional and national Native American communities towards the activism necessary to bring about policy changes in all of the spheres that affect Native American women's lives."[14] Consistent with NAWHERC's roundtable-consensus approach, participants are mailed a copy of the compiled report for input prior to general dissemination to the public. Thereafter, the reports are sent out to participating tribes, tribal councils, tribal health boards, community-based organizations, members of the US Congress, national women's organizations, and other groups. The concerns raised by participants in the roundtables determine the center's research priorities and activities, inform the development of their educational materials, and direct the training of community activists.

In 1999, NAWHERC convened a focus group, using the roundtable process, to investigate the status of reproductive health care services provided by the Indian Health Service (IHS). The focus group consisted of eight women—representing six different Lakota and Dakota nations—who used IHS as their primary and reproductive health care provider. The focus group served as a study tool to craft effective and accurate ways to improve IHS delivery of reproductive health services to Native women and community members. The focus group report made many recommendations, including that direct training for practitioners be made more culturally sensitive. It notes:

> It is important to understand that within Native American culture, Elders and people of high accomplishment, such as health care practitioners, are in a position to be treated with respect. Thus, the recipient of care respects the position of the health care provider and trusts the person to keep them informed about their condition. Because of this Native women are often necessarily viewed as passive participants in their health management.[15]

Among its recommendations was the need for IHS to demonstrate commitment to

> following policies and procedures and disciplining aberrant behavior among service providers. This includes everything from informed consent forms to confidentiality policies. Patients need to know that going into the IHS clinic won't violate their civil rights. This, too, will serve to reduce the gap between provider and patient and encourage trust in the IHS system.[16]

The report also recommended that the IHS provide more information about reproductive tract infections, sexually transmitted diseases, and contraception and make condoms more easily available.

Thus, the roundtable process and ensuing report placed pressure on the IHS to provide better-quality health care services and be alert to the culture and perceptions of its clients. The report itemized the services clients wanted. Improvements in the attitudes and behavior of health care providers were underlined. This report is a good example of how

NAWHERC used community-based research to improve IHS health care and services to make them more culturally appropriate.

NAWHERC's research and roundtable reports have been circulated widely to draw attention to Native needs. Asetoyer reports that they have affected IHS policies:

> And we have taken our realities, documented them, moved them forward with or without the permission of Indian Health Service all the way to IHS Headquarters, to senators, to foundations, and all the way to the UN so that we can share our realities and the way some policies have affected our lives.
>
> We've gotten some incredible feedback...We have a program committee member who recently retired from IHS and who still has access to information. She said: "Do you know that you've changed policy? You've got them all scurrying around changing things because they're getting inquiries from senators' offices, from the press; they've been calling." ... Whenever I get ready to go to an international meeting, I get a call from IHS asking for an advance copy of whatever we're going to release there. They've learned to respect the work we do.[17]

NAWHERC's research has also been effective in changing the way that the Centers for Disease Control (CDC) collects statistics about Native women. Through its research and documentation efforts, the center has proved to be a voice to be reckoned with and has impacted the development of health policy and practice in Indian communities.

In its first decade, the center carried out many community research projects to better address the reproductive health concerns and needs of Native women in Aberdeen and throughout the United States. It conducted studies on fetal alcohol syndrome (1986 to the present), the impact of Norplant in the Native American community (1992), the abuse of Depo-Provera and Norplant by the IHS (1993), and the revictimization of battered women (1994). Using a community-based research approach and the roundtable process, NAWHERC has been able to gather data and document various inequities and their effects on Native American women. Through its advocacy and reporting, NAWHERC has advanced a critique of the Indian Health Service that stimulated Native activists to demand better health care. It forced the IHS to revise its approach to health care to be more attentive and culturally sensitive to the needs of Native peoples, to improve its data collection, and to adopt culturally appropriate health care practices as well as changes in some of its protocols.

Direct Services to the Community

NAWHERC has about ten full-time staff, four three-quarter-time positions, and four to six volunteers. The staff and volunteers provide a wide range of women's health and education services in the Yankton Sioux-Aberdeen community that reflect the center's broad vision of health and the relationship between health rights and cultural integrity. These services address community needs identified through research and engagement in the community. The center's projects cover a wide swath of activities, including leadership and youth development. It operates a hotline and runs a domestic violence shelter and food pantry. The center conducts AIDS awareness programs and runs a variety of other health programs, such as diabetic nutrition, child health, and cancer prevention. It also conducts an environmental issues program. This impressive range of activities shows how the center is involved in most facets of women's lives on the reservation.

Coalition Work

Over the last decade, the center has made strategic alliances with other Native women's groups (such as the Women's Circle on the Sisseton Reservation and the White Buffalo Calf Society) and several tribal colleges on reservations in South and North Dakota, as well as with organizations outside the Dakotas.[18] One example of the center's power in coalition was its joining with other groups of women of color to monitor the federal government's guidelines regarding Depo-Provera and Norplant. Charon Asetoyer found that the IHS has not followed protocol regarding Depo-Provera and Norplant distribution, and that women using these devices have not been systematically tracked or monitored. The center also keeps a close watch on IHS promotion of Norplant in many Native communities. The center has brought attention to the fact that the IHS lacks uniform policies and procedures regarding the use of these contraceptives. Since Depo-Provera must be administered quarterly to be effective, and Norplant users have to remove the implants after five years to avoid ectopic pregnancies, it is imperative that the women who use this type of contraception be monitored. The center continues to fight for a uniform federal protocol that is followed consistently in all IHS clinics.

Participation in the SisterSong Collective has enabled NAWHERC to work with a select group of Native women's organizations and other women of color to share learning and develop education, outreach, and advocacy strategies that aim to increase awareness among indigenous women and women of color on reproductive health issues, inform health care practitioners about culturally appropriate treatment, and advocate for better legislation to improve women's health. In 2002, the four Native American groups of the SisterSong Collective spent time reassessing the 1990 health agenda put forward at Pierre and plan to move forward with that set of principles.

NAWHERC has also engaged in international collaborations. During the Cairo and Beijing conferences, it worked with women from the Indigenous Women's Working Group—Mothers of Nations—to place the issues of Native communities on the international agenda. These included issues of health and reproductive rights, violence against women, land and environmental rights, and self-determination.

The Significance of NAWHERC

The center has provided much-needed reproductive health care advocacy and education to Native women. Due to the center's public education and outreach programs, and because of the influence it has had on IHS policies, Native women are better informed about their health and their rights. More indigenous women have become knowledgeable advocates for their health care. The center has brought national attention to the health needs of Native American women and enriched thinking and practice on cross-culturally competent health care.

The center has been prolific in producing research and policy recommendations and educational materials of remarkably high quality. Its research plays an integral role in illuminating community needs from within—to both fellow Native Americans and non-Native people—and in devising appropriate health care interventions. The center's numerous reports cover a range of topics, giving much needed information on mental, physical, and environmental health concerns. NAWHERC has influenced the development of activist agendas and policy initiatives in Indian nations across the country and engaged Native women in establishing research priorities. Its recommendations have been used in the

development of IHS protocols and in the training of health practitioners. The research serves as an important source of information about
the health of Native Americans and has implications far beyond the
reservation.

NAWHERC's educational materials contain up-to-date, practical
information about how people can improve their health. Pamphlets are
written in accessible language and are widely available in the community.
Its culturally appropriate sexual and reproductive health programs serve
as a model for other communities. It looks to the elders as a source of
knowledge on traditional health practices and culturally relevant teachings on coming of age, childbirth, breastfeeding and child rearing, sexuality, and sexually transmitted diseases. Many of the center's reports
and roundtables pay particular attention to the teachings of elders, and
NAWHERC always looks for ways to incorporate traditional practices
into its work.

NAWHERC is impressive in its ability to consistently and simultaneously work at many different levels. The particular concerns of indigenous women are quite distinct from those of other women of color, and
the center has brought that awareness to other women of color groups. It
has also brought this sensitivity to mainstream groups, and often serves
as a representative of Native American women's issues in these forums.

With Asetoyer as its primary spokesperson, the center has been
an inexhaustible advocate for Native American women's health in the
United States. NAWHERC's work on women's health and rights, economic development, land and water rights, and cultural preservation
provides a solid foundation for further Native activism on this set of
issues and shows us how broad based an organization must and can be to
adequately address the complex and multidimensional needs of underserved communities.

NOTES

1   Level of Need Funded Workgroup, *Phase Two Technical Report* (Rockville, MD: Indian Health Service), http://www.ihs.gov/NonMedicalPrograms/Lnf/PIIDHstatus.htm.

2   Native American activist, Sarah Littlecrow-Russell, pointed this out in her thoughtful reading of an early draft of this chapter.

3   NAWHERC, *Moving Forward: The Native Women's Reproductive Rights Agenda* (Lake Andes, SD: NAWHERC, 2001), 37. This information also appears on Indigenous Women's Reproductive Rights and Pro-Choice Page at http://www.nativeshop.org/pro-choice.html.

4   Wilhelmina A. Leigh and Malinda A Lindquist, *Women of Color Health Data Book* (Bethesda, MD: Office of Research on Women's Health at the National Institute of Health, 1998), 4. These mortality rates were for the period from 1990–1992.

5   M. Annette Jaimes with Theresa Halsley, "American Indian Women," in *The State of Native America*, ed. M. Annette Jaimes (Boston: South End Press, 1992), 325.

6   Leigh and Lindquist, *Women of Color Health Data Book, 4.*

7   In fact, as Elizabeth M. Armstrong shows in her article "Diagnosing Moral Disorder: The Discovery and Evolution of Fetal Alcohol Syndrome," *Social Science Medicine* 47, no. 12 (1998): 2025–2042, the very construction of FAS as a medically recognized syndrome is problematic, since the original studies involved a very small number of cases and tended to ignore other conditions (such as poverty, malnutrition, etc.) that can also contribute to poor health in newborns, preferring instead to focus on the moral deficiencies of "alcoholic" mothers.

8   This is the way in which the Pierre meeting is discussed in several NAWHERC publications.

9   This agenda was set in Pierre on May 18, 1990. It can viewed in its entirety, including amendments, at http://www.nativeshop.org/pro-choice.html.

10 From a statement issued on July 7, 1992 by the the women of color meeting co-sponsored by the Religious Coalition of Abortion Rights, the Ms. Foundation, and the NAWHERC held in Washington, DC.

11 Some of these native societies include the Treaty Council, Tribal Councils, the South Dakota Coalition Against Domestic Violence, and the Minnesota Women's Task Force. Included among the progressive women they work with are Cecilia Fire Thunder and Karen and Sharon Day, who work on women's health issues.

12 This process is similar to the Latina Roundtable process. Many aspects of the Latina Roundtable process were influenced by Chicana history, and the indigenous histories shared between many Chicana and Native women create some overlap in their approaches.

13 In the appendices for *Moving Forward* there is a note on women's societies, from which the roundtable has consciously drawn. Traditionally, matters

pertaining to women, including all decisions concerning reproductive health care, were the business of women. Each individual woman's decision on these matters was final and respected. However, women would often turn to other women within the society for advice, mentoring, and assistance.

14   NAWHERC, *Dakota Roundtable II: A Report on the Status of Native American Women in the Aberdeen Area* (Lake Andes, SD: NAWHERC, 1994), 4.

15   NAWHERC, *The Current Status of Indian Health Services Reproductive Health Care: Report 1: A Focus Group Examining the Indian Health Service's Reproductive Health Care for Native American Women in the Aberdeen Area* (Lake Andes, SD: NAWHERC, 1999), 20.

16   Ibid.

17   NAWHERC, *Moving Forward*, 22.

18   These organizations include the American Indian Community House and the American Indian Law Alliance in New York City, the Minnesota American Indian AIDS Task Force, the Indigenous Women's Network and the American Indian Center in San Francisco, and the Gibson Foundation of Hawaii.

9

Organizing by Asian and Pacific Islander Women

Immigration, Racism, and Activism

O F the communities documented in this book, Asian and Pacific
Islander (API) women began organizing for reproductive freedom
the most recently, and their efforts are the least visible. While individual API women have been active in struggles for their rights for a long
time, it was in the 1960s that API women began organizing on a larger
scale to address issues of particular concern to women in their communities, such as trafficking, reproductive rights, gay and lesbian rights, and
domestic violence. API women have also participated and held leadership positions in coalitions working on civil and labor rights, environmental justice, and a host of other social justice campaigns. According
to professor and activist Shamita Das Dasgupta, Western conceptions of
API women hide their history of resistance and activism. Retrieving that
history is important for contemporary activists.[1] Dasgupta states that
"All cultures contain elements that disenfranchise women as well as ones
that empower them.... As activists, we need to salvage those parts of our
culture that uplift women as a group."[2] As part of that effort, this chapter
places API women's activism in the context of discrimination, oppression, and ongoing reproductive abuses, while highlighting both the mul-
titude of issues that make up the API reproductive justice agenda and
the organizing achievements of the API community.

Over 60 ethnic and national groups comprise the Asian and Pacific
Islander population in the US, with each having different immigration histories, needs, and resources.[3] However, government studies and

popular stereotypes do not differentiate among groups within this enormously diverse body of people. Instead, they have provided a composite picture that masks great differences in acculturation, language, education, culture, and reasons for migration to the United States. While appreciating that the API categorization does not designate a single, monolithic culture, this book uses API to refer to women and men from all of these groups, including both immigrant and American-born.

This diversity itself has presented special challenges for API activists. In their analysis of Asian women's health organizing, Sia Nowrojee and Jael Silliman suggest the simultaneous need for community-specific as well as pan-Asian organizing.[4] The vast language and cultural differences among API women necessitate strategies tailored to particular communities, while the small number of people in each community requires that API women to work together to make gains in health services access, to secure culturally appropriate services, and to obtain welfare benefits. Nowrojee and Silliman also encourage API groups to be honest about acknowledging their differences, and to recognize that working together is only possible when people are given the time and opportunity to learn about each other's cultures.[5] As activist Milyoung Cho points out, there is also strength in this diversity: "If we could just break through the many differences we have, we could capitalize on how we are so [accustomed] to dealing with so many facets of reality within our lives."[6] In the history of API activism chronicled in this chapter, we explore aspects of both diversity and unity while trying not to lose sensitivity to the nuances of either. In the case studies presented in the following two chapters, we see how the groups profiled—Asian Pacific Islanders for Reproductive Health (APIRH) and the National Asian Women's Health Organization (NAWHO)—put this approach to work.

Controlling API Women Through Restrictions on Immigration

The experiences of Asians and Pacific Islanders in the US have been shaped by a long history of restrictive anti-immigration policies. Though the policies have varied in strictness and degree of enforcement, all were ultimately aimed at controlling the number of API people allowed into the US.[7] As a form of population control, US immigration policy had short- and long-term consequences for API women's reproductive freedom, rights, and lives.

Other effects of the policies were also gender specific, with API men and women having profoundly different immigration experiences. Asian immigration to the US began with thousands of Chinese men coming to California when gold was discovered in the Sierra Nevada foothills in 1848. However, upon arrival, they found that gold was hard to get, and many of the Chinese immigrants became railroad workers.[8] Low wages, unstable living conditions on the frontier, and tight controls on immigration prevented many of the men from bringing their families. In the 1870s, after the transcontinental railroad was completed and the Gold Rush fizzled, economic depression set in. Jobs were scarce, and white workers coming to California from the East saw Chinese workers as competitors. Anti-Chinese sentiments were virulent, and beatings and lynchings of Chinese men were not uncommon. This wave of hostility to Chinese immigrants culminated in the banning of Chinese labor through the Chinese Exclusion Act of 1882—the first federal law directed at a specific nationality.[9] With the Chinese excluded, other API workers came from Japan, India, the Philippines, and Korea, most settling in the Western part of the country, the majority in California. Like the Chinese men, they were used as sources of cheap labor to work on farms in Hawaii, on the railroads in California, and in the lumber and mining industries throughout the rest of the West.[10]

From the mid-1800s until the mid-1960s, API women's entry to the US was even more strictly controlled than that of their male counterparts. For example, by 1870 there were 56,625 Chinese men in the US, compared with 4,574 Chinese women.[11] Asian American feminist writer Sonia Shah remarks that "the first Asian women to come to the US in the mid-1800s were disadvantaged Chinese women, who were tricked, kidnapped, or smuggled into the country to serve the predominantly male Chinese community as prostitutes."[12] But for the most part, the women were just kept out. Even wives were prohibited from joining their husbands.[13] For example, in 1914, of 5,000 Indian workers in California, only 12 were women, even though one-half to one-third of the men were married.[14]

As racism against the Chinese increased, Chinese women were characterized as prostitutes and singled out for moral condemnation and control by legislators and the police:

The impressions that *all* Asian women were prostitutes, born at that time, "colored the public perception of, attitude toward, and action against all Chinese women for almost a century." …Police and legislators singled out Chinese women for special restrictions and opprobriums, "not so much because they were prostitutes as such (since there were also many white prostitutes around plying their trade) but because—as Chinese—they allegedly brought in especially virulent strains of venereal diseases, introduced opium addiction, and enticed white boys to a life of sin."[15]

Additional research by Connie Yung Yu found that US Senate hearings on Chinese immigration "resounded with harangues about prostitutes and slave girls corrupting the morals of young white boys."[16] One lawyer argued in support of the Chinese Exclusion Act in 1882 by claiming the immorality of Chinese women as evidence of the overall debauched nature of Chinese people: "They bring no decent women with them."[17]

Other API women—Japanese, Korean, Filipino, and Indian—have had exclusionary experiences similar to those of Chinese women. At one time or another, each group was denied entry to the US, and if they did succeed in emigrating, they faced discrimination, stigmatization, and exploitation. Additionally, coming to the US later than their husbands meant that API women encountered a world that was familiar to their husbands, but not to them. They were severely disadvantaged by language, law, and custom and were economically dependent on their husbands. Entering the US as wives has also meant that their legal status is contingent on their husband's sponsorship, further increasing their vulnerability in the home as well as in the larger society.[18]

Immigration restrictions eased somewhat after World War II, and by the early 1960s "approximately 500,000 Asians lived in the United States."[19] When the Immigration Act was passed in 1965, it abolished quotas based on national origin and replaced them with ones based on professional status. At that time, the picture of API immigrants in the US became more complex. Over the past four decades, the educational and economic resources of API immigrants have varied drastically, even among people coming from similar locations. On the one hand, there were refugees from the wars and conflicts the US was waging in Asia, including large numbers of Cambodians, Laotians, and Vietnamese. On the other, there were professionals from South Asia, especially India and Pakistan, who were not able to find suitable jobs in their home countries. Overall, this second group of immigrants was educated and had greater economic resources than those who came before and after them.[20] Furthermore, immigration after the Immigration Act included many women and children. Between 1970 and 1990, 4.5 million Asians immigrated to the US.[21] In the following decade, the Asian American population increased 52 percent, from 6.6 million to 10 million.

Many Asians who emigrated in the 1980s and 90s lacked educational and economic resources. And similar to their predecessors, they were seen as a source of cheap labor for garment and high-tech sweatshops, domestic services, and restaurants. For example, Chinese, Korean, Vietnamese, and Filipina women, together with Latinas, were among the lowest paid workers in the high-tech industries of Silicon Valley. Activists and the Immigration and Naturalization Service estimate that 25 percent of domestic workers in New Jersey, New York, and Connecticut are API women, primarily from the Philippines, Tibet, Nepal, Bangladesh, India, Pakistan, and Malaysia.[22] With the exception of Tibetans, most of these women are undocumented, which makes them especially vulnerable to exploitation—experiencing low wages, isolation, lack of health care, and sexual harassment.[23]

Asian immigrants of the last two decades were greeted with overt anti-immigrant sentiment and activism. The not-so-new nativism sounded the same racist themes that have historically characterized anti-immigrant politics. These prejudices were used to legitimize a new round of anti-immigrant policies and rhetoric that focused on immigrant women and their children. New immigrants—primarily Asian Pacific Islanders and Latinos—were seen as depleting economic and natural resources.[24] This was especially the case in California, home to 36 percent of all Asian Pacific Islanders.[25] "Overuse" of the welfare system by immigrants, especially those who were undocumented/"illegal," was characterized as a threat to the access for "Americans."[26]

"While much of the media attention during the 1980s and 90s focused on Mexican immigrants, API and other immigrant women also bore the brunt of anti-immigrant policies, which fell into two categories: restricting spousal immigration and limiting access to social services by both documented and undocumented immigrants.[27] The Immigration Marriage Fraud Amendment of 1986 was designed to curb phony marriages, even though this was not a significant problem.[28] However, the amendment did make it more difficult for legal immigrants to sponsor their legitimate spouses,[29] and in 1998, critical provisions of the Immigration and Nationality Act, which made it possible for spouses to stay in the US while approval of their residency status was pending, were allowed to expire. As a result, family members applying for residency had to return home while they waited for approval, which could take up to ten years. At the same time, the income level required to sponsor family members was raised to 125 percent of the poverty line—$24,675 for a family of four—a standard that many immigrant families could not meet.[30] These provisions fall more heavily on immigrant women, since most who gain legal residency do so through their spouse or other family members and thus tend to be the primary beneficiaries of marriages to legal immigrants.[31]

Federal and state policies also limited immigrants' access to social services, which led to increased hardships specifically for women. For example, in 1994, California passed Proposition 187, which sought to prohibit local and state agencies from providing publicly funded social services, education, welfare, and non-emergency health care to anyone who was not verified as a US citizen or documented immigrant. It also stressed a ban on public support for prenatal care for undocumented women. Though passed by the voters, it was declared unconstitutional.[32] Regardless of the final decision, Proposition 187 increased anti-immigrant sentiment and made immigrants afraid to use social services.

Two years later, the federal Personal Responsibility and Work Opportunity Reconciliation Act (PRWORA) – also known as "the welfare reform act," dramatically changed the nation's welfare system. The law ended, Aid to Families with Dependent Children (AFDC), a 60 year old federal entitlement program, and replaced it with Temporary Assistance to Needy Families (TANF), a decentralized, state-run, block-grant program. The bill had several provisions targeting legal immigrants who were not citizens, thus elevating the importance of formal citizenship in a way that it had not been before.[33] As originally passed, it made most legal immigrants ineligible for all federal means-tested programs during their first five years of residency in the US. Included in the prohibition were Food Stamps, Supplemental Social Security Income (SSI), Medicaid and State Children' Health Insurance Program (SCHIP), and TANF.[34] Immigrants coming to the US after the bill was passed were also to be ineligible to receive benefits for five years. Immigrants who are undocumented cannot receive benefits unless their legal status changes.

Under this legislation, states retained the discretionary power to decide whether or not to use state funds to provide certain TANF benefits and Medicaid to immigrants.

While subsequent federal and state legislation restored some benefits for immigrants who were in the US prior to 1996, the overall framework and exclusions remain substantially the same. Not only did this bill restrict eligibility, it imposed new proof of citizenship requirements for receiving federal benefits. Overall, it created confusion and a good deal of fear so that many immigrants who are eligible do not access services. For example, immigrants whose children are eligible often are not aware of this. Thus, many immigrants are afraid to access assistance for their children or have been incorrectly denied.[35]

In addition to legal restrictions, API women face other obstacles to basic health care access. Many Asian immigrants are concentrated in low-wage jobs that do not provide health insurance, and approximately 36 percent of Asian American women under the age of 65 have no health insurance at all.[36] Furthermore, language barriers constitute another impediment to health care. Over 60 percent of the Asian immigrant population is limited English proficient, and though activists have worked to establish language standards for health care providers, full access remains a long way off.[37] Additionally, some Asian American women are likely to use traditional, non-Western health practices and herbal medicines, which are not covered by most insurance plans. In these and other ways, health care services tend not to be culturally appropriate. Culturally competent care would integrate systems of care and would make what is currently available linguistically accessible without fear of arrest or other legal reprisals, such as deportation.

Overcoming Stereotypes

Persistent racist and sexist stereotypes about API women, emanating from within and outside API communities, continue to have negative consequences for their overall sexual and reproductive health. One of the most pervasive, externally imposed stereotypes that activists have exposed is the myth of the "model minority." Among other pitfalls, the myth presumes that all Asians are economically successful, obscuring the inequalities and differences among Asian-American communities. It leads health policy-makers to underestimate or ignore problems and risk factors and to invest fewer resources than are needed by API communities. It also perpetuates the view that, insofar as API women have health problems, they also have the necessary economic and medical resources to address them. These false assumptions translate "into little funding for services earmarked for Asian communities. Asian women's health needs, in particular, have not been identified as research priorities in any advocacy or policy arena."[38]

The myth has psychological and sociological implications, as many Asians who have been socially and economically successful have internalized it. This often results in a lack of sympathy for those who have not. Asian American activist Anannya Bhattacharjee observes that the model minority myth can blind successful Asian groups to racism. She has noted this tendency specifically among immigrants from India: "Not infrequently intoxicated by its success as a model minority, [the Indian community] fails to perceive racism towards itself...The Indian immigrant bourgeoisie disregards an analysis of power and ideology which is crucial to its understanding of its own history."[39]

Other external stereotypes also inflict harm. The sexualized stereotypes of API women promulgated over a century ago are reflected in the demographics of the global traffick in women. When promoting international sex tourism to Americans, specialized marketing identifies API women as exotic and willing to please. This translates domestically to API women being viewed and treated as commodities.

At the same time, API women are oppressed by messages from within their own communities that good Asian women are asexual. The predominant view within many Asian American cultures is that sex is a duty of wives that should occur only in heterosexual marriage, solely for the purpose of reproduction. Such cultural messages prevent discussion of and attention to women's sexual health issues.[40] Efforts are made to socialize API women to be "obedient daughters," "faithful wives," and "caring mothers."[41] These social norms require women's conformity to certain behavioral standards: subservience, propriety, and self-sacrifice.[42] The stereotype of the selfless Asian woman, whose role is to take care of others and be the primary caregiver in her family and community, leads Asian women to give their own health lower priority.

At the first national Asian women's health conference in 1995, Sia Nowrojee spoke about devaluing API women's sexual health as a consequence of these behavioral expectations. She chided the community for its silence regarding the heavy toll these attitudes had taken on women's lives and well-being. She found the assumptions about proper sexual behavior especially restrictive in immigrant communities, where "women's sexual purity and loyalty are seen as instruments of community control and strength."[43] These stereotypes do not capture the reality of API women's lives, in which a spectrum of sexual behaviors exists. Left out of this picture are "the good, that is consensual, responsible and pleasurable sex between partners, both heterosexual and homosexual—and the bad, that is violence and sexual abuse, infection, unwanted pregnancy, unsafe abortion, and poor-quality services."[44] As Dasgupta states, "Our lives go beyond images of the proverbial 'good' daughter, the asexual, all-enduring mother who walks three steps behind her man. Passive and insulated womanhood is not our reality."[45] By challenging these myths and stereotypes, API women have resisted racism and challenged sexism within their own communities.

Roots of Contemporary Reproductive Rights Activism

As mentioned earlier, advocacy and organizing specifically around women's issues came later in API communities than in the others examined in this book and built on earlier activism in other areas. From the time of their arrival in the United States, Asian American women activists have been involved in a variety of political causes, including resisting the appropriation of land in Hawaii by the US in 1893 and participating in the labor movement during the 1930s and 40s. In the 1960s and 70s, Asian women engaged in struggles for peace, civil rights, and immigrant rights. API women also participated in radical efforts to combat racism and promote racial unity.[46] Unfortunately, they also faced gender inequalities within these movements. Sonia Shah reveals that "Leftist Asian women in Yellow Power and other Asian American groups often found themselves left out of the decision-making process and their ideas and concerns relegated to 'women's auxiliary' groups that were marginal to the larger projects at hand."[47]

In the late 1970s, primarily middle-class East Asian women organized church groups, social service centers, and professional societies that initially focused on educational and service projects but sometimes evolved into social justice advocacy organizations.[48] For example, in 1976, Asian Women United (AWU) started in New York City as a social club and grew into a major clearinghouse and support agency for API women. AWU continues to create and distribute materials that expose the racist and sexist views advanced about API women. Other groups formed at that time included the Organization of Chinese American Women, a business group, and the Organization of pan-Asian American Women, the oldest public policy organization devoted to concerns of API women. The National Network of Asian and Pacific Women, founded in 1982, has helped Asian women obtain and keep better socioeconomic status via better paying jobs. These groups were important for enabling women to develop leadership skills and political experience and to evolve organizing models for the Asian American community.

In August 1980, more than 500 Asian women met in Washington, DC, for the first National Asian Pacific American Women's Conference, sponsored by the National Education Association. Speaking to the importance of the conference, participant Juanita Tamayo Lott writes, "We met other pan-Asian women, older women, younger women, women who did not grow up in the US in the 1960s but who shared similar hopes and dreams. We all realized the overwhelming magnitude of tasks we had chosen to tackle whether health, education, employment, sex roles, or international relations."[49] Although conference delegates were predominantly middle-class professionals, sessions were focused on economic disparities and the needs of new immigrants. In the words of one advocate, "The most serious problems are not with the professionals. They are with the recent immigrants, the garment workers, the dim sum girls in Chinatown who often do not even make the minimum wage."[50]

Along with Latinas, API women make up the majority of the sweatshop labor force. They comprise one-third of sweatshop workers in California and about half of the sweatshop labor force in New York.[51] Their jobs often require them to work ten to twelve hour days, six to seven days a week in dangerous conditions while receiving low wages and no overtime compensation. For these reasons, opposing sweatshops was an important women's issue, and some API women became leaders in the anti-sweatshop movement. For example, the Asian Immigrant Women Advocates (AIWA), an Oakland-based organization, worked with Chinese garment workers to improve conditions in their shop. They began a campaign against the designer Jessica McClintock in 1992, bringing national attention to the sweatshop issue. In New York, the Chinese Staff and Workers Association led a similar campaign against Donna Karan in 1999.[52] These campaigns were successful not only in securing settlements and rights for workers but also in politicizing hundreds of young API women.[53]

South Asian women began organizing in the 1980s, focusing on the problems of immigrant women. Between 1980 and 1985, more than a dozen South Asian women's groups were founded in the US and Canada, by women from India, Pakistan, Nepal, Sri Lanka, and Bangladesh. Professor Jyotsna Vaid categorizes the organizations according to the different factors leading to their formation.[54]

First, there were those organizations that addressed specific problems faced by South Asian women immigrants, including domestic violence, unequal social and economic opportunity, and discrimination. Groups such as Samaanta in Vancouver and Sakhi in New York City offered information and referrals, crisis intervention and counseling, direct services, and advocacy. Second, there were those organizations that focused on building a visible progressive identity for South Asian women. Included in this category are groups like Manavi in New Jersey and the New York–based Asian Indian Women's Network. One of the members of the group describes their impetus for organizing: "We felt there were many Indian groups that organized cultural events and family oriented activities. We knew there was a tremendous need for a group to be dedicated to women's issues. Our goal is to work towards social change and create a visible ethnic identity for Asian Indian women."[55] Finally, there were those organizations that worked on legal advocacy and combating oppressive traditional practices on the Indian subcontinent, such as dowry-related deaths and the impact of Islamic fundamentalism on women's legal rights. The Committee on South Asian Women in Texas and Wisconsin were examples of the latter.

By combating the submissive and model minority stereotypes of their communities, these groups allowed South Asian women to express a range of identities and exercise various cultural options. For example, Anamika, a lesbian group, started a publication by the same name because the members felt "the isolation and the reality of our lives, which was never acknowledged either by groups 'back home' or by South Asian groups here, have propelled us to start the newsletter."[56] Asian American lesbians began organizing in 1980, initially forming groups with Asian American gay men such as the Asian/Pacific Lesbians and Gays (A/PLG). However, because women were so outnumbered in these organizations, they did not provide the community lesbians needed, so women

engaged in their own activities and ultimately created their own organizations, such as Asian/Pacific Lesbians and Friends and Asian Lesbians
of the East Coast, which began in 1983 in New York City as a strictly
lesbian group.[57]

Since the majority of victims of trafficking are from Southeast Asia,
Southeast Asian women have taken the lead is in raising awareness of
and organizing against all forms of trafficking—including the trading
of women for both sexual and economic exploitation. The Coalition
to Abolish Slavery and Trafficking (CAST), formed in 1998 in Los
Angeles, was the first organization to provide direct services, technical
assistance, and training for victims of trafficking. Though not an API
organization, CAST has many Asian staff, and the majority of its clients
are from Southeast Asia.[58]

Organizing for Reproductive Health

Many of the South Asian activists who came to reproductive rights
organizing in the late 1980s had worked in other progressive social justice movements either in their countries of origin or in the US. Many
brought more radical politics to bear on their work.[59] During the 1990s,
the rapid increase of second-generation South Asians living and studying in the US drew many of them to activism. Young API women, as well
as those from other ethnicities, were inspired by the feminist writings
of South Asian activist scholars like Gayatri Spivak, Chandra Mohanty,
Shamita Das Dasgupta, and Uma Narayan, and by women's movement
organizing in South Asia, much of which came out of Left movements
on the subcontinent. Thus, both South Asian immigrants and first-gen-
eration women incorporated radical politics into their organizing around
sexual and reproductive rights.

For Asian and Pacific Islander women activists, the intensification of
anti-abortion activities in the late 1980s (described in Chapter 2) was a
catalyst to their reproductive rights organizing. Reflecting on the time,
Juanita Tamayo Lott, who grew up in San Francisco's Japantown and
worked for decades on policy issues, writes:

> As individuals, many women—including young Asian American
> women—rejoiced in [*Roe v. Wade*]. We celebrated this freedom, perhaps
> overindulged. Then we watched the generation of young women after us
> assume reproductive choice, and later held their hands as they rebounded

from harsh legislative, judicial, and civilian attempts to restrict abortion and other contraceptive options.[60]

In 1989, API women from various cultures who attended the "In Defense of *Roe*"[61] conference wrote the first ever statement on the reproductive health of API women:

> This is a historic moment for us. Recognizing the tradition of family and community, including alternative lifestyles, we, as Asian Pacific American Women, underscore the importance of a reproductive health agenda for our communities.
>
> One definition of reproductive health includes issues of access to health care, abortion, sterilization, pre- and post-natal care, AIDS, forced abortions, teen pregnancy, and sex education.
>
> The particular needs of our community can only be met through bilingual and generation-sensitive information and sex education. It is also necessary for us to confront the sexual objectification of our people. For example, military prostitution, sex tourism, mail order brides, geishas, and other exotica.[62]

Soon after this gathering, the first API reproductive rights organization, Asians and Pacific Islanders for Choice (APIC), was formed. APIC was the mother of both APIRH and NAWHO. While abortion politics catalyzed their organizing, as with the other groups in this book, reproductive freedom for API women goes well beyond abortion to include their right to establish families and communities.

In addition to the racist population control efforts discussed earlier in the chapter, API women have faced and resisted other attempts to control their reproduction. For example, cultural pressure to bear male children can urge API women to have more children than they want or push them to abort female fetuses.[63] This has been documented in some of the Asian countries from which API women emigrate, including China and India.[64] In Canada, South Asian women activists successfully shut down private prenatal testing clinics which were used to determine the gender of a fetus so that women could abort females.[65] API immigrant women have also lost power in the birthing process. Traditional practices used by some API women such as squatting during birth, not "cutting" (episiotomy), and burying the placenta, which give more control to women, are denied because they conflict with Western medical practices.[66]

Activist Cheng Imm Tan summarizes how the specific history and experiences of API women and girls have shaped their definition of the issues, posed particular problems, and provided unique opportunities for organizing:

> As an Asian woman, culture and history also inform my activism and my spirituality. I am connected to and affected by the history and experiences of my ancestors and my people. It has been a history affected by oppression, war, colonialism, and modern-day economic and cultural imperialism. The hopes, aspirations, struggles, and fears of my people, passed down from generation to generation, still live within my veins and haunt my subconscious dreams.[67]

In the following two cases studies of APIRH and NAWHO, we see organizations that are creating new meanings of reproductive rights that more aptly reflect the complex and overlapping realities of API life in the US. In the words of Professor Karin Aguilar-San Juan's analysis, API feminists are creating their own paradigm that acts as neither "an 'addendum' to Asian American politics or as a 'variant' of white feminism, because those terms force Asian American feminism into the margins of other political frameworks."[68] APIRH and NAWHO are redefining reproductive freedom in order to confront the realities of API America, firmly situating themselves in the context of, and in partnership with, other women of color in the US.

NOTES

1   Shamita Das Dasgupta talks about the importance of "becoming reacquainted with our own heroines" as a key aspect of activist history in her introduction to *A Patchwork Shawl: Chronicles of South Asian Women in America* (New Brunswick, NJ: Rutgers University Press, 1998), 12. Echoing the same idea, Yuri Kochiyama tells about Queen Liliuokalani, a native Hawaiian who called her people to action after she was dethroned by US military action in 1893 in the preface to *Dragon Ladies: Asian American Feminists Breath Fire*, ed. Sonia Shah (Boston: South End Press, 1997).

2   Dasgupta, *A Patchwork Shawl*, 10.

3   API includes people from many countries in the East Asia, Southeast Asia, South Asia, and the Pacific Islands.

4   Both women were early board members of the National Asian Women's Health Organization.

5   Sia Nowrojee and Jael Silliman, "Asian Women's Health: Organizing a Movement," in *Dragon Ladies*, 84.

6   Pamela Chiang et al., "On Asian America, Feminism, and Agenda-Making: A Roundtable Discussion," in *Dragon Ladies*, 58.

7   In addition to the Chinese Exclusion Act of 1882, other restrictions included the Act to Prevent the Kidnapping and Importation of Mongolian, Chinese, and Japanese Females for Criminal and Demoralizing Purposes (1879); the Gentleman's Agreement capped Japanese and Korean immigration (1907); The Immigration Act of 1917 curbed Asian Indian immigration; the Oriental Exclusion Act of 1924 stopped labor immigration from mainland Asia; and the Tydings-McDuffie Act restricted Filipino immigration (1934). Citizenship through naturalization was denied to all Asians between 1924 and 1943. The pattern here was to welcome Asians when their labor was needed and to exclude them when the economy stagnated. Sucheta Mazumdar discusses this in "General Introduction: A Woman-Centered Perspective on Asian American History," in *Making Waves: An Anthology of Writings by and about Asian American Women*, ed. Asian Women United of California (Boston: Beacon Press, 1989), 1–3.

8   Mazumdar, "General Introduction," 1.

9   The law suspended Chinese labor immigration and excluded all Chinese, other than merchants, students, diplomats, and visitors, from immigrating to the United States. Other restrictive legislation followed.

10   Lora Jo Foo, *Asian American Women: Issues, Concerns, and Responsive Human and Civil Rights Advocacy*, Ford Foundation Report (New York: Ford Foundation Report, 2002), 13.

11   Mazumdar, "General Introduction," 2.

12   Shah, *Dragon Ladies*, xiv.

13   Karen Isaksen Leonard, *Making Ethnic Choices: California's Punjabi Mexican Americans* (Philadelphia: Temple University Press, 1992), chapter 2.

14   Sonia Shah, "Three Hot Meals and a Full Day at Work: South Asian Women's Labor in the United States," in *A Patchwork Shawl*, 214.

15   Sucheng Chan, "The Exclusion of Chinese Women, 1870–1943" in *Entry Denied: Exclusion and the Chinese Community in America, 1882–1943*, ed. Sucheng Chan (Philadelphia: Temple University Press, 1991), 97–99, 138 quoted in Shah, *Dragon Ladies*, xiv.

16   Connie Yung Yu, "The World of Our Grandmothers," in *Making Waves*, 35.

17   Ibid.

18   Anannya Bhattacharjee, "The Habit of Ex-nomination: Nation, Woman, and the Indian Immigrant Bourgeoisie," in *A Patchwork Shawl*, 177.

19   Foo, *Asian American Women*, 13.

20   NAWHO, *Learning From Communities: A Guide to Addressing the Reproductive Health Needs of Vietnamese American Women*, April 1998, 7.

21   Foo, *Asian American Women*, 14.

22   Ibid., 86–87.

23   Ibid.

24   Syd Lyndsley, "The Gendered Assault on Immigrants," in *Policing the National Body*, ed. Jael Silliman and Anannya Bhattacharjee (Boston: South End Press, 2002), 176.

25   Foo, *Asian American Women*, 14.

26   Lyndsley, "The Gendered Assault," 176.

27   Ibid., 181.

28   Ibid.

29   Ibid.

30   Ibid.

31   Ibid.

32   The decision was made in November 1997 in *League of United Latin American Citizens v. Wilson*, 908 F.Supp 755, 763 (C. D. Cal. 1995).

33   Audrey Singer, *Welfare Reform and Immigrants: A Policy Review* (Washington, DC: Brookings Institution, 2004), 22.

34   Exceptions to the prohibition included refugees, asylees, Amerasians, persons granted withholding of deportation or removal, Cuban/Haitian entrants, legal permanent residents with forty quarters of work (for Food Stamps and SSI only), or people who physically entered the US before August 22, 1996 (for TANF and Medicaid), and those in the military.

35   Legal Momentum, "Welfare Reform: After Five Years, Is It Working?" in *Welfare and Poverty* at http://www.legalmomentum.org/issues/wel/welfareworkingshtuml.

36   Foo, *Asian American Women*, 107.

37   NAWHO, *Conference Program for Coming Together, Moving Strong: Mobilizing an Asian Women's Health Movement* (San Francisco: NAWHO, 1995), 30–32.

38   Nowrojee and Silliman, "Asian Women's Health," 73.

39   Anannya Bhattacharjee, "Private Fists and Public Force: Race, Gender and Surveillance," in *Policing*, 33–34.

40   Nowrojee and Silliman, "Asian Women's Health," 77.

41   Satya P. Krishnan et al., "Lifting the Veil of Secrecy," in *A Patchwork Shawl*, 151.

42   Ibid.

43   Sia Nowrojee, "Coming Together," 36.

44   Ibid.

45   Dasgupta, *A Patchwork Shawl*, 1–2.

46   Esther Ngan-Ling Chow, "The Feminist Movement: Where Are All the Asian American Women?," in *Making Waves*, 363–364.

47   Shah, *Dragon Ladies*, xvi.

48   William Wei, quoted in Shah, *Dragon Ladies*, xvi.

49   Juanita Tamayo Lott, "Growing Up, 1968–1985," in *Making Waves*, 360.

50   Margaret Fung, quoted in Carolyn Weaver's "Asian-American Women: A Bid for Visibility," *New York Times*, August 19, 1990.

51   Foo, *Asian American Women*, 63.

52   Ibid., 76.

53   Shah, *Dragon Ladies*, xviii.

54   Jyotsna Vaid, "Seeking a Voice: South Asian Women's Groups in North America," in *Making Waves*, 395–405.

55   Ibid., 400.

56   Ibid.

57   Pamela H., "Asian American Lesbians: An Emerging Voice in the Asian American Community," in *Making Waves*, 288–289.

58   Foo, *Asian American Women*, 56–57.

59   Dasgupta, *A Patchwork Shawl*, 11–12.

60   Juanita Tamayo Lott, "Growing Up" in *Making Waves*, 356.

61   The statement was written at the "In Defense of *Roe*" conference. For more information on the conference see Chapter 2, 37–38.

62   Women of Color Partnership Program, *Common Ground, Different Planes* (Washington, DC: Religious Coalition for Abortion Rights, August 1989), 13.

63   Foo, *Asian American Women*, 118.

64   It is worth noting that in India feminists succeeded in making abortion for reasons of sex selection illegal.

65   Foo, *Asian American Women*, 118.

66   Ibid., 120.

67   Cheng Imm Tan, "Searching for the Ox: The Spiritual Journey of an Asian American Feminist Activist," in *Dragon Ladies*, 210.

68   San Juan sees "API women activists as caught between not wanting to alienate API men by embracing feminism, and not wanting to identify with a feminism that carries with it the insensitivity and racism of white European feminists," quoted in Shah in *Dragon Ladies*, x.

10

Asians and Pacific Islanders for Reproductive Health

U NTIL the creation of Asians and Pacific Islanders for Reproductive Choice (APIC) in 1989, Asian and Pacific Islander (API) women had no organized voice or visibility in the pro-choice movement. APIC co-founder Peggy Saika expressed the impetus for action in this way: "How much longer could we be invisible on such a fundamental issue as abortion? We needed to have an explicitly pro-choice vehicle to inject our voice into the movement."[1] Three years later, seeing the need for a broader framework to convey the organization's own definition of choice, APIC changed its name to Asians and Pacific Islanders for Reproductive Health (APIRH).

Founding Asian Pacific Islanders for Choice

Asian Pacific Islanders for Choice was part of a new wave of pro-choice organizing catalyzed by the 1989 Supreme Court decision in *Webster v. Reproductive Health Services*. In the wake of *Webster*, large numbers of abortion rights supporters from diverse communities felt the fragility of abortion rights and were inspired to organize. In California, Mary Luke, executive director of Bay Area Planned Parenthood, called together a group of educated, professional East Asian women who were active in both feminist and Asian Pacific progressive organizations,[2] because she felt it was time for API women to become visible on the choice issue and to mobilize to defend reproductive rights. This meeting led to the creation of Asian and Pacific Islanders for Choice (APIC). Of the founding group members, only Peggy Saika and Audrey Shoji remained throughout the organization's evolution. Like other APIC founders, they were experienced and respected activists, but Mary Luke was the only one

181

who had focused her activism on reproductive rights before. However, as threats to abortion rights intensified, they felt compelled to act.

APIC was immediately welcomed by API women and the national mainstream pro-choice movement. Saika remembers:

> It was exciting. Wherever we went there were API women who wanted to do something... We understood that having a presence could not be achieved with one or two voices. So we looked for opportunities to increase the number of API women involved in the movement. For example, we were invited to send a representative to a conference organized by the Ms. Foundation for all of their state coalitions. We agreed to participate on the condition that [the foundation] would fund a delegation of six women. And they did![3]

APIC was run by volunteers until 1992, when Mary Chung, a young activist, was hired to perform administrative work for the board. Over the next two years she went on to become APIC's state coordinator and then the organization's first executive director in 1993.

From APIC to APIRH

APIC's mission originally focused on abortion, family planning, and better access to reproductive health services for low-income and immigrant API women. However, as the group engaged with other API organizations, its outlook changed. Peggy Saika remembers:

> We soon realized that "choice" conceived solely in terms of abortion access did not address the myriad of ways in which reproductive choice for API women is limited. We saw that the mainstream reproductive rights movement did not consider the ways in which racism, class segregation, patriarchy, and immigration status impact and limit the multitude of reproductive choices a woman must make in her lifetime.[4]

APIC chairperson Audrey Shoji also notes the complexity of reproductive rights for API women: "The reality of our lives is that Asians and Pacific Islanders face reproductive health choices as only one aspect of a complex struggle to survive in a society where we are often still perceived as 'foreign.'"[5]

Shoji saw reproductive rights as civil rights. From this perspective, API women could connect their definition of choice to "the historical denial of rights and liberties suffered by sectors of our community as well as the community as a whole."[6] For Shoji, the connection was painfully apparent: "For communities who have been forbidden from immigrating to this country, owning land, interracial marriage; who have endured internment based solely on ancestry, and forced or coerced sterilization and birth control, access to reproductive health care is indeed a basic civil right essential to self-determination and survival."[7]

Chung shared the perception articulated by Saika and Shoji that APIC needed to adopt a larger reproductive health frame in order to work with Asian community and health organizations. The women believed that other issues, including access to basic health care, language and cultural barriers to access, and poverty, ranked much higher on the community's agenda than abortion alone. In 1992, reflecting the need for a broader framework and a shift in focus, APIC became APIRH— Asians and Pacific Islanders for Reproductive Health. The name change delivered the message that the organization had a wider vision and program. Throughout its existence, APIRH has continued to develop and build on its expanded vision. That same year, APIRH co-founded the Women of Color Coalition for Reproductive Health Rights, in which Chung played a key leadership role (for more about WOCCRHR see Chapter 2, page 40).

Challenging Assumptions About API Communities and Reproductive Rights

While APIRH members were committed to an expanded definition of reproductive health, they remained vocal abortion rights advocates. They wanted to demonstrate that API communities supported abortion rights. There was no printed information about API views on abortion. "No one was talking about these issues in our communities. We were activists. We wanted to do something right away, even though we had very few resources. We weren't waiting for the grant to come in."[8] APIRH decided to do a reproductive health survey, the first study of its kind conducted by the API community about API attitudes toward reproductive health. This was a genuine grassroots, community-based effort. Approximately 20 women, all volunteers, carried out the survey, interviewing 1,215 adults in Los Angeles, Sacramento, and San Francisco. "Everyone pitched in to do the survey. I brought the results to Christmas dinner. After we ate everyone helped sort them by zip code."[9] The survey confirmed APIRH members' view that API women and men supported abortion. Results showed that 85 percent of those surveyed "supported a woman's right to choose abortion under varying conditions."[10]

In 1993, for the 20th anniversary of *Roe v. Wade*, APIRH held a press conference to present the survey results. Beckie Masaki, executive director of the Asian Women's Shelter, pointed to the importance of the survey results:

> Without this kind of data, the myth that Asians are not largely pro-choice ... is prevalent. Therefore, services have not emerged for Asian Americans as a priority What the finding points to is that there is strong support and interest in the Asian American community for a woman's right to choose, and services, community education, and advocacy must begin to match that.[11]

APIRH gained tremendous publicity for the survey. Coverage by the *San Francisco Examiner, Nichi Bei Times*, and *Hokubei Mainichi* stressed the findings that API communities are pro-choice and that poor access to health care limits their choices. Mary Chung and APIRH board chair Audrey Shoji emphasized that language and cultural barriers, poverty, and the lack of health information all contribute to depriving API women of early abortions.[12]

In her remarks at the press conference, Shoji highlighted the importance of respecting diversity when she said, "While *Roe* was intended to protect the rights of all women in this country, the fact is that API women face problems that even the wisdom of the Supreme Court could not comprehend...API women come from 30 distinct populations and each of these ethnic populations has its own language, culture, and customs."[13] Failure to understand the distinctions among the different communities obscures the issues facing each one. For example, compared with other racial groups, teen pregnancy rates appear to be low when API communities in California are lumped together. However, if the rates are broken down by ethnicity and poverty statistics, there are significant differences among API communities.[14] Policy recommendations based on the survey called for further research to address the appropriate cultural perspectives of the 14 largest communities identified by the 1990 US Census.[15] The recommendations underlined the need to conduct research in native languages by native speakers, and for it to reflect different socioeconomic backgrounds.[16] The APIRH report was widely circulated among pro-choice organizations.

Getting to the Grassroots

As APIRH's report circulated, Chung and APIRH gained national visibility. Chung was sought out by mainstream organizations and groups of women of color alike to bring an Asian voice to the choice issue. She quickly became a prominent spokeswoman in national and international reproductive rights politics. In turn, APIRH's organizational ambitions grew. Inspired by the organizational chapter structure of the National Black Women's Health Project (NBWHP), APIRH began to think nationally. Chung and the APIRH board created a plan to become a national organization with initial chapters to be located in Sacramento, Los Angeles, San Francisco, San Jose, and New York City.

The expansion plans were put on hold in 1993 when Chung left APIRH and founded the National Asian Women's Health Organization (NAWHO) to promote the health and reproductive rights of Asian America.[17] Those interviewed for this book who were involved in APIRH at that time provide differing accounts of the separation. Some saw it as the result of disagreements between Chung and the board over the vision and future of the organization. Others disagree, saying that because the reasons were never clarified, it is only speculation to conclude that such differences were the cause. Still others saw it as a split that was divisive within the API women's activist community. There were concerns that the organizing base was not large enough to support two organizations focused on API women's reproductive rights and health and that there would be competition for funding and about which group would be the authentic voice of API women. After an unsuccessful effort to reconcile the two organizations, a few board members of NAWHO resigned. As we shall see, APIRH and NAWHO have evolved quite distinctively, with differences in priorities, leadership models, and strategic focus.

Following Chung's departure, APIRH's board reorganized, several of the core founders moved on, and new, younger women became involved. Once again the volunteer board ran the organization until Yin Ling Leung, who had been a volunteer board member, was hired in 1997. At that time, APIRH decided that it could best serve the API community if it was grounded in a grassroots strategy of community organizing and leadership development, focusing on those API women and girls most in need of "choice" in their lives. The chapter model was set aside with this shift in priorities from national concerns to grassroots engagement, and community organizing became central to APIRH's programmatic work.

Throughout its history, APIRH's analysis and vision of reproductive rights within the context and realities of API communities has been evolving. A comprehensive definition of reproductive freedom for API women and girls is at the core of its work. APIRH's 2003 vision statement builds on earlier definitions:

> Women and girls have Reproductive Freedom when we have the social, economic, and political power to make healthy decisions for ourselves and our families at home, work, and in all other areas of our lives. Reproductive Freedom is not just a matter of individual choice. Reproductive decisions are made within a social context, which includes inequalities of wealth and power.
>
> Reproductive Freedom is central to quality of life issues for API women and girls—having reproductive freedom allows women to have self-determination for herself, her family and her community.
>
> Regulation of Reproductive Freedom of API women and other women of color has been a central aspect of racial, class, and gender oppression in the US and continues to become more restrictive and punitive.[18]

Eveline Shen, who became APIRH executive director in 1999, talked about the implications of this definition for APIRH's organizing:

> We are looking to address reproductive freedom within a social justice context. This means that we can bring people into discussion with us on a variety of issues that intersect with reproductive freedom, including immigrant rights, welfare rights, queer rights, and environmental justice. Our definition of reproductive freedom allows us to work on the issues that are most pressing or important to the people we work with in our communities—parents, youth, service workers, churches, schools, etc. while using an API feminist framework.[19]

Today APIRH is "a social, political and economic justice organization fighting for Asian and Pacific Islander women's and girl's liberation through the lens of reproductive freedom."[20] The organization's evolution shows that it has been consistently guided by an integrated approach to social change using eight core strategies: community organizing, leadership development, popular education, participatory action research, community building, movement building, policy analysis, and advocacy. The success and extent to which APIRH's organizational agenda has been grounded in priorities identified by the community provides a working model for other reproductive rights organizations looking to do similar work. Connection to the community was critical at every stage—identifying needs and problems, researching the issues, developing organizing projects to address needs, and setting policy goals.

Identifying the Issues, Grounding Their Activism

Opening Doors Project

In 1994, APIRH created the Opening Doors Project, a community organizing approach to gaining information about API women's health. The group worked for one year with a wide range of community-based organizations, community activists, legal and legislative advocates, direct service providers, and community leaders from the fields of health care, social services, mental health, domestic violence, children's health, alcohol and substance abuse, HIV/AIDS, environmental health, and job training programs to develop a network of individuals and organizations willing to do the hard work of helping API women improve the quality of their fives. Together, these groups held numerous community forums, focus groups, and roundtable discussions throughout California, gathering information about the needs of API women and the barriers to meeting them. Through this inclusive process, APIRH wanted to develop a multilingual, multicultural community organizing model and establish an API women's health agenda articulated and defined by API women in California.

Hosting an Unconference

In April 1995, APIRH held a landmark conference, "Opening Doors to Health and Well-Being." Over 150 API women came to Sacramento to be part of this first statewide gathering on API women's health.[21] Because of APIRH's commitment to involving the community in the definition of problems and in efforts to solve them, the gathering was organized in a nontraditional way. The organizers talked about it as an "unconference." The community women participating in the gathering were acknowledged as the experts best qualified to talk about what it would take to move the community on issues of choice and reproductive rights. Thus, everyone was both an expert and a learner:

> We want to "open the doors" between those of us on the same side of
> the door (Asian and Pacific Islander women and other women of color)
> and invite and encourage dialogue, so that we may inform and educate

ourselves about our health and well-being...We want to develop strategies to "open the doors" leading to those currently holding positions of economic and political power to ensure that our voices are heard and fundamental changes are effected. We want to develop mechanisms by which those on the other side of the door (those in positions of power) will eventually want to eliminate the door altogether, and recognize, respect and incorporate our perspectives as Asians and Pacific Islanders and people of color.[22]

The unconference was well attended by women from many different parts of the community and various ethnic groups, including Cambodian, Chinese, Filipino, Hawaiian, Hmong, Japanese, Korean, Lao, Mien, Pacific Islander, South Asian/Indian, Sri Lankan, Taiwanese, Thai, Tongan, and Vietnamese representatives, and those of mixed Asian heritage. Most participants were born outside the US and described themselves as immigrants. Their ages ranged from 12 to 74, with the majority between the ages of 25 and 50.

Participants discussed the need for training, resources, and services to help recent immigrants adjust to life in the US. Widespread depression and other mental health problems and the prevalence of violence against women were associated with adjusting to life in a new society. They noted that elderly Chinese and Japanese women have the highest suicide rates of all racial and ethnic groups, including whites.[23] Furthermore, women in immigrant and refugee families who are cut off from help by their inability to speak English are especially vulnerable to domestic violence.

Through discussions, research, and the unconference, APIRH identified these and other health concerns of Asian and Pacific Islanders. Underlying all of the specific issues were recurrent themes: the fact that ethnic identity affects a woman's mental and physical health; the difficult challenge women face in reconciling dominant US values, norms, and beliefs with API cultural roots; the need for culturally appropriate information and services; and the desire for a holistic view of health which encompasses the need to care for body, mind, spirit, and emotions.[24] Participants in the project wanted to utilize both Western medical knowledge and traditional health care systems.

While there was an understanding that addressing the underlying issues requires long-term organizing to build and sustain empowered and healthy communities, participants also sought concrete ways to move forward immediately. Women asked for assistance with banking and money management, job seeking, legal matters, and educational resources, including one-on-one mentoring programs and outreach. Teens wanted their schools to provide them with resources about sexuality, family planning, contraceptives, and sexually transmitted diseases (STDs).[25] These suggestions were part of a grassroots effort to deal directly with the daily challenges of living life in the US as immigrants with limited English language ability and financial resources.

After the unconference, APIRH released *The Health and Well-Being of Asian and Pacific Islander American Women* as "a counterpoint to health agendas define by others on behalf of [API] women…It is but one response to address the paucity of Asian or Pacific Islander ethnic- and gender-specific information."[26] The report highlighted the importance of researching and understanding health problems from the vantage point of API populations, rather than extrapolating findings from other groups. This is imperative to understanding health practices as well as to designing health and education programs and services. In explaining why they did not always seek care, API women pointed to difficulties in communication, being treated disrespectfully, and not knowing where to go for services.[27]

The women also emphasized the tremendous need for more health information. One survey showed that although almost all the women interviewed had heard of cancer, over half thought there is little one can do to prevent it. When public health information is not presented bilingually or in other culturally inclusive ways, it can be misleading.

Internal cultural values and the externally imposed stereotypes discussed in Chapter 9 are also relevant. The report found that modesty and shame prevent API women from seeking breast and cervical cancer screenings, as well as information on birth control, STDs, and HIV/AIDS. Because the public expression of women's sexuality in their communities is perceived as dangerous and inappropriate, Asian women are less likely than white women to speak about sex. Chinese women, for example, tend to be reluctant to share reproductive health problems with male providers. Such sociocultural considerations are critical to understanding and trying to change women's behavior.

Shifting the Focus to Southeast Asian Women and Girls

In 1995, APIRH decided to focus on youth in Southeast Asian communities and to adopt grassroots organizing as its primary tool for social change. This decision was based on APIRH's understanding of the economic situation of recent Southeast Asian immigrants to the US, who had come as political refugees and whose communities' health needs were largely invisible. APIRH felt a moral and political imperative to assist these people. The founders of APIRH were East Asian, from the most privileged of the API communities. APIRH board chair Lisa Ikemoto explained that the "ethics of privilege" require people with relative privilege to assist people who have the least.[28] The decision to focus on young Southeast Asians was an acknowledgement of the changing contours of Asian America and APIRH's belief that improving life for the most marginalized people would help the entire community.

Further, APIRH thought that youth would be more receptive to organizing. They saw that young people were open and engaged in the US and as such, would be able to help connect APIRH to the adults in the community. Youth are more at ease speaking English, not as influenced by religion in their daily lives, and less afraid of political activism.[29]

APIRH was well positioned to work with Southeast Asian youth. Through the Opening Doors Project, it had developed connections to Southeast Asian community organizations. APIRH had learned a good deal about influential institutions in those communities, including mutual aid societies and churches. Churches have tremendous credibility in the community because they provide direct assistance such as food pantries. The churches are then able to use their legitimacy to disseminate anti-abortion politics. Yin Ling Leung sees the need for progressives to do more community investment and empowerment work: "My feeling is that we do not do enough of this kind of work...We are often too driven by our own agendas and not able to hear and listen and respect the agenda of the community first."[30]

In the years following 1995, APIRH created three projects that reflected their commitment to Southeast Asian communities: the Health, Opportunities, Problem-Solving, and Empowerment Project (now called HOPE for Girls), the HOPE Environmental Justice Initiative, and the Asian and Pacific Islander Teen Pregnancy Prevention Initiative. All three projects demonstrate APIRH's integrative approach and its efforts to develop leaders and activists who work for social change and reproductive freedom within their own communities. The HOPE for Girls project was the first effort towards realizing this goal.

The HOPE for Girls Project

In 1997, APIRH launched HOPE. Designed for girls between the ages of 14 to 18, HOPE is youth driven. Its major goal is to "develop the capacity of API young women and girls to take action to improve their lives and their community."[31] In HOPE, members connected reproductive freedom with other social justice issues, including environmental justice, welfare rights, school safety, and teen pregnancy prevention.

APIRH first piloted a model project in Richmond, California, an industrial community north of Berkeley, and then took the project to Long Beach and Oakland. The overall goals and strategies were the same in each site and included leadership development, popular education, community-based participatory research, and community building. Through HOPE principles and the support of the staff, the girls were empowered to make important decisions and to take action.[32]

The Participatory Action Research (PAR) model was essential to keeping the girls at the center of all aspects of the project.[33] For example, in Long Beach the girls conducted a survey to determine the extent of sexual harassment. "This survey report therefore embodies the leadership of Cambodian American young women who identified an issue affecting them personally—the problem of sexual harassment in school—and took initiative to investigate it with the hope of making school safer for all students."[34] In HOPE and through PAR, girls articulated their problems and developed the skills and confidence to address them.

Transforming the girls into organizers was part of the community organizing strategy. In order to support their organizing efforts, APIRH offered support and resources. For example, APIRH staff offered tutoring, college preparation, counseling, writing classes, and a summer program with stipends. Sometimes they helped by talking to the girls' teachers, dealing with possible pregnancies, and assisting the girls in getting to doctors' appointments. HOPE offered training programs to develop grassroots organizing and critical thinking skills as well as political analysis. These programs enhanced the girl's political and self-awareness. They created a cohesive group that serves as a resource for support, problem-solving, and development.

In each community where HOPE has operated, the program has evolved according to the priorities of the girls involved in the project. In Richmond, the focus was on Laotian girls and young women, and it evolved as a collaboration between APIRH and Asian Pacific

Environmental Network (APEN). HOPE created its popular education and leadership development model through this partnership. Because of HOPE, a strong young women's component exists within all of APEN's work, and young women are in leadership positions in the organization. HOPE in Long Beach initially took up issues of deportation, civil rights, and racism, which were particularly pressing after the events of September 11, 2001. In Oakland, HOPE functioned as an environmental justice and reproductive freedom initiative, specifically documenting and organizing against community exposure to toxic emissions. All the projects placed reproductive rights in a broader context.

In 2002, APIRH discontinued its HOPE work in Long Beach. Eveline Shen cited the reasons for this as "the challenges stemming from maintaining large projects in two very different geographic locations as well as increasing tension among board members, staff, and participants over organization strategies and direction." Fortunately, the work HOPE took up has continued with young women in Long Beach via the organization Khmer Girls in Action.[35] APIRH's only continuing youth organizing is the HOPE project in Oakland.

About 80 percent of the girls stay in the program through high school, and APIRH wants to find ways to keep them involved after graduation. In one effort to capitalize on the leadership and activism cultivated through HOPE, APIRH is currently developing a Youth Advisory Committee. The committee will consist of youth who have graduated from the HOPE program and, with over 200 graduates, it will have a large base group to draw upon. The goals of the Youth Advisory Committee will be to guide the ongoing youth organizing at APIRH as well as to support current youth leaders in their development as activists. Furthermore, APIRH works with other API, social justice, and reproductive rights organizations to apply and replicate aspects of the HOPE model and expand the base of the reproductive rights movement. APIRH is also using its experience with HOPE to develop a strategy for organizing adult women.

Whether its participants learn their own history, set out their vision of reproductive freedom, or get schools to improve sexual harassment policies, HOPE's ultimate goals are to empower API girls and develop a new generation of activists with a political perspective that uses reproductive rights as a framework for analyzing the issues that affect their lives.[36]

Environmental Justice and Reproductive Rights

APIRH has a long history of linking reproductive rights and environmental justice. Since APIRH members have roots in both movements, they can build an integrated understanding of the connections between the two and create innovative organizing projects.

In the Oakland HOPE project, environmental justice issues were integral to the understanding of reproductive rights. The girls developed a Reproductive Freedom Tour, highlighting sites in the community that have an adverse impact on the reproductive health and overall well-being of API girls and women.[37] Tour stops included a toxic medical waste incinerator, a garment factory, the prisons, a local high school, and the welfare office. In addition to the abandoned houses and dilapidated buildings, the tour highlighted the fact that there are 29 liquor stores and only one food store, nine check-cashing places, and one library. The girls produced a tour guide that provided graphic images of these problems. The tour brought 20 organizations and 100 activists together to learn about key environmental health issues in the Oakland School District. HOPE's work dovetailed with APIRH's participation in an environmental justice coalition in Oakland.

From 1999 to 2003, APIRH played a leading role in an environmental justice campaign focused on the largest medical waste incinerator in California, which was located in Oakland. A coalition was created to document the fact that the company that owned it was using some of the most harmful technologies and methods of waste disposal, which are especially linked to endometriosis and ovarian cancer in women. The coalition publicized its findings in order to mobilize the community to take action. APIRH and the coalition held a series of forums and gave other presentations to raise awareness and draw new supporters. APIRH members also met with representatives of the company that owned and operated the incinerator, Integrated Environmental Systems (IES). The goal was to have IES adopt cleaner technology and reduce emission rates. Ultimately, this effort was successful. Not only was the facility shut down, but the general public and policy-makers were educated about environmental hazards and the need for cleaner and safer technologies, especially as they related to reproductive health. In the words of one APIRH member, "Before I came to APIRH, I had no idea about the toxins in our environment. Now I understand that we have to work together—with all races and everyone in our community—to make sure that we have clean air and water. We deserve it."[38]

The Asian and Pacific Islander Teen Pregnancy Prevention Initiative

API communities have been left out of the national focus on teen pregnancy. By aggregating the diversity of Asian populations, researchers have alleged that teen pregnancy is not a significant issue for API girls. Because of its community work, APIRH knew this was not an accurate picture; it was clear that teen pregnancy is an important issue for API communities.[39] In 2000, the group developed the Asian and Pacific Islander Teen Pregnancy Prevention Initiative (API–TPPI),[40] a community research and advocacy project. They worked in collaboration with two programs at the University of California at San Francisco—the National Centers of Excellence in Women's Health and the Center for Reproductive Health Research and Policy. API-TPPI is another example of APIRH reaching out to Southeast Asian youth in an effort to both educate and learn from them.

The program engaged API women, girls, and community leaders in discussions about teen pregnancy and teen pregnancy prevention, in order to understand their perspectives on the issues and to develop policy recommendations. The focus groups with young API women yielded important insights into how they saw healthy sexuality. While the girls included the ideas of monogamy, safe sex, and no STDs—themes from the mainstream teen pregnancy prevention programs—they also had broader perspectives. They related priorities like "taking care of your body," being "proud of being a girl," and "having freedom to make good choices" to not getting pregnant.[41] They also felt that low self-esteem and lack of power encouraged teen pregnancy. One girl explained it this way:

> I see a lot of my girlfriends who think lowly of themselves and don't see a future. Sometimes, getting a boyfriend and doing what he wants no matter what is the most important thing in their lives. We have awful schools, no jobs, and no way out—at least that's how it feels to me sometimes.[42]

Community leaders and the youth made the connection between economic opportunities, the deficient state of welfare, and teen pregnancy in API communities. As one participant explained:

Families on welfare are in a system which doesn't allow them to get out of poverty. If you have no economic resources, you aren't able to access quality reproductive health care. Also, if teenagers feel that there is no hope of getting out of their situation and making their lives better, then they are more likely to engage in high-risk behavior, like having unsafe sex.[43]

The power of API-TPPI was threefold. It provided a forum for API girls to talk about teen pregnancy and prevention and educated them on the subject. It synthesized the significant information garnered about teen pregnancy from API communities into a report and made important policy recommendations for future research and action.[44]

Contributions and Challenges of APIRH

One of APIRH's most significant contributions to the reproductive rights movement has been its analysis of reproductive rights at the intersection of multiple oppressions. APIRH's comprehensive definition of reproductive rights is grounded in the community and is meant to be relevant to women whose lives are profoundly affected not only by their race, class, and gender but also by their experiences as refugees and immigrants. Through its struggles with issues of culture, power, and oppression, APIRH has a grasp on how to work in these communities in meaningful ways. The organization's decision to organize in the most vulnerable communities is unusual in the prochoice movement and provides invaluable lessons for organizing and for developing a comprehensive and inclusive reproductive rights agenda.

APIRH's work, like that of other groups in this study, challenges the view that women living on the margins are not interested in feminism and reproductive rights. When the issues are defined by the women themselves and articulated in terms that are relevant to their communities, it is possible to involve them in organizing for change and advocating for themselves. APIRH is overtly committed to feminism and social justice. The organization's ability to frame reproductive rights in terms that are meaningful to women in these communities is crucial for drawing these women to the movement. APIRH has managed to respond to the issues identified by the community and then connect those issues (sexual harassment, education rights, and environmental justice) to reproductive freedom. These connections are made not only in ideological or rhetorical ways but also concretely, in projects and policy changes at the local level.

Like other organizations that are closely attuned to the changing needs of their communities, APIRH is constantly evolving and refining its strategy and analysis. APIRH has had three major leadership changes through its 14-year existence—from Mary Chung to Yin Ling Leung to Eveline Shen—more than the other organizations in this study These have not been easy. APIRH has had to go through intense periods of re-examination of leadership, organizational structure, and programmatic work, particularly as it has tried to figure out what an API feminist model of leading and organizing looks like. Eveline Shen, APIRH's executive director for the past five years, sees this as part of APIRH's ongoing evolution in developing culturally specific models of leadership and organization which facilitate staying in touch with API communities. An example of the organization's evolution is the name change that took place in May 2004 when APIRH became Asian Communities for Reproductive Justice (ACRJ). Shen asserts that this change better reflected the reproductive issues and needs identified within API communities. The new name was symbolic for other reasons: "We have become ACRJ in solidarity with our sisters of color working on reproductive justice across the country."[45]

APIRH has consistently posed difficult questions for itself that are basic to its identity and efficacy as an API reproductive freedom organization. It asks: What does an API feminist model of organizing look like? What does it means to organize the most marginalized segments of the API community? How can APIRH members relate to and work with mainstream reproductive rights and pro-choice organizations, given the complexity of issues they struggle with on a daily basis? How can they stay focused on a community-rooted mission and locate API women's interests at the center of the larger reproductive rights movement? These questions do not necessarily have one right answer. As the organization grows and develops we can look forward to hearing their responses to some of these complex and yet important questions.

Both the challenges and APIRH's impact are seen in its major areas of work with youth, movement building, and raising awareness of reproductive rights in API communities. APIRH wants to develop young women leaders who have a feminist, class, and race analysis.[46] Though mentoring, developing leadership in, and empowering girls are very hard to quantify or measure, APIRH has done significant work on this front. In a short period of time it has worked with many young women and girls who accomplished significant organizing in their communities. Fourteen-year-old Amy Saephan put it this way: "At HOPE I learned that I have another person inside of me who can stand up for herself."[47] APIRH's success can also be measured partly by the impact it has had on public policy. For example, the Long Beach schools adopted ideas proposed by the girls in HOPE,[48] including teacher and student training, monitoring, and addressing incidents of sexual harassment.

Movement Building

APIRH is committed to building the reproductive rights movement and to ensuring that issues that are at the core of women's existence will be an essential part of any vision of human rights and social justice. This makes reproductive and sexual issues less vulnerable to dismissal by those who want to characterize them as Western and middle-class preoccupations. Their analysis of the interconnections is one of APIRH's most important political contributions. APIRH works with reproductive rights, civil rights, environmental justice, and anti-racist groups. It is on the Management Circle of SisterSong and a member of the Reproductive Rights Task Force of INCITE! Women of Color Against Violence.[49] It is also a member of the California Coalition for Reproductive Freedom and most often is the only API reproductive rights group in pro-choice coalitions.

In working with larger organizations, the inequality of financial resources can be a barrier to creating partnerships. While APIRH is called upon to work in solidarity and coalition with, for example, Planned Parenthood and NARAL Pro-Choice California, it cannot be equal financial partners because of the disparity in their resources. As APIRH sees it, one of its roles is to challenge reproductive rights groups to think about race and class, to work with social justice groups to include issues of gender, and to support API service providers to consider organizing as a strategy for increasing access to health care. This is no easy task, and APIRH is rightfully concerned about crafting realistic goals.

Being a community-based organization is an essential part of APIRH's identity and vision of social change. It is committed to listening to its constituencies and trying to balance this with its organizational commitment to feminism and reproductive rights. Within APIRH there have been conflicts over strategies, pace, and priorities, exacerbated by the scarcity of resources.

At the same time, since APIRH is one of only two API reproductive health organizations, it has been called upon to function in national circles. APIRH's present director, Eveline Shen, is recognized locally, statewide, and nationally in reproductive rights circles as well as social justice organizing arenas. The breadth of issues and activism incorporated into the APIRH vision is both a strength and a challenge. APIRH is committed to movement building, organizing, and advocacy. Despite the fact that it is focused on grassroots organizing, it continues to be sought as a partner by state and national organizations and coalitions. For example, in spring 2004 organizing for the March for Women's Lives in Washington, DC, APIRH was one of the lead organizers of a women of color contingent. The effort to engage in all of these arenas is challenging and within each area difficulties are confronted.

While APIRH's national profile sometimes conflicts with its goal of community organizing, co-founder Peggy Saika thinks that the original APIC mission of bringing an Asian voice to the pro-choice movement is still necessary and largely unfulfilled: "We need courageous and cohesive organizations that will set out a new vision around choice and reproductive rights that is explicit. We can't let our fears of alienating some constituencies prevent us from being out there in the way we need to be."[50] APIRH has definitely brought an API women's voice to the movement by participating in coalitions in California and nationally. Perhaps the local/national distinction evaporates when we consider that 40 percent of all Asians and Pacific Islanders live in California. Hence, work done by APIRH at the local level has a national impact.

APIRH's infrastructure was too fragile to support its rapid growth. Its youth work puts relatively large resources into what might seem to be relatively few women. While APIRH is committed to organizing on the issues brought forward as priorities by the communities it works in, foundations have their own agendas. The foundations that support reproductive rights organizations emphasize abortion rights. APIRH has aimed at trying to balance all these pressures and build the organization's core infrastructure. While the organization has been supported by some of the major reproductive rights foundations, APIRH leaders, like those of other nonprofit organizations, see the need to expand and diversify their funding base. They are currently trying to build an individual donor base. This work is very labor intensive.

APIRH is playing a unique and essential role in API communities and in the reproductive rights movement. It has a long-term social change vision for API communities and for building a reproductive justice movement. Its members want to expose people in the fast-growing immigrant communities to pro-choice and reproductive rights politics because they see reproductive rights as a central concern for women of color. They also see that API youth have no direct connection to the mainstream reproductive rights movement and see filling this gap as a critical organizational goal. All of this work is long-term and slow. As former staff member Rina Mehta observed, "I have no doubt that the girls in the Long Beach project will be pro-choice—but it doesn't happen overnight."[51]

APIRH's vision includes reproductive rights for all women and builds the base of the social justice movement. Shen summed up APIRH's view about the importance of generating a wide base of support for reproductive rights:

> During these challenging times, it is more critical than ever that we invest in building a strong base of women of color committed to reproductive freedom, that we forge alliances across our differences and build new and innovative partnerships, and that we develop a strong clear vision of reproductive freedom for all women and girls.[52]

NOTES

1 Peggy Saika, interview by Marlene Gerber Fried, January 2002.
2 These organizations included Planned Parenthood, the Asian Law Caucus, and the Asian Civil Rights Organization.
3 Saika, interview.
4 Ibid.
5 Audrey Shoji, introductory letter to *The Asian/Pacific Islander Reproductive Health Survey, 1991–1992* (Oakland: APIC, 1992).
6 Ibid.
7 Ibid.
8 Saika, interview.
9 Ibid.
10 APIC, *The Asian/Pacific Islander Reproductive Health Survey, 1991–1992* (Oakland: APIC, 1992), 2.
11 Quoted in Hokubei Mainichi, *North American Daily*, January 27, 1993, 1.
12 Ibid.
13 Ibid.
14 APIRH, *Teen Birth Rates in California* (Oakland: APIRH, 1993).
15 The 1990 US Census identified the 14 largest API communites to be Filipino, Japanese, Chinese, Asian Indian, Korean, Vietnamese, Laotian, Cambodian, Thai, Hmong, Hawaiian, Samoan, Guamanian, and Fijian.
16 APIC, *Reproductive Health Survey*, 17.
17 Those who were involved in this transition provide differing accounts of it. Some saw it as the result of tensions between Chung and the board over vision for the organization. Others feel that the reasons have never been clarified.
18 APIRH, "Join Us!," (Oakland: APIRH, 2003).
19 Eveline Shen, interview by Marlene Gerber Fried, January, 2001.
20 APIRH, "Community Manual," (Oakland: APIRH, 2003), 2.
21 APIRH, *The Health and Well-Being of Asian and Pacific Islander Women* (Oakland: APIRH, 1995).
22 Ibid., 12.
23 Ibid., 25.
24 Ibid., 12–13.
25 Ibid., 38.
26 Ibid., 2.
27 Ibid., 19.
28 Lisa Ikemoto, talk presented at the National Network of Abortion Funds annual conference in Memphis, June 9, 2001.
29 Eveline Shen, interview by Marlene Gerber Fried, January 2001.
30 Yin Ling Leung, email to Marlene Gerber Fried, July 22, 2003.
31 APIRH Newsletter, Summer 2000.
    Que Dang, winner of the 2000 Ms. Foundation's Gloria Steinem Leadership Award, was its first coordinator. Eveline Shen, APIRH's current executive director, worked on the pilot curriculum and leadership training as

an intern in Richmond and developed the project in Oakland. This became the APIRH's Organizers-in-Training Program, which uses participatory action research to gather information and as the basis for analyzing issues.

32   Ann Cheatham and Eveline Shen, "Community Based Participatory Research with Cambodian Girls in Long Beach, California: A Case Study," in *Community-Based Participatory Research for Health*, ed. Nina Wallerstein and Meredith Winkler (Somerset, NJ: Jossey Bass, 2002).

33   Participatory Action Research (PAR) is a research strategy that is grounded in political context and which seeks social change. The key aspects of PAR include that it is a collaborative process, not a method, of researchers and affected community members working together; that its purpose is knowledge which will lead to greater access; that it is rooted in building relationships; and that the researcher and community members are co-learners.

34   APIRH, *Making Schools Safer for Girls: Sexual Harassment and the Impact on Girls' Right to Learn* (Oakland: APIRH, 2000), 2.

35   Former APIRH staff member and HOPE creator Que Dang created Khmer Girls in Action.

36   Ann Cheatham, *HOPE Project for Girls Presents a Reproductive Freedom Tour of Oakland* (Oakland: APIRH, 2001), 7.

37   APIRH, "Dear Friend and Ally," letter, March 5, 2001.

38   APIRH, Progress Report, October 2001–September 2002 (Oakland: APIRH, 2002).

39   Disaggregating the data was a necessary step. For example, while only 0.8 percent of births to Chinese women are to teenagers, 18.9 percent of births to Laotian women are to teenagers.

40   The information about the API-TPPI project and the direct quotations are based on "Summary Findings" in *Teen Pregnancy Among Asians and Pacific Islanders in California: Final Report* (Berkeley: The Regents of the University of California, 2001).

41   Ibid.

42   Ibid., 7.

43   APIRH, *Asians and Pacific Islanders for Reproductive Health Teen Pregnancy Prevention Initiative*, Final Report to the California Wellness Foundation (Oakland: APIRH, January 2000–December 2001), 6.

44   Ibid., 8.

45   Eveline Shen, email to Marlene Gerber Fried, August 2004.

46   Eveline Shen, interview by Marlene Gerber Fried, October 2002.

47   Oakland HOPE Project, flyer.

48   Theary Chhay et al., "Dear Friend," letter, October 11, 2000.

49   INCITE! Women of Color Against Violence is a national activist organization of radical feminists of color advancing a movement to end violence against women of color and their communities through direct action, critical dialogue and grassroots organizing.

50   Saika, interview.

51   Rina Mehta, interview by Marlene Gerber Fried, February 2001.
52   Eveline Shen, unpublished speech given at the California Coalition for Reproductive Freedom Lobby Day, January 21, 2003.

11

The National Asian Women's Health Organization

I N 1993, Mary Chung, a 26-year-old Korean immigrant, founded the National Asian Women's Health Organization (NAWHO). Believing in the need for Asian American women to become advocates for their health and reproductive rights, Chung set out to make visible the health needs of Asian and Pacific Islander (API) women and to influence health and reproductive rights policies that affected them. Chung is a dedicated and strong leader, who writes:

> Sometimes I think it's inaccurate for me to be called the "founder" of the National Asian Women's Health Organization. Because, in many ways, I think the organization—or at least the need for it—found me.[1]

As we shall see, Chung created an organization that is a distinctive combination of grassroots and national organizational styles and politics. NAWHO has mobilized thousands of API women at both grassroots and national levels. It has also created partnerships with mainstream and community-based health institutions. NAWHO has exposed the damage done to API women's health by stereotypes and cultural norms (see Chapter 9) such as those which tell API women to put everyone before themselves. Chung drives home the dangers: "Why should we be surprised when a 65-year-old Chinese American woman in Chicago who has breast cancer drinks bleach trying to kill herself so that she won't be a burden on her family?"[2] Chung and NAWHO challenge these stereotypes and make it possible for API women to acknowledge their own health needs, feel that they are entitled to seek care, and become their own advocates. Speaking out is the first step. For Chung, this was a deeply personal mission. She had experienced firsthand the cost of community silence and the oppressiveness of the model minority stereotype. Chung broke her own silence at NAWHO's first conference with a very personal report:

> These are the statistics that make the work of organizations like NAWHO necessary and critical. But as the women's movement has always said, the personal is political. So I want to share with you my reason for starting this organization. When I was 13 years old, I lost my older sister to suicide. She was just 17. NAWHO is for my sister and others just like her.[3]

Getting Started

Like the other groups in this study, NAWHO's vision of women's health was ambitious and inclusive. NAWHO set out to be

> a community-based health advocacy organization committed to improving the overall health status of Asian women and girls. NAWHO develops and implements a broad agenda for Asian women's and girls' health, addressing the numerous factors that impact the physical, emotional, mental, social, and spiritual well-being of Asian women and girls. Through on-going activities, NAWHO provides a foundation on which women can proactively determine and advocate for our health, our lifestyles, and ourselves—on our terms.[4]

Mary Chung wrote that "NAWHO was formed to address the health needs of the diverse populations of Asian women. The founders of NAWHO recognized the absence of comprehensive and proactive research and the lack of programs focused on Asian women's health needs."[5]

Chung was inspired by the organizing that surrounded her in the Bay Area. Her first job was as a bookkeeper in an Asian American civil rights organization, and she had volunteered for the National Organization for Women (NOW) in San Francisco and for Korean American women's projects and battered women's shelters. Through this work as well as her time at Asian and Pacific Islanders for Choice (APIC), Chung was connected to other women of color organizing for reproductive health. Byllye Avery and Julia Scott of the National Black Women's Health Project (NBWHP) and Luz Alvarez Martínez from the National Latina Health Organization (NLHO), among others, supported her vision to create a national Asian American women's health organization.[6] They gave advice and support on a daily basis; Alvarez Martínez even opened her office space to Chung.[7]

These influential and experienced activists introduced Chung to potential funders. Initial financial support for NAWHO came from two smaller foundations.[8] As it developed, NAWHO attracted funding from government, corporate, and nonprofit sources—including pro-choice, feminist, and health foundations. Today, NAWHO is one of the best-funded reproductive rights and health organizations for women of color.

Chung was committed to pan-Asian organizing, recognizing both similarities and differences among API communities. "The needs and concerns of Asian women are at the same time specific and diverse, and they must be addressed within community, cultural, and linguistic contexts."[9] Building a strong movement of women of color was another priority for Chung, and she saw NAWHO as part of that effort. This was reflected in the diverse composition of its original board of directors: Sia Nowrojee, Luz Alvarez Martínez, D. Tosi Sasao, Grace Sison, Byllye Avery, and Mary Chung herself. This was a group of professionals with backgrounds in activism, policy work, politics, and research. They were well-known leaders who brought credibility, experience, and skills to this new organization and shared Chung's vision of a racially and ethnically inclusive movement.

Organizing an Asian American Health Constituency

Chung knew that improvements in the reproductive rights and health of Asian American women would come about only when they became a vocal and visible constituency. To help Asian American women articulate their own priorities, NAWHO organized two major national conferences on Asian and Pacific Islander women's health. These gatherings attracted large numbers of API women, generated awareness and visibility about their health issues, and helped set an API women's health agenda. Perhaps most important, women who attended experienced a sense of collective empowerment about the possibilities for change and their ability to create their own health agenda.

In November 1995, the first national conference ever held on the health of Asian and Pacific Islander women, "Coming Together, Moving Strong: Mobilizing an Asian Women's Health Movement." It was attended by 300 API women in San Francisco's Japantown. Chung articulated the organization's goal in her opening statement: "It is our vision that this conference will foster a movement that will maintain this focus on the health needs of Asian American women, that we will no longer allow the marginalization of our community in the national health care agenda."[10] Miriam Ching Louie, a longtime activist, expressed the tremendous achievement that the conference represented: "Even being able to have this Asian women's health conference is something that absolutely could not have been imagined 10 or 15 years ago, when the US women's health movement and the way it cut issues were very, very different."[11] Louie was pointing to the growing consciousness of the diverse health needs and issues of women of color as well as the US women's health movement's inability to adequately incorporate race. At workshops and plenary sessions, discussing health issues also meant discussing healthy environments, substance abuse, and mental health. An array of government officials, health professionals and advocates, community leaders, and members of the greater Asian American community participated, giving the conference legitimacy and making it an inclusive initiative.

The importance of breaking silences was a key theme: "The conference provided an unprecedented forum for Asian women to discuss a range of health issues that are rarely discussed in our communities."[12] Poet Janice Mirikitani powerfully expressed the significance of the gathering:

...We are not silent in dark closets and barns and bedrooms,
fondled, raped, battered, incested, molested, murdered.
My words will shield my sons from bullets and war,
my protests still cradle my daughters from pimps of self hate,
generational poverty, perversion, prostitution, unwanted pregnancy,
diseases and infant mortality.

I break this cycle of oppression.
My body belongs to me.[13]

The conference accomplished for API women what the NBWHP conference had done for African American women almost 15 years earlier: "It gave us a gathering place, [it gave] us the space to recognize the reality of our problems, our needs, our pain, and to work together to find solutions to better our own lives as Asian American women."[14] The participants reflected a range of politics, ethnicities, and socio-economic positions. Radical and mainstream voices were merged and mobilized into a powerful constituency for Asian women's health.

For the first time, health information on a wide range of issues affect-ing API women was brought together. The synthesis provided a sober-ing and angering picture, which revealed inadequate insurance coverage as well as deficits in every aspect of health care from routine health checkups and prenatal care to information about HIV/AIDS. Failure to attend to the needs of specific API communities, as well as economic barriers, had led to lower rates of using health services. Thus, although cervical cancer is more pervasive among Chinese and Southeast Asian women than among white women, and the nationwide rate of breast cancer in Asian American women is approaching that of white women,[15] few Asian women use screening services for cervical or breast cancer. API women had lower rates of Pap test screening, mammography, and clinical breast examination than any other racial or ethnic population in the United States.[16] Studies cited by researcher Sia Nowrojee showed that only 18 percent of Chinese American women had an annual pelvic exam, which allows for early detection of abnormal cells and the poten-tial to avoid developing cervical cancer or at least benefit from early diagnosis.[17]

The health needs identified at the conference became the focus for subsequent programs organized by NAWHO and others. Several ideas for action emerged which informed NAWHO's future agenda, includ-ing the conviction that API women should define their health needs and work for implementation of appropriate government policy; the importance of API women organizing themselves in opposition to wel-fare reform and other damaging public policies; ensuring that women's sexual health is a priority in national and Asian women's health agen-das; increasing funding for services, education, and research; and raising awareness about the existence and needs of API lesbians.

In 1997, NAWHO organized a second conference, "The Quality of Our Lives: Empowering Asian American Women for the 21st Century." Chung credits Patsy Mink, the first Asian American woman in Congress and a NAWHO supporter, with providing the impetus for a conference that would bring together API women in political leadership.[18] The sec-ond conference had the specific goals of making elected officials advo-cates for API women's health and building a network of leaders who could support each other and the next generation of leaders.[19]

NAWHO was committed to developing grassroots leadership. At the conferences, it trained Asian women to be effective community leaders and advocates. Panels focused on partnerships and other forms of activism at the national, state, and community levels. Scholarships were given to 100 immigrant and refugee women and girls, and the NAWHO National Leadership Network was born.

The second conference was oriented toward having an impact on public policy. Two-thirds of the panelists were office holders, public health officials, or researchers. There were letters of support from elected officials, including President Clinton, the governor of California, the mayor of Los Angeles, and several members of Congress, who, along with state legislators, were featured speakers.

Both conferences played a crucial role in developing an Asian women's health movement and integrating API women's needs into the reproductive rights movement. They also drew the attention of policy-makers to the health needs of API women and established NAWHO as a significant force both in the women's health and pro-choice movements and in government health research and policy-making organizations. As a result, NAWHO went on to create significant partnerships with the Centers for Disease Control and Prevention (CDC) and played a role on Capitol Hill and in the White House on the issue of racial disparities in health care.

Reproductive Health and Beyond

When NAWHO began, there was a profound lack of awareness and information about the reproductive and sexual health of API women. Organizing to pressure the government to increase information and access to care for API women was especially complex given the diversity of a population comprised of over 40 distinct cultures with many different languages and dialects. In addition, non-Asians had masked these differences and needs by applying the model minority stereotype to all API Americans.[20]

NAWHO addressed this complex situation by employing a multipronged approach that included conducting community-based research; working in partnership with state and federal organizations; producing and disseminating research reports with findings and recommendations; and training health professionals in culturally competent approaches to API communities. NAWHO has added to the public's understanding of "culturally competent":

Cultural competency refers to the continually developing ability to respond to individuals of different cultures in a way that is sensitive to and respectful of the differences that exist between cultures. In a health care setting this requires providers to be aware of the cultural values and beliefs of clients and to understand how these factors influence their health-seeking attitudes and behaviors.[21]

NAWHO has brought together policy-makers and community activists to identify the health problems of API communities, which include cancer, depression, diabetes, heart disease, and smoking—in addition to inadequate reproductive and sexual health. All of NAWHO's activities have raised awareness about the health status of Asian and Pacific Islander American women. Based on its research, NAWHO has published a series of reports on sexually transmitted diseases, reproductive health, heart disease, and breast cancer. These studies broke new ground in data collection on API health and were the foundation for new intervention programs. For example, NAWHO's study of smoking was the first national multilingual smoking-habits survey. The results were given to the federal government, which led to more accurate perceptions about tobacco use among API Americans, a necessary step towards achieving more culturally specific avenues of intervention to increase health.

Similarly, NAWHO's South Asian Women's Health Project, which documented the difficulties women have when they try to obtain health services, was also a first.[22] Using personal narratives based on interviews with 85 women, NAWHO examined South Asian women's perspectives about their own health needs and problems, the influence of their cultures on their perceptions, and how women, health advocates, and providers can overcome barriers to addressing South Asian women's specific needs.[23] The project recognized the importance of supporting South Asian women's advocacy on behalf of their own health. It recommended that health policy-makers and service providers work with South Asian women "to collect gender, cultural, generational, and income disaggregated information on the health needs of South Asian communities."[24] Based on the notion that health must be approached comprehensively, the study identified broad areas requiring attention, including mental health, nutrition, occupational health, violence, and reproductive and sexual health issues. This was one of the first studies to identify specific health concerns of lesbian and bisexual women who, in addition to experiencing problems common to API women, suffered alienation from their families and isolation from the community.[25] These recommendations can be generalized to other communities.

In all, NAWHO has published over 20 research reports. Initially, its research focused on reproductive rights, but its agenda quickly expanded to include other women's health issues and ultimately men's health too. NAWHO recognized that the absence of knowledge about the reproductive health practices and behavior of API men had a profound impact on efforts to promote women's health; in 1999 NAWHO released *Sharing Responsibility*, the first study of API men's reproductive health attitudes and behaviors.[26]

With insight into API men's health and its data on API women, NAWHO has been able to construct a comprehensive account of API women's health. Its work demonstrates the value of ethnically/racially and culturally specific research.[27] It highlights health problems that are of very high incidence in Asians. Because these conditions do not show up in the general population, mainstream providers would not be likely to look for them in the absence of NAWHO's important work.

From Research to Action

NAWHO used its research to advocate for improving API health outcomes. Its findings and recommendations have been used by many agencies to create new intervention programs and have motivated institutions and API communities to take action to eradicate racial and ethnic health disparities. Challenging prevailing understandings about access to services, NAWHO connected the lack of information on API women's health to the fact that culturally competent health services were inadequate or nonexistent. The low usage rate of health services by Asian and Pacific Islander Americans had been interpreted by mainstream health institutions as a lack of need for these services rather than a lack of access. NAWHO's work led to a very different conclusion. For example, NAWHO argued that the fact that API Americans do not use mental health services does not mean that there is no need for them. Instead, lack of usage reveals barriers to access that can be overcome by creating culturally appropriate services, better outreach, more insurance coverage, and extending free care where possible. The following quote illustrates NAWHO's perspective: "My mom was in a deep depression and she wouldn't talk about it. Asian American families don't realize that women are depressed, so [Asian American women] won't seek help...In Asian cultures you're not supposed to express your feelings. You're supposed to keep them inside and deal with it."[28] NAWHO drew attention to the previously unattended problem of API women's mental health.

To ensure that API health issues would be addressed, NAWHO made it a priority to work with federal and state officials and agencies to raise awareness about the need for, and increase access to, health services, While critics felt that these activities came at the expense of community building and grassroots organizing, the organization was extremely successful in this area. For two years (1998–2000), NAWHO had a second office in Washington, DC, to facilitate its national advocacy work. Ultimately, it decided to close the office and consolidate its resources in California, this effort contributed to building its national presence. Chung was one of only ten Asian American leaders selected to represent Asian American health concerns in a White House meeting with President Clinton and Vice President Gore. She served on the Steering Committee of the National Initiative to Eliminate Racial and Ethnic Health Disparities, a partnership between the Department of Health and Human Services and the American Public Health Association, and she was invited to Clinton's weekly radio address when he publicly cited the fact that Vietnamese women have five times the rate of cervical cancer of white women.

NAWHO played a leadership role in developing a plan to address the breast cancer issue among API women. In 1996, NAWHO convened the first National Asian American Breast Cancer Summit to create a comprehensive national plan of action.[29] Subsequently, NAWHO formed partnerships with state-sponsored cancer control projects, funded by the CDC, national cancer agencies, and local and regional community-based organizations, to improve screening outreach and cancer education for Asian American communities. NAWHO set up a toll-free number in five languages to inform women about the importance of early detection screenings such as mammograms and Pap tests. NAWHO has been working with health department directors in eight states on improving access to services and cultural competency and raising awareness among API women about the importance of screenings.

In similar efforts, NAWHO has created agreements with the CDC to work collaboratively on a range of issues including diabetes, immunization, and tobacco control.[30] These efforts have brought visibility to API health issues at the national policy level. And NAWHO's work is now part of an important body of research on API health, which has led to improved awareness among health care providers who work with API communities.[31] NAWHO has raised a great deal of money for further research by the CDC for screenings for breast cancer and diabetes and other health issues affecting API women and communities. Between 1998 and 2004, it gave $1.4 million in grants to grassroots API organizations and expanded the research pool for API health. NAWHO was the first organization to have multiple federal partnership agreements in areas such as breast and cervical cancer and immunization.

Working with the Pro-Choice Movement

NAWHO consistently worked within the movement in order to raise API women's visibility, address issues pertinent to them, and fight against their marginalization and isolation. Although Chung was critical of the mainstream movement for not being more focused on the needs of API women, she was seen as an important ally and leader. She served on several boards of leading pro-choice organizations and worked closely with leaders of major pro-choice groups.[32]

Chung collaborated with other women of color who were leaders of reproductive rights organizations to enhance the visibility and position of women of color in the movement. She and the other leaders saw the need to join together both to support each other and to have a greater impact on both the movement and public policy. In 1992, Chung was one of seven leaders who founded the Women of Color Coalition for Reproductive Health Rights (WOCCRHR), and in 1994 NAWHO took over the coordination of the group. Through WOCCRHR, NAWHO participated in both the International Conference on Population and Development (ICDP) in Cairo in 1994 and the Fourth World Conference on Women in Beijing in 1995. The coalition played a critical role in ensuring that US women of color were heard in both domestic and global negotiations and that other Asian health groups were also included. For the first time, API perspectives on immigration, reproductive and sexual health and rights, violence against women, community organizing, and sustainable development were represented in national and international policy dialogues.[33]

These coalition partners and other organizations worked together again in 1998, when NAWHO organized a policy briefing on women of color for media representatives, foundations, and health advocates at the

National Press Club in Washington, DC. NAWHO invited other women's health groups to participate including the National Abortion and Reproductive Rights Action League (NARAL), the NBWHP, and the National Latina Institute for Reproductive Health. NAWHO presented a paper detailing recent congressional actions on reproductive rights and their impact on Asian American communities.[34] The briefing was part of NAWHO's overall goal of protecting and advancing the reproductive health rights of API women and their families.

NAWHO staff members have spoken at national demonstrations, press events, and many conferences and panels sponsored by other organizations. They trained leaders of federal agencies and representatives of the Clinton administration to work more effectively and sensitively with the API community. In her history of the women's health movement, Sandra Morgen describes NAWHO's role: "Now, like the other women's health movement organizations that offered support and encouragement, NAWHO was playing a key role in creating and building on linkages among women's health organizations and between these organizations and the women, the health professionals, and the public policy makers it hoped to influence."[35]

NAWHO leaders see these efforts as having made important changes in API, women of color, and mainstream movements. "We feel we have become equal partners and that mainstream groups have an understanding about the need to include Asian Americans in reproductive rights issues."[36] NAWHO staff believe that their work has made it impossible to exclude API women from any gathering on reproductive rights. They see NAWHO as having established a solid presence in mainstream consciousness and activism.

Development of Youth Leadership

Developing the leadership of young women has been a priority for NAWHO from the beginning. Because of the challenges she faced as a young leader, Chung talked about being especially sensitive to the need to trust in young leadership.[37] Her youth distinguishes her from virtually all the other heads of national organizations in the pro-choice and women's health movements, both mainstream and women of color. NAWHO staff, all women in their 20s and 30s, talk about Chung as an important mentor and role model for them as young women.[38]

In 1997, NAWHO created the Leadership Network in order to more systematically support and develop new API community health leaders. The network brings community-based health and social justice advocates together as a national body to promote improved health policies. Young women and men are recruited to the network from around the country with the overall goals of empowering emerging Asian American leaders and giving them the skills to become effective health advocates at national, regional, and community levels; establishing a strong, cohesive national Asian American health network; fostering social changes at the community level; and having an impact on relevant institutions in order to promote the health and well-being of Asian Americans.[39]

NAWHO held training conferences in 1998, 1999, and 2000, each time bringing 100 young API leaders from across the country together for networking and skill building. These gatherings were opportunities for young participants to meet established leaders and laid the groundwork for future relationships which would support community-level work. The significance of NAWHO's Leadership Network was affirmed when the White House Office of Management and Budget and the director of the National Institute of Mental Health co-sponsored an executive branch briefing for the network to discuss new policy commitments that would have an impact on Asian American communities.

The network functions in an ongoing way and has been successful in helping emerging leaders become more effective advocates in public policy and community health. Network members have obtained state funding for health outreach programs, research in their states, and support for API medical students and have been appointed to National Institutes of Health panels. In Michigan, affiliates organized a statewide Asian women's health day and held discussion forums. In Seattle, network members organized meetings with policy-makers to discuss language-related health issues. In Los Angeles, members started meeting regularly after NAWHO's second national conference.

The network includes over 170 leaders from 19 states. By being part of the network, they learn about health disparities, grassroots organizing, and the policy-making process, gaining valuable skills and knowledge that lead to community empowerment and improved health. Representatives of the network serve on NAWHO's National Policy Council, which works with the NAWHO board and staff to formulate policies and define principles grounded in the needs of their constituencies to guide those making health policy at the state and national level.

NAWHO's Contributions

In only 11 years of existence, NAWHO has grown tremendously, and has an impressive list of accomplishments. In a relatively short time, NAWHO has become an important advocate for API women's health within the mainstream pro-choice movement, in policy circles, and among major health policy organizations, including the CDC. NAWHO has helped to give API women and men a voice in the political system and has raised the priority of dealing with API health issues among government, foundations, health care and research institutions, and other nonprofit organizations. Its research on health problems ranging from breast cancer to tobacco use has brought API issues to state and national attention. NAWHO can also take credit for increasing cultural competency among health professionals, substantial leadership development, and expanding resources for API health concerns. It has 4,000 members and supporters and it provides significant grants to community-based health organizations.[40] Central to all of its projects is building capacity at the community level. The organization has trained hundreds of API women and men around the country in advocacy and policy work.

Within the reproductive rights movement, NAWHO has been both a gadfly and team player as it brings together ideas and strategies from the mainstream organizations and more radical and community-based groups. For example, its positions in opposition to population control and coercive contraception and its understanding of the need to include reproductive rights in the broader context of health distinguished it from the mainstream pro-choice movement. At the same time, NAWHO has been highly visible on the abortion issue and its focus on policy and legislative change is more typical of mainstream groups. NAWHO conferences, which featured established politicians and heads of agencies, also included many radical and grassroots activists from the Asian American community who determined the programs and developed the policy recommendations. Thus, NAWHO effectively combined mainstream and radical voices.

From its inception, gaining the attention of politicians and other influential people has been a consistent NAWHO strategy to combat the invisibility of API women in politics and policy. For example, a highlight of the first conference in 1996 was a town meeting chaired by Congresswoman Patsy Mink. Furthermore, the San Francisco Board of Supervisors declared the days of NAWHO's first conference as Asian Women's Health Days. At the conference NAWHO highlighted the fact that Asian American women were a political constituency:

> There are those who believe that the Asian American community is apolitical, that we do not vote, that we have no interest in organizing around the very issues we will be discussing this weekend. But by our very presence here today, we will prove them wrong. It is here that we begin a dialogue among Asian American women, health care providers, advocates and policy makers, to break down the barriers of stereotypes, of racism, of sexism, and of silence, that stand between Asian American women and healthy, safe lives.[41]

In 1997 NAWHO organized "Silent Epidemics: A National Policy Summit on Depression and Asian American Women." This first gathering of mental health experts to focus on Asian American women's health sought and attained the recognition and attention of the mainstream reproductive rights movement and influential politicians in California and Washington, DC.

NAWHO was one of the only organizations in the API community representing a cross-section of API women that had the capacity to work in this way. Congressman Robert Matsui spoke about the importance of NAWHO's role:

> What NAWHO is doing is larger than representing the issue at hand—they are demonstrating that Asian Americans are leaders, are involved, and have the influence to challenge or support the policies of this country. This presence is the factor that will create a significantly different future for our children.[42]

NAWHO has been a magnet for a younger generation of Asian women interested in reproductive rights and political advocacy. Almost immediately after NAWHO was founded, younger women from this rapidly growing population volunteered their services in order to help their communities and to develop their networking and political skills. NAWHO also attracted the support of Asian American politicians who could identify with its mission and who were keen to gain the support of this burgeoning constituency.

The breadth of issues NAWHO works on and its extensive research and publications record are impressive. It has been able to branch into new areas of concern as they arise. "Even though there are tensions when allocating time and resources among advocacy health education and research, we see all of our work as organically connected...Research generates the need for advocacy and the energy to make it happen."[43] As we have seen, NAWHO's research reports spotlight health disparities and include concrete recommendations for change. NAWHO created partnerships to help effect the changes it champions. For example, after holding community forums and other educational and policy activities about breast cancer, NAWHO worked with the CDC to create Communicating Across Boundaries, the first cultural competency training and curriculum for health care professionals. Originally NAWHO had eight state health departments as partners to pilot and test the training; it is now being used in 22 states.

When NAWHO began, even the most basic health information about API women was sketchy when it existed at all. "Our research agenda is huge and growing, because the health needs of our communities have been so neglected, we have to prove to the public that they exist."[44] Unwavering in its commitment to continue to fill these gaps, NAWHO has demonstrated an ability to follow needs as they arise rather than work from a preconceived agenda. For example, in attempting to "uncover and document an accurate picture of the reproductive and sexual health status of Asian American women,"[45] NAWHO organized a focus group to examine the life and health experiences of immigrant women in their countries of origin, which follows the women as they move to new countries.

For eight years, founder Mary Chung was the driving force of the organization, as well as its public face. In 2001, she stepped down as executive director and was succeeded by Afton Hirohama, who brought seven years of experience with NAWHO to the leadership position. This was a challenging and significant transition. Like some of the other organizations documented here, NAWHO has been very much identified with its founder. For eight years Chung was the driving force of the organization as well as its public face and voice. While changes in leadership present difficulties, as we have noted elsewhere it is also critical to develop new leaders.

NAWHO has had a tremendous impact on public health policy circles, in health service delivery, in the pro-choice movement, and in the lives of API women. It has built a constituency for API health advocacy and made sure that the needs and concerns of API communities are visible. It has more than fulfilled the hopes and needs expressed by Sia Nowrojee, NAWHO's board chair, speaking at the organization's first conference:

> Through your participation, we believe that you will contribute your important voice and experience to a movement that desperately needs to hear from you. We also hope that when you go home, you will share this experience with the women in your life who were not able to be here... Asian women of all communities, of different ages and immigration status, from all over the country, are coming together to say we are important, we will no longer be separated and we will no longer be silent.[46]

NOTES

1   Mary Chung Hayashi, *Far From Home: Shattering the Myth of the Model Minority* (Irving, TX: Tapestry Press, 2003), 43.

2   Ibid., 83.

3   Mary Chung, "Conference Speech," in NAWHO, *Conference Proceedings from Coming Together, Moving Strong: Mobilizing an Asian Women's Health Movement* (San Francisco: NAWHO, 1995), 12.

4   NAWHO, *1993–1994 Annual Report* (San Francisco: NAWHO), 1.

5   Mary Chung, letter to Marlene Gerber Fried, October 9, 1993.

6   Others included Cynthia Newbille-Marsh of NBWHP and current director (as of 2004) of Planned Parenthood of the Golden Gate, Dian Harrison (Chung Hayashi, *Far From Home*, 44).

7   Ibid., 45.

8   The early small foundation support came on behalf of the Jessie Smith Noyes Foundation and the Moriah Fund via program officers Jael Silliman and Shira Saperstein, respectively, who were committed to supporting the activism and leadership of women of color.

9   Mary Chung quoted in Sandra Morgen, *Into Our Own Hands: The Women's Health Movement in the US, 1969–1990* (New Brunswick, NJ: Rutgers University Press, 2002), 64.

10   Mary Chung, "Opening Statement," in NAWHO, *Conference Program for Coming Together, Moving Strong: Mobilizing an Asian Women's Health Movement* (San Francisco: NAWHO, 1995), 2.

11   NAWHO, *Conference Proceedings*, 75.

12   Afton Hirohama and Priya Jagannathan, "Introduction," in NAWHO, *Conference Proceedings*, 3.

13   Janice Mirikitani, "A Man Talking to Himself; The Woman Who Replies," in NAWHO, *Conference Proceedings*, 2.

14   Hirohama and Jagannathan, "Introduction," 3.

15   NAWHO, *Conference Proceedings*, 36.

16   NAWHO, *National Plan of Action on Asian American Women and Breast Cancer* (San Francisco: NAWHO, May 1997), 2.

17   NAWHO, *Conference Proceedings*, 35.

18   Chung Hayashi, *Far From Home*, 51.

19   Ibid.

20   Ibid., 10–11.

21   Ibid., 89.

22   NAWHO, *Emerging Communities: A Health Needs Assessment of South Asian Women in Three California Counties* (San Francisco: NAWHO, January 1996).

23   Ibid.

24   Ibid., 22.

25   Ibid., 12.

26   NAWHO, *The Asian American Men's Health Survey: Sharing Responsibility* (San Francisco: NAWHO, October 1999).

27   For example, they drew attention to problems specific to API women, including Hepatitis B (a precursor to liver cancer), which is five times more prevalent in Asian Americans, and Thalessemia, which can result in still births and is a genetic condition carried by about 10 percent of Chinese and 40 percent of Southeast Asians.

28   NAWHO, *Breaking the Silence: A Study of Depression Among Asian American Women* (San Francisco: NAWHO, 2000), 8.

29   NAWHO, *National Plan of Action.*

30   In 2002–2003, NAWHO initiated several campaigns, including the National Asian American Immunization Program, the National Asian American Diabetes Education campaign, the National Collaborative for Asian American Women's Mental Health, and a violence prevention project working with student leaders and college administrators.

31   Afton Hirohama, memo to Marlene Gerber Fried, March 7, 2003.

32   These organizations include Planned Parenthood, NARAL, Alan Guttmacher Institute, NOW, the Reproductive Health Technologies Project and the Pro-Choice Resource Center.

33   Sia Nowrojee and Jael Silliman, "Asian Women's Health: Organizing a Movement," in *Dragon Ladies: Asian American Feminists Breathe Fire*, ed. Sonia Shah (Boston: South End Press, 1997), 86.

34   NAWHO, *1997–1999 Report of Activities* (San Francisco: NAWHO), 21.

35   Morgen, *Into Our Own Hands*, 67.

36   Hirohama, memo.

37   NAWHO, *1999–2000 Annual Report* (San Francisco: NAWHO), 3; and Mary Chung, interview by Marlene Gerber Fried, February 2001.

38   Mary Chung, interview.

39   Chung Hayashi, Far From Home, 57–58.

40   Ibid., 17.

41   NAWHO, *Conference Proceedings*, 6.

42   NAWHO, "1998 National Leadership Training Conference," *1997–1999 Report of Activities*, 20.

43   Cindy Moon, Lucy Ngyuen, and Jennifer Stoll, interview by Marlene Fried, January 2001.

44   Mary Chung, interview.

45   NAWHO, *Global Perspectives: A Report on International Asian American Women's Reproductive Health* (San Francisco: NAWHO, 2001), 1.

46   Sia Nowrojee, letter, in NAWHO, *Conference Program*, 3.

12

"We Will No Longer be Silent or Invisible"

Latinas Organizing for Reproductive Justice

I T is commonly believed that issues of reproductive health and sexuality are not of concern to Latinas or their communities. As Latinas are predominantly Catholic, it is assumed that they are all against abortion, do not use birth control, and are not active participants in political struggles for reproductive freedom. These ideas persist not only among the general public but in the pro-choice movement and feminist scholarship as well.[1]

The continual marginalization of women of color in organizing wholly erases the significant roles that Latinas have played in the development of both mainstream reproductive rights efforts and community-based reproductive health and sexuality agendas. In fact, as activist-historian Elizabeth Martínez points out, "Latinas' views on reproductive rights are often more radical than Anglo women's views and not 'conservative,' as some people say, because their definition of choice requires more profound social change than just abortion rights or preventing pregnancy."[2] Grounded in the realities of their communities, Latinas insist that broader issues, such as racism and classism, influence their reproductive lives, and that true reproductive freedom necessitates an end to all forms of social inequality. As this and the following two chapters demonstrate, Latinas *are* organizing for their reproductive and sexual health

*This chapter was researched and written by Elena R. Gutiérrez.

rights and have developed innovative organizing strategies, principles, and practices grounded in the needs and cultures of their communities.

A challenge in documenting the activism of Latinas, however, is the diversity of communities and individuals that are placed within the category.[3] With national origins from countries in Central and South America and the Caribbean, Latinas have a wide variety of racial, ethnic, religious, and linguistic traditions. Latino communities are geographically dispersed throughout the US, and their cultures are regionally distinct and complex. Totaling more than 40 million, Latinas and Latinos are members of communities and families with various citizenship statuses, great intergenerational differences in acculturation, identity formation, and socioeconomic status. With the 2000 Census, Latinos became the largest minority group in the US, at 12.5 percent of the population,[4] and are expected to comprise 25 percent of the US population by 2050.

As some of the first scholarship attempting to document Latina organizing for reproductive justice, this analysis focuses primarily on the two largest Latino groups in the nation, Puerto Ricans (9.6 percent) and Mexicans (58 percent), about whom the most written material is available.[5]

Myths and Misconceptions

Images of Latinas circulating in popular media and academic research promote the idea of a "generic Latina," ignoring the complex social, historical, and cultural contexts within which Latinas live.[6] In place of nuanced and multidimensional representations of Latinas are a handful of highly exaggerated and conflicting stereotypes upon which many people base their understanding of Latinas in the US. Generally, the images are of passive, childlike females who are subservient to their husbands in particular and men in general. Latinas are represented as traditional women—heavily influenced by Catholicism—and therefore sexually repressed.[7] Or, when depicted as sexual beings, their sexuality is explicitly linked to their being Latina—meaning that they are characterized as tropically "exotic" and hypersexual. When depicted as sexually liberated, their liberation is written off as acculturation into the white mainstream society, reinforcing the idea that white women's sexuality is the norm and all others are aberrations.[8] Always heterosexual, Latinas are defined by a strict virgin/whore dichotomy of sexuality and reproductive behavior. In both cases, a Latina is believed incapable of using birth control.[9]

These stereotypes serve to justify state, medical, and social intervention in their reproduction.

These core images shift and assume different meanings when applied to particular communities in different historical moments and social contexts. For example, Puerto Rican women have historically been cast in a variety of hypersexualized images that classify them as sexually deviant.[10] Extending beyond the island to Puerto Rican women living on the US mainland, various social and political representations present them as exotically sexual beings who carelessly bear many children who will ultimately become welfare dependents and drain social resources.[11]

Mexican-origin women are also ideologically associated with their fertility, but in contrast to the hypersexuality of Puerto Rican women, a strict Catholic traditionalism and over-identification as mothers is emphasized.[12] The childbearing of Mexican immigrant women is increasingly suspect and often criminalized. For example, Proposition 187[13] in California targeted poor, pregnant Mexican immigrant women, blaming them for the state's and the nation's problems. Mexican women were depicted as purposely crossing the border to give birth in publicly financed county hospitals to gain citizenship status and thus eligibility for public assistance.[14] These representations provide the ideological justification for punitive policies that shape Latinas' reproductive experiences.[15] They also influence how health care professionals treat Latinas.[16]

The Reproductive and Sexual Health Status of Latinas

Although research on Latinas and their health is sparse, studies report that, overall, they experience poor health,[17] with disproportionately high rates of cervical cancer, sexually transmitted diseases, HIV/AIDS, teenage pregnancy, obesity, diabetes, domestic violence, and unintentional injuries compared to other women.[18] These circumstances are exacerbated by the extremely low rates of health care delivery to Latinas caused by financial, institutional, and cultural barriers. Low levels of education and income contribute to high poverty rates in Latino communities and, concomitantly, poor health status. Almost one-third of Latinos report no health insurance coverage and Latinas are the least likely of any group to have access to regular health care or health insurance coverage.[19] Since many Latinas communicate in Spanish, the predominantly English-speaking health care system presents significant challenges to health care delivery.[20] Recent anti-immigrant sentiment has also increasingly discouraged many Latinos from seeking health care. As many providers have limited knowledge and understanding of Latina cultures, when immigrant and US-born Latinos do receive medical attention, many report high dissatisfaction with the health care they receive. Few feel that their health care providers genuinely care about their wellbeing.[21]

Latinas are more likely to have children at younger ages.[22] Almost 17 percent of births to Latinas are to adolescents under the age of 20, with Puerto Ricans having the highest percentage of teen births (21.9 percent) of all racial or ethnic groups.[23] Latinas have historically received low rates of prenatal care. In the past ten years, their use of prenatal services during the first trimester has increased significantly.[24] When they do receive prenatal care, however, Latinas experience a low level of satisfaction, and complain of a poor quality of care and a lack of culturally sensitive treatment.[25]

Latinas also experience a high incidence of and mortality due to cervical cancer.[26] The high rates may be tied to a host of environmental factors. Due to their concentration in service and agriculture industries, Latinas have high exposure to toxins. They are at high risk from the effects of teratogenic chemicals (known to cause malformation in a fetus) in the workplace and home because they are over-represented in three of the major labor market categories in which exposure is high: clerical (radiation), service (cleaning chemicals), and operatives and laborers (pesticides, herbicides, and chemicals). Agricultural laborers are also at high risk for exposure, and many communities experience high rates of infertility, stillbirths, fetal abnormalities, and cancers.[27]

Latinas face additional sexual health risks; perhaps the cause for most concern is that Latinas currently represent 20.2 percent of the total AIDS cases among women.[28] AIDS is the third leading cause of death for Latinas between the ages of 15 and 24. Latinas also have among the highest rates of chlamydia, gonorrhea, and human papilloma virus (HPV).[29] Lack of basic knowledge about sexually transmitted diseases (STDs), lack of health insurance, and cultural and linguistic barriers to the health care system prevent Latinas from being able to prevent and/ or treat STDs.

Research consistently shows that Latinas are pro-choice. Furthermore, they have abortions at a rate proportionately higher than any other group,[30] with 20.1 percent of all abortions being obtained by Latinas.[31] They are 2.5 times as likely to have an abortion as white women.[32] While

Latinas are actively seeking abortion services, they are among that group of poor women most likely to suffer from lack of access to safe abortions. When they do have abortions, Latinas disproportionately suffer from medical complications. Rosie Jiménez, an important symbol in the reproductive rights movement, is a clear reminder to Latinas that abortion is about more than choice.[33]

History of Reproductive Oppression
Puerto Rican Women: Legacies of Colonialism

> But the first and most important site of Puertorriquena struggle is the female body. The body represents the unique and culturally revered capacity to procreate, symbolizes the taboo realm of sexuality, and carries with it the honor or shame of the family. The body is at once a valued (often exploited) instrument for social survival and an object for enforcing social control...Sexuality, reproduction, motherhood, and family need to be redefined in light of the experiences of colonization, inter-lingualism, and the development of capitalism in Puerto Rico.[34]

While the population control policies that have been implemented in Puerto Rico by the US government have gained some attention, issues of reproduction and sexuality were in fact at the center of Puerto Rican politics even before North American involvement.[35] Control of women's sexuality and reproduction was central to the colonial relationship the island's residents first experienced with the Spanish, beginning in 1508, and continues to be a key factor in the neocolonial status it maintains with the US.[36] Activist-historian Aurora Levins Morales contends that "from the first treaty with Ponce de Leon to the present, successive invaders of our country have tried to control our people by controlling our wombs."[37] Over the centuries and through today, colonialism, neocolonialism, and capitalism have shaped the sexual and reproductive politics of Puerto Rican women.[38] Beginning with Spanish colonization, legislation was enacted to contain the reproductive and sexual behaviors of women. According to Levins Morales, "From the earliest days an astonishing proportion of the laws, decrees, and government correspondence coming out of Spain concern women's sexuality and reproduction, and their movements from one place to another," all in an effort to prevent interracial sex and reproduction in the colony. Spanish women were encouraged to migrate to the island, and in 1526 a brothel was established to deter

Spanish soldiers from having sex with women from the island. When African slaves were brought to the island, it also became a capital crime for Spanish men to have sex with African women.[39]

Although more research is needed on the control of women's sexuality since Spanish colonization, it has been well documented that for the last 100 years the land and population of Puerto Rico has been used as a base upon which to conduct social and scientific experiments. In 1898, following the Spanish-American War, the US claimed Puerto Rico as its territory. Since then, reproductive and other social experiments on the island were fundamental to the relationship between the US and Puerto Rico. Essentially, Puerto Rico and its people have served as a laboratory for American contraceptive policies and products. For example, the contraceptive foam, the intrauterine device (IUD), and many varieties of the pill were all tested on the bodies of Puerto Rican women before ever making their way to the mainland US market.[40] When laws against birth control prevented medical trials of the contraceptive pill on the mainland US during the 1950s, pharmaceutical companies conducted field trials in Puerto Rico. There were several experimental studies testing various birth control pills that often led to dangerous consequences. In one experimental study of the birth control pill on 838 Puerto Rican women, five women died. The incident was not reported to the Food and Drug Administration (FDA), and the drug was declared safe.[41]

The United States government has also sponsored population control in Puerto Rico. Designed to remedy unemployment, a dragging economy, and "overpopulation," the program centrally promoted sterilization of women.[42] Although federal funding of other contraceptives was not widely available in Puerto Rico until 1968, and abortion was illegal until 1973, tubal ligation—the most popularly performed method of sterilization—had been available, for little or no cost, to most women since 1937. Because sterilization was available in Puerto Rico and not in the United States, Puerto Rican women provided an opportunity for surgeons to practice and refine the technology before it was marketed in the US. Although these policies were generally accepted by Puerto Rico's ruling class, the support of United States funders and policy-makers catapulted their development. In the mid-1940s, Clarence Gamble, a leader in the US eugenics movement, with political connections and a financial empire, implemented a full program of sterilization in Puerto Rico. Within a few years tubal ligation was so common that sterilizing Puerto

Rican women after childbirth was almost routine, with consent often obtained either during labor or right after childbirth. Legally, women were to be "well-advised" of the medical justifications for sterilization, but in reality they seldom were and many of the women didn't understand the procedure was irreversible.

Campaigns to sterilize women were often tied to development. During the 1950s, Operation Bootstrap efforts to boost the Puerto Rican economy encouraged women to enter the workforce to increase manufacturer productivity. As the procedure became common for most Puerto Rican women, "Puerto Rican women became *predisposed* to sterilization because of its widespread availability and convenience, social acceptance, and overall lack of [other] viable options."[43] Some women agreed to sterilizations only after doctors told them that the procedure could be reversed and that they could have children later. Others were simply uninformed, not knowing of or being told about other birth control options. Still others were economically coerced. Such practices continued without much public reaction until Puerto Rican Nationalists and Catholics joined together to expose the genocidal campaign of sterilization. By 1965 about 35 percent of the women in Puerto Rico had been sterilized, two-thirds of them in their 20s.[44]

Although there are important distinctions between the realities of Puerto Ricans living on the island and those who settle in the continental US, statistics show that the reproductive experiences of both groups are similar. Like Puerto Rican women living on the island, those in the New York area have rates of sterilization much higher than the level for all women in the US.[45] It is suspected that, for Puerto Rican women, sterilization has replaced other methods of birth control, as many Puerto Rican women wish to be sterilized whether living in the US or Puerto Rico. Anthropologist Iris Lopez argues that the continued high rates of sterilization for Puerto Rican women living on the island and in the continental US are a direct effect of population control policies of the US government in Puerto Rico.[46]

Mexican American Women in the Southwest

While sexual and reproductive abuse of Native women began during the Spanish colonization of Mexico, Mexican-origin women's reproduction has been an issue of public concern in the United States since at least the turn of the 20th century. During the 1920s, national debates raged about increased immigration to the US and its impact upon the "racial stock" of the nation. Fears grew among whites about the effects immigration might have upon the cultural and social fabric of the country. During the heyday of eugenics, racist ideas about the cultural inferiorities of Mexicans and their excessive fertility became part of the political discourse in the Southwest. Questioning whether newly arrived Mexican immigrants would shed their native (and presumably inferior) cultures to adopt mainstream Anglo-Saxon values, habits, and customs, Americanists (who believed that immigrants could succeed in the United States only if they gave up their own cultural habits and adopted "Anglo" practices) and public health officials designed programs to promote the assimilation process. These programs specifically targeted Mexican immigrant women and their children, identifying them as the primary agents for cultural change.[47] Mexican American families were inculcated with American ideals of family planning and family size in hopes that this would ultimately convince women to have fewer children. While perhaps intended to facilitate their integration into the country, the underlying message of these programs to alter Mexican women's reproductive and childrearing practices was that, without direction, Mexican women would not be proper mothers or citizens.

Like Puerto Rican women, Mexican-origin women were also used as guinea pigs for contraceptive trials. In 1971, Dr. Joseph Goldzheir, of the Southwest Foundation for Research and Education, conducted a study designed to test whether symptoms associated with the pill (nervousness, depression, and headache) were direct effects of the pill or psychological. The trial, sponsored by Syntex Labs and the Agency for International Development, included a total of 398 women, all of whom were poor and 80 percent of whom were Mexican American. Half the women were given one of three actual prescription birth control pills, and the other half a placebo. The women were told that the pills might not be 100 percent effective and that they should also apply vaginal cream. Though the women were never fully informed that they were involved in a medical experiment, Goldzheir argued that the experiment was entirely ethical. When asked why clinic clients were not fully informed, Goldzheir replied, "If you think you can explain a placebo test to women like these, you've never met Mrs. Gomez from the west side." All of the women involved already had two or more children, had gone to the clinic for the specific purpose of obtaining contraceptives to avoid another pregnancy, and had never before used an oral contraceptive. Of the 74 who were prescribed the placebo, 10 became pregnant. As residents of Texas, where abortion was illegal, all were forced to bear children they had specifically visited the clinic to prevent.[48]

Also like Puerto Rican women, throughout the Southwest, Mexican-origin women were targeted for sterilization. Hundreds of women were sterilized without their knowledge between the years of 1969 and 1973 at the University of Southern California–Los Angeles County Medical Center.[49] Many of the women were coerced into signing permission forms during labor, after doctors had threatened to withhold pain medication unless they agreed to sterilization, or were never asked for their consent. They described being approached during labor by primarily English-speaking personnel who coerced and harassed them to "consent" to a tubal ligation. If a patient would not consent, some doctors performed the procedure anyway, without telling the woman. Sometimes doctors would lie, telling a woman that she would die if she were not sterilized, or that the state of California only allowed three children born by cesarean section before sterilization was necessary.

As other chapters in this book document, poor women of color bore the brunt of the abuse, and many have argued that sterilization abuse of poor women and women of color in the 1970s was a direct outgrowth of eugenics.[50] In addition to Puerto Rican and Mexican-origin women, other Latinas, poor women, and women of color were sterilized in teaching hospitals across the nation.[51]

As individuals and in collective organizing, Latina activists have resisted these abuses and promoted reproductive freedom. In past decades, Latinas throughout the nation have planted the seeds of organizing to improve the reproductive and sexual health experiences of their communities.

Latina Organizing for Reproductive Freedom

Latinas' resistance to reproductive oppression occurs as part of broader community resistance to the social, economic, and political exploitation that Latinos face in the US. Alongside other activists, Latinas have actively struggled and organized around labor and education issues, sexism within their own communities, and environmental and social discrimination. And although the historical record may not highlight their achievements, Latinas have also fought for reproductive freedoms.[52]

The widespread exposure of the reproductive abuse of Latinas catalyzed concerted efforts that coalesced as part of the social justice movements of the 1960s and 70s. In that period, Latina activism occurred within and outside of Latino Nationalist and mainstream women's rights organizations, both of which tended to marginalize the issues of women of color. Beginning locally and within grassroots organizations, these efforts provided the basis for the development of a distinctive Latina reproductive rights platform that emerged in the more formal, national-level organizations during the 1980s and 90s.

Organizing During the 1960s and 70s

Throughout the second half of the 20th century Latinas fought for their right to bear children in addition to struggling around a host of other issues such as labor organizing, welfare rights, education, and childcare.[53] At times, Latina efforts to organize around issues of birth control or sexuality from a liberatory framework challenged Nationalist agendas that so often proscribed that women's role in community advancement was to produce lots of children. These pronatalist agendas stemmed from historic and contemporary birth control experimentation and sterilization abuses. Believing that their communities were literally at risk of being demolished by state efforts, Nationalists considered these abuses tantamount to genocide.

However, while Chicano and Puerto Rican Nationalists denounced the abuses that occurred, they ultimately adopted differing stances toward abortion. For example, shortly after the New York State abortion law legalizing pregnancy termination up to 24 weeks went into effect on July 1, 1970, Carmen Rodríguez became the first woman to die from a legal abortion. Leaders of the Young Lords Party (YLP), a Nationalist organization, argued that, within a racist medical system that already mistreated Puerto Ricans, the new abortion law promised to be yet another form of genocide. Upon Rodríguez's death, Gloria Cruz, the YLP health captain, warned:

> A new plan for the limitation of our population was passed—the abortion law. Under this new method we are now supposed to be able to go to any of the city butcher shops (the municipal hospitals) and receive an abortion. These are the same hospitals that have been killing our people for years.[54]

In response to these concerns, the Young Lords opened community-run clinics that offered a broad range of birth control options, including abortion. Similar community-based clinics were opened in Los Angeles, some created by the Brown Berets, a Chicano Nationalist organization like the Young Lords. However, while the Young Lords believed that abortion was an important component of comprehensive health care, the Brown Berets were adamantly anti-abortion and pushed a more traditional pronatalist Nationalist agenda. They argued that all forms of birth control were tools of genocide, and any attempt to end a pregnancy that might result in future revolutionaries was decried.[55]

The divergent stances on abortion taken by two Latino grassroots organizations indicate that there is no singular Latino stance on abortion or reproductive politics. It also demonstrates the difficult situation Latinas and others face in reproductive politics. As expressed in the Young Lords' statement on women:

> Third World sisters are caught up in a complex situation. On the one hand, we feel that genocide is being committed against our people... On the other hand, we believe that abortions should be legal if they are community controlled, if they are safe, if our people are educated about the risks, and if doctors do not sterilize our sisters while performing abortions.[56]

While Puerto Rican women were able to successfully integrate the struggle for reproductive freedom into the Young Lords Party platform, Chicanas more often developed their own complementary organizations. However, they did not retreat into a separate entity but continued to demand that so called "women's" issues be acknowledged in the struggle for Chicano equality. Despite efforts to stifle women's issues in the Chicano movement, the first National Chicana Conference was held in May 1971 in Houston, Texas. At this meeting, discussions of abortion, birth control, marriage, and other feminist issues were central.

In her recollections of the proceedings at the conference, Francisca Flores regards issues of family size as fundamentally an issue of bodily self-determination:[57]

> The issue of birth control, abortions, information on sex, and the pill are considered "white" women's lib issues and should be rejected by Chicanas according to the Chicano philosophy which believes that the Chicana women's place is in the home and that her role is that of a mother with a

large family. Women who do not accept this philosophy are charged with betrayal of our culture and heritage—OUR CULTURE HELL![58]

On another level, part of Chicana efforts to fight for their reproductive autonomy was to counter the Nationalist narrative, which prescribed that their role in the revolution was to produce lots of brown babies. Chicana writers such as Sylvia Delgado questioned the Nationalist prerogative of procreation:

> We accuse genocide. La Raza's cry. So we turn to increasing the population. But what kind of padres are we, if we are going to see our sons raised in slavery, with cut-rate education, poverty, and to watch our children die? I say no to fools who say women are tools for copulation and birth. Unwanted babies are not loved in the mother nor by those who must toil for them. Don't people think that 15- and 16-year-olds are listening to their ban on birth control? While parents and peers taboo sex, they know what they are feeling in sexual terms. Are we going to go down as saying intercourse is to make babies while in our heads we are glad that in the past lays we had, there was no pregnancy?[59]

Breaking the silence about Chicana sexuality and the right to make their own reproductive decisions, activists ignited a discussion that has helped to envision different roles for women from those traditionally defined by the Nationalist movement. The development of a Chicana feminist consciousness led to the establishment of many new grassroots organizations focused upon the issues women found central to gaining equality. Latinas became involved in all areas of women's organizing—in domestic violence and sexual assault movements, educational and social policy efforts, and the fight for welfare rights.

Opposing Sterilization Abuse

Latinas across ethnicities in Los Angeles, San Francisco, and New York came together to organize legal, grassroots, and legislative measures against the sterilization abuse of Latinas and other women of color. While individual efforts took place on both the East and West Coasts, ultimately Latinas began communicating and working together. In New York, many Puerto Rican anti-sterilization abuse activists were previously involved in similar organizing in Puerto Rico. Others had come to be involved in reproductive rights issues as an outgrowth of their work within the Puerto Rican Socialist Party. Similar to the women within the Chicano movement, many women struggled to bring women's issues to the forefront of a decidedly Nationalist agenda. With reproductive rights at the center of their women's platform, women like Maria Sanchez, Martina Santiago, Elsa Rios, and Eugenia Acuña organized and attended demonstrations and mobilized against sterilization abuse and the lack of informed consent procedures.[60]

The Committee to End Sterilization Abuse (CESA) was founded in 1974, spearheaded by Dr. Helen Rodríguez-Trías, Dr. Raymond Rakow, and Maritza Arrastia, editor of *Claridad*. Although CESA was a multi-ethnic coalition, Latinas were crucial to the group's efforts. Comprised of a coalition of individuals and groups, including the Puerto Rican Independence Movement, the Puerto Rican Socialist Party, the Center for Constitutional Rights, the Marxist Education Collective, and the Committee for the Decolonization of Puerto Rico, the group was formed on the basis of rumors of sterilization abuse and recent statistics showing that sterilizations in public hospitals in primarily Puerto Rican neighborhoods had increased 180 percent. CESA initially organized to collect information about sterilization to document abuse and educate others about the issue, developing fact sheets and statistics. Largely due to CESA's mobilization and the community outcry against sterilization abuse, sterilization guidelines for the state of New York were developed, with CESA's influence strongly represented on the advisory committee. These laws and regulations ultimately became a model for many other state regulations and the federal regulations that were later established.

In 1979, CESA united with the Committee for Abortion Rights and Against Sterilization Abuse (CARASA) and several other organizations, such as the Mexican American Women's National Association, the Center for Constitutional Rights, and the Chicana Nurses Association in a coalition to monitor the compliance of New York City hospitals with new city laws. This New York coalition became part of the Reproductive Rights National Network (R2N2) in 1981.[61]

Meanwhile, much of the activism in California revolved around a particular case of abuse at Los Angeles County Medical Center and the lawsuits that followed. In 1975, 11 Mexican-origin women filed a civil suit against the Los Angeles County Medical Center, claiming that each of them had been involuntarily sterilized between 1971 and 1974. The women asked the court to require the US Department of Health, Education, and Welfare to mandate that hospitals receiving federal funds provide sterilization counseling and consent forms in Spanish. The court ruled against the women, attributing the nonconsensual sterilization to a "communication breakdown" between the women and their doctors. The appeal of the court's decision was also denied. In large part, this legal effort, and the connected attempts to bring attention to the issue and raise money for the case, resulted from an already established network of Chicana grassroots organizations fighting for issues of childcare, health care, and educational opportunities for their children.[62]

The Mexican American Legal Defense and Education Fund (MALDEF) Chicana Rights Project worked with this network to file a petition with the State of California Department of Health for the adoption of more strenuous regulation of consent procedures for sterilization operations. Organizers in San Francisco and around the state turned to CESA in New York for advice and assistance. Although Latina organizing against sterilization abuse occurred on both coasts, this was perhaps the first prolonged national communication between Latinas concerned about reproductive and sexual rights.

In addition to legislative battles, Latina activists staged protests, held rallies, circulated petitions, and gave speeches in order to educate the public and the women's movement about sterilization abuse in their communities. They also broadened the meaning of reproductive rights and identified the value of women organizing along racial-ethnic lines. As Dagmaris Cabezas wrote in 1977:

> This is a struggle where Puerto Rican women have to lead the way, because only the Puerto Rican woman can best understand her own reality. I don't think any one has the right to tell her what position she must take. There are women who opt for sterilization or abortion because their economic reality pushes them in that direction. Therefore, one can't separate that struggle from the struggle for better day care centers, for equal pay for equal work, for a better education, and for all rights that a woman must have to make a free choice in this society.[63]

Although not solely Latina, CESA was perhaps the most significant reproductive rights development on the East Coast, and a significant step in the development of a national Latina reproductive rights agenda because it was founded and largely run by Latinas. According to Eugenia Acuña, who was a member of a CESA chapter in Connecticut, CESA was important because for the first time she was able to connect issues of national liberation and women and work with other Latinas:

> We did research on sterilization rates in New Haven. We organized women in the community and got at least one community clinic to look at what it was doing. The thing about CESA that was so important was that here were some Latinas who were also feminist, and cared about reproductive rights but from a Latina point of view. That was like coming home.[64]

For others like Acuña, coming together with other Latinas to struggle against reproductive abuse was a significant event. Until that point, many Latina health workers and activists had experienced isolation. With new connections and experience working together, CESA led to the founding of the first Latina-specific reproductive rights organizations in the US and to coalition work among various organizations.

Organizing from the 1980s to the Present

Before discussing the evolution of a number of Latina reproductive health entities over the past 30 years, it is important to emphasize that, even before Latinas came together to work in collaboration, many were already individually doing the hard work of health education or providing health services in their communities, often in addition to activism against reproductive abuse. Usually working in isolation, and with very limited resources or support, during the 1980s and 90s a cadre of Latina health professionals grew across the nation. Those who were drawn to women's health education and services were usually the first to develop a reproductive and sexual health curriculum for Latinas and the only ones in their clinics or organizations voicing those concerns.

Many of these health educators worked in both Latino communities and mainstream reproductive rights networks. For example, Eugenia Acuña, a Chilean who migrated to the US and received a masters in public health from the University of Puerto Rico, worked in a wide variety of positions in New York City, some at the same time: health department, bureau of maternity services, community centers, coordinator of Hunter College reproductive rights education project, health education, and the International Reproductive Rights and Health Action Group. Many other Latinas followed similar paths in their own communities, providing health care information at different forums, developing curricula, and training other educators. As these practitioners developed their expertise and became acquainted with one another, many realized the need to begin organizing formally together to share information, combine agendas, and provide mutual support.

The Latina Roundtable on Health and Reproductive Rights (LRHRR) was founded in October 1989 by a number of women—mostly Puerto Rican and Dominican—including Jenny Rivera, Diana Correa, Celina Romany, and Elsa Rios.[65] These community leaders were concerned about the health crisis among Latinas and felt the need to organize a Latina response to escalating attacks against their reproductive rights. Being the only Latina reproductive rights organization in New York, LRHRR quickly emerged as a major community education and health policy group, addressing Latina health and reproductive rights issues on a local, state, and national level. At the time, LRHRR was the only visible women of color organization in the state exclusively devoted to advocating for increased access to a full range of quality and affordable health services and reproductive options for Latinas. Its first executive director was Wilma Montañez, a longtime reproductive rights advocate who started her career as a community health worker and family planning counselor working with youth and immigrant communities. Her involvement with issues of HIV/AIDS and women, along with her commitment to include community-based input in public policy, positioned the organization as a critical player in the reproductive rights movement, locally and nationally. Composed of Latina health providers, attorneys, community activists, educators, and policy analysts, the LRHRR was instrumental in providing a Latina analysis and action plan on the most restrictive reproductive rights policies of the late 1980s and 90s, which included waiting periods for abortion, parental involvement in abortion decisions, welfare reform, mandatory HIV/AIDS testing, and treatment of pregnant women. Although many social service agencies within the New York City Latino community were concerned with some of these issues, there was reluctance to adding a gender lens to issues such as HIV/AIDS; reproductive rights continued to be considered a white woman's issue that did have a place on the long list of other community concerns.

The LRHRR's coalition-building and networking efforts provided a safe place for Latinas to meet and collaboratively develop advocacy strategies to be used to influence public policy. LRHRR meetings provided much-needed support to activists who felt that their desires to include and strengthen the voice of women within their own organizations were not always welcomed. One of LRHRR's most memorable activities was organizing clinic defense efforts in the South Bronx in response to Operation Rescue in July 1992. This event marked the first time a group of Latinos took a public position defending abortion services in the community. When Montañez left LRHRR in 1996 to become the reproductive rights program officer at the Jessie Smith Noyes Foundation, Luz Rodríguez took the helm. Under her leadership, LRHRR received a grant from the Ford Foundation that helped initiate the SisterSong Collective, which has since gained national recognition as a force for women of color working for reproductive justice. Consistent with other nonprofit organizations with fragile infrastructures, LRHRR closed its doors in 1998. During its short stint, LRHRR succeeded in proving that Latinas on a local level could have an impact on national policies and, most importantly, that Latinas are involved in the reproductive rights movement.[66]

In the 1990s, Amigas Latinas en Acción, a Latina feminist collective in Boston, advanced its Latina perspective on reproductive health through Mujeres en Acción Pro Salud Reproductiva: Northeast Project on Latina Women and Reproductive Health.[67] They used data collected from women to advocate for policy changes. They promoted Latina leadership and distributed bilingual, bicultural informational materials on reproductive health and sexuality. Ultimately, these programs developed into a support group in which women discussed issues of sexuality and the body. Many participants said it was the first time that they had ever talked about such topics, and its developers considered it "the first step in empowering women to articulate their unique identities and to reclaim their rights as Puerto Rican women."[68]

National Latina Institute for Reproductive Health

The National Latina Institute for Reproductive Health (NLIRH) established itself in 1994 as the first independent national organization for Latinas on reproductive rights issues. Initiated by the Hispanic Outreach Project of Catholics for a Free Choice in 1991, its primary objectives were to provide information and technical assistance to national Latina/o organizations that wished to work on issues of reproductive health, and to promote the involvement of Latina/o organizations in pro-choice efforts. Starting with a four-member advisory committee, the group rapidly grew.[69] Developing audiovisual and written materials that encompassed the cultural attitudes, values, perspectives, and languages of Latinas with regard to issues of choice, the project was also centrally involved in the mainstream pro-choice movement. The NLIRH newsletter, *Instantes*, featured educational articles about reproductive health and rights from a Latina viewpoint and included legislative analysis. The group's first director, Aracely Panameño, developed the organization to more broadly define its mission to include a broad array of health issues that spoke to the diversity of Latina/o communities in the US.

From 1996 through 1999, the NLIRH held a series of forums across the nation to bring Latinas interested in working on reproductive and general health issues together and to promote regional and national collaboration in the development of a Latina reproductive politics platform. The NLIRH agenda was driven by the needs and voices of Latinas at the grassroots rather than being directed from the top down.[70] The goal was to encourage the formation of state coalitions, networking circles, and statewide reproductive rights agendas. The delegates invited to each forum included health care providers and policy-makers, teachers, clinic staff, activists, and others concerned with Latina reproductive rights. They presented a summary of the health status of Latinas in their region and strategized about how to implement policy changes based upon their findings. Regional health leaders also addressed the delegates and spoke of the reproductive health concerns experienced in the region. For example, Olga Sanchez from the Mexican American Legal Defense and Education Fund discussed the ties between welfare reform and anti-immigrant legislation in California. Other speakers showed how access to dental care and environmental degradation are related to reproductive health. Skill-building for those who provide health services to Latino populations was also part of the agenda.

The forums brought Latina reproductive health practitioners together for the first time ever and planted seeds for activist collaboration in advocating for Latina reproductive health rights in their own communities. However, maintaining collaborations proved difficult, as scheduling, distance, and lack of financial and other resources prevented groups from developing. Many regions struggled to continue this work beyond the forums. In 1998, the NLIRH expanded its efforts to strengthen and institutionalize state coalitions. By providing funding and technical assistance, it hoped to empower state coalitions to undertake outreach and educational projects and to participate in local and state health policy discussions. This effort was deliberately aimed to "grow" the movement: "Recognizing the high rate of burnout experienced by many of us involved in activist work, NLIRH's intent in working with coalitions was to create permanent, staffed, and funded entities designed around a common overall goal—to improve Latinas' health."[71] Unfortunately, NLIRH's quick expansion, together with its ever-broadening scope, ultimately spread the still-young organization too thin. Although the NLIRH was forced to close its doors for a few years, it reopened in 2003, and recently moved into the forefront of organizing for Latina reproductive and sexual freedom as one of the co-sponsors of the 2004 March for Women's Lives. Moreover, the NLIRH has spawned other organizations, one of them being the Colorado Organization for Latina Opportunity and Reproductive Rights (COLOR), which is featured in Chapter 14.

The two case studies which follow demonstrate that Latina efforts have successfully reframed reproductive issues to reflect their cultural and political realities and developed innovative organizing strategies and principles. Perhaps more importantly, as Dr. Helen Rodríguez-Trías pointed out, "The ingenuity of women in grassroots community organizations was the main factor enabling the continuation of reproductive health services to women."[72] The next chapter discusses the oldest organization working on behalf of Latinas and their reproductive rights—the National Latina Health Organization.

NOTES

* This essay is written en memoria de Helen Rodríguez-Trías, who was dedicated to improving the health conditions and life circumstances of US Latinas. In the 1970s, Rodríguez-Trías spoke out tirelessly against sterilization abuse of Puerto Ricans. A founder of the Committee to End Sterilization Abuse, her efforts were crucial in establishing informed consent guidelines for sterilization that protect all women. Throughout her career she was active in the Women's Health Movement, serving on the boards of the National Women's Health Network and the Boston Women's Health Book Collective. An expert in maternal and child health, she was the first female director of pediatrics at Lincoln Hospital in the Bronx, New York in 1970, the first Latina medical director of the New York State Department of Health AIDS Institute in the 1980s, and the first Latina president of the American Public Health Association in 1992. In 1996, she helped found and co-direct the Pacific Institute of Women's Health, a non-profit dedicated to improving women's health and well-being. She was awarded a presidential Citizen's Medal of Honor for her work on behalf of women and children, AIDS patients, and the poor. An inspiration to many, this history is written so that her work, and the efforts of so many others who strive to better the life circumstances of their communities will not go unknown.

1 For example, Angela Pattatucci-Aragon's entry "Hispanic/Latina Women and Reproductive Rights" in the *Historical and Multicultural Encyclopedia of Women's Reproductive Rights in the US*, ed. Judith Baer (Westport, CT: Greenwood Press, 2002), 103–106, asserts that: "While reproductive autonomy has been top priority among non-Hispanic feminists, it has been of secondary importance to Latina feminists. They have concentrated upon basic survival issues such as adequate childcare, and public safety. Thus, Latinas have often been the subjects, but not the participants, in discussions focusing on reproductive rights."

2 Elizabeth Sutherland Martínez, "Listen Up, Anglo Sisters," in *De Colores Means All of Us: Latina Views for a Multi-Colored Century* (Cambridge, MA: South End Press, 1998), 188.

3 The terms Latino and Hispanic were created by the US government to categorize people of Latin American descent living in the US. However, as markers they erase differences in national origin and racial/ethnic status, citizenship status, etc., and promote the representation of Latinos as a monolithic group. Moreover, while they may be defined as such through this definition, individuals who officially fall into this group may or may not personally identify as Latina/o, though research shows that Latinos are increasingly self-identifying as Latina/o: see Nilda Flores-Gonzalez, "The Racialization of Latinos: The Meaning of Latino Identity for the Second Generation," *Latino Studies Journal* 10, no. 3 (1999): 3–31 and Suzanne Oboler, *Ethnic Labels, Latino Lives: Identity and the Politics of Representation in the US* (Minneapolis: University of Minnesota Press, 1995).

4   US Census Bureau, *The Hispanic Population: Census 2000 Brief* (Washington, DC: Bureau of the Census, May 2001), 1.

5   Ibid., 2.

6   The term, "generic Latina" is borrowed from a play with the same title by Chicago's Teatro Luna, an all-Latina troupe. Their play demonstrates that media images often treat Latinas as caricatures and stereotypes, flattening the deep diversity within Latina cultures. Judith Ortiz Cofer also writes of the homogenization of Latinas in "The Myth of the Latin Woman: I Just Met a Girl Named Maria," in *One World, Many Cultures*, ed. Stuart Hirschberg and Terry Hirschberg (Boston: Allyn and Bacon, 1998), 167–175.

7   Susana Chavez-Silverman, "Tropicolada: Inside the US Latino/a Gender B(l)ender," in *Tropicalizations: Transcultural Representations of Latinidad (Re-Encounters with Colonialism)*, ed. Frances R. Aparicio and Susana Chavez-Silverman (Hanover, NH: University Press of New England for Dartmouth College, 1997).

8   Ana Maria Juarez and Stella Beatriz Kerl, "What Is the Right (White) Way to Sexual? Reconceptualizing Latina Sexuality," *Aztlán* 28, no. 1 (2003): 7–37.

9   Lourdes Miranda King, "Puertorriqueñas in the US," *Civil Rights Digest* 6, no. 3 (1974): 20–27.

10   Laura Briggs, *Reproducing Empire: Race, Sex, and US Imperialism in Puerto Rico* (Berkeley: University of California Press, 2002), 4.

11   For an extended discussion, see Briggs, *Reproducing Empire*.

12   Sally J. Andrade, "Social Science Stereotypes of Mexican American Women: Policy Implications for Research," *Hispanic Journal of Behavioral Sciences* 4, no. 2 (1982): 223–244.

13   Passed in 1994, but later overturned, Proposition 187 was a statewide referendum that barred undocumented immigrants from public services such as non-emergency health care, welfare and public schools.

14   The so-called "Save Our State" initiative constructed the high fertility of Mexican women as emblematic of the myriad problems caused by increasing immigration from Mexico.

15   Leith Mullings, "Images, Ideology, and Women of Color," in *Women of Color in US Society*, ed. Maxine Baca Zinn and Bonnie Thornton Dill (Philadelphia: Temple University Press, 1994), 265–289.

16   Susan C. M. Scrimshaw, Ruth E. Zambrana and Christine Dunkel-Schetter, "Issues in Latino Women's Health: Myths and Challenges," in *Women's Health: Complexities and Differences*, ed. Sheryl Burt Ruzek et al. (Columbus: Ohio State University Press, 1997), 329–347.

17   While I will highlight some of the major trends in the reproductive health status of Latinas here, a thorough analysis is beyond the scope of this chapter. For a more complete assessment of the status of Latina reproductive health, see Aida L. Giachello, "The Reproductive Years: The Health of Latinas," in *Latina Health in the United States: A Public Health Reader*, ed. Carlos W. Molina and Marilyn Aquirre-Molina (San Francisco: Jossey-Bass, 2003), 77–131.

18   Hortensia Amaro and Adela de la Torre, "Public Health Needs and Scientific Opportunities in Research on Latinas," *American Journal of Public Health* 92, no. 4 (2002): 526.

19   Although Latinos have very high labor force participation, they are in great part members of the working poor and are concentrated in low wage jobs that do not offer health insurance. In 1995, 21 percent of Latinos ages 15–44 reported no health insurance coverage, compared with 7.5 percent of whites and 9.3 percent of African Americans of that age group. (J. Abma et al., "Fertility, Family Planning and Women's Health: New Data from the 1995 National Survey of Family Growth," *Vital and Health Statistics* 23 (1997): 19. Also see de Adela de la Torre et al., "The Health Insurance Status of US Latino Women: A profile from the 1982–1984 Hispanic HHANES," *American Journal of Public Health* 86, no. 4 (1996): 534–537.

20   Kathryn P. Derose and David W. Baker, "Limited English Proficiency and Latinos' Use of Physician Services," *Medical Care Research and Review* 57, no. 1 (2000): 76–91.

21   Hortensia Amaro, "Psychological Determinants of Abortion Attitudes Among Mexican American Women" (PhD dissertation, University of California Los Angeles, 1982) and Giachello, "The Reproductive Years."

22   This may partially be explained by the fact that most Latino births are to Mexican American women, who represent roughly 70 percent of Latinas of childbearing age. They also have the highest fertility rate of any racial/ethnic group. Birthrates (the number of births per 1,000 population) of Latino origin were as follows, 26.4 for Mexican Americans, 19.0 for Puerto Ricans, 10.0 for Cubans, and 23.2 for Central and South American women in the United States. Stephanie J. Ventura et al., "Births: Final Data for 1998," *National Vital Statistics Reports* 48, no. 3 (2000), http://www.cdc.gov/nchs/data/nvsrnvsr48/nvs48_03.pdf.

23   Ibid.

24   Ibid. There are significant intra-group differences; however, "in 1998, about 6.3 percent of all Latino mothers had late or no prenatal care at all, compared to 2.4 percent and 7 percent of white and African American mothers, respectively. Within the Latino population, Mexican American mothers (6.8 percent), those from Central and South America (4.9 percent), and Puerto Ricans (5.1 percent) were most likely to delay or not receive prenatal care at all. The percentage for Cuban mothers was the lowest of any other racial and ethnic group (1.2 percent)." Mexican mothers reported the lowest use of early prenatal care (72.8 percent).

25   A. Handler et al., "Women's Satisfaction with Prenatal Care Settings: A Focus Group Study," *Birth* 23, no. 1 (1996): 31–37.

26   A. Napoles-Springer and E. Pérez-Stable, "Risk Factors for Invasive Cervical Cancer in Latino Women," *Journal of Medical Systems* 20, no. 5 (1996): 277–294.

27   Adaljiza Sosa Riddell, "The Bioethics of Reproductive Technologies: Impacts and Implications for Latinas," in *Chicana Critical Issues*, ed. Norma Alarcon

(Berkeley: Third Woman Press, 1993), 189; See also Nancy San Martin, "Children of the Fields; Birth Defects Occur at an Alarming Rate Among Guatemalan Migrant Workers," South Florida *Sun-Sentinel*, July 14, 1996.

28   Centers for Disease Control and Prevention, *HIV/AIDS Surveillance Report: US HIV/AIDS Cases Reported Through December 1998* (Atlanta: CDC, 1999) cited in Giachello, "The Reproductive Years," 119.

29   Centers for Disease Control and Prevention, *National HIV Seroprevalence Surveys: Summary for Results of Data from Serosurveillance Activities Through 1998* (Atlanta: CDC, 1999) cited in Giachello, "The Reproductive Years," 121.

30   See Beatríz Pesquera and Denise Segura, "'It's Her Body, It's Definitely Her Right': Chicanas/Latinas and Abortion," *Voces: A Journal of Latina Studies* 2, no. 1: 103–127, for an overview of recent studies on Latina attitudes towards abortion. Also see National Latina Institute for Reproductive Health, *Latinas and Abortion* (Washington, DC: NLIRH, 1999).

31   Physicians for Reproductive Choice and Health and the Alan Guttmacher Institute, *Overview of Abortion in the US* (2003), http://www.prch.org. Also see Pamela Erickson and Celia Patricia Kaplan, "Latinos and Abortion," in *The New Civil War: The Psychology, Culture, and Politics of Abortion*, ed. L.J. Beckman and S.M. Harvey (Washington, DC: American Psychological Association, 1998).

32   Alan Guttmacher Institute, *Facts in Brief: Induced Abortion*, http://www.agi-usa.org/pubs/fb_induced_abortion.html

33   See Ellen Frankfort with Frances Kissling, *Rosie: The Investigation of a Wrongful Death* (New York: Dial Press, 1979).

34   Candida Flores et al., "La Mujer Puertorriqueña, Su Cuerpo, y Su Lucha por la Vida: Experiences With Empowerment in Hartford, Connecticut," in *From Abortion to Reproductive Freedom*, ed. Marlene Gerber Fried (Boston: South End Press, 1990), 221.

35   Briggs, *Reproducing Empire*.

36   For a discussion of the neocolonial status of Puerto Rico, see Pedro A. Cabán, *Constructing a Colonial People: Puerto Rico and the US, 1898–1932* (Boulder: Westview Press, 1999); and Edwin and Edgardo Meléndez, *Colonial Dilemma: Critical Perspectives on Contemporary Puerto Rico* (Boston: South End Press, 1993).

37   Aurora Levins Morales, "Piecing a History Together: the Women of Boriken," *Women's Review of Books* 9, nos. 10–11 (1992): 7.

38   Yamila Azize-Vargas and Luis A. Avilés, "Abortion in Puerto Rico: The Limits of a Colonial Legality," *Puerto Rico Health Sciences Journal* 17 (1998):   27–36; Iris Lopez, "An Ethnography of the Medicalization of Puerto Rican Women's Reproduction," in *Pragmatic Women and Body Politics*, ed. Margaret Lock and Patricia A. Kaufert (New York: Cambridge Studies in Medical Anthropology, 1997), 240–259; and Briggs, *Reproducing Empire*.

39   Levins Morales, "Piecing a History Together," 7.

40   Bonnie Mass, "Puerto Rico: A Case Study of Population Control," *Latin American Perspectives* 5, no. 4 (1977): 73.

41   Ibid., 26.

42   Briggs, *Reproducing Empire.*

43   Lopez, "An Ethnography," 242–243.

44   Ibid., 240–241.

45   Joseph J. Salvo, Mary G. Powers, and Rosemary Santana Cooney, "Contraceptive Use and Sterilization Among Puerto Rican Women," *Family Planning Perspectives* 24, no. 5 (1992): 219–223.

46   Lopez, "An Ethnography," 240–241.

47   George J. Sanchez Jr., "'Go After the Women': Americanization and the Mexican Immigrant Woman, 1915–1929," in *Unequal Sisters: A Multicultural Reader in US Women's History*, ed. Ellen Carol Dubois and Vicki L. Ruiz (New York: Routledge, 1990), 250–263.

48   Goldzheir, who was considered a pioneer in testing oral contraceptives and was a consultant to several drug companies, refused to accept any responsibility for the impact of the experiment on these women's lives, attributing their pregnancies to their carelessness in using the cream. He announced his findings at the American Fertility Society meetings in New Orleans in April 1971. From "Placebo Stirs Pill 'Side Effects'" in *Medical Wold News* (1971), 19.

49   Carlos G. Velez-Ibañez, "Se Me Acabó La Canción: An Ethnography of Non-Consenting Sterilizations Among Mexican Women in Los Angeles," in *Mexican Women in the US: Struggles Past and Present*, ed. Magdalena Mora and Adelaida Del Castillo (Los Angeles: Chicano Studies Research Center, UCLA, 1980), 71–91; Virgina Espino, "Women Sterilized as You Give Birth: Forced Sterilization and Chicana Resistance in the 1970s," in *Las Obreras: Chicana Politics of Work and Family*, ed. Vicki Ruiz (Los Angeles: UCLA Chicano Studies Research Center Publications, 2000); Elena R. Gutiérrez, "Policing 'Pregnant Pilgrims': Situating the Sterilization Abuse of Mexican-Origin Women in Los Angeles County," in *Women, Health, and Nation: Canada and the US Since 1945*, ed. Georgina Feldberg et al. (Montreal: McGill-Queen's University Press, 2003), 379–403.

50   Adelaida Del Castillo, "Sterilization: An Overview," in *Mexican women in the United States: Struggles Past and Present*, ed. Magdalena Mora and Adelaida Del Castillo (Los Angeles: UCLA Chicano Studies Research Center Publications, 1980): 65–69.

51   For example, Dominican women were also sterilized at Gouvenor Hospital and Beth Israel Hospital on the Lower East Side of New York City. From "Sterilization: Dominican Women in NYC," in *Triple Jeopardy* (December 1973).

52   Although this history focuses on public organizing, we must begin to acknowledge the other ways in which women have actively participated in the struggle for reproductive rights. As suggested by Mary Pardo, women's activism not only occurs at the organizational level but also often takes place in individual

interaction. Latinas are politically active not only in public spheres—for example, in mobilizing a grassroots effort to stop the building of an incinerator in their neighborhood—but also in their everyday lives. See Mary Pardo, "Creating Community: Mexican American Women in Eastside Los Angeles," in *Community Activism and Feminist Politics: Organizing Across Race, Class, and Gender*, ed. Nancy A. Naples (New York: Routledge, 1998), 266–300. For example, keeping the control of reproductive and sexual health in their own hands has been a priority for many Latinas. The birthing of children by *parteras*, or midwives, occurs in many Latino communities. Moreover, as Latinos are increasingly dependent upon Western medicine, women's friendship and communication networks provide another primary means of obtaining and sharing information about health care options and negotiation of the health care system. These "informal" communications also serve an important purpose of allowing women to exchange important information with others, such as whether experiences at particular health clinics have been positive or negative, or in which hospitals Latinos have been treated poorly.

53   For a more elaborate discussion of Chicana feminist organizing see Vicki L. Ruiz, "La Nueva Chicana: Women and the Movement," in *From Out of the Shadows: Mexican Women in Twentieth-Century America*, ed. Vicki L. Ruiz (New York: Oxford University Press, 1998), 99–126; and Denise A. Segura and Beatriz M. Pesquera, "Beyond Indifference and Antipathy: The Chicana Movement and Chicana Feminist Discourse," in *The Chicano Studies Reader: An Anthology of Aztlán, 1970–2000*, ed. Chon A. Noriega et al. (Los Angeles: UCLA Chicano Studies Research Center Publications, 2001), 389–410.

54   Gloria Cruz, "Murder at Lincoln," *Palante* (July 1970): 3, cited in Jennifer A. Nelson, "Abortions Under Community Control: Feminism, Nationalism, and the Politics of Reproduction Among New York City's Young Lords," *Journal of Women's History* 13, no. 1 (2001): 114.

55   The roles of women in the Young Lords Party and within Chicano Nationalist groups such as the Brown Berets varied; differences arose in part, but not completely, due to the groups' differing perspectives on women's roles in revolution. Young Lords had a very outwardly promujer position—see their position paper on women. For more on the Young Lord's position on reproductive politics, see Nelson, "Abortions Under Community Control." For more on Chicano Nationalist positions see, Elena R. Gutiérrez, *Fertile Matters: The Racial Politics of Mexican Origin Women's Reproduction* (Austin: University of Texas Press, Forthcoming).

56   The Young Lords Party position is cited in Dorinda Moreno Gladden's book, *Mujer en Pie de Lucha* (Mexico City: Espina del Norte Publications, 1973), 53–54.

57   For more extensive coverage of the events at the Conferencia de Mujeres Por La Raza, see Anonymous, "Chicanas of Today Say What They Want," *El Grito Del Norte*, October 2, 1971, 16; Elizabeth Olivarez, "Women's Rights and the Mexican American Woman," *Regeneración* 2, no. 4 (1974): 40–42.

58   Francisca Flores, "Conference of Mexican Women: *Un Remolino*," *Regeneración* 1 (1971): 1–5.

59   Sylvia Delgado, "Chicana: The Forgotten Woman," *Regeneración 2* (1971): 3.

60   Elsa Rios, interview with Elena R. Gutiérrez, September 4, 2002.

61   Linda Gordon, *Woman's Body, Woman's Right: A Social History of Birth Control in America*, rev. ed. (New York: Penguin Books, 1990), 434–435.

62   For more thorough discussions of these events, see Espino, "Women Sterilized" and Gutiérrez, "Policing Pregnant Pilgrims."

63   Dagmaris Cabezas, "Mañana is Not Good Enough," *Nuestro* 1, no. 4 (1997): 19.

64   Eugenia Acuña, interview by Elena R. Gutiérrez, September, 4, 2002.

65   Wilma Montanez, interview by Elena R. Gutiérrez, July 30, 2002.

66   Ibid.

67   This project was based out of the Hispanic Health Council in Hartford, Connecticut.

68   Flores et al., "La Mujer Puertorriqueña," 227.

69   The committee was originally comprised of Sally Martínez (vice president of the Women's Division of the League of United Latin American Citizens), Bambi Cárdenas Ramírez (member of the US Commission on Civil Rights), Alice Cardona (assistant director of the New York State Division of Women) and Aida Giachello (professor of sociology at the Jane Addams School of Social Work at the University of Illinois, Chicago).

70   NLIRH, "West Latina Reproductive Health Forum: Conference Proceedings" (draft, June 1998), 7.

71   COLOR, letter to forum participants, April 1998.

72   Helen Rodríguez-Trías, "Women Are Organizing: Environmental and Population Policies Will Never Be the Same," *American Journal of Public Health* 84, no. 9 (1994): 1379–1382.

13

The National Latina Health Organization

Organización Nacional de la Salud de la Mujer Latina

O N International Women's Day, March 8, 1986, four Latinas pooled their collective strength to found the National Latina Health Organization (NLHO). The NLHO combines direct service with public policy and health advocacy and was modeled on the National Black Women's Health Project (NBWHP). The group promotes self-empowerment for Latinas through educational programs, outreach, and research. The women have built a nontraditional organizational culture which, together with the programs, reflects a direct understanding of and appreciation for the complexity of the roles and status of Latinas, their family health and reproductive issues, and their socioeconomic realities.

Prior to creating the NLHO, each of the founders had previous experience working to improve the health of her community. Elisabeth Gastelumendi, a Peruvian immigrant, was a longtime community activist. Alicia Bejarano was a health educator at Planned Parenthood where she designed the sex education program *Entre Nosotros* (Between Us) for Latino families. Luz Alvarez Martínez worked at IBM but maintained connections to the women's health community and was on the board of Berkeley Women's Health Collective. Paulita Ortiz was actively involved in Re-evaluation Counseling (RC). She grew up translating for

*This chapter was researched and written by Elena R. Gutiérrez.

her Spanish-speaking parents, who were migrant farmworkers. Doing this she realized the need for bilingual and accessible health care:

> I was the interpreter in the family very early on...As a child, it always felt like a big project to communicate for the parents. So I remember I was feeling like it was a matter of life or death, and I wanted to make sure my mother and father got the health care we needed...Children have to take care of their parents.[1]

Through working at the Berkeley Women's Health Collective (BWHC), Alvarez Martínez heard Byllye Avery speak about the upcoming first national conference of the National Black Women's Health Project in 1983. When Alvarez Martínez learned that the conference was being created for African American women by African American women, she knew that she had to go. She borrowed money from a fellow BWHC board member and made her first trip across the country. For Alvarez Martínez, the conference was a life-changing experience: "It was amazing to see workshops facilitated by African American women—women of color were doing everything, although I don't remember seeing any Latinas. I kept thinking, why am I here?"[2] As she has come to believe, Alvarez Martínez was there to experience and meet people who would eventually be instrumental in establishing the NLHO. At the conference, Alvarez Martínez learned about the group's model of Self-Help—women telling their stories and coming to realizations about their own lives. The women were using Self-Help as a model to connect the personal and the political, the micro and the macro. After the conference, Alvarez Martínez attended a gathering hosted by Avery, where she got to know several women more closely and maintained strong ties with them after the conference. Oakland happened to be one of the places where the NBWHP was developing a state chapter of the organization. Alvarez Martínez would attend NBWHP events and often volunteered for the project. She was close to several of the organization's local members. Although she was invited to join as a founding member of the NBWHP-Oakland chapter, Alvarez Martínez declined because she was not African American. As an advocate for coalition and solidarity work, Alvarez Martínez implicitly understood the value of race-based organizing. She supported the work they were doing to create an African American women's organization, not a women of color organization.

Following Lillie Allen's recommendation, however, she joined a women's group based on RC in Oakland. There she met Paulita Ortiz, who was a trainer of the Self-Help process. When Alvarez Martínez moderated a panel on women of color and reproductive health for International Women's Day in 1986, she invited Ortiz to attend with her. Alicia Bejarano, who worked at Planned Parenthood, was also in the audience. After the panel Bejarano ran up to Alvarez Martínez, very enthusiastic about the idea of women of color directly addressing their own health concerns that the panel had generated. She wanted to see something similar happen for Latinas, in Spanish. Bejarano, Alvarez Martínez, and Ortiz had lunch together later that day, and shared their vision of creating a space where Latinas could address their own health concerns. From that moment, the NLHO grew from an idea into an organization.

A few months later, Alvarez Martínez and Ortiz met again with Alicia Bejarano and Elizabeth Gastelumendi (who had heard of the group's vision and wanted to join) to discuss how they could create such an organization and what it would look like. At the first meeting in May 1986, the founders acknowledged the need for Latinas to tell their own stories. They thought this was particularly important, as Self-Help was really about women taking an active role in their own healing. Strongly committed to using Self-Help as a technique for transforming internalized oppression into action for social change, they planned to incorporate Self-Help in both their programs and the group's organizational culture.

After meeting for four months, the group developed a written statement of purpose and goals. According to Alvarez Martínez, "once we started, it took on a life of its own."[3] Their founding statement reads:

> The National Latina Health Organization was formed to raise Latina consciousness about our health and health problems. The NLHO promotes Self-Help methods and self-empowerment processes as a vehicle for taking greater control of our health practices and lifestyles. We are committed to work toward the goal of bilingual access to quality health care and self-empowerment of Latinas through educational programs, outreach, and research.[4]

In addition to promoting Self-Help as a tool for individual empowerment and social change, a primary goal of the organization was to raise consciousness among Latinas, their families and communities, and the general public about Latina health. The NLHO intended to fill the void left by the medical establishment, which ignored Latina health issues. Beyond raising consciousness, the group aimed to "act as a catalyst for all of us to take control over our health and our lives."[5] In response to the lack of Latina health professionals, which contributed to poor health care, it also promoted a model of "Latinas helping Latinas." Based on many of their own experiences in the health care field, the founders believed that Latinas would respond affirmatively to improving their physical, mental, and emotional health and wellbeing if the information, training, and program content were presented to them by other Latinas.

The four women believed that Latinas faced discrimination in receiving health care. They knew that most Latinas did not even have access to bilingual or culturally proficient health care information. Directly attributing current Latina health disparities to living in a racist society they wrote:

> The history of Latina women is filled with struggle to preserve our families, our communities and our own identity... As daughters, we are the unwelcome ones; as wives we lose our identities and become second class citizens; as members of our society we are trained to take a decorative and servile role. Moreover, as members of a prevalent white society, we are considered incapable of being anything but domestic servants. Even our language has been used to humiliate and oppress us.[6]

Citing the higher rates of sterilization abuse, death rates, and unequal medical treatment in Latina experiences, they wanted to emphasize "the connection in the health care we receive and our general state of health to the racism that is practiced in this country against people of color."[7] The NLHO not only called for bilingual services but a much broader definition of what is necessary for an individual's true access to good health:

> NLHO's definition of good health is holistic and includes not only freedom from disease but a wellness approach that encompasses access to quality education, the right to jobs that are environmentally safe and afford us the economic means to good, safe housing; the fundamental right to accessible quality health care and services that are culturally sensitive and language appropriate; and physical and spiritual well-being. Most broadly, health is about the self-empowerment of Latinas. Learning

that the way to effect change and improve our physical, mental, and emotional health is to initiate the process ourselves.[8]

Despite their focus on the discrimination Latinas face as a group, they were well aware of the diversity among Latinas, as the four of them came from different migratory, country, and class backgrounds.[9]

By November 1986, 15 women had joined the NLHO. They were "teachers, lawyers, housewives, farm workers, health care workers, students, businesswomen, domestics, and other professionals." They declared, "Some of us were native born, some are immigrants and some refugees. We are Puerto Ricans, Cubans, Mexicans, Chicanas, South Americans, and Central Americans."[10] Their diversity meant that they had to work especially hard at the beginning to get to know each other.[11] Despite their differences, as the founders had predicted, health was an issue that could and would draw many types of women together to organize for social change. When differences arose, they were able to rely on Self-Help to see them through.

Self-Help
Women in the NLHO see Self-Help as integral to the process of social change. Believing that women must first change themselves if they are to change society, they see Self-Help methods and self-empowerment processes as a way for Latinas to take greater control of their own health practices. Self-Help is not individualized; it is a collective process which makes possible, and is simultaneous with, combating structural oppression.

The founders' adoption of Self-Help theory was not just theoretical, or intended for their "clients," but a working practice that they themselves relied upon. From the outset, the founders realized that they needed a process that would support their working together to develop the organization. Paulita Ortiz, with her strong background in RC, became primarily responsible for developing the NLHO's Self-Help model. She explained:

> We believed that as long as women were communicating from a place of being aware of themselves and their surroundings, we could succeed in making social change. Because many of us had seen and experienced what envy, our own needs and hurts can do to an organization, we wanted something in place to help us during those times. The more we processed

the more it evolved and the more natural it becomes...Early on we didn't understand Self-Help as we do now. But we knew we had to make a commitment to have a process to keep ourselves working together, because we had seen how things can fall apart... We didn't know what we meant by it or how we were going to use it; we just knew we needed it.[12]

According to Alvarez Martínez, Self-Help really helped her and the other women to be able to continue the hard work of the organization in the early years. As none of the founders had experience running an organization, it helped them to work through their own fears and emotions about taking leadership and to negotiate internal relationships.

The NLHO also integrated Self-Help in all of its educational programs. This meant that women not only received health information but were also given the opportunity to evaluate the information in terms of their own lives. Women were encouraged to share their stories with each other in a supportive, nonjudgmental group setting. As the founders imagined it early on:

The groups will give women the attention we have never gotten; it will give us a place where we can feel safe enough to tell our own story...what has been causing our stress and affecting our health. Our life stresses can cause us high blood pressure, ulcers, heart conditions, etc. Stress can cause us to eat badly, smoke or abuse drugs...These in turn can cause health conditions. We are not used to others wanting to listen to us. It is amazing what heavy burdens we can unload by verbalizing what we may never have been able to talk about before. Something that we may have thought no one else would understand.[13]

As women began to realize their agency in creating their life circumstances, the Self-Help process has had a significant impact on many who utilize it. Ortiz states, "We have often said that the more we become aware of and know our own self-worth the more we will make an informed, healthier life choice and the more we will contribute in whatever situation we are in."[14] Rather than tell women what nutritional choices they should make, or overloading them with sexual health information, the NLHO believes that women will come to the best decisions for themselves when they have been listened to and supported, and realize their own power.

Moreover, support groups provide a space where Latinas can discharge their feelings and express their joy, pain, anger, sadness, or whatever emotions arise as they explore topics such as poverty, oppression, health, and family. This is critical, according to the NLHO, because Latinas are often so busy taking care of others and struggling to survive that they do not have the opportunity to express themselves and be heard. The very act of two or more women expressing themselves and listening to each other provides an interruption in this pattern, and often in and of itself can be meaningful.

When combined with educational information, or self-empowerment curricula, Self-Help is used to encourage individuals to process how what they have learned is meaningful for their own lives. Laura Jiménez, a staff member for many years, pointed out that because Self-Help emphasizes personal and emotional response to any given issue, it actually facilitates transformational learning. Jiménez explains how this works with an example related to sexual health:

> I sat in a group of women who said, "This is herpes; this is how I got it." Hearing that changes the way you think and conceptualize sexually transmitted diseases and the work we have to do. It takes things out of the rhetoric, abstinence–protection–safe sex and just makes it very personal, and shows that it is not that complicated. It is about bodies, desire, and health.[15]

A powerful transformative experience, Self-Help is the tool that would guide both the organization's educational efforts and internal relationships. As such, all who are involved closely with the organization or its programs are expected to train in and practice Self-Help.

The Early Years

With an initial grant from the Ruth Mott Foundation, in April 1987, just over a year after the women first met, the organization opened its offices in the Spanish-Speaking Unity Council building in the heart of the Fruitvale neighborhood in Oakland. Up until that time, the founders and a number of volunteers had established the organization while working full-time in other jobs. In October 1987, Alvarez Martínez was awarded a Social Service Leave of Absence: she was given full pay for nine months from her job at IBM in order to become the full-time director of the NLHO. Paulita Ortiz also joined the NLHO staff as a half-time administrative assistant.

The board took on an increasingly local composition at this time, as all founding members believed that the organization should be directly responsive to the needs of their immediate community. Having a local board also allowed for a directing body upon which Alvarez Martínez could rely to accomplish some of the everyday tasks of the organization, and most volunteered significant time. Carmelita La Roche contributed her services in the office twice a week for over five years and served as the organization's treasurer. Like many other women, La Roche dedicated long hours to the organization to help take care of her community. Although essential to the organization's sustenance, maintaining a dedicated local board that can represent a national agenda has been hard.

Local Programming

During the spring of 1988, NLHO began co-sponsoring classes and workshops that covered a Variety of health subjects in the Latino community through Merritt College in Oakland. One course, Latina Health Issues: Better Health Through Self-Empowerment, addressed topics such as mental health, patients' rights, birth control, sexuality, *curanderismo* (a form of traditional healing), cancer prevention, sexuality, homophobia, teen pregnancy, HIV/AIDS, domestic violence, and alcohol abuse over a series of classes. Led by Latina health professionals and community members, the course integrated the Self-Help process into every class. After hearing a speaker, each woman would have a chance to share how the information impacted her own life. The NLHO programs were successful and became increasingly popular. The NLHO had created a space that allowed women to speak, share their stories, and receive support. Plus, free childcare was always provided, making it all the more accessible to participants. For some women, participating in an NLHO program was a gateway to their becoming members of the organization. It was through these classes that the Self-Help process became more directed to helping Latinas understand and utilize health information and integral to the organization's programming. Based upon her own educational experiences, Ortiz designed an alternative model of health education, one in which women could deal with the realities of their daily lives and respond to the information they were receiving. Ortiz recalls:

I went back to school and took two classes at Laney College. I took a Chicano studies class. I would go to class and get all this information about oppression, and I would feel bad...I would say this isn't right—and I stopped taking classes. And I remember thinking, "And we want our kids to go to school and learn? We want them to go to those classes?" And that's where I got the idea for "better health through self-empowerment." At every meeting we would have a facilitator and we used the process. It got real clear to me that women were not going to listen to health information when they have to worry about their life—if they don't have food, or money, they couldn't learn about AIDS.[16]

Not only did utilizing the Self-Help process as an educational tool help women to understand their oppression, but hearing the experiences of others also helped NLHO members to understand what kind of information and resources community members needed. Through developing the course curricula, members gathered existing information on Latina health, built up a network of Latina health specialists, and ultimately developed a resource library on Latina health. Moreover, they drew hundreds of women and their families to learn, think, feel, and speak about their health.

The First National Conference on Latina Health Issues

Shortly after its founding, the group immediately focused on meeting its first goal: planning a national conference on Latina health issues. It recognized that there were many other Latinas throughout the country who were devoted to Latina health issues. The conference was geared toward bringing together Latina health professionals and activists to share and learn from one another. It focused on education and consciousness-raising, which the NLHO considered the first step to health improvement.

To plan a conference that was truly national in scope, the NLHO extended its outreach widely to ensure broad representation. They received much support from women all over the country, and members of a national advisory board actively helped shape the conference agenda. Individuals and groups across the country co-sponsored the conference, helped recruit participants, and participated in the workshops.[17]

Ads in both English and Spanish-language media advertised the conference to local women:

Good health is not a privilege for the few. But it can seem that way if you are poor, Spanish-speaking and female. As Hispanic women we face special health care needs that too often have not been addressed by existing health care systems. It's time for us to meet our own needs. On September 23rd Hispanic women from across the country will gather for the first National Conference on Latina Health Issues. Latina health professionals will join forces with Latinas who need health care to find new approaches to issues that threaten our communities: epidemic teenage pregnancy, drug-abuse, AIDS, poor nutrition, and job safety in high-tech and agricultural industries...Good health is not a privilege for the few.[18]

Over 350 women came from all over the country to learn, discuss, and strategize about issues affecting Latina health. All of the workshops were run, organized, and presented by Latinas—not only by professionals or those women with degrees, but also *curanderas, parteras, hierberas,*[19] and others with valuable information to share. Workshops provided participants with health resources and information on how to access them. The conference also presented an orientation to Self-Help, creating an opportunity for women to consider how this information impacted their own lives. All sessions and keynote speakers were directly translated in either English or Spanish. Food and childcare were provided to enable Latinas and their families to attend the conference. The conference was a historic milestone. It was the first time Latinas from across the nation came together to learn about their health concerns. The gathering promoted a strong feeling of solidarity among many attendees and facilitated connections between women who shared similar concerns. At the same time, tensions arose around issues of sexuality. The conference included workshops and panels related to lesbian health and sexuality. However, lesbian participants expressed disappointment that their issues were often segregated and their panels not widely attended by heterosexual participants.

Following the conference, the group's efforts were spent in networking and outreach activities across the nation. Through her strong connection with Byllye Avery of the NBWHP, and the women she met at their first conference, Alvarez Martínez became involved in national reproductive rights circles, and she began traveling nationwide to meet with other activists. She joined the board of the National Abortion Rights and Action League (NARAL), constantly advocating for the inclusion of more women of color in the organization and expanding the abortion issue to address other reproductive health issues and include the needs of women of color. Alvarez Martínez quickly became a national spokesperson for Latina perspectives on reproductive rights. While the NLHO developed a national reputation, its members also concentrated on developing their educational programs in California. It was during a presentation on reproductive health for the Bay Area Network of Latinas (BANELA) that the momentum to start Latinas for Reproductive Choice (LRC) gained force. During her talk, Alvarez Martínez expressed her belief that Latinas must take a stronger role in reproductive rights issues because their perspectives and experiences needed to be voiced. A number of women began meeting and formed LRC, which ultimately became a project of the NLHO. The primary mission of LRC was to break the silence among Latinas about abortion and other issues of reproductive choice. The main message that they wanted to convey was that many Latinas *are* pro-choice.

Latinas and Abortion Rights

The NLHO was explicitly pro-choice in many ways, although reproductive health issues have not been central to the organization's programming. This commitment is highlighted in Latinas for Reproductive Choice (LRC), a short-lived program of the NLHO, and its coalition work with other mainstream and women of color organizations. At a press conference in October 1990, the NLHO announced its intention to "break the silence on reproductive rights issues within the Latina community."[20] On the 13th anniversary of Rosie Jiménez's death, the group declared that Latinas "will no longer stand on the sidelines and let others decide our fate." Instead, they would express their reproductive attitudes without fear.[21] As the NLHO worked to break the silence, Rachel Vargas joined the LRC. Vargas had recently been excommunicated from the Catholic Church for being clinic administrator at the Reproductive Services Clinic in Corpus Christi, Texas. Vargas believed that her treatment was intended as a lesson to pro-choice Latinas not to defy the church's position. Using her excommunication as a platform, the LRC encouraged dialogue about reproductive health, and abortion in particular, in Latina communities. The women of LRC were boldly pro-choice. Through openly talking about abortion themselves, they hoped to "help women to be open and talking about it and making it a public issue that we can do something about. We need to be open about it if we're going to keep it legal in this country."[22] They strongly believed that Latinas needed to become more active in order to keep abortion legal.

In order to do this, they put considerable efforts into serving as a link between Latinas and the larger pro-choice community. LRC/NLHO was one of the strongest voices advocating for mainstream organizations to address the needs of Latinas. "We have given our support to pro-choice activities and organizations with mixed emotions because we often feel that we are not really incorporated into the defining, articulating, planning, and decision-making of those organizations. For too long we have been mere tokens."[23] They demanded that the mainstream reproductive rights movement protect the bodies of all women and worked to place more Latinas on the boards of reproductive rights organizations to make sure their perspectives were included.

They joined other women of color organizations in calling for the redefinition of choice to include the range of reproductive needs, from contraception to prenatal care. As they put it:

> Access to abortion is only half the issue for Latinas. Reproductive choice for us is much more than abortion—it is the ability to have healthy babies, when, and if, we want. It means the freedom to have one child or ten. Or even none. Reproductive choice means access to culturally relevant, quality health care and information, education about sexuality and contraception for our daughters, and access to alternative forms of birth control, regardless of cost.[24]

LRC also wanted to bring attention to the inequities Latinas face in relation to health care and spoke out on the historical reproductive abuse of Latinas:

> We are subtly and sometimes overtly coerced to believe that sterilization is the only alternative to the inferior, degrading reproductive health care we receive, which often denies us access to safe and effective contraception or to abortion. Sometimes a woman must agree to sterilization in order to receive an abortion. We are sterilized by doctors who regard excessive childbearing by poor women and women of color as deviant or inappropriate.[25]

In addition to its education and outreach programs, LRC planned to increase representation and participation of Latinas in other health organizations. LRC also gathered signatures from more than 40 prominent pro-choice Latinas across many fields to demonstrate that Latinas were pro-choice. After this initial effort, however, LRC did not continue as a distinct project of NLHO. Faced with dwindling resources and increasing member burnout, the NLHO opted to continue its reproductive rights work in coalition with other national organizations.

The NLHO worked almost exclusively within networks of women of color to accomplish its reproductive rights agenda. It was a founding member and active participant in the Women of Color Coalition for Reproductive Health Rights (WOCCRHR), which began as an informal network in 1987 and was formalized in 1992 to influence public policy, research, and education on reproductive health issues. It was through this network that the NLHO spearheaded a petition drive to call for a moratorium on the usage of Depo-Provera. In November 1993, it organized Defend Women's Health! Day of Outreach and Community Mobilization to Stop Depo-Provera, did community organizing, and met with the commissioner of the Food and Drug Administration (FDA) and representatives of the Department of Health and Human Services to directly express its concerns on behalf of women of color. Though a moratorium was never called, the publicity around the event was an opportunity to educate Latinas and other women of color about the dangers of Depo-Provera.

Throughout the following decade, the NLHO was involved with a broad range of women's health issues, as it struggled to establish itself as a national organization. Because there was such a dearth of resources on Latinas and health, the organization's presence was sought in many arenas outside of reproductive health, including tobacco prevention. As the only full-time staff member, Alvarez Martínez increasingly represented the organization and became critical to its operations.

Las Jovenes

During the mid-1990s, the NLHO began youth programming, which has become the hallmark of the organization. The NLHO was awarded funding to work with 11- to 14-year-old girls from predominantly Latino neighborhoods on a campaign to make smoking unacceptable and unattractive to youth and prevent experimentation with tobacco. With this charge, the NLHO designed a holistic program that focused on health education, building self-esteem, and incorporating the Self-Help process. In January 1994, the NLHO started a group of 11- to 14-year-old girls at Horace Mann Academic Middle School in the Mission District, a predominantly Latino neighborhood in San Francisco.

NLHO staff member Susana Renaud developed a holistic, culturally proficient curriculum that integrated consideration of ethnicity, culture, social, family, and school environments. In addition to learning about physiology, all aspects of tobacco information, and how advertising targets girls, the girls also explored their own cultural identity through arts and exercise. For example, a Native elder from the community visited the group and introduced the sacred, healing, and indigenous symbolism of tobacco use. The program aimed to prevent girls from using tobacco and provide them with methods of self-empowerment.

The girls launched a successful letter campaign to a tobacco company that advertised on a billboard located near their school. Their efforts led to the ad's removal, with the NLHO drawing much praise, media attention, and further funding for a six-week program during the summer. Because of their work, several of the girls were asked to participate on panels, television talk shows, and at city council meetings to share information about tobacco and alcohol dangers. This experience ultimately provided a blueprint for the several youth programs that the NLHO currently runs. All the youth programs incorporate Self-Help and self-empowerment theory and provide supportive group settings in which to discuss the health curriculum.

Political Alliances

During the mid-1990s, the NLHO was increasingly less national in scope and more tied to the Bay Area and California political context. Similar to many other Latina organizations, the NLHO devoted most of its energies to defending its community against right-wing attacks. The NLHO's task was all the more serious in California, where a number of policy measures targeting immigrant communities were pushed. For example, the NLHO opposed Proposition 187, an initiative to end all health, educational, and social services for undocumented immigrants. It was active in supporting grassroots and legal challenges to the initiative and worked with local, state, and national organizations "to stop the inhumane, racist action of Governor Wilson, the creators of Proposition 187 and all those that support the initiative."[26] Despite massive resistance, voters passed the act and the first executive order Governor Pete Wilson made was to discontinue prenatal care to undocumented immigrants.

However, the law was eventually prevented from being enacted, largely due to critics who challenged its constitutionality. Proposition 187 provides a powerful example of why it is important to have a Latina voice dedicated to supporting reproductive rights. The NLHO's efforts directly respond to critical community needs that perhaps do not fall under the traditional purview of reproductive health and help to illuminate to both Latino community activists and reproductive health activists alike that Latinas' needs are crucial to consider.

Despite its growing visibility, during the organization's first decade, it had more and more difficulty getting all of the necessary work done. During these early years, the organization experienced significant stress due to decreasing financial resources coupled with increased programs. The organization focused on much of the day-to-day work to keep current programs running and was not able to develop its infrastructure or fundraising.

The late 1990s brought greater financial stability to the organization, as it received significant funding for the development of Latina adolescent programs. The NLHO has received a lion's share of current funding from state and national programs geared toward decreasing adolescent pregnancy. For example, the California State Department of Health granted the organization significant funding for the development of Latina adolescent programs. While the intended goal of the program was to delay the initiation of sex, the NLHO drew from its early tobacco prevention initiatives to develop a holistic program stressing mentorship and empowerment: instead of focusing programs on girls' sexuality, it stressed the correlation of adolescent pregnancy with the socioeconomic and educational status of the girls and their families. Their program was designed to reduce the incidence of pregnancy during teenage years through providing teens with the information, education, skills, and support they need to make the best decisions for themselves. Unlike mainstream directives that insist that the cultural norms of the youth must be changed, NLHO programs draw from a basis of self-knowledge which emphasizes the positive aspects of culture and ethnic consciousness in empowering young women.

Recalling the needs of the youth they first worked with in San Francisco, the NLHO staff knew that Latina girls are not only at risk for pregnancy, but also at risk for abuse, violence, educational deprivation, and neglect. Moreover, they often lack the support of a compassionate adult in their lives. The staff wanted to provide a program that could respond to these realities. According to Laura Jiménez, one of the program's designers and coordinators, the girls were up front in saying that they needed the guidance of an adult in their lives. Toward this end, the organization developed a one-on-one mentorship program matching Latina youth from area schools with local Latina volunteer mentors. Managing the logistics of one-on-one mentorship proved difficult given limited staff, and the program ultimately developed into an on-site school group program in order to reach more girls, called Nahui Ollin Teotl (the Essence of the Four Movements).

Created for young Latinas in middle school and high school, the program aims to give the participants the skills and support they need to make healthful life decisions for themselves. The program particularly focused on raising their awareness of issues that put them at risk for pregnancy and sexually transmitted diseases; its goal was empowerment. The curriculum included topics such as drug and alcohol use, racism, sexism, and spirituality; it also included guest speakers, projects, field trips, and activities.

Alongside the health education curriculum, the Self-Help process was used to create a safe environment where the girls could build trust between themselves, their peers, and the program coordinators. Perhaps because they were provided with an opportunity to talk honestly about subjects that directly impacted their lives, such as environmental racism, adultism, and tracking in schools, the groups grew in popularity and the program expanded to six schools in Oakland, including alternative high schools for parenting teens. The groups have been very successful in impacting the girls' lives; at one school of 59 girls participating in the afterschool program, 100 percent of them reported improvements in their grade point averages.[27]

Haciendose Mujeres: The Intergenerational Latina Health Leadership Project

The organization's financial stability was significantly boosted when it became a founding member of the SisterSong Women of Color Reproductive Health Collective in 1998 and formed Canción Latina, its Latina subgroup. Because SisterSong has secured long-term funding, it is able to make more significant planning decisions, as it is less driven by financial insecurity. The NLHO then began collaboration with the

Chicana/Latina Studies Working Group at the University of California at Berkeley to design a course entitled Redefining Latina Health: Body, Mind, and Spirit. The course was first taught at Berkeley in the fall of 1998, by University of California at Berkeley ethnic studies students and NLHO staff. Students learned about health issues from a variety of perspectives and were introduced to the Self-Help process. Providing a holistic introduction to Latina health, the class was designed to promote participatory education, and some students were able to intern with the National Latina Health Organization as well.

Assured of funding over three years, Alvarez Martínez wanted to finally realize a goal she had set after the first conference that the organization held in 1988: a multigenerational reproductive health conference for Latinas. Focused on youth, the sessions were designed to celebrate their learning and talking about their reproduction and sexuality with each other, their families, and peers.

The conference was held in April 1999 on the campus of the University of California at Berkeley. More than 300 women and men of all ages participated in workshops on desire and the erotic, power and sexuality, health rights education, substance abuse, intimate violence, and youth empowerment. Laura Jiménez, who first began working with the NLHO in 1996 after she graduated from college, organized the conference. She remembered that it felt groundbreaking for many of those involved, because the sessions opened up dialogues between women, friends, sisters, mothers, and daughters:

> I think a lot of young people, a lot of people period, talked about things that related to sex and reproductive health that they had not before felt comfortable or [been] given the opportunity to talk about. And it was presented to them in a natural way so that it wasn't irritating, intimidating, or embarrassing. I think it was successful in that we were able to bring so many people from the community to the university and make them feel that they belonged there. It was successful in that we had families come together. It was successful in that we had a group of teen moms that came from LA. We had a young man that came from inside the Youth Authority to the conference.[28]

The conference was a huge success and offered many lessons. Chief among them was that planning a conference was hard work; clearly it would be a significant challenge to organize other conferences in locations outside of the group's home town. In the fall of 1999, Laura Jiménez moved to New York City to establish the organization's New York office, which was located at Hunter College.[29] When Alvarez Martínez and Jiménez first spoke to officials from the college's departments of women's studies and community health to tell them about the Latina health course and sponsoring a conference, their response was overwhelmingly enthusiastic. Alvarez Martínez recalled that one faculty member said, "It would be like bringing water to a dry place."[30]

The NLHO drew upon its connections to collaborate with many others and pull off the East Coast conference held in October 2000 at the City College of New York.[31] Although there were fewer participants at this conference than the one in Berkeley the year before, more workshops were youth led. According to Jiménez, it was a challenge to move to New York City as a West Coast-based organization because the group had not established legitimacy in the community, or with funders. She recalls:

> Some of the funders wanted to know what our track record in New York was—we had none. They wanted to see proof of our work in New York, and we didn't have any yet. I think they saw us as an organization that came to New York and just started a project as an isolated incident. And we weren't in the community, serving the community. Trying to say we were a community-based organization but working out of the university was not good.[32]

Learning from this experience and drawing upon its strength in developing youth programs, the NLHO hopes to collaborate with other organizations in New York City to continue establishing a bicoastal presence. However, given current government budget cuts to health programs and the NLHO's inability to hire a grant-writing fundraiser, it is uncertain when a fully operational New York branch of the NLHO will be realized. Nevertheless, conference outreach and multidimensional coalition work have been invaluable in building a national Latina reproductive rights agenda—both in determining issues and establishing networks.

Through their involvement with Canción Latina, the NLHO has continued to build strong relationships with other women of color organizations. These networks have not only facilitated community building but strengthened the NLHO's understanding of and commitment to a pan-Latina organization. Working with groups such as Casa Atabex Aché (South Bronx, New York), Grupo Pro Derechos Reproductivos (Puerto Rico), and Women's House of Learning and Empowerment (Oxnard, California), the NLHO collected information on Latina's health in those particular communities. As the resulting policy brief emphasized, despite their differences, Latinas across ethnicities voiced similar concerns:

> From the clinics of Oakland, California, to the streets of Loiza in Puerto Rico, Latinas of all backgrounds tell us they suffer consistent violence and abuse, that they remain unaware of how to protect themselves from unplanned pregnancies and sexually transmitted diseases. Furthermore, they both shun and are shunned by the very institutions that supposedly exist to prevent and respond to these issues.[33]

Since joining SisterSong, the organization has focused on health education. Outside of its work with SisterSong, the organization has finally received funds to build on its previous work in reproductive health policy and develop an infrastructure. Since April 2003, it has cultivated a national advisory board of experts in Latina reproductive health that meets monthly, via teleconferencing, to discuss national reproductive heath policy matters and their implications for Latinas.

Stability and Evolution

Since its inception in March 1986, the National Latina Health Organization went from being a shared dream of four women in Oakland to a bicoastal, nationally recognized organization. Perhaps one of its greatest achievements is its longevity. At times operating with very low funds, the organization has functioned since it was founded and celebrates its 19th birthday in spring 2005. Given the difficulties of funding, the lack of support for general and reproductive health work in Latino communities, and the broad scope of its mission, the NLHO's resilience is a triumph. That its success was accomplished while promoting alternative models of health and offering a nontraditional organizational culture is particularly noteworthy.

The NLHO has unequivocally brought Latina voices to national reproductive rights politics and expanded the focus of reproductive rights beyond abortion. Through their 18 years of organizing, NLHO members have played a significant role in helping the reproductive rights movement and Latino communities understand that reproductive health is experienced differently among Latina subgroups and compared with white women and other women of color. They have also been able to educate their constituencies. The NLHO has made it clear that reproductive health is a significant issue in Latinas' lives.

The organization has also advanced a Self-Help training program specific to Latinas and implemented the Self-Help process at all levels of its operation. With the training of a core group of Self-Help facilitators in preparation for its national conferences, at one point the NLHO was running several weekly support groups consecutively throughout the year. Although the number of groups has significantly decreased since the late 1990s, the organization's continued collaborations with other groups have helped the process spread. This alternative perspective has provided a tool for hundreds of women to be empowered to improve their own health. Providing discussions which are based in women's realities, rather than on the myths which so often inform policy, is the deliberate way in which the NLHO hopes to make social change.

While many women who have trained in Self-Help say it has made a significant impact in their lives, there are many other community women who are unable to participate in these groups because of the time commitment they demand. Because both Self-Help and including all women in its programs are priorities, the organization continues to make efforts to acquire funding that will allow it to specifically develop Self-Help work. Although it is written into almost all of the grant applications (costs such as paying facilitators, paying childcare, meals for women who come in for trainings), the NLHO has never received funding for this specific purpose. Despite this, the organization maintains a steady number of facilitators and groups often run on their own steam because women are committed to each other and the process. Many women commit many hours to Self-Help work without pay, because they believe and experience positive effects in the work.

In this way, the work and vision of the NLHO, "is unstoppable. There is always going to be a group going on somewhere. It's gotten past the organization because other groups are now using the process and crediting the organization for teaching those tools."[34] According to Alvarez Martínez, it is simply the only way she can imagine working, because it embodies the core principles of the organization's foundation—to empower women to do what is best for their lives:

Well, we are very clear that this is the core. If you are going to work here, you have to use it. And for some people it takes a long time to commit and see the importance of it. But it keeps us grounded. So this is the only way I know that it will work. It's how we keep our personal and organizational integrity.[35]

As Alvarez Martínez's statement indicates, Self-Help is central to the organization's identity and the key to making the group's programs work. As the organization continues to follow this vision, significant challenges remain to ensuring that the NLHO will grow and become the national organization that its name implies.

Challenges

The continuous challenge of being a community-based but nationally focused organization has been most evidenced by the difficulty in maintaining an effective board of directors. The NLHO was founded as a grassroots organization and was built from the ground up by a group of energetic and resourceful women. All of its founders were doing professional or volunteer health work in their communities and became members of a working board for the first years of the organization's existence. However, the organization's vision and mission was national in scope, and as such necessitated a national board.

Although a national advisory board was constituted to plan the first National Conference on Latina Health Issues, and over the years several high-profile experts in women's health have served on the board, limited resources made it difficult to bring a national board together on a consistent basis. Trying to effectively plan the organization's direction through conference calls has at times contributed to an ineffective board. At different times this has led to the development of a local board serving as the de facto national board, because local boards are easier to convene and community interests are always represented. However, a local board for a national organization severely limits the organization's scope. A local board composition is additionally challenging for the organization when it applies for national funding. Alvarez Martínez feels that the board composition puts the organization in the position of "trying to please everybody"—meaning that local board members feel required to answer to communities where they live and at the same time have a vision for transformative change on the national level, a level of focus that runs the risk of making local organizations feel alienated or insignificant.

Having participated in national boards herself, Alvarez Martínez has witnessed groups that are well funded and able to effectively involve board members. While it would be optimal to have a national board that could come together regularly, at this point, she has been forced to recognize the funding limitations of the organization. The NLHO's current board is composed of locally based advocates, activists, and professionals.

It has been a struggle to find members with fundraising skills. Moreover, because of the NLHO board's instability, the organization has often lacked leadership and vision other than that of its executive director. There is no larger body responsible for fundraising or accountability. Not only does this amount to added pressure for Alvarez Martínez and her staff, but the long-term result is that the organization has not developed to its potential in the 18 years of its existence. As the group itself recognized in its 1995 annual report, "Our significant challenge continues to be developing the means to create a stable infrastructure."[36] Given the constant challenges of scarce resources and funding in the context of a wide array of local and community needs, the NLHO is stretched incredibly thin for a national organization.

Beyond the boardroom, the NLHO is further challenged with developing identities as both a national and a local organization. For example, because it is largely West Coast and California based, the group overrepresents women of Mexican origin. If it is to continue its status as a national organization, it must clarify its priorities in this regard. Straddling both national and community concerns will likely continue to overwhelm the organization unless strategic decisions are made.

The lack of organizational infrastructure along with the competing demands of local and national organizational agendas may also be having a long-term impact in the form of low retention of women who come to the organization to volunteer. The organization has had difficulty developing a national membership base and over the years has seen many women pass through its doors. Unfortunately, the majority of these women do not maintain long-term contact, especially those who do not want to be involved in the Self-Help process. The NLHO appreciates that in order to realize its goals, it must tap broader constituencies, access more resources, and promote a more national scope and vision.

While the organization was originally run by a cross-section of women of varying ages, its current staff is largely between 20 and 30 years old. Many of the women are still in the process of completing their education and do not stay long. Although the NLHO provides full health benefits for its staff, its budget makes competing with jobs with higher salaries difficult. After the connection between the NLHO and Berkeley was established, a large number of NLHO staff were current or recently graduated students from the university. While this provides NLHO with well-prepared interns and staff, it also tends to be a fairly consistent revolving door. Inevitably, students return to school, seek further training, or move on to employment with increased pay and benefits.

The National Latina Health Organization is committed to social change and demands that Latinas achieve their needs on their own terms. With a holistic vision that truly centers on women's empowerment, the organization challenges the mainstream frameworks that shape current funding patterns and traditions. Although the NLHO sometimes struggles to keep running within this context, it has consistently offered programs that help women and girls improve their lives.

By continuing to build its powerful educational and Self-Help programs and its commitment to youth, the NLHO has already helped empower the leadership that can push its visionary agenda forward.

NOTES

1   Paulita Ortiz, interview by Elena R. Gutiérrez, January 18, 2004.

2   Luz Alvarez Martínez, interview by Elena R. Gutiérrez, July 24, 2002.

3   Ibid.

4   NLHO, "Founding Statement" (organizational files, 1986).

5   NLHO, Ruth Mott Foundation proposal (organizational files, November 24, 1986).

6   NLHO, "Introduction Statement" (organizational files, 1986).

7   NLHO, "First Leaflet" (organizational files).

8   NLHO, "Essential Principles for Responsible Health Care Reform" (organizational files).

9   As Luz Alvarez Martínez wrote in one of their early statements, "I am first generation, Paulita is second generation Mexican American. Alicia is from Ecuador and came here as an adult. And Elizabeth is from Peru and also as adult here...Paulita grew up as a migrant farm worker with her family. I grew up in San Leandro, which is a pretty white area. So we were pretty different. Paulita grew up in the fields, I grew up in this white city, and the other two grew up in their own countries. It was very interesting." Alvarez Martínez as quoted in Sandra Morgen, *Into Our Own Hands: The Women's Health Movement in the US, 1969–1990* (New Brunswick, NJ: Rutgers University Press, 2002), 57.

10   NLHO, Ruth Mott Foundation proposal, 3.

11   Gwen Roberts, "Latinas on the Move" (organizational files), 17–18.

12   Ortiz, interview.

13   Luz Alvarez Martínez, interview by KNBR radio, transcript, n. d.

14   Ortiz, interview.

15   Laura Jiménez, interview by Elena R. Gutiérrez, September 3, 2002.

16   Ortiz, interview.

17   Outreach expanded to MADRE, an organization of 28,000 members in New York; the National Conference of Puerto Rican Women Inc., an organization with 15 chapters throughout the Northeast; Taller Salud in Puerto Rico; Chicano Advocates for Equality; NOW; COSSMO; United Farm Workers; Amigas Latinas en Accion pro Salud; and more. The conference planning committee included women from Texas, New Mexico, California, Illinois, Massachusetts, Colorado, Florida, Wisconsin, New Jersey, Pennsylvania, New York, and Puerto Rico.

18   NLHO, "Free Speech Message" (organizational files).

19   Literally translated to mean "healers, midwives, herbalists."

20   Latinas for Reproductive Choice, leaflet (organizational files, 1990).

21   Ibid.

22   Vicki Larson, "Coast to Coast: California, Making Choices" (organizational files).

23   Luz Alvarez Martínez, "*Webster* and Women of Color: 'We Are Still Invisible'" (organizational files), 6.

24 Latinas for Reproductive Choice, leaflet.

25 Alvarez Martínez, "We Are Still Invisible," 6.

26 NLHO, press release (organizational files, 1995).

27 Alvarez Martínez, interview.

28 Jiménez, interview.

29 The office space was donated by El Centro de Estudios Puertorriqueños at Hunter College.

30 Alvarez Martínez, interview.

31 Co-sponsoring organizations included Casa Atabex Aché, SIECUS, the Institute for the Puerto Rican and Hispanic Elderly, and the Dominican Women's Development Center.

32 Jiménez, interview.

33 Canción Latina, "In the Eye of the Storm: A Latina Women's Health Action Agenda" (organizational files), 12.

34 Alvarez Martínez, interview.

35 Ibid.

36 NLHO, Annual Report (1995).

14

The Colorado Organization for Latina Opportunity and Reproductive Rights

C OLOR is one of the youngest organizations in this book. It was founded in 1998 by seven deeply committed sexual and reproductive health practitioners and activists who were "troubled by the high teenage birth rate and high HIV rate among Latinas."[1] Their mission is "to educate on, advocate for, and promote quality of health and reproductive rights for the sisterhood of Latinas. Through direct service, education, and outreach, each of COLOR'S actions promotes awareness of Latina reproductive rights and aims to improve the quality of reproductive health care received by Latinas."[2] COLOR is a grassroots organization with a broad agenda. It plays a central role in mainstream reproductive rights politics in Colorado and, increasingly, at a national level, while simultaneously developing a uniquely Latina voice and approach to reproductive health issues.

Latinas/os are the largest minority group in Colorado—17.1 percent and 31.7 percent of Colorado's and Denver's populations, respectively—yet they receive the poorest health care in the state. The conditions are so dismal that COLOR often refers to them as "epidemic."[3]

Many of COLOR'S founders worked in teen pregnancy and STD/HIV prevention and witnessed firsthand the difficulties Latinas face when seeking reproductive care. Most became politically active because of the high incidence of young motherhood in their community. Gloria Sanchez, a founding member of COLOR who grew up during the time

*This chapter was researched and written by Elena R. Gutiérrez.

of the Chicano movement in Denver, was committed to the organization because of her experiences working with young mothers:

> I used to work with teenagers, girls who got pregnant. And I would talk to them, and one girl told me one time, "I never even saw a penis until my son was born." I was talking with another girl at the high school one time and she told me that she had got pregnant when she was 13 and she said that her mom called her a bitch, a whore, a slut, all these things. And then I asked her, I said, "did she talk to you about birth control or anything?" She said, "Oh, no, I didn't even want to have sex." She was pretty much forced; she said it was "kind of like rape." I said, "But did you ever tell your mom that, that he had forced you?" She said "oh no, I just took it all. I just let my mom think that I was a slut, and all those kinds of things." So it was those kinds of conversations that I had with teens that really made me believe in the work that COLOR was doing.[4]

Other founding members had similar experiences while working with Latina youth groups and pregnancy prevention. Charlene Ortiz, who had her first child when she was a teen, ran young women's intervention groups at Planned Parenthood. Two of her brothers died after becoming HIV-positive. Melanie Herrera Bortz's mother had an arranged marriage. She had 8 living children out of 12 pregnancies.

> While my mother had different aspirations, she never questioned my father, and never had control over her own fertility...But this was how she was raised, and she felt that this was what she should do... I saw how lack of choice affected my mother, and I want to ensure that Latinas have what they need to control their own bodies.[5]

As these examples illustrate, COLOR members aren't just motivated by abstract health statistics, but by their own experiences as Latinas in the United States.

Drawing from this knowledge, COLOR asserts that the poor health status of Latinas is a result of social oppression and consequently places social justice at the heart of its mission. Its members believe that reproductive and sexual rights are central to achieving full equity and opportunity for Latinas/os in the United States, and that Latinas have the fundamental right to determine their reproductive experiences. COLOR'S board president, Herrera Bortz, explains: "Having the right to control your body is no different than having the right to vote, or having the right to practice the religion of your choice or freedom of speech."[6]

COLOR'S members consider their efforts part of a long legacy of activism to achieve social, political, and economic equality for Latina/o communities. In fact, COLOR'S very existence is a direct result of previous Latina organizing for sexual and reproductive health rights.

Origins

Three founding members of COLOR—Melanie Herrera Bortz, Charlene Ortiz, and Flora Rodríguez Russel—first met in 1996 at a forum sponsored by the National Latina Institute for Reproductive Health (NLIRH) in Albuquerque, New Mexico. Previously unacquainted, the women had much in common. They all lived in Denver and were already professionally and politically involved in Latina/o health education and advocacy work. Herrera Bortz was then working at the Latin American Research and Service Organization. Ortiz and Rodríguez Russel both worked at the Denver Department of Public Health and Hospitals. Ortiz had worked for over 13 years in the areas of HIV, sexually transmitted diseases, and teen pregnancy. Rodríguez Russel was also a lawyer, longtime activist in reproductive rights, and board member of the NLIRH.

The Southwest NLIRH forum was crucial to bringing together women who shared a commitment to improving the reproductive health status of Latinas, often for the first time. Ortiz recalled that during the forum the delegates worked closely together to devise a plan for improving Latina reproductive health in Colorado, and it was the "seed planting" of COLOR.[7] Several attempts were made to continue the work begun at this forum when they returned to Denver. However, Colorado, like other NLIRH state caucuses, was having difficulty implementing the strategies developed at various forums. The NLIRH began to provide $5,000 dollars of seed money and on-site technical assistance to some delegations. In 1998, the NLIRH-Colorado Caucus was one of the first funded, with Rodríguez Russel asking, on behalf of the NLIRH, if Herrera Bortz would take leadership in establishing the state coalition. With Planned Parenthood of the Rocky Mountains as its fiscal sponsor, and a total of $12,000 of financial support from the NLIRH, the group went to work to envision a strategy for organizing in Colorado.

In December 1999 the group separated from both NLIRH and Planned Parenthood and became an independent organization, taking the name Colorado Organization for Latina Opportunity and Reproductive Rights (COLOR). Members of COLOR stressed that the move to independence was not meant to distance the group from the NLIRH. On the contrary, the NLIRH is indisputably considered the organizational *abuela* (grandmother) of COLOR by all its current members.[8] COLOR members were motivated to independence by their need to ensure regional control of the organization's agenda. Herrera Bortz described it this way:

> I truly believe that communities know best, know their issues and their problems, and know what's best for them. I don't believe in top down. I definitely believe in local control. And not that NLIRH in any way was trying to guide us or tell us what we needed to do, but we felt in order to make COLOR part of Colorado—part of the community in this state— we needed our own issues that we focused on and our own name that we created ourselves.[9]

Although COLOR evolved into its own organization, members view the NLIRH as directly responsible for providing the conditions within which it was able to develop. COLOR is governed by an all-Latina board of directors.

A Latina Voice on Choice

"'Choice' is a very privileged word. We throw it around casually, but we must remember to stay aware of other cultures and their impact on women's choices," says Herrera Bortz.[10]

Of the organizations covered in this book, COLOR is one of those most directly involved with the mainstream reproductive rights movement. Providing a Latina voice in the mainstream reproductive health movement in Colorado is central to the group's mission. Each member of COLOR had previously experienced being the only Latina or woman of color in their respective organizations and agreed that little attention was being paid to the health crisis facing Latina/o communities. According to Herrera Bortz,

> Latinas' health in general was being very ignored...There are so many problems around HIV infection rates, around teenage pregnancy and fertility rates that to me it has hit, in my opinion, epidemic proportions... And I didn't think there was enough of a voice in the pro-choice movement in this state to the point where there was not a Latina voice at all.[11]

Founding board member Ortiz speaks to why Latinas needed their own organization:

> We already knew that there were women out there to fight for reproductive rights...But they didn't look like us...All the fights were strong. They helped women overall, but they did not help Latinas specifically. And we have strong, cultural connections to our bodies, to our minds, and our souls. We see that holistically. And not everyone sees that. And right away, that is who we are. And when you look at our health, and when you look at it holistically, and you have people who don't connect all of those parts,...we just didn't feel represented...There were pieces missing. I definitely acknowledge that those struggles, and those fights, clearly helped us, clearly,...but those other pieces were missing for us.[12]

COLOR members believe that Latinas themselves should define the issues important to their communities and how those issues should be handled. "Most mainstream reproductive rights work does not take place in the context of culture," Herrera Bortz explained.[13] Undeniably, they argue, their cultural context demands a broad perspective on reproductive health. COLOR literature states, "For many women, the term 'pro-choice' equals abortion. As Latinas, we approach reproductive health from many different perspectives and believe that being pro-choice also means being concerned about birth control, HIV/AIDS, and sexuality education as well as having safe access to abortion."[14]

COLOR promotes a program that integrates body, mind, and spirit as important facets of Latina/o reproductive and sexual health. As Jacinta Montoya, a board member, conveys, "We look at it from a holistic viewpoint. So, having the physical and psychological abilities to get care and to have sexual relations if you choose, or not to have them, and also, choosing when and if to have a child."[15] While focusing upon the individual physical and spiritual influences that impact a Latina's reproductive health, COLOR also recognizes that today most Latinas do not experience actual reproductive freedom because of economic and political barriers that limit their access.

Thus, a majority of the organization's efforts reach beyond mainstream strategies to secure abortion rights that incorporate broader issues of access to culturally proficient health care for Latinas and their families. Its work currently focuses on the economic barriers that impact Latinas' health and on developing a sexual and reproductive health curriculum for multigenerational Latina communities. It has recently completed a policy analysis of the harsh impacts of welfare reform on Latinas, and it is currently developing a comprehensive sexual education plan for Latina youth.

At the same time, many of COLOR'S projects sit squarely within the concerns of the mainstream reproductive rights movement, and several individual members are active in pro-choice efforts in Colorado in addition to their work with COLOR. As a member organization of the Protect Families, Protect Choice Coalition, a group of organizations working together to defend abortion rights in the state, COLOR worked to defeat anti-choice ballot initiatives in the November 1998 and 2000 elections. The organization also took a lead role in the last four years of the annual *Roe v. Wade* Anniversary Pro-Choice Lobby and Rally Day. COLOR'S contributions to this and subsequent events have demonstrated Latina leadership and organizing ability to the pro-choice community of Colorado. According to Herrera Bortz, COLOR'S work is important not just for Latinas and the organization itself but for the mainstream reproductive rights movement:

> Not only does it bring visibility to the organization, but it also provides an opportunity for white women to see that Latinas are involved in this movement, and I think that far outweighs anything else. Even though there aren't many Latinas who go yet, it's getting into their psyche that they are not the only ones in this movement. And moreover, it may also influence more women of color to join the movement.[16]

Not everyone in COLOR would agree with Herrera Bortz, as some members are ambivalent about whether or not Latinas should be involved with mainstream reproductive rights organizations. Similar to the experiences of other women of color, much of the ambivalence stems from COLOR members' belief that struggles for reproductive freedom must move beyond the narrow focus on abortion rights. However, most members think that the larger mainstream movement and COLOR can have mutually beneficial relationships. This is particularly critical in a state such as Colorado, where they must constantly defend themselves against conservative forces. Montoya points out, "Since [Colorado] is so conservative, and since the anti-choice community has vowed to bring legislation every two years, we know there's a constant battle there against choice. So there are those common issues that we can work on with the mainstream community, and be more effective."[17] COLOR thus attempts to educate mainstream reproductive rights activists as they work with them against anti-choice forces in the state.

Organizational Culture

COLOR'S board members envisioned an organization infused with Latino cultural values, something different from what they could experience in the mainstream. From the outset, they adopted many of the practices used in *razalogía*, a Chicano approach to community learning focusing on transformative knowledge and cultural activism. Razalogía, which means "knowledge of and for the people," was first practiced during the 1970s by Chicano activists seeking to understand how Mexican Americans could effect social transformation. In contrast to individualistic models of knowledge attainment, it sees learning and knowledge as a communal process which should be used toward the purpose of community healing and creating a more just society. One of the core principles of razalogía is that all individuals can strive toward social justice by drawing from their own experiences and knowledge of self.[18] Through shared realization of internalized oppression, it is believed many can come to awareness of their personal value and group power and then utilize this knowledge to work together for social change.

Razalogía employs *conocimiento* as the most basic principle of the group. Conocimiento helps people to learn how to see their "common unity" as an enhancement of personal and group power. According to razalogía's founders:

> The Conocimiento Principle recognizes that common unity begins with the process of shared awareness and understanding, or conocimiento. In essence, we must learn the basics of who each person is before we can evolve the trust and bonding required for unity and shared group power. With this principle in mind, all group efforts balance the focus on a task with a conscious effort to maximize relationships of shared awareness among participants.[19]

COLOR has adopted this principle as a core tenet, as it strives to bring women who often come from very different backgrounds to work together. Ortiz, a razalogía trainer, introduced the process to the group.

> We use that model because it incorporates values—Latino values. And the very, very first value that we put on is conocimiento, which is "to

get to know you." And we basically say that this is who we are. And in our community, if we know where you are, and we can get a picture of where you come from, we'll know who you are. So, we do that amongst each other, and...it allows us to start opening up. There's a connection there because we know what our cultures are like. And [the] mainstream doesn't do that.[20]

The conocimiento exercise is used when new people join the organization, giving members the opportunity to tell each other who they are and to learn about one another. Through this naturalized process of culturally based community building, members are able to acknowledge the similarities and differences each of them brings to Latina reproductive political activism. They are able to achieve an increased commitment to action after sharing in the process of realizing that they are not alone; they are part of a community and can learn from each other and work together to enact social change.

Based upon this framework, COLOR promotes the idea that all members of the organization are leaders, and that each person has unique skills, abilities, and contributions to make. All members are empowered and expected to take responsibility for significant tasks, and leadership development and skills building of the board members, staff, and volunteers are part of the organization's core commitments. In this way, the organization contributes to both movement and community development through building the capacity and abilities of each one of its members. While put into practice at every level, implementation of these values is particularly evident in the group's strategic planning and yearly work plan process, in which every member is expected to participate and lead.

Strategic Planning

During the NLIRH-Colorado Caucus strategic planning process, members met monthly for a year to develop a budget and define a mission, goals, and infrastructure for the organization. Herrera Bortz led the group through the process of constructing a mission and vision statement and developing a five-year work plan. This was challenging for many. Although most members were sexual and reproductive health direct services providers and activists, only one had previous board experience. Herrera Bortz describes how the arduous and sometimes overwhelming process became a tool of empowerment:

Some people had a hard time with that process. [They were saying] "Where do I fit in here? I don't understand what my role is!" "I don't get this strategic plan. How do I do this?" And my response to them was, "In your job, at some point, you're going to have to sit down with your board or with your boss and you're going to have to work on a strategic plan. So right now, you're learning what a strategic plan is. So you can take the tools that you learned here, and apply them in the real world." In my opinion, that is one way for Latinas to have even more power...They come to the table, they know how to form a goal, and they know how to develop a mission statement, and they know what an objective is, and they know what time lines are, and they know what evaluation means. To me, that is power. To me, that is knowledge. And to me, knowledge is power. And so that's how I explained it to women who were frustrated. And some of them stayed. And they are still there at the table.[21]

As Herrera Bortz suggests, for many board members, feelings of accomplishment, "ownership" of the organization, the sense of "making a difference," and feeling part of a community were fostered through the strategic planning process. This is particularly significant, as many of the board members felt alienated from these important processes when working within mainstream organizations. Montoya explains:

Even though the strategic planning was so mind numbing, you could see results. We had a mission statement, we had a name, we had the things that you need, the foundation, the infrastructure that you need in order to have an organization. And I felt like I was making more of a differ- ence. I'm having problems with Planned Parenthood right now, because I don't see where I can really affect much change, or contribute very much. Whereas with COLOR all along, my ideas have been listened to, and I've had input, and we've been forming an infrastructure, and doing stuff, which is really important, is actually taking action.[22]

Other COLOR members also experienced the unique satisfaction that came from completing the strategic planning process. Like Montoya, many had worked within mainstream reproductive rights organizations but felt that they were not able to be as involved as they would have liked. Core Latino values of razalogía—community learning, empower- ment, and social change—and conocimiento—shared awareness of each other's abilities and culture—were integrated and actively present in COLOR'S organizational planning.

Healthy Women, Healthy Families, and Future Programming

COLOR'S first major programmatic effort was a media campaign for the Latino community that it launched in the fall of 2002. Designed to raise social awareness of the importance of Latina health issues, the campaign also aimed to more formally introduce COLOR and its mission to the community. The first priority of the campaign was to focus on the community's needs, as identified by the community.[23] Because of lack of academic scholarship on Latina health, members felt that they needed to conduct their own community research to design an effective campaign. A volunteer with a PhD in anthropology trained COLOR members in some basic skills of social science research. Members then conducted a series of focus groups in both English and Spanish to canvass the needs community women expressed around issues of reproductive health.

Based on the focus groups, COLOR designed the media campaign with a simple message: the crucial connection between the health of a mother and the health of the entire family. The tag line that the group created, "Healthy Women, Healthy Families," stressed that because women are often mothers who care for many people, their health and well-being are crucial to maintaining the health of all other members of the family. COLOR members believed that focusing on the family was the best way to introduce issues of women's health into Latino communities, and all phases of the campaign focused on this general point. Drawing this message directly from focus group participants, COLOR developed and promoted a campaign directly responsive to the community, with the hope that the message would resonate more effectively.

The campaign promoted the Latina Information Line, a bilingual referral service offering information on abortion providers, safe sex practices, and general information about COLOR. The organization also developed a brochure listing resources in Colorado, including community health clinics, rape awareness and assistance, battered women's shelters, and places for getting HIV testing.

Based on the success of "Healthy Women, Healthy Families" and feedback from community members, COLOR has created Lesbianas Latinas Para la Salud Reproductiva (Latina Lesbians for Reproductive Health). COLOR is aware that Latina lesbians access health care and routine gynecological services less often than others and are therefore less likely to receive regular screening exams. The project promotes knowledge and awareness around reproductive health, particularly breast cancer, HIV, sexually transmitted infections, and domestic violence. That the initiative was proposed to the group by a community member who was also a COLOR volunteer and has now come to fruition speaks both to the success of the media campaign and COLOR'S visionary leadership. It not only significantly raised individual awareness of COLOR and its commitment to promoting health in Latino communities but also provided a forum for further community-driven work and health promotion to occur. Moreover, the program is unique in its explicit integration of issues of sexuality and lesbianism into a Latina reproductive health framework. This is notable, as COLOR is organizing in one of the most conservative states in the nation.

Education, Representation, and Transformation

As COLOR'S primary goal is to promote awareness of Latina reproductive health and rights, its main programmatic efforts focus on education. COLOR members have spoken at numerous professional and community organizations and national forums. In Denver, advocates and volunteers take a Latina perspective into the policy arena through their volunteer work with other organizations and networking. Although their broad directive offers distinct challenges, COLOR advocates believe that it is the only way to make effective change. As former board member Elicia Gonzales states, "We're trying to educate Latinas, and then the larger community, which are very different, but both important if we're going to enact any change."[24]

As board president, Herrera Bortz represents the organization both nationally and in the Colorado community. She gives several presentations per year on the status of Latina reproductive health to Latina/o and mainstream reproductive rights organizations alike. COLOR'S commitment to educating mainstream organizations about Latina issues is reflected in Herrera Bortz's presentations to Planned Parenthood and NARAL Pro-Choice America. At a Planned Parenthood of the Rocky Mountains training, Herrera Bortz presented "Is Choice a Diversities Issue?" which emphasized the cultural values that influence how Latinas make health choices, and how those decision-making processes influence their reproductive health. Often COLOR'S work includes providing basic education on who Latinas/os are, and the diversity of experiences that fit within this category. Herrera Bortz explains that many

times members of the general public are unaware that Latinas/os are a
diverse group:

> In Denver there's this whole myth that we are homogeneous... And we're
> not. And so that's very clear and evident to me. But I don't think it's evi-
> dent to non-Latinos and so I try to educate people on that. Every time I
> do a talk, I talk about demographics and subgroups and so forth to make
> people realize that. And people always thank me for that, they always
> come to me and say, "Oh, I was unaware, I didn't know."[25]

Much of the work of promoting awareness of Latina reproductive
health and rights occurs less formally, outside of specific COLOR directives. Since COLOR board members are involved with several other
health and community organizations, they have been able to introduce
Latina perspectives on reproductive politics to a larger audience through
the other organizations they are associated with.[26] In both paid and
volunteer work, COLOR members increase awareness of and promote
culturally proficient services for Latinas and their families, using tools
such as networking and education. COLOR members are able to bring
a critical Latina lens to all aspects of their work. For example, Darcí
Martínez was a COLOR board member for just over two years and also
the manager of a local Planned Parenthood clinic. In that role, Martínez
was always sure to educate the staff about the particularity of serving
Latina clients: "I constantly try to bring to my senior staff the status of
women in our community right now. Open your eyes; look at the issues.
Just bring it to the table. I think COLOR does that more than anything,
makes people aware."[27] While each of these efforts is not part of a deliberate strategy employed by COLOR, all board members are expected to
be present and actively advocate on behalf of Latina reproductive health
in whatever capacity they can.

COLOR'S Significance

COLOR has accomplished much in its first six years. In addition to its
programmatic work, members have built a solid infrastructure essential
to COLOR'S long-term viability. All members are proud of the work
they have accomplished, are incredibly fond of the organization, share
mutual respect for each other, and have experienced a bond that has been
absent in their other working relationships. Elicia Gonzales explains,
"We all had such different backgrounds, but similarities too. It felt more

like a family than any other group I've been in."[28] This close relationship has undeniably enabled the group to accomplish all the work that it has despite its limited resources.

COLOR has also stayed true to its goal of building leaders in the movement through skills building and training. In the process of fighting for reproductive health equity and bringing awareness to the health status of Latinas in Colorado and in the nation in general, COLOR simultaneously provides a place where Latina health professionals and activists find a supportive community where they can develop their organizing skills. This training has been crucial for all COLOR members, as they have found that mobilizing around Latinas' diverse reproductive needs is indeed challenging.

While attracting and retaining members and funding presents a significant challenge for most nonprofit organizations, the complications surrounding Latina reproductive politics can be additionally weighty. Part of this is the complexity of Latina reproductive health politics. As board member Montoya states:

> We're fighting a battle on many fronts, because we're fighting the sexism that exists in the Latino community, and we're fighting the racism that exists in the pro-choice community, and all of those things make it hard to attract members, and to attract funding and to move forward.[29]

Indeed, the pure broadness of the categories the group is trying to encompass—Latinas and reproductive and sexual health and rights—provide seemingly endless issues to work on. Moreover, COLOR'S vision considers reproductive health issues from the multiple standpoints of Latina lives. Montoya explains:

> It's kind of broad when we think of it. It's Latinas, so women from preteen up to grandma age, from all walks of life, recent immigrants up to people who have been here for generations, Spanish speakers and English speakers. Because I think that although a big array of people have different roadblocks to access to reproductive health, there's roadblocks all the way.[30]

As her reflections indicate, one of the challenges COLOR faces in its work is the large and diverse constituency. At the same time, it is forced to decide where to place the energies of the few individuals who carry on the work. Currently, there are simply not enough board members or volunteers to do all of the work that is necessary for the organization to grow. According to board member Gloria Sanchez, "[We] definitely need to recruit more members, and do more to keep more."[31]

All board members are aware that their capacity to effect change is hindered by their small size. On the other hand, since board members are also the organization's primary workers, they are clear that incoming members need to be able to commit the hours and energy necessary to do the hard work of the organization. Although limited resources are sometimes frustrating, Herrera Bortz believes that acknowledging and accepting these limitations is important, especially for a relatively new organization, as it provides some context for the important successes they do have and some understanding for when they feel as if they are not doing enough. The decision to grow slowly, focusing more on infrastructure and less on recruiting and retaining members, has presented an additional challenge, as they acknowledged themselves in 2000.

> An on-going problem with COLOR is recruitment. Due to the sensitive nature of being a Latina pro-choice organization many Latinas are unwilling to join. The reasons given by these women are that they feel that joining a pro-choice group will alienate them in the community and their jobs. We have accepted that the work we do can sometimes be controversial in our community, nevertheless we are committed to COLOR'S mission.[32]

Through their experience, board members found that while some women were reluctant to join a pro-choice organization, others became involved because of all of COLOR'S non-abortion-related programming. Although drawn to these other issues, many eventually leave because they experience personal conflict working on issues related to abortion.[33]

Low retention may be something those working on issues of reproductive freedom within the Latina communities must accept until reproductive health outreach is more widely acceptable in those communities. Herrera Bortz encourages other members to focus on the commitment of those who do participate, not the numbers. However, organizations with small member bases and big agendas often struggle with burnout. For many who have been involved in COLOR since its inception, building a nonprofit has entailed many more long hours of hard work than they had initially expected. Because each member is involved in every part of any project, many admit to feeling overwhelmed by the amount of time they put in. However, many stay committed for fear that if they do not do it, no one else will pick up this crucial work. There is concern that there is not a large pool of activists to replace them, which constantly reinforces that training the next generation of Latina leadership is also a critical part of their mission.

Another possible contributor to the lack of retention may be the stage COLOR is at in its development. COLOR has been able to start, maintain, and grow with a strong organizational infrastructure—something often neglected in newly started nonprofits. New nonprofits tend to focus more on the programs they want to institute and less on structure, which often leads to the demise of an organization. COLOR founders wanted to avoid that pattern, so they spent much of the group's first few years of existence establishing the infrastructure and ensuring that programming was of a high quality. Though it had the support of a larger, more experienced organization, in many ways, COLOR started from scratch and learned the skills of institutional development while building an organization from the ground up. This has resulted in a strong foundation and the empowerment of individual members but has led to varying degrees of burnout for some. It also likely contributed to the dropping out of individuals who were not able to make the same commitment of time and energy or who were not drawn to the work of organizational development. In the future, COLOR must think about how to integrate, utilize, and build community with those who have different strengths and abilities.

As Montoya suggested earlier, the lack of availability of funding for abortion and reproductive rights work also challenges the continuation of COLOR's work. Although COLOR has solicited funding from prominent Latino organizations, its requests have been denied because many Latino organizations are unwilling to promote a reproductive rights agenda for fear of alienation from Latina/o community members. According to Herrera Bortz, "It's limiting to be pro-choice because it really impacts funding. I can't tell you how many requests have been turned down, especially from Latinos...Two Latino-based funding requests were turned down. I know it's because we are pro-choice."[34] With such limited foundation support available, COLOR must build up the donations and fundraising efforts of the organization.

The organization also needs to establish an independent organizational and work space. To date, all of the organizational files, materials, and supplies have been located at board member and staff homes. Many of the board members hope that they can change this situation as soon as possible. As Montoya states that having "a home base makes you feel permanent."[35]

Board members are additionally coming to realize that one person cannot shoulder all of the administrative, fundraising, and programmatic tasks of COLOR, even in a funded position. Other than a brief period during which the organization had a program manager, all of the administrative tasks, including grant writing, were done by Herrera Bortz and sometimes Montoya, COLOR'S incoming president. An independent office would complement their goal of spreading organizational responsibility among members. As a working board, individual members must commit to doing more of the day-to-day work of the organization. With the transition of Herrera Bortz from this position, the organization faces a lot of change. One of the group's priorities should be to continue to develop the skills of the other board members.

While the organization has been recognized nationally,[36] it plans to develop a presence and network in the larger region of the Southwest. A larger networking circle would not only bring the group visibility, but help them find support from similar organizations that may be able to provide an advisory role or possibilities for coalition work.

Toward this end, COLOR must develop broader outreach to other Latina communities so that the organization truly reflects a multidimensional Latina voice. At present, all board members are of Mexican origin, and most identify as Chicana, though past members have been of other Latino origins. While their composition reflects the predominance of Mexican-origin communities in Colorado, the group strives to more fully address the full range of Latina experiences.

COLOR has made significant contributions to Latina reproductive and sexual health. Centering its cultural values and putting them into practice, COLOR has indeed made major steps toward bringing awareness to Latina perspectives on reproductive and sexual health rights and developing culturally proficient curriculum and health care models that will benefit Latino communities. As a group working within mainstream reproductive rights circles, COLOR is also developing a strong model of a culturally-based organization. In the process of fighting for reproductive health equity and bringing awareness to the status of Latinas in Colorado and in the nation in general, COLOR simultaneously provides an organizational forum within which Latina health professionals and activists have found mentorship and are learning organizational skills and capacity building.

COLOR is a direct descendant of past and current efforts to bring Latina voices to the table of organizing for reproductive and sexual health. It is determined to honor this legacy and continue this important work, despite the many challenges. As Herrera Bortz so effectively states, present conditions for the lives of many Latinas simply demand that the work must continue: "When the teenage pregnancy rate goes down and when Latinas do not have the highest HIV infection rate, when you know our women are getting prenatal care, and when our abortion rate goes down, then we'll stop working."[37]

NOTES

1   COLOR, "Pro-Choice Latina Organization Launches Media Campaign," news release, October 17, 2001.

2   COLOR, "Mission Statement" (organizational files).

3   COLOR, "Colorado Caucus Statement," Southwest NLIRH Forum, January 13, 1996.

4   Gloria Sanchez, interview by Elena R. Gutiérrez, July 12, 2002.

5   COLOR, "Profile: Melanie Herrera Bortz," (2003).

6   Melanie Herrera Bortz, interview by Elena R. Gutiérrez, July 12, 2002.

7   Charlene Ortiz, interview by Elena R. Gutiérrez, July 7, 2002.

8   Ibid.

9   Herrera Bortz, interview.

10   Ibid.

11   Ibid.

12   Ortiz, interview.

13   COLOR, "Profile."

14   "Pro-Choice Latina Organization Launches Education Campaign," *Hola Colorado*, October 26, 2001.

15   Jacinta Montoya, interview by Elena R. Gutiérrez, July 10, 2002.

16   Herrera Bortz, interview.

17   Montoya, interview.

18   Roberto Vargas and Samuel Martínez, *Razalogia: Community Learning for a New Society* (Oakland, CA: Razagente Associates, 1985).

19   Ibid.

20   Ortiz, interview.

21   Herrera Bortz, interview.

22   Montoya, interview.

23   Ibid.

24   Elicia Gonzales, interview by Elena R. Gutiérrez, July 22, 2002.

25   Herrera Bortz, interview.

26   A few of the organizations to which COLOR members belong are the Colorado Families Resource Network, the NARAL Pro-Choice Colorado, the Colorado Women's Agenda, the Latino STD/HIV Advocacy Coalition, the HIV Resources Planning Council, Planned Parenthood of the Rocky Mountains, and the Protect Families Protect Choice Coalition.

27   Darcí Martínez, interview by Elena R. Gutiérrez, July 13, 2002.

28   Gonzales, interview.

29   Montoya, interview.

30   Ibid.

31   Sanchez, interview.

32   Melanie Herrera Bortz et al., *Jessie Smith Noyes Foundation Final Report* (Denver, CO: COLOR, December 20, 2000), 3.

33   Herrera Bortz, interview.

34   Ibid.

35 Montoya, interview.

36 The hard work and vision of COLOR members is indeed being recognized nationally. Herrera Bortz was granted a 2003 Gloria Steinem Women of Vision Award from the Ms. Foundation for Women in recognition of her work with COLOR and her tireless efforts to fight for the reproductive and sexual rights of Latinas.

37 Herrera Bortz, interview.

15

Too Much to Deny

THE vibrant histories of resistance and activism presented here demonstrate that women of color have been deeply engaged in the struggle for reproductive justice. As researchers, we recovered, reflected upon, and sought to convey these histories and to draw lessons from the struggles they represent. We hope this work will lead to a deeper understanding of the contributions and perspectives of women of color regarding issues of reproductive justice. As activists, we want these narratives to inform the ways in which organizing takes place and to strengthen organizing efforts by women of color. We also hope they encourage multiracial organizations and women of color organizations to find additional ways to work together, in coalition and across lines of difference, to extend the sexual and reproductive health of all women.

In this concluding chapter, we assess the importance of organizing by women of color, first examining the role of identity politics in their struggle. We analyze why, and how, women of color redefined the meanings of reproductive rights and turned conferences and research into organizing tools. We analyze their organizing strategies and tactics, underlining the role of culture and community traditions. We outline the strategic alliances they fostered with the communities of color and the mainstream reproductive rights and social justice movements to advance their political agendas. We comment on the influence that women of color have had on pro-choice organizations, reproductive health discourses, and policy interventions at the local as well as the national level. Key organizational challenges they face, including funding, are analyzed. Finally, we explore the future directions that these women of color organizations are charting and suggest ways to enhance their important work.

Identity Politics Revisited

Contrary to broadly based critiques, which argue that identity politics fracture movements, we found that women of color organizations, by defining themselves through race and ethnicity, created spaces that nurtured their activism. The organizations they established served as retreats from the battles waged to get their perspectives across and issues raised in the mainstream pro-choice movement, within their own communities, and in other movements. Whereas the larger society and the pro-choice movement marginalize women of color perspectives and concerns, these identity-based organizations validate their particular perceptions of reality. Organizing around race and ethnicity enabled activists to regroup, re-enter, and engage in reproductive rights struggles. In these separate spaces they defined reproductive rights on their own terms, took leadership and action to realize these rights, and mobilized new constituencies and movements. They determined their own struggles and sites for action, thus resisting domination. Through this process, they developed culturally based styles of organizing and communicating and created focal points for action. Though not utopian, these spaces facilitated the imagining of alternative paths to achieve reproductive freedom.

Women of color have brought diverse voices and concerns to the political arena, broadening both the understanding of reproductive rights and the constituencies supporting them. In this way they have democratized the reproductive rights movement. By virtue of being embedded in the changing needs and concerns of their communities, they revitalize the meaning of reproductive rights on an on-going basis to include the concerns of those who are often overlooked. In general, their focus on the least privileged benefits all women. For example, the activism spearheaded by women of color to end sterilization abuse led to the development of guidelines and regulatory processes that provide protection for all women. Even if women of color agendas are incorporated by the mainstream, we think it is essential to maintain their autonomous organizations to play these pivotal and radical roles.

Women of color organizations need to be affirmed and seen neither as competing with other struggles to promote reproductive health and rights nor as a step in the process of integrating into the mainstream movement. Ideally, the independent organizing by women of color would be complemented by multiracial and multiethnic organizing that equitably distributes power and resources to benefit and empower women of color.

Multiracial organizations and collaborations should allow a broad range of groups to bring their concerns to bear in the articulation of reproductive health and sexual rights. Only through the sharing and exchange of ideas and experiences can the needs of all women be acknowledged and addressed. Otherwise, as we have seen time and again, what may represent an expansion of reproductive freedom for one group could be a diminution of freedom for another. In multiracial spaces, a cross-section of women is able to debate reproductive rights and technology issues from a variety of perspectives and take appropriate action that benefits all and does not compromise any woman's rights. Anti-racist work can also be conducted here. Such organizations enable the work done in women of color organizations to be known to and addressed by a broader constituency. This bridging work is crucial for forging common ground among different groups who have both shared concerns and particular interests.

Multiracial organizing efforts do exist in the reproductive rights movement, especially among younger activists and new organizations such as National Women's Alliance, Third Wave, and Choice USA. Their commitment to multiracial organizing signals a new development in reproductive rights organizing and is an encouraging development. However, as of now, multiracial organizations and coalitions are not sufficiently strong voices in the pro-choice movement, which is still dominated by middle-class white women and the politics of liberal feminism. If the pro-choice movement is to be more effective, it must be more inclusive of diverse reproductive rights perspectives and concerns beyond abortion. As we have heard from all of the groups in this book, a narrow abortion rights message and agenda alienates women of color; it also alienates low-income white women who share many of the same concerns as women of color. A sole focus on abortion is separated from the lives and daily concerns of most women. While a low-income woman may have one or two abortions in her life, she also must deal with poor, unsafe housing, inept medical care, lack of health insurance, pay inequities, and a host of other issues on an ongoing basis. Severing abortion from these day-to-day concerns casts the pro-choice movement as overprivileged, elitist, and insensitive to the realities of many women's lives. Whereas liberal feminism basically addresses gender-based economic inequalities and seeks reform through legal changes, a more radical feminist politics challenges the entire system, linking all forms of oppression. The reproductive rights agenda that women of color propose cannot be disengaged from structural economic violence, inequality, and racism, and it is on this point that these two political philosophies—a radical versus a liberal feminist agenda—clash. But it is this challenge to economic injustice that opens up the most promising opportunities for revitalizing and broadening the pro-choice movement.

Political Roots of Women of Color Struggles

The radical agenda that women of color pursue has its roots in other progressive social movements. The majority of the founders of the women of color organizations we examined were involved in broader social justice movements—civil rights, feminism, women's health, and Native American sovereignty. Leadership opportunities for women of color within these movements were lacking and they had to contend with a considerable amount of sexism.

The commitment of women of color to reproductive rights often generated controversy in their communities. Most Nationalist organizations failed to address gender issues, with the exception of two groups, the Puerto Rican Young Lords Party and the Black Panther Party. Bitter and divisive debate continues in communities of color over whether the struggle for reproductive rights diverts attention from anti-racist and sovereignty struggles. Thus, reproductive justice advocates face resistance in their communities, as well as from the pro-choice movement, and walk a fine line in both spaces. In pro-choice circles, they are often the only women of color and the ones who raised race-related concerns. In their own communities, they are the only ones talking about issues of sexual and reproductive rights. Peggy Saika, board chair of Asians and Pacific Islanders for Reproductive Health, said that APIRH had to be the affirmative action people within the pro-choice movement, a sentiment echoed by many of the other leaders we featured here. Facing resistance at both ends led women of color to feel embattled, isolated, and vulnerable.

Despite these problems, progressive movements shaped the psyches and the organizational mandates of women of color groups. The philosophies and political agendas of these movements were the foundations upon which these organizations built. In addition to working within mainstream pro-choice organizations and their communities, some women of color organizations made connections with evolving social justice movements such as the environmental justice, anti-sweatshop, and immigrant rights movements.

Women of color organizations have affected and been affected by those women's health and reproductive rights movements that made the politics of race/ethnicity and class integral to their organizing. Many white women in the women's health movement of the 1960s and 70s were engaged with or sympathetic to the civil rights movement, which made them realize the importance of anti-racist work. Organizations that were, or attempted to be, explicitly attuned to addressing race within predominantly white organizations were the earliest supporters of the women of color activists and organizations in this book, in particular the National Women's Health Network (NWHN).[1] In addition to having women of color on the NWHN's board of directors, the NWHN supplied organizational support, provided funds directly, and shared its funding contacts as well as field networks that opened doors for women of color activists.

To advance their agendas and perspectives, women of color sought out the support of women of color and white women allies working in mainstream institutions. The ally role that white women in mainstream groups played allowed for some significant action, such as sponsoring national conferences and meetings of women of color, like the "In Defense of *Roe*" conference in 1989. Race-conscious white women allies also served as bridge builders between autonomous women of color organizations and the movements for choice and women's health.

Redefining Reproductive Rights

As the varied histories of women of color organizations described here illustrate, women of color are not the subjects of a single experience or history of racism. Each group had to address its particular history of reproductive oppression and to articulate its particular positive vision and agenda for reproductive freedom, which included demanding the right to have children free from coercion, either by the state or through community pressure. Claiming reproductive rights in a culturally specific and meaningful way was essential to developing a political agenda and a constituency base. Thus, defining the meaning of reproductive rights was a highly charged, politicized exercise and a key step in the organization-building process of each group.

The Native American groups emphasize land sovereignty and the right to maintain and sustain their communities and culture. The historical trauma of having their children taken away from them to be brought up in boarding schools and foster homes shaped their reproductive rights agenda, which also includes cultural and spiritual development and the right to live as Native peoples. Colorado Organization for Latina Opportunity and Reproductive Rights (COLOR) believes that reproductive and sexual rights are central to achieving full equality and opportunity for Latinas in the US. They see their work to secure reproductive rights as part of a long history of Latino activism on issues of social justice. For African American women, bodily integrity is crucial, as this right was wrenched from them during slavery. Immigration restrictions and abuses frame the reproductive rights agendas of Latinas and Asian Americans. Medical experimentation, discriminatory treatment, poor quality of care, and abuse, as well as issues of population control, were concerns across communities of color. Similarly, as people of color communities are disproportionately poor, the right to have the financial resources to maintain their families is crucial for women of color to realize their reproductive rights. Cultural competency—the idea that providers should understand and respect the languages, customs, and traditions of the communities they serve—has been an important demand across women of color groups.

The organizations in this book that initially formed by organizing around issues of abortion and contraception never separated these issues from other reproductive health concerns. As a result, they moved quickly to action on a broader range of needs and rights. Their communities have different reproductive rights realities and needs, and "choice" is not where they enter the movement. To be relevant in their own communities, they adopted a broad approach that encompassed a range of reproductive rights and wrongs. We see this in the names of the groups, their missions, and their agendas, which are holistic, with reproductive rights being part of a broader health and social justice framework. Casting their names and mission in terms of reproductive health, and most recently reproductive justice, offers an opportunity for dialogue that can include choice but not be restricted by it. Access to basic health services, issues of poverty, and language and cultural barriers were core concerns across women of color organizations that a politicized health framework encapsulates.

Mainstream society has classified women of color broadly into four ethnic categories, ignoring the differences these definitions span. Furthermore, narrowing the women of color to four categories eliminates entire groups altogether. With whom do immigrant women from Africa, the Middle East, and the non-Latin Caribbean, or women of color who identify as multiracial find solidarity? Keenly aware of the problems inherent in such an arbitrary and sweeping classification system, activists attended to the multiplicity of identities encompassed within each grouping. For example, the National Latina Health Organization (NLHO) and COLOR strive to be sensitive to the differing needs, cultures, language nuances, and immigrant experiences among Latinas, who include Puerto Ricans and women of Mexican and Central American origin as well as Cuban Americans. Native groups respect the different tribal histories and sovereign authority of indigenous nations. Asian women's groups strive to be pan-Asian in staffing and to organize around health concerns in specific communities. For example, the National Asian Women's Health Organization (NAWHO) had separate outreach and research efforts to accommodate the different cultural and language needs of the various Asian communities it serves. It has different organizers for the South Asian and Southeast Asian communities, who know the language and culture of each group. Organizing priorities also differ depending upon community identified needs.

Cultural struggle—finding their voice and framing issues in ways that resonate within their communities—is part and parcel of the political struggle of women of color organizations. All of the activists sought to preserve the connection to their culture and community, consciously drawing on those resources and traditions. Where possible, women of color activists work with community institutions, leaders, and organizations that share their objectives. They reach out to spiritual leaders and draw on spiritual and traditional practices, indigenous knowledge, music, and dance in their organizing efforts that enable a cross-section of the community members to contribute or participate in cultural activities.

Women of color developed culturally specific tools and organizing strategies to advance their work, such as the Self-Help approach pioneered by the National Black Women's Health Project (NBWHP). Self-Help enables women to come to terms with internalized racism and to develop the confidence to undertake advocacy and organizing to improve their health status. This emotional process is liberatory: it provides a space to raise and share fear and trauma and work with others to overcome these impediments. The NLHO also adopted these methods, adapting them for Latinas. Native women in Akwesasne, by connecting with cultural traditions associated with dance and midwifery, were able to start the process of self and community healing. APIRH embarked on a year-long set of dialogues with community members and leaders to formulate its organizational agenda. COLOR adopted *conocimiento* to enhance personal and group power. Working one-on-one, in small group sessions, and in circles on issues of internalized oppression and self-esteem were essential features of their reproductive rights work.

By defining their work in the context of political and cultural struggles in their communities, activists have reached new constituencies and actors to support reproductive freedom. For instance, the NBWHP has developed an ongoing relationship with African American leaders in Congress and educates them about black women's health status, concerns, and needs. By doing so the group has garnered congressional support for a reproductive health agenda. Similarly, NAWHO works with Asian American elected officials and Asian community leaders and members, and Native American activists have brought reproductive health concerns to the attention of public health agencies as well as to their communities and social movements.

Working within the confines of community has its drawbacks too. In the community arena, issues of race and ethnicity are privileged as the primary categories of oppression. This ignores how different systems of stratification intersect in the construction of identity and the meaning and experiences of reproductive rights. Differences of sexuality, disability, and class were mostly glossed over among the women of color groups we examined. It is noteworthy, for example, that though sexuality and sexuality education has been an important component of their work, many women of color organizations have not dealt directly with lesbian issues. Some of this is related to the homophobia that exists in their communities. Despite the fact that some of the leaders of the organizations were lesbian, they chose not to organize on lesbian, bisexual, and transgender issues, and there did not seem to be significant internal pressure to take clear stands on lesbian concerns. While lesbians participated in the organizations, were often in leadership positions, and presented at conferences, issues of sexual orientation and homophobia were not largely integrated into organizational agendas.

The lack of attention to homophobia represents a missed opportunity among women of color organization as it is among mainstream groups. Sexual rights are the part of the human rights framework that speaks more directly to the right of bodily integrity and freedom from sexual abuse and challenges discrimination based on gender and/or sexual orientation. They are also affirmative rights and include the right to sexual pleasure, self-expression, and intimacy. Sexual rights were very central in the development of the women's health movement, but the hegemonic and more liberal pro-choice agenda pushed issues of sexuality to the margins of the movement. Pro-choice and reproductive rights became synonymous and, in the process, issues of sexuality were peeled away from reproductive rights. Women of color organizations also failed to tie sexual rights securely to their definitions of reproductive rights. However, had they confronted the lesbian question, perhaps this disjuncture between sexual and reproductive rights would not have occurred. In the ongoing constructions of a collective identity, "deciding who we are requires deciding who we are not. All social movements, and identity movements in particular, are thus in the business, at least sometimes of exclusion."[2] These exclusions are often strategic. Clearly, there were groups of women, such as lesbians within ethnic groups, whose concerns were marginalized in women of color organizations. It is among the newer multiracial formations like National Women's Alliance, Third Wave, and Choice USA that sexual orientation and sexual rights are being more seriously engaged.

Coming Together: The Impetus for Organizing

The conference as a space for education and discussion was adopted and transformed by communities of color as a critical organizing tool. Conferences served as catalysts to community-based organizing. The initial conferences were large inspirational gatherings that drew women from an identity-based group together for the first time around issues of reproductive rights and were defining or "movement moments" for each of the groups. The exhilaration and enormous energy palpable in the first gathering, the Black Women's Health Conference at Spelman, was experienced by the other groups at their early conferences as well. They drew diverse women within each community around a common purpose, enabling political agendas for action to emerge. All of the groups worked extensively to ensure that their conferences reached out broadly within their respective communities, which they saw as crucial for forging an inclusive agenda.

Coming together to learn more about themselves and to chart an agenda for other women who shared their racial/ethnic identity enabled participants to develop new understandings of themselves as individuals and as part of a community. Particular attention was directed toward bringing economically vulnerable women to the conferences. Learning from one another's experiences was revelatory, with the dialogues between poor and middle-class and professional women being among the most powerful exchanges. However, the organizations we studied found it difficult to sustain the momentum generated by these conferences. A different set of skills and significant organizational infrastructure are necessary to build on conference energy and create networks and programs to implement the vision that is so inspirational for conference participants. Conferences are resource-intensive in terms of labor and finances and are not adaptable to creating regular channels for movement building and outreach. Repeated conferences, without the interim organizational building necessary, can lead to overextension, disillusion, and dissolution. Thus, it is not surprising that many of the groups have abandoned the conference structure or employ it much less as an organizing force.

The NBWHP stood the longest by its commitment to host annual conferences, but it had to abandon these meetings due to financial difficulties. Other groups like the NLHO, NAWHO, APIRH, and African American Women Evolving (AAWE) tapped the conference process in their initial development stage to identify and energize their constituencies. However, withdrawing from using the conference as a mobilizing vehicle, and instead relying on electronic and newsletter outreach together with mobilization on a program and project basis, may have made the organizations less open to new ideas and new leadership as well as more distant from their membership. While these digital-age outreach strategies reach greater numbers of people, they are less effective for encouraging a new and diverse set of recruits and encourage passivity among supporters. It remains a challenge for women of color organizations to find ways to raise resources to strategically utilize the conference mobilizing process to enhance program development and institution building activities, as well as to encourage a new and diverse set of recruits to this movement and to respond to the emerging concerns their constituencies.

Outreach within and Across Communities

Beyond the conferences, activists reached out to women in their communities as well as to women they saw as allies within the US and beyond. They paid special attention to the needs of economically vulnerable women, who are disproportionately represented in communities of people of color and immigrants.[3] However, although most of the groups have tried to address the needs of economically disadvantaged women, they are not primarily poor women's organizations. The rank and file members, staff, and leaders are mainly middle-class, educated women, many of whom are health practitioners or advocates. The emphasis on reaching and bringing in low-income women as key organizational actors, which some of the groups emphasized at the outset, was not operationalized. Systematic efforts are still needed to give low-income women greater presence and voice.

Most of the organizations viewed young people as a key constituency and were committed to developing the next generation of leaders. Several incorporated this commitment in their leadership, organizational structures, boards, and activities. NAWHO, APIRH, and AAWE are all led and staffed by women in their 20s and 30s. APIRH and NAWHO focused on building youth leadership, which was particularly evident in APIRH's Health, Opportunities, Problem-Solving, and Empowerment Project (HOPE) for girls and the NAWHO National Leadership Network.

Intergenerational work is also valued across women of color groups. Among NBWHP's first projects was a film featuring African American women and their daughters talking about menstruation and sexuality. More recently, AAWE has produced a video of mothers and daughters talking about reproductive health and sexuality, which is used to encourage intergenerational understanding. Native American Women's Health Education Resource Center (NAWHERC) consciously builds on the elders model, in which activists relearn and draw sustenance from the wisdom of their elders and from traditional culture. NBWHP has a college-based program, and the Walking for Wellness Project draws on a cross-generational constituency. The NLHO has developed an intergenerational conference model where women of all ages can come together to learn about and share their concerns. NAWHO has embarked on a project to talk about sexuality with kids.

International connections have also been important for US women of color involved in reproductive rights. Charon Asetoyer of NAWHERC made links with indigenous movements in other parts of the world and was active in the Indigenous Women's Network (IWN). Through these organizations and their leadership, women of color had an organized, collective presence at the United Nations' Cairo (1994) and Beijing (1995) conferences, the World Conference Against Racism (2001), the series of UN conferences on HIV/AIDS, and the International Women's Health Meetings, where they brought unique women of color perspectives to the deliberations. They found that they shared many of the same experiences of coercion with regards to population control with women around the world and joined in efforts to challenge reproductive oppression through international conference declarations and other joint statements.

Researchers of Their Own Reality

The dearth of data regarding the reproductive and sexual health of women of color compelled activists in all of the organizations to undertake primary research for their respective constituencies. This was essential to determining community outreach and intervention strategies as well as to developing appropriate policy advocacy positions. For example, the Mother's Milk Project, NAWHERC, and NAWHO developed extensive research agendas, partnering with academic, national, and state health researchers at places such as Cornell University, the Centers for Disease Control, and the Office of Minority Health. Through such initiatives, they have pressured the government to undertake research and programming that addresses the reproductive health of women of color. These efforts have had a broad impact on national health policy, especially with regard to racial disparities in health and health care. APIRH employed the Participatory Action Research (PAR) model in all of its work and developed the Reproductive Freedom Tour as well as the HOPE project for girls to enable community members to identify community problems. Using PAR, they devised community based solutions to reproductive health hazards in the community and to sexual harassment in the schools. AAWE, too, conducted research on access to emergency contraception for African American women and worked to make it more available.

The research that has been carried out by women of color groups is action oriented, participatory, and serves numerous objectives, sometimes simultaneously. The research process itself often drew on community traditions: for example, NAWHERC used the roundtable process to talk about and document the personal experiences of Native American women. In this way, women of color activists transformed the research process and broke down the barriers between researchers and their subjects. Their findings—high incidence of infertility among African American women, fetal alcohol syndrome among Native American women, breast cancer among Asian and Pacific Islander (API) women— have been used to galvanize their constituencies to advocate for changes in policies and programs to address critical health needs.[4] For example, the research conducted at Akwesasne on birthing and breast milk contamination conceptualized the women's body as the "first environment." It made the direct connection between a woman's body and environmental toxins that has been pivotal in developing further studies by national health agencies in the US and Canada on environmental impacts on reproductive health.

The research process—design, methods employed, researchers, and partnerships forged—and the ways in which the results were used, were also forms of political activism. For example, Katsi Cook trained Native women to "become researchers of their own reality" and in so doing empowered them to conduct community health research and advocate on their own behalf and inspired a few Native women to attain advanced academic training and degrees. Similarly, the findings were used to inform and mobilize the communities and ultimately to change health policies and practices by securing more health resources for those communities.

Organizational Structures

The organizations represented here run the gamut in terms of their size, agenda emphasis, organizational structures, and leadership styles. Some, like NAWHO and the NBWHP, have centralized organizational structures and over time have garnered impressive resources for their work. Others, including Mother's Milk Project, APIRH, COLOR, and the NLHO, are more loosely structured, and less formal or professionalized. For example, both NAWHO and the NBWHP have more hierarchical leadership and organizational styles and tend to be staff run.

They have presidents or executive directors who earn comparatively high professional salaries, while the grassroots organizations tend to rely more on volunteers for both staffing and board members. The offices of some organizations are well appointed and their board meetings and other formal gatherings are upscale compared with the more grassroots women of color groups.

The need to develop strong institutions is an ongoing challenge for women of color groups. Pursuing work on several fronts, taking on a holistic agenda, and developing the internal structures necessary to facilitate the work, all coupled with a consistent lack of steady funding, is daunting. The organizations have tried different structures with varying degrees of success, including organizing chapters, functioning as loose networks, developing membership models, being volunteer driven, and creating staff-driven organizations. However, with the pressure to play so many roles at once, they have paid insufficient attention to issues of transparency and accountability, which has led to dissatisfaction and disillusionment among staff members in several instances. Staff development as well as setting in place institutional policies and procedures to make sure that these organizations are not dominated and controlled by a founding leader are important to address.

These women of color organizations were founded by strong and charismatic leaders and have not been able to adequately develop the next line of leadership and ways to share responsibility and authority. The women of color movement suffers from the "founders syndrome," where a few leaders become the face of the organizations they represent. This, however, is not unique to reproductive rights organizations led by women of color. It tends to be a problem shared by many of the grassroots nonprofit organizations. This is beginning to change, as the number of women of color leaders and organizations is increasing steadily with time, allowing more diverse voices to speak out on the issues. Developing leadership beyond the founding ranks and bringing in the next generation of leaders are critical challenges, in which several of the organizations are now engaged, as a few founding "mothers" have stepped aside. Among them are Byllye Avery, Peggy Saika, and Mary Chung, who continue to play a supportive role. Thus, while they have made room for new leadership to emerge, their organizations have not lost their expertise and dedication.

There have been some ideological tensions between the professional versus the grassroots orientations of women of color groups, both within and between women of color groups. A few organizations are more policy focused than based in community organizing. However, women of color are redefining what it means to be engaged in policy work by underlining the importance of bringing local voices to national attention. Disagreements have arisen among women of color regarding whether those working on the policy level or grassroots base-building groups are better placed to speak on behalf of or represent the community. More professional or national groups, due to their access to resources, have an advantage as spokespersons, while grassroots organizations are closer to the community and thus more representative and better able to speak on community issues. Again, each has a distinct space and contribution to make, but due to the competition for funds, there is often jockeying among women of color groups regarding who should speak on behalf of or represent a community.

A shift from grassroots political work toward more emphasis on policy level and professional organizational style could reflect a political shift away from an oppositional and radical politics. However, we contend that the lines between what constitutes a radical or a mainstream group are blurred or less meaningful among women of color reproductive rights groups. No matter what the organization's offices, staff hierarchies, or budget size, advocacy on behalf of the rights of women of color, especially low-income women, constitutes a radical agenda. It is the content of the agenda, the alliances and analysis that ground the work, and the constituencies mobilized that make for a radical agenda.

Working with Mainstream Pro-Choice Organizations to Advance a Policy Agenda

Most of the women of color activists who were involved in reproductive rights and health policy brought with them experiences of frustration from their attempts to include their issues in mainstream pro-choice agendas. Even when their efforts were successful, the work took its toll. Cherríe Moraga discusses the challenges that women of color confront when working in the mainstream:

> Our strategy is how we cope, on an everyday basis, how we measure and weigh what is to be said and when, what is to be done and how, and to

whom...daily deciding/risking who it is we can call an ally, call a friend, whatever that person's skin, sex or sexuality. We are women without a line. We are women who contradict each other.[5]

Constantly negotiating shifting currents of power is an untaught method of survival.[6] In our research, we found activists were at once engaged in and drained by such survival strategies in their relationships with white feminists and the mainstream pro-choice movement.

Once women of color formed their own groups, they thought they would be in a better position to pressure pro-choice organizations to address their concerns. Newly formed women of color groups banded together in the late 1980s and early 90s to promote a women of color agenda. They demanded to have a seat at policy tables and in marches, programs, and legislative policies to promote reproductive rights, because decisions about agendas and strategies were made by the large, mainstream pro-choice organizations with little input from women of color. However, at that time, fledgling women of color organizations did not command the political or economic clout in terms of organizational resources to negotiate a place at the policy table, and their attempts to influence the pro-choice movement bore little fruit. While women of color believed they should be included regardless of their organizational resources, the mainstream groups did not operate in this way; they excluded other white organizations that lacked resources as well. Sometimes this led to public critiques of mainstream organizations by women of color. However, their complaints about being excluded from decision making did not lead to their inclusion.

It was not until the 1990s that the NBWHP and NAWHO were able to command a place at pro-choice policy tables. NBWHP established its Public Policy and Education Office in Washington, DC, in 1990 so that it could promote a broad range of policies to improve black women's health and serve as a voice for African American women in national policy deliberations. NAWHO had a Washington office for the same purposes. NAWHO and the NBWHP started to build congressional support for their advocacy work. This increased their bargaining power vis-à-vis the mainstream groups that were legislatively focused. The National Latina Institute for Reproductive Health also tried to cultivate this political capacity, but the effort overextended the resources of the organization, causing it to shut down for a period of time. Native

American groups focused on sovereignty in attempts to address main-stream public policy agendas.

A great deal of effort and time was spent by women of color activists to ensure the presence of women of color at pro-choice events and decision-making circles. To date these issues have not been resolved. No organizations of women of color were originally included in the decision to hold the 2004 March for Women's Lives when it was planned by the National Organization for Women, Planned Parenthood, the Feminist Majority, NARAL Pro-Choice America, and ACLU. A storm of criticism over the lack of inclusion led to important changes. The name had originally been the March for Choice and it was changed to reflect a broader reproductive rights agenda. Co-author Loretta Ross was hired as the co-director for the march and the four-person steering committee was expanded to include the National Latina Institute for Reproductive Health and the Black Women's Health Imperative (formerly the National Black Women's Health Project).

Other problems arose when women of color tried to bring their perspectives to the pro-choice movement. Mainstream organizations often viewed individual leaders of women of color organizations as representatives or spokespersons for entire communities. Consequently, a handful of representatives were called on repeatedly to serve in this capacity. While the reliance on a few women of color as representatives to the mainstream made for continuity and familiarity for the mainstream groups, this tactic had its drawbacks. Already slim resources were stretched further, as women of color leaders were pulled out of the work that needed to be done in their communities to play the role of national spokesperson for their identity group. It also led to some jockeying among women of color to ensure their group was represented, and this was sometimes divisive in terms of relationships with other women of color.

The issue of appropriate spokespersons was compounded by the perception that the so-called "representatives" of women of color were not selected by women of color but were "anointed" from outside. Frequently a well-meaning foundation officer or member of a mainstream group would select a person as a spokeswoman for an ethnic group. Typically the person selected was someone who was either familiar or whose style and politics they recognized. This in turn produced the "star" syndrome among a few women of color, who sometimes had disproportionate access to information, resources, and wider networks. This underlines the catch-22 situation that many women of color organizations face: demanding to be "at the table," when there are few representatives that are constantly called upon, carries its own burdens. This issue needs to be addressed by both white women and women of color. White women must be willing to increase the representation of women of color; women of color must be willing to make space for others to participate.

Reflecting on these experiences, we see the pressure on thinly staffed and poorly funded groups to be active on yet another front. Their work with mainstream organizations was in addition to their core activities, which included doing research and outreach in their communities and trying to affect state and federal legislative public health policy. Few mainstream pro-choice groups play all these roles at once, except for the very large ones.

The forays that women of color made into the mainstream underline the importance of simultaneously continuing to work in their own organizations and networks and where they think it is expedient, to ally with other mainstream or women of color organizations to advance their objectives. However, serving as a/the voice for women of color in mainstream circles—from a position of inequality—was onerous and sometimes even undermined efforts to consolidate their own work. It took time and energy away from other tasks necessary to meet the needs of their own organizations and constituencies. This led activists to question whether their efforts were warranted, especially when the mainstream seemed resistant to change. COLOR, AAWE, and APIRH were concerned about this problem but felt obligated to keep trying to affect mainstream discourses and policies. For example, Julia Scott, as the head of the NBWHP at the Washington office, was regularly asked to be the representative for all women of color, which hampered her efforts to develop a political agenda for her own organization. Mary Chung, Luz Alvarez Martínez, and Charon Asetoyer were repeatedly being called upon to speak for Asian Americans, Latinas, and Native Americans respectively. Thus, the selecting of representatives could be viewed as a double-edged sword—while it was useful in promoting women of color perspectives in the mainstream, it also led to the depletion of women of color resources.

Challenges of Funding

The lack of steady and consistent funding for the core operations of their organizations has plagued the development of women of color groups. The funding community has been less hospitable to the broad agenda of reproductive rights that women of color organizations embrace. In part this is a structural issue. Small foundations are often single-issue oriented and the larger foundations are structured into various programs with different program officers in charge. Thus, groups that work across issues often do not fit foundation program guidelines and structures. Foundations are typically more responsive to the single-issue abortion and contraception rights and access funding requests of most mainstream pro-choice organizations than to the broad political agendas of women of color organizations. For example, while the NBWHP focused on Self-Help, empowerment, and constructing an African American health agenda through the convening of large conferences, it had a hard time raising funds from donors for these activities. It is easier to raise funds for a single issue or legal advocacy work around a single issue, which is why most foundations were more interested in funding the NBWHP Public Education Policy office over the base-building mobilization using the Self-Help model that characterized the work of the Atlanta Mother House. Committed to Self-Help, the NBWHP has never been able to fund this core activity.

While we think that work at both the base-building and policy level is important, reproductive rights funders have been more supportive of traditional and professional organizations over base-building efforts. This preference has ramifications in the field, as women of color groups must compete with mainstream groups for scarce resources that at best do not really support their holistic agendas and at worst actually undermine them. Despite the funding challenges, the advantages of a broad strategy outweighed the difficulties. It brings an organization a greater number of potential allies. Working to improve women's health in a social justice or human rights framework meant that groups could more easily build alliances with other movements working on civil rights, community empowerment, environment, and health care access, whether or not there was a reproductive rights or gender component.

Foundation staff are under pressure from their boards to show that their grant making is having significant impact. While it is relatively easier to measure whether or not an organization makes a difference in the legislative sphere, it is harder to assess the grassroots work in which women of color are often engaged. Working on issues of internalized oppression, which is so important to enable women of color to take action on other fronts, is a vital part of reproductive rights work among the groups we studied but is much harder to evaluate. Different evaluation measures are needed if women of color are to be supported in their multilayered strategies.

The Ms. Foundation, though its grants were usually small, was crucial for almost all of the organizations. In the early 1980s, Ms. and the Ruth Mott Foundation were among the few funders that were ready to invest in women of color organizing. The Ms. grants were invaluable because of the leverage they gave organizations to reach out for other funds and for the networking and technical assistance that they provided the grantees. During the mid-1980s, the advent of several women of color program officers to positions in small and larger foundations was also important for women of color organizations to garner funds for their work. For the most part, women of color funders were open to the particular needs confronting the groups and were more sympathetic to the inclusive analysis and vision of reproductive rights organizing.[7] The education and lobbying efforts with other funders to understand the importance of the work that women of color were doing was as important as direct financial assistance. These foundations continue to provide core support for women of color groups and to be advocates for women of color in the funding community.

Sometimes funders' strategies, however inadvertent, put groups in competition with each other. For example, it seemed that there was a cap on the number of women of color groups from each community that would be supported. Providing funds to only one African American organization rather than a range of African American groups working on reproductive rights meant that one voice from each community would often get unduly amplified and others would not be heard. Once there was one Latina reproductive rights organization, it was hard to raise funds for another one, as a funding portfolio already had Latina representation. Such an approach is racist to women of color since donors do not just support one white women's organization to serve as the representative or token voice. They typically fund a diversity of pro-choice organizations to capture a range of issues and approaches. Only recently are foundations becoming more open to seeking a diversity of voices and strategies within the women of color reproductive rights and health movement.

The politics of funding white women's groups to organize women of color also caused considerable tensions. It reinforced white hegemony because the white organizations held the purse strings. This strategy created resentment among women of color groups, who felt used rather than being equal partners. It also meant that there was less money to directly fund women of color groups.

Cobbling together many small grants is a very labor-intensive and time-consuming process, especially for groups that do not have staff fundraisers. Fundraising is an enormous burden on the director of any non-profit, but it is intensified for women of color who have all the regular functions of directors and, in addition, serve as the token person of color in numerous situations.

One promising development is the Funders Network Women of Color Strategy Group. This initiative by the Funders Network represents a group of funders committed to strengthening the role and leadership of women of color within the reproductive health and rights movement. The group has organized sessions at the network meetings and commissioned research to "understand better the barriers to experiences in, and importance of women of color in reproductive rights organizations and leadership."[8] Women of color are also trying to change the way in which donors and grantees interact and to make this relationship more of a partnership. Through their work in the SisterSong Collective and Third Wave Foundation, women of color are trying to envision what a partnership between donors and grantees would look like and are questioning the way it would affect the traditional power relationship. They are exploring the risks entailed in such a partnership as well as the promises.

Women of Color Organizing—Outcomes

The impact of women of color organizing around reproductive rights has been far-reaching. Women of color organizations have made sure that concerns and issues central to women from their communities are defined, registered, and represented. They have drawn increased government attention, resources, and services to their communities, especially to the reproductive health needs of the most underserved in those communities, and brought about important policy changes. New research has been carried out on topics that were not addressed by the mainstream movement or health institutions. Creating and developing new program interventions, initiating reproductive health and education services that previously did not exist in their communities, raising state and federal attention, and creating programs and generating funds to address the needs of their constituencies, these organizations have provided an essential voice to health policy formulation and decision making.

Through the development of women of color organizations, an entire new set of leaders has emerged. They have become commanding voices for expanding and promoting reproductive rights and have developed a new agenda for action. They are dedicated to extending leadership, training, and mentoring for the next generations, who will come into a movement that values their participation and provides mentorship and support. This will insure that there is a cadre of leaders who can articulate the reproductive health needs of their communities, engage in outreach, research, and education, and have greater political education and connections to promote the reproductive health needs of their communities. We are already seeing the impact of their work both in the organizations profiled here and in new multiracial groups. Younger activists are increasingly drawing on the holistic perspective that women of color have articulated. They employ many of the techniques and tools that women of color have created to advance a more inclusive agenda.

There are more women of color working in senior positions in mainstream pro-choice organizations who are allying with women of color groups to build a broader-based movement. The demands by women of color, coupled with the pressure exerted by some foundations for greater representation of women of color in the movement, have resulted in more women of color leaders on the boards and staff of mainstream organizations.

Within the mainstream organizations and movement, the organizing of women of color has raised awareness of their communities' reproductive rights issues. Women of color have spotlighted issues of marginalization, discrimination, and inequity and raised important new perspectives. The organizing by women of color around the Hyde Amendment and welfare reform, and the critical approaches they brought to the promotion of Norplant and Depo-Provera, have made pro-choice organizations more sensitive to discriminatory reproductive health policies. Women of color have also been somewhat successful in making issues of infant mortality, drug use during pregnancy, infertility, and reproductive tract infections important elements of a comprehensive reproductive health agenda. In a recent survey commissioned by the Funders Network, most representatives of mainstream organizations interviewed said they thought "women of color look at reproductive health and rights issues in ways that differ from the prevailing mainstream perspectives."[9] The differences included looking at access rather than rights and having a holistic way of seeing reproductive rights issues which goes beyond health care issues to include housing, jobs, and safety for their children.

Many of the activists whose work is represented in this book were in Atlanta at the SisterSong National Reproductive Health and Sexual Rights conference in the fall of 2003 that brought together a wider circle of women, service providers, policy-makers, and allies to discuss and develop strategies to improve the reproductive health of women of color in the US. Since the last time women of color met nationally in 1989, many more women of color activists and organizations are involved in organizing and advocacy for reproductive justice. The 600 women at Atlanta are rejuvenating a movement for the reproductive rights of all women. Linda Burnham of the Women of Color Resource Center described it as "a touchstone event in the struggle for reproductive rights and the development of women of color organizing."[10] The sheer range of sexual and reproductive rights work being done by women of color in mainstream movements, in their own organizations, and in other social justice and human rights organizing, as well as the variety of forms in which this takes place, indicates that the activism of women of color has entered a new phase. For many of the attendees, it felt like a reproductive rights movement was aflame outside of the mainstream.

This new phase of organizing for reproductive rights must address an enormous range of urgent health issues. Women of color work in a world in which their people lack access to basic health care while killer pandemics like AIDS ravage their communities. They have to guard against and challenge new and devious twists in population control such as the "war on terrorism,"[11] and they will have to confront more covert forms of racism and sexism threatening their right to safe and healthy lives. Activists must somehow extend their limited resources to engage in public policy debates as health care access becomes increasingly limited for vulnerable and underserved populations. They have to continually point out and sustain the spiritual dimensions of reproductive justice organizing, and ensure that their cultures and traditions are not extinguished in the drive to homogenize the American population. Women of color have to be the tellers of their own stories, and more among them must document their own activism to maintain the authenticity of their voices and experiences.

Activists must be firm in their support for abortion rights, but at the same time not let abortion politics eclipse equally pressing issues such as access to health care or racial disparities in health care delivery. We are beyond the point of merely claiming that the pro-choice movement must include the perspectives of women of color. For the reproductive rights and pro-choice movements to make a difference in the lives of all women, the voices of all women must be heard. Appeasing conservative forces will not do. Only comprehensive, inclusive, and action-oriented agendas will redirect the reproductive and sexual rights movement in a way that is relevant and compelling to the diversity of women who constitute America today.

The activists and the organizations discussed in this book have seeded a movement. They have provided it with new models for organizing, demonstrated ways to draw in broader constituencies and engage other social justice movements, and developed a holistic vision of reproductive justice which refuses to allow rights to be divided.

NOTES

1   Several of the early leaders like Byllye Avery, Katsi Cook, Charon Asetoyer, and Loretta Ross speak warmly of the nourishing role the NWHN played in their development.

2   Joshua Gamson, "Messages of Exclusion: Gender, Movements, and Symbolic Boundaries," *Gender & Society 11*, no. 2 (1997): 178–199.

3   NAWHO and APIRH, for example, paid particular attention to the needs of immigrant women and to the economically weaker Asian community members. The NBWHP and AAWE made special efforts to bring poor women to their events.

4   For example, there was little research on the high rates of infertility among African American women until the NBWHP highlighted this issue. NAWHO's path-breaking community-based studies of API health and sexuality broke stereotypes regarding Asian attitudes towards abortion and contraception.

5   Cherríe Moraga and Gloria Anzaldúa, *This Bridge Called My Back: Writings by Radical Women of Color* (New York: Kitchen Table Women of Color Press, 1983), xix.

6   Susan Stanford Friedman, "Beyond White and Other: Relationality and Narratives of Race in Feminist Discourse," *Signs: Journal of Women in Culture and Society* 21, no. 1 (1995): 1–41.

7   Women of Color Strategy Group, *Views From the Field: Women of Color and the Reproductive Health and Rights Movement* (Takoma Park, MD: Funders Network on Population, Reproductive Health and Rights, 2003), 6.

8   Ibid.

9   Ibid.

10   Burnham, Linda, "Reproductive Rights Not Just About Choice: SisterSong Report Back," *Sister to Sister 9*, no. 3 (Winter 2003).

11   Some argue that the rise in terrorism is related to population growth in poor countries. The theory goes that growing populations without access to sustainable livelihoods and secure futures turn to terrorism. Thus, the growth in population in third world countries represents a security threat to the US and the world. For a more detailed analysis of this trend, see Anne Hendrixson, "Superpredator Meets Teenage Mom: Exploding the Myth of the Out-of-Control Youth," in *Policing the National Body: Race, Gender, and Criminalization*, ed. Jael Silliman and Anannya Bhattacharjee (Cambridge, MA: South End Press, 2002), 231–258.

Bibliography

Abma, J., et al. "Fertility, Family Planning and Women's Health: New Data From the 1995 National Survey of Family Growth," *Vital and Health Statistics* 23 (1997).

Abramovitz, Mimi. *Regulating the Lives of Women: Social Welfare Policy From Colonial Times to the Present.* Boston: South End Press, 1996.

African American Women for Reproductive Freedom. *We Remember.* In *Our Bodies, Ourselves for the New Century*, edited by the Boston Women's Health Book Collective, 413–414. New York: Touchstone Press, 1998.

Almaguer, Tomas. *Racial Fault Lines: The Historical Origins of White Supremacy in California.* Berkeley: University of California Press, 1994.

Amaro, Hortensia. "Psychological Determinants of Abortion Attitudes Among Mexican American Women." PhD diss., University of California Los Angeles, 1982.

Amaro, Hortensia, and Adela de la Torre. "Public Health Needs and Scientific Opportunities in Research on Latinas." *American Journal of Public Health* 92, no. 4 (2002): 525–529.

Amott, Teresa and Julie Matthaei, eds. *Race, Gender and Work: A Multicultural Economic History of Women in the United States.* Rev. ed. Boston: South End Press, 1996.

Andrade, Sally J. "Social Science Stereotypes of Mexican American Women: Policy Implications for Research." *Hispanic Journal of Behavioral Sciences* 4, no. 2 (1982): 223–244.

APIRH. *The Health and Well-Being of Asian Pacific Islander Women.* Oakland, CA: APIRH, November 1995.

Appel, Linda, and Charon Asetoyer, eds. *Report on and Analysis of the Yankton Sioux Reservation Community Health Fairs*. Winter 1993–1994. Lake Andes, SD: NAWHERC, 1994.

Armstrong, Elizabeth M. "Diagnosing Moral Disorder: The Discovery and Evolution of Fetal Alcohol Syndrome." *Social Science Medicine* 47, no. 12 (1998): 2025–2042.

Avery, Byllye. "A Question of Survival/A Conspiracy of Silence: Abortion and Black Women's Health." In *From Abortion to Reproductive Freedom: Transforming a Movement*, edited by Marlene Gerber Fried, 75–81. Boston: South End Press, 1990.

———. "Who Does the Work of Public Health?" *American Journal of Public Health* 92, no. 4 (2002): 570–576.

Azize-Vargas, Yamila, and Luis A. Avilés. "Abortion in Puerto Rico: The Limits of a Colonial Legality." *Puerto Rico Health Sciences Journal* 17 (1998): 27–36

Baehr, Ninia. *Abortion Without Apology: A Radical History for the 1990s*. Boston: South End Press, 1990.

Baer, Judith A. *Historical and Multicultural Encyclopedia of Women's Reproductive Rights in the US*. Westport CT: Greenwood Press, 2002.

Baird-Windle, Patricia, and Eleanor J. Bader. *Targets of Hatred*. New York: Palgrave / St. Martin's Press, 2001.

Baker, Ann. "Pro-choice Activism Springs From Many Sources." In *From Abortion to Reproductive Freedom: Transforming a Movement*, edited by Marlene Gerber Fried, 179–186. Boston: South End Press, 1990.

Bandarage, Asoka. *Women, Population and Global Crisis: A Political-Economic Analysis*. London: Zed Books, 1997.

Baxandall, Rosalyn, Linda Gordon, and Susan Reverby, eds. *America's Working Women*. New York: Random House, 1976.

Beal, Frances. "Double Jeopardy: To Be Black and Female." In *Sisterhood Is Powerful: An Anthology of Writings From the Women's Liberation Movement*, edited by Robin Morgan. New York: Vintage Books, 1970.

———. "Women in Black Liberation." In *Sisterhood Is Powerful: An Anthology of Writings From the Women's Liberation Movement*, edited by Robin Morgan. New York: Vintage Books, 1970.

Bhattacharjee, Anannya "The Habit of Ex-nomination: Nation, Woman and the Indian Immigrant Bourgeoisie." In *A Patchwork Shawl: Chronicles of South Asian Women in America*, edited by Shamita Das Dasgupta. New Brunswick, NJ: Rutgers University Press, 1998.

———. "Private Fists and Public Force: Race, Gender and Surveillance." In *Policing the National Body: Race, Gender and Criminalization*, edited by Jael Silliman and Anannya Bhattacharjee, 1–54. Cambridge, MA: South End Press, 2002.

Bond, Toni. "Barriers Between Black Women and the Reproductive Rights Movement." *Political Environments* 8 (Winter–Spring 2001): 1–5.

Boyd, Leslie, and Charon Asetoyer. *Health Survey for the Yankton Sioux Reservation Community*. Lake Andes, SD: NAWHERC, 1993.

Briggs, Laura. *Reproducing Empire: Race, Sex, Science and US Imperialism in Puerto Rico*. Berkeley: University of California Press, 2002.

Cabán, Pedro A. *Constructing a Colonial People: Puerto Rico and the United States: 1898–1932*. Boulder, CO: Westview Press, 1999.

Cabezas, Dagmaris. "Manana Is Not Good Enough." *Nuestro* 1, no. 4 (1997): 19.

Cade, Toni. "The Pill: Genocide or Liberation?" In *The Black Woman: An Anthology*, edited by Toni Cade. New York: Mentor Books, 1970.

Carson, Rachel. *Silent Spring*. Boston: Houghton Mifflin, 1962.

Castañeda, Antonia. "Sexual Violence in the Politics and Policies of Conquest: Amerindian Women and the Spanish Conquest of Alta California." In *Building With Our Hands: New Directions in Chicana Studies*, edited by Adela de la Torre and Beatriz M. Pesquera. Berkeley: University of California Press, 1993.

Castle, Elizabeth A. "Black and Native American Women's Activism in the Black Panther Party and the American Indian Movement." PhD diss., University of Cambridge, 2000.

Center for Democratic Renewal. "Indian Issues and Anti-Indian Organizing." In *When Hate Groups Come to Town: A Handbook of Effective Community Responses*. Atlanta: CDR, 1992.

Centers for Disease Control. "Abortion Surveillance—US, 1996." *Morbidity and Mortality Weekly Report* 48, SS-4 (1999): 5.

Centers for Disease Control and Prevention. *Tracking the Hidden Epidemics: Trends in STDs in the US*. Atlanta: CDC, 1998.

Chamberlain, Pam, and Jean Hardisty. "Reproducing Patriarchy: Reproductive Rights Under Siege" In *Defending Reproductive Rights: An Activist Resource Kit*. Somerville, MA: Political Research Associates, 2000.

Chan, Sucheng. "The Exclusion of Chinese Women, 1870–1943." In *Entry Denied: Exclusion and the Chinese Community in America, 1882–1943*, edited by Sucheng Chang. Philadelphia: Temple University Press, 1991.

Chavez-Silverman, Susana. "Tropicolada: Inside the US Latino/a Gender B(l)ender." In *Tropicalizations: Transcultural Representations of Latinidad (Re-Encounters with Colonialism)*, edited by Frances R. Aparicio and Susana Chavez-Silverman. Hanover, NH: University Press of New England, 1997.

Cheatham, Ann, and Eveline Shen. "Community Based Participatory Research With Cambodian Girls in Long Beach, California: A Case Study." In *Community-Based Participatory Research for Health*, edited by Nina Wallerstein and Meredith Winkler. Somerset, NJ: Jossey Bass, 2002.

Chow, Esther Ngan-Ling. "The Feminist Movement: Where Are All the Asian American Women?" In *Making Waves: An Anthology By and About Asian American Women*, edited by Asian Women United of California. Boston: Beacon Press, 1989.

Churchill, Ward. *A Little Matter of Genocide: Holocaust and Denial in the Americas, 1492 to the Present*. San Francisco: City Lights Books, 1997.

Churchill, Ward, and Winona LaDuke. "Native North America: The Political Economy of Radioactive Colonialism." In *The State of Native America*, edited by M. Annette Jaimes, 241–266. Boston: South End Press, 1992.

Cisler, Lucinda. "Unfinished Business: Birth Control and Women's Liberation." In *Sisterhood Is Powerful: An Anthology of Writings From the Women's Liberation Movement*, edited by Robin Morgan. New York: Vintage Books, 1970.

Cofer, Judith Ortiz. "The Myth of the Latin Woman: I Just Met a Girl Named Maria." In *One World, Many Cultures*, edited by Stuart and Terry Hirschenberg. 4th ed. Boston: Allyn and Bacon, 1998.

Cohen, Jean. "Strategy or Identity." *Social Research* 52, no. 4 (1985): 663–716.

Combahee River Collective. "Combahee River Collective Statement." In *Home Girls: A Black Feminist Anthology*, edited by Barbara Smith. New York: Kitchen Table Press, 1983.

Cook, Katsi. "Into Our Hands." *Yes! A Journal of Positive Futures* 13 (Spring 2000): 17.

———. "Women Are the First Environment." *Native Americas*, Fall 1997.

Critchlow, Donald T. *Intended Consequences: Birth Control, Abortion, and the Federal Government in Modern America*. New York: Oxford University Press, 1999.

Daniels, Janean Aceveda. "Court Ordered Caesareans: A Growing Concern for Indigent Women." In *From Abortion to Reproductive Freedom: Transforming A Movement*, edited by Marlene Gerber Fried, 255–261. Boston: South End Press, 1990.

Dasgupta, Shamita Das. *A Patchwork Shawl: Chronicles of South Asian Women in America*. New Brunswick, NJ: Rutgers University Press, 1998.

Davis, Angela. *Women, Race, and Class*. New York: Vintage Books, 1983.

———. "Racism and Reproductive Rights." In *From Abortion to Reproductive Freedom: Transforming a Movement*, edited by Marlene Gerber Fried, 15–26. Boston: South End Press, 1990.

———. "Violence Against Women and the Ongoing Challenge to Racism." In *Freedom Organizing Series Pamphlet no. 5*. New York: Kitchen Table Women of Color Press, 1985.

Davis, Susan E., and the Committee for Abortion Rights and Against Sterilization Abuse (CARASA). *Women Under Attack: Victories, Backlash and the Fight for Reproduction Freedom*. Boston: South End Press, 1988.

De la Torre, Adela, et al. The Health Insurance Status of US Latino Women: A Profile From the 1982–1984 Hispanic HANES. *American Journal of Public Health* 86 (1996): 534–537.

Del Castillo, Adelaida R. "Sterilization: An Overview." In *Mexican Women in the United States: Struggles Past and Present*, edited by Magdalena Mora and Adelaida Del Castillo. Los Angeles: UCLA Chicano Studies Research Center Publications, 1980.

Delgado, Sylvia. "Chicana: The Forgotten Woman." *Regeneración* 2 (1971).

Derose, K. P., and D. W. Baker. "Limited English Proficiency and Latinos' Use of Physician Services." *Medical Care Research and Review* 57, no. 1 (2002): 76–91.

Dickson, Michele, and Charon Asetoyer. Radon in My Community: The Impact of Radon in the Yankton Sioux Communities. Lake Andes, SD: NAWHERC, 1992.

Dixon, Dázon. "Operation Oppress You: Women's Rights Under Siege." In *From Abortion to Reproductive Freedom: Transforming a Movement*, edited by Marlene Gerber Fried, 185–186. Boston: South End Press, 1990.

Dobbing, John, ed. *Infant Feeding: Anatomy of a Controversy: 1973–1984*. London: Springer-Verlag, 1988.

Easthope, Tracey, and Charon Asetoyer. *The Impact of AIDS in the Native American Community*. Lake Andes, SD: NAWHERC, 1998.

Ehrlich, Gillian, and Charon Asetoyer. *The Current Status of Indian Health Service's Reproductive Health Care, Report 1: A Focus Group Examining the Indian Health Service's Reproductive Health Care for Native American Women in the Aberdeen Area*. Lake Andes, SD: NAWHERC, 1999.

Erickson, Pamela, and Celia Patricia Kaplan. "Latinos and Abortion." In *The New Civil War: The Psychology, Culture, and Politics of Abortion*, edited by L.J. Beckman and S.M. Harvey. Washington DC: American Psychological Association, 1998.

Espino, Virginia. "Women Sterilized as You Give Birth: Forced Sterilization and Chicana Resistance in the 1970s." In *Las Obreras: Chicana Politics of Work and Family*, edited by Vicki Ruiz. Los Angeles: UCLA Chicano Studies Research Center Publications, 2000.

Feagin, Joe R. "Old Poison in New Bottles: The Deep Roots of Modern Nativism." In *Immigrants Out! The New Nativism and the Anti-immigrant Impulse in the United States*, edited by Juan F. Perea. New York: NYU Press, 1977.

Feiner, Susan F. *Race and Gender in the American Economy: Views Across the Spectrum*. Englewood Cliffs, NJ: Prentice Hall, 1994.

Ferber, Abby L. *White Men Falling: Race, Gender and White Supremacy*. New York: Rowman & Littlefield Publishers, 1998.

Flores, Candida, et al. "La Mujer Puertorriqueña, Su Cuerpo, y Su Lucha por la Vida: Experiences with Empowerment in Hartford,

Connecticut." In *From Abortion to Reproductive Freedom: Transforming a Movement*, edited by Marlene Gerber Fried, 221–231. Boston: South End Press, 1990.

Flores, Francisca "Conference of Mexican Women: Un Remolino." *Regeneración* 1 (1971).

Flores-Gonzalez, Nilda. "The Racialization of Latinos: The Meaning of Latino Identity for the Second Generation." *Latino Studies Journal* 10, no. 3 (1999): 3–31

Foo, Lora Jo. *Asian American Women: Issues, Concerns, and Responsive Human and Civil Rights Advocacy*. New York: Ford Foundation, 2002.

Frankfort, Ellen, with Frances Kissling. *Rosie: The Investigation of a Wrongful Death*. New York, Dial Press, 1979.

Franklin, John Hope, and Alfred A. Moss Jr. From Slavery to Freedom: A History of African Americans. 7th ed. New York: Knopf, 1994.

Friedman, Susan Stanford. "Beyond White and Other: Relationality and Narratives of Race in Feminist Discourse." *Signs: Journal of Women in Culture and Society* 21, no. 1 (1995): 1–41.

Gafori, Liza Haale, and Charon Asetoyer. *Revictimizing the Battered: An Investigation of the Charles Mix County Criminal Justice System's Management of Domestic Violence Cases*. Lake Andes, SD: NAWHERC, 1994.

Gaines, Kevin K. *Uplifting the Race: Black Leadership, Politics, and Culture in the Twentieth Century*. Chapel Hill: University of North Carolina Press, 1996.

Gamson, Joshua. "Messages of Exclusion: Gender, Movements, and Symbolic Boundaries." *Gender & Society* 11, no. 2 (1997): 178–199.

Garcia, Ana Maria. *La Operación*. Cinema Guild, VHS, 39 minutes, 1982.

Giachello, Aida L. "The Reproductive Years." In *Health Issues in the Latino Community*, edited by Marilyn Aquirre-Molina, Carlos W. Molina, and Ruth Zambrana. San Francisco: Jossey-Bass, 2001.

Giddings, Paula. *When and Where I Enter: The Impact of Black Women on Race and Sex in America*. New York: Harper Collins, 1984.

Gilbert, Heather, and Charon Asetoyer. *Recycling or Alleged Recycling? A Review of The Hydromex Waste Processing System*. Lake Andes, SD: NAWHERC, 1994.

Gladden Moreno, Dorinda. *Mujer en Pie de Lucha*. Mexico: Espina del Norte Publications, 1973.

Glasgow, Douglas G. *The Black Underclass: Poverty Employment and Entrapment of Ghetto Youth*. San Francisco: Jossey-Bass, 1980.

Gordon, Linda. *Woman's Body, Woman's Right: Birth Control in America*. Rev. ed. New York: Penguin Books, 1977.

Grewal, Shabnam, et al., eds. *Charting the Journey: Writings by Black and Third World Women*. London: Sheba Feminist Publishers, 1988.

Guha, Ramchandra. *Environmentalism: A Global History*. New York: Longman, 2000.

Gunn Allen, Paula. *Grandmothers of the Light: A Medicine Woman's Sourcebook*. Boston: Beacon Press, 1991.

———. *The Sacred Hoop: Recovering the Feminine in American Indian Traditions*. Boston: Beacon Press, 1986.

Gutierrez, David. *Walls and Mirrors: Mexican Americans, Mexican Immigrants, and the Politics of Ethnicity*. Los Angeles: University of California Press, 1995.

Gutiérrez, Elena. *Fertile Matters: The Racial Politics of Mexican Origin Women's Reproduction*. Austin: University of Texas Press, forthcoming.

———. "Policing 'Pregnant Pilgrims': Situating the Sterilization Abuse of Mexican-Origin Women in Los Angeles County." In *Women, Health, and Nation: Canada and the US Since 1945*, edited by Georgina Feldberg et al., 379–403. Montreal: McGill-Queen's University Press, 2003.

———. "The Racial Politics of Reproduction: The Social Construction of Mexican Origin Women's Fertility." PhD diss., University of Michigan, 1999.

Guy-Sheftall, Beverly, ed. *Words of Fire: An Anthology of African American Feminist Thought*. New York: New Press, 1995.

H., Pamela. "Asian American Lesbians: An Emerging Voice in the Asian American Community." In *Making Waves: An Anthology By and About Asian American Women*, edited by Asian Women United of California. Boston: Beacon Press, 1989.

Hader, Shannon L., et al. "HIV Infection in Women in the United States: Status at the Millennium." *Journal of the American Medical Association* 285 (2002): 1186–1192.

Hall, Ruth E. *Ask Any Woman: A London Inquiry Into Rape and Sexual Assault.* Bristol, England: Falling Wall Press, 1985.

Handler, et al. Women's Satisfaction With Prenatal Care Settings: A Focus Group Study. *Birth* 23, no. 1 (2001).

Hartmann, Betsy. *Reproductive Rights and Wrongs.* New York: Harper and Row, 1987.

Harvey, Neil, and Jeff Wessman. "An Interview with Katsi Cook." *Talking Leaves* 10, no. 1 (2000).

Hatcher, Robert, ed. *Contraceptive Technology: International Edition.* Atlanta: Printed Matter Inc., 1989.

Hayashi, Mary Chung. *Far From Home: Shattering the Myth of the Model Minority.* Irving, TX: Tapestry Press, 2003.

Hendrixson, Anne. "Superpredator Meets Teenage Mom: Exploding the Myth of the Out-of-Control Youth." In *Policing the National Body: Race, Gender and Criminalization,* edited by Jael Silliman and Anannya Bhattacharjee, 231–258. Cambridge, MA: South End Press, 2002.

Henshaw, Stanley, and K. Kost. "Abortion Patients in 1994–1995: Characteristics and Contraceptive Use of US Abortion Patients." *Family Planning Perspectives* 20, no. 4 (1998): 140–147

Hine, Darlene Clark, and Kathleen Thompson. *A Shining Thread of Hope: The History of Black Women in America.* New York: Broadway Books, 1998.

Holmes, Linda Janet. "Thank You Jesus to Myself: The Life of a Traditional Black Midwife." In *The Black Women's Health Book: Speaking for Ourselves,* edited by Evelyn C. White. Seattle: Seal Press, 1990.

Huntington, Samuel. *Who Are We? The Challenges to America's National Identity.* New York: Simon & Schuster, 2004.

Institute of Women and Ethnic Studies. *Reproductive Health Bill of Rights.* 2nd ed. New Orleans: Women of Color and the Emerging Reproductive Health Technologies Project, IWES, 2000.

Jaimes, M. Annette. "Federal Indian Identification Policy: A Usurpation of Indigenous Sovereignty in North America." In *The State of Native America,* edited by M. Annette Jaimes. Boston: South End Press, 1992.

Jaimes, M. Annette, with Theresa Halsey. "American Indian Women." In *The State of Native America*, edited by M. Annette Jaimes, 331–344. Boston: South End Press, 1992.

Jennings, Jennifer, and Charon Asetoyer. *The Impact of AIDS in the Native American Community*. Rev. ed. Lake Andes, SD: NAWHERC, 1996.

Joyner, Brenda. "Fighting Back to Save Women's Lives." In *From Abortion to Reproductive Freedom: Transforming a Movement*, edited by Marlene Gerber Fried, 205–211. Boston: South End Press, 1990.

Juarez, Ana Maria, and Stella Beatriz Kerl, "What Is the Right (White) Way to Sexual? Reconceptualizing Latina Sexuality." *Aztlán* 2, no. 1 (2003): 7–37.

Keemer, Edgar. *Confessions of a Pro-Life Abortionist*. Detroit: Vinco Press, 1980.

King, Lourdes Mirandas. "Puertorriquenas in the United States: The Impact of Double Discrimination." *Civil Rights Digest* 6, no. 3 (1974): 20–35.

Kolbert, Kathryn, and Andrea Miller. "Legal Strategies for Abortion Rights in the Twenty-First Century." In *Abortion Wars: A Half Century of Struggle, 1950–2000*, edited by Rickie Solinger. Berkeley: University of California Press, 1998.

Krishnan, Satya P., and Malahat Baig-Amin. "Lifting the Veil of Secrecy." In *A Patchwork Shawl: Chronicles of South Asian Women in America*, edited by Shamita Das Dasgupta. New Brunswick, NJ: Rutgers University Press, 1998.

LaDuke, Winona. *All Our Relations: Native Struggles for Land and Life*. Boston: South End Press, 1999.

Lawrence, Jane. "The Indian Health Service and the Sterilization of Native American Women." *American Indian Quarterly* 24, no. 3 (2000): 400–419.

Leonard, Karen Isaksen. *Making Ethnic Choices: California's Punjabi Mexican Americans*. Philadelphia: Temple University Press, 1992.

Lerner, Gerda. *Black Women in White America*. New York: Vintage Books, 1972.

Lewry, Natasha, and Charon Asetoyer. *The Impact of Norplant in the Native American Community*. Lake Andes, SD: NAWHERC, 1992.

Lim, Susie, and Charon Asetoyer. *A Study of the Herbicide and Pesticide Use Within the Lake Andes Watershed On The Yankton Sioux Reservation*. Lake Andes, SD: NAWHERC, 1996.

Lindstrom, Sia, and Charon Asetoyer. *A Report on Southern Missouri Waste Management Association's Proposed Landfill Project in the Lake Andes Area, South Dakota*. Lake Andes, SD: NAWHERC, 1993.

Ling, Huping. *Surviving on the Gold Mountain: A History of Chinese American Women and Their Lives*. New York: State University of New York Press, 1998.

Littlecrow-Russel, Sara. "Depo-Provera and Norplant Usage by the Indian Health Services Monitoring Present Day Practices in the Wake of Historic Abuses and Past Litigation." *Aboriginal Woman* (forthcoming).

Littlewood, Thomas B. *The Politics of Population Control*. Notre Dame, IN: University of Notre Dame Press, 1977.

Lopez, Iris. "An Ethnography of the Medicalization of Puerto Rican Women's Reproduction." In *Pragmatic Women and Body Politics*, edited by Margaret Lock and Patricia A. Kaufert, 240–259. New York: Cambridge Studies in Medical Anthropology, 1997.

Lott, Juanita Tamayo. "Growing Up, 1968–1985." In *Making Waves: An Anthology of Writings by and About Asian American Women*, edited by Asian Women United of California. Boston: Beacon Press, 1989.

Lyndsley, Syd. "The Gendered Assault on Immigrants." In *Policing the National Body: Race, Gender and Criminalization*, edited by Jael Silliman and Anannya Bhattacharjee, 175–196. Boston: South End Press, 2002.

Mankiller, Wilma, and Micheal Wallis. *Mankiller: A Chief and Her People*. New York: St. Martin's Press, 1993.

Marks Jarvis, Gail. "The Fate of the Indian." *National Catholic Reporter*, 1977.

Martinez, Elizabeth Sutherland. *De Colores Means All of Us: Latina Views for a Multi-colored Century*. Cambridge, MA: South End Press, 1998.

Mass, Bonnie. "Puerto Rico: A Case Study of Population Control." *Latin American Perspectives* 5, no. 4 (1977): 66–81.

Mazumdar, Sucheta. "General Introduction: A Woman-Centered Perspective on Asian American History." In *Making Waves: An Anthology of Writings by and About Asian American Women*, edited by Asian Women United of California, 1–3. Boston: Beacon Press, 1989.

McKeegan, Michele. *Abortion Politics: Mutiny in the Ranks of the Right.* New York: Free Press, 1992.

Meléndez, Edwin, and Edgardo Meléndez. *Colonial Dilemma: Critical Perspectives on Contemporary Puerto Rico.* Boston: South End Press, 1993.

Metcalf, Ann. "Old Woes, Old Ways, New Dawn: Native American Women's Health Issues." In *Women's Health: Complexities and Differences,* edited by Sheryl Burt Ruzek et al. Columbus: Ohio State University Press, 1997.

Molina, Natalia. "Illustrating Cultural Authority: Medicalized Representations of Mexican Communities in Early-Twentieth-Century Los Angeles." *Aztlán* 28, no.1 (2003): 129–143.

Moore, Patricia A. "Indian Woman's Sterilization Suit Starts." *National Catholic Reporter,* January 19, 1979.

Moraga, Cherríe, and Gloria Anzaldúa, eds. *This Bridge Called My Back: Writings by Radical Women of Color.* New York: Kitchen Table Women of Color Press, 1983.

Morales, Aurora Levins. "Piecing a History Together: The Women of Boriken." *Women's Review of Books 9,* nos. 10–11 (1992).

Morgen, Sandra. *Into Our Own Hands: The Women's Health Movement in the US 1969–1990.* New Brunswick, NJ: Rutgers University Press, 2002.

Mullings, Leith. "Images, Ideology, and Women of Color." In *Women of Color in US Society,* edited by Maxine Baca Zinn and Bonnie Thornton Dill, 265–289. Philadelphia: Temple University Press, 1994.

Napoles-Springer, A., and E. Perez-Stable. "Risk Factors for Invasive Cervical Cancer for Latino Women." *Journal for Medical Systems* 20, no.5 (1996): 277–294.

NLIRH. *Latinas and Abortion.* Washington DC: NLIRH, 1999.

NAWHERC. *Dakota Roundtable: A Report on the Status of Native American Youth in the Aberdeen Area.* Lake Andes, SD: NAWHERC, 1993.

———. *Dakota Roundtable II: A Report on the Status of Native American Women in the Aberdeen Area.* Lake Andes, SD: NAWHERC, 1994.

———. *Wicozanni Wowapi* (Good Health Newsletter). 1995–2000.

————. *Dakota Roundtable III: A Report on the Status of Young Native American Women in the Aberdeen Area.* Lake Andes, SD: NAWHERC, 1996.

————. *Moving Forward the Native Women's Reproductive Rights Agenda.* SisterSong Native Women's Reproductive Health and Rights Roundtable. Lake Andes, SD: NAWHERC, 2001.

————. *Indigenous Women's Reproductive Rights: The Indian Health Service and Its Inconsistent Applications of the Hyde Amendment.* Lake Andes, SD: NAWHERC, October 2002.

NAWHO. *Emerging Communities: A Health Needs Assessment of South Asian Women in Three California Counties.* San Francisco: NAWHO, January 1996.

————. *National Plan of Action on Asian American Women and Breast Cancer.*" San Francisco: NAWHO, 1997.

————. *Learning from Communities: A Guide to Addressing the Reproductive Health Needs of Vietnamese American Women.* San Francisco: NAWHO, April 1998.

————. *The Asian American Men's Health Survey: Sharing Responsibility.* San Francisco: NAWHO, October 1999.

————. *Breaking the Silence: A Study of Depression Among Asian American Women.* San Francisco: NAWHO, 2000.

————. *Global Perspectives: A Report on International Asian American Women's Reproductive Health.* San Francisco: NAWHO, 2001.

Nelson, Jennifer. *Women of Color and the Reproductive Rights Movement.* New York: NYU Press, 2003.

————. "Abortions Under Community Control: Feminism, Nationalism, and the Politics of Reproduction Among New York City's Young Lords." *Journal of Women's History* 13, no. 1 (2001): 157–180.

Nowrojee, Sia, and Jael Silliman. "Asian Women's Health: Organizing a Movement." In *Dragon Ladies: Asian American Feminists Breathe Fire,* edited by Sonia Shah, 73–89. Boston: South End Press, 1997.

Oboler, Suzanne. *Ethnic Labels, Latino Lives: Identity and the Politics of Representation in the US.* Minneapolis: University of Minnesota Press, 1995.

Olivarez, Elizabeth. "Women's Rights and the Mexican American Woman." *Regeneración* 2, no.4 (1974): 40–42.

Omolade, Barbara. *The Rising Song of African American Women.* New York: Routledge, 1994.

O'Neil, J.D. "The Politics of Health in the Fourth World: A Northern Canadian Example." *Human Organization* 45, no.2 (1986):119–128.

Paltrow, Lynn. "Policing Pregnancy." *Tompaine.com*, April 24, 2004. http://www.tompaine.com.

———. "Pregnant Drug Users, Fetal Persons, and the Threat to *Roe v. Wade.*" *Albany Law Review* 62 (1999): 1000.

Pardo, Mary. "Creating Community: Mexican American Women in Eastside Los Angeles." In *Community Activism and Feminist Politics: Organizing Across Race, Class, and Gender*, edited by Nancy A. Naples, 266–300. New York: Routledge, 1998.

Park, Lisa Sun-Hee. "Navigating the Anti-immigrant Wave: The Korean Women's Hotline and the Politics of Community." In *Community Activism and Feminist Politics: Organizing Across Race, Class, and Gender*, edited by Nancy A. Naples. New York: Routledge, 1998.

Pascoe, Peggy. "Miscegenation Law, Court Cases, and Ideologies of Race in Twentieth Century America." In *Unequal Sisters, A Multicultural Reader in US Women's History*, edited by Vicki L. Ruis and Ellen Carol Dubois. New York: Routledge, 2000.

Pesquera, Beatriz, and Denise Segura. "'It's Her Body, It's Definitely Her Right': Chicanas/Latinas and Abortion." *Voces: A Journal of Latina Studies* 2, no. 1:103–127.

Petchesky, Rosalind. *Abortion and Woman's Choice: The State, Sexuality and Reproductive Freedom*. Boston: Northeastern University Press, 1990.

Pollitt, Katha. "Fetal Rights." In *"Bad" Mothers: The Politics of Blame in Twentieth-Century America*, edited by Molly Ladd-Taylor and Lauri Umansky. New York: NYU Press, 1998.

Riddell, Adaljiza Sosa. "The Bioethics of Reproductive Technologies: Impacts and Implications for Latinas." In *Chicana Critical Issues*, edited by Norma Alarcon. Berkeley: Third Woman Press, 1993.

———. "Chicanas and El Movimiento." In *Chicana Feminist Thought: The Basic Historical Writings*, edited by Alma M. Garcia. New York: Routledge, 1997.

Riddle, John M. *Eve's Herbs: A History of Contraception and Abortion in the West*. Cambridge, MA: Harvard University Press, 1997.

Risen, James, and Judy L. Thomas. *Wrath of Angels: The American Abortion War*. New York: Basic Books, 1998.

Robbins, Rebecca L. "Self Determination and Subordination." In *The State of Native America*, edited by M. Annette Jaimes, 87–121. Boston: South End Press, 1992.

Roberts, Dorothy. *Killing the Black Body*. New York: Pantheon Books, 1997.

———. "Punishing Drug Addicts With Babies." In *Abortion Wars: A Half Century of Struggle, 1950–2000*, edited by Rickie Solinger. Berkeley: University of California Press, 1998.

Rodríguez-Trías, Helen. "Women Are Organizing: Environmental and Population Policies Will Never Be the Same" (1993 presidential address to the American Public Health Association) *American Journal of Public Health* 84, no. 9 (1994): 1379–1382.

Ross, Loretta. "African American Women and Abortion: A Neglected History." *Journal of Health Care for the Poor and Underserved* 3, no. 2 (1992).

———. "African American Women and Abortion." In *Abortion Wars: A Half Century of Struggle, 1950–2000*, edited by Rickie Solinger. Berkeley: University of California Press, 1998.

———. "Blacks and Fertility." *Point of View: Magazine of the Congressional Black Caucus*, Winter 1988.

Ross, Loretta, et al. "The SisterSong Collective: Women of Color, Reproductive Health and Human Rights." In "Health of Women of Color," special issue, *American Journal of Health* 17 (2001): 85–100

———. "Just Choices: Women of Color, Reproductive Health, and Human Rights." In *Policing the National Body: Race, Gender and Criminalization*, edited by Jael Silliman and Anannya Bhattacharjee, 147–174. Boston: South End Press, 2002.

Ross, Loretta, Sherrilyn Ifill, and Sabrae Jenkins. "Emergency Memorandum to Women of Color." In *From Abortion to Reproductive Freedom: Transforming a Movement*, edited by Marlene Gerber Fried, 147–150. Boston: South End Press, 1990.

Roth, Rachel. *Making Women Pay: The Hidden Costs of Fetal Rights*. Ithaca, NY: Cornell University Press, 2000.

Roubideaux, Yvette. "Perspectives on American Indian Health." *American Journal of Public Health* 92, no. 9 (2002): 1401–1403.

Rubin, Lillian. *Families on the Fault Line: America's Working Class Speaks About the Family, the Economy, Race, and Ethnicity*. New York: Harper Collins, 1994.

Ruiz, Vicki L. "La Nueva Chicana: Women and the Movement." In *From Out of the Shadows: Mexican Women in Twentieth-Century America*, edited by Vicki L. Ruiz, 99–126. New York: Oxford University Press, 1998.

Saletan, William. "Electoral Politics and Abortion: Narrowing the Message." In *Abortion Wars: A Half Century of Struggle, 1950–2000*, edited by Rickie Solinger. Berkeley: University of California Press, 1998.

———. *Bearing Right: How Conservatives Won the Abortion War.* Berkeley: University of California Press, 2003.

Salvo, Joseph J., Mary G. Powers, and Rosemary Santana Cooney. "Contraceptive Use and Sterilization Among Puerto Rican Women." *Family Planning Perspectives* 24, no. 5 (1992): 219–223.

Sanchez Jr., George J. "'Go After the Women': Americanization and the Mexican Immigrant Woman, 1915–1929." In *Unequal Sisters: A Multicultural Reader in US Women's History*, edited by Ellen Carol Dubois and Vicki L. Ruiz. New York: Routledge, 1990.

Sandoval, Chela. *Methodology of the Oppressed.* Minneapolis: University of Minnesota Press, 2000.

Schroedel, Jean Reith. *Is the Fetus a Person? A Comparison of Policies Across the Fifty States.* Ithaca, NY: Cornell University Press, 2000.

Scrimshaw, Susan C.M., Ruth E. Zambrana, and Christine Dunkel-Schetter. "Issues in Latino Women's Health: Myths and Challenges." In *Women's Health: Complexities and Differences*, edited by Sheryl Burt Ruzek et al., 329–347. Columbus: Ohio State University Press, 1997.

Scully, Judith A.M. "Killing the Black Community: A Commentary on the United States War on Drugs." In *Policing the National Body: Race, Gender and Criminalization*, edited by Jael Silliman and Anannya Bhattacharjee, 55–80. Cambridge, MA: South End Press, 2002.

Seaman, Barbara. *The Doctor's Case Against the Pill.* Alameda, CA: Hunter House, 1969.

———. *Free and Female.* New York: Coward, McCann & Geoghegan, 1972.

———. *Women and the Crisis in Sex Hormones.* New York: Rawson Associates, 1977.

Segura, Denise A., and Beatriz M. Pesquera. "Beyond Indifference and Antipathy: The Chicana Movement and Chicana Feminist Discourse." In *The Chicano Studies Reader: An Anthology of Aztlán, 1970–2000,* edited by Chon A. Noriega et al, 389–410. Los Angeles: UCLA Chicano Studies Research Center, 2001.

Shah, Sonia. "Three Hot Meals and a Full Day at Work: South Asian Women's Labor in the United States." In *A Patchwork Shawl: Chronicles of South Asian Women in America,* edited by Shamita Das Dasgupta. New Brunswick, NJ: Rutgers University Press, 1998.

———. ed. *Dragon Ladies: Asian American Feminists Breathe Fire.* Boston: South End Press, 1997.

Simpson, Leanne. "Listening to Our Ancestors: Rebuilding Aboriginal Nations in the Face of Environmental Destruction." Snowchange. org. http://www.snowchange.org/views/indigenous/leanne_list_en.html (accessed November 25, 2002).

SisterSong Women of Color Reproductive Health Collective. *A Reproductive Health Agenda for Women of Color.* NY: Casa Atabex Ache, 2001.

Sklar, Holly. *Chaos or Community: Seeking Solutions, Not Scapegoats for Bad Economics.* Boston: South End Press, 1995.

Smeal, Eleanor. *Why and How Women Will Elect the Next President.* New York: Harper and Row, 1984.

Smith, Andrea. "Sexual Violence and American Indian Genocide." *Journal of Religion and Abuse* 1, no. 2 (1999): 31–52.

———. "Better Dead Than Pregnant: The Colonization of Native Women's Reproductive Health." In *Policing the National Body: Race, Gender and Criminalization,* edited by Jael Silliman and Anannya Bhattacharjee, 123–146. Cambridge, MA: South End Press, 2002.

Solinger, Rickie *The Abortionist: A Woman Against the Law.* New York: Free Press, 1994.

———. *Beggars and Choosers: How the Politics of Choice Shapes Adoption, Abortion, and Welfare in the United States.* New York: Hill and Wang, 2001.

———. "Poisonous Choice." In *"Bad" Mothers: The Politics of Blame in Twentieth-Century America,* edited by Molly Ladd-Taylor and Lauri Umansky. New York: NYU Press, 1998.

———. *Wake Up Little Susie: Single Pregnancy and Race Before Roe v. Wade.* New York: Routledge, 1992.

Staggenborg, Suzanne. *The Pro-choice Movement: Organization and Activism in the Abortion Conflict.* New York: Oxford University Press, 1991.

Stannard, David. *American Holocaust.* Oxford: Oxford University Press, 1992.

Stiffman, Lenore A., and Phil Lane Jr. "The Demography of Native North American: A Question of American Indian Survival." In *The State of Native America,* edited by M. Annette Jaimes, 23–53. Boston: South End Press, 1992.

Tan, Cheng Imm. "Searching for the Ox: The Spiritual Journey of an Asian American Feminist Activist." In *Dragon Ladies: Asian American Feminists Breathe Fire,* edited by Sonia Shah, 200–215. Boston: South End Press, 1997.

Tillmon, Johnnie. "Welfare Is a Woman's Issue." In *America's Working Women,* edited by Rosalyn Baxandall, Linda Gordon and Susan Reverby. New York: Random House, 1976. (Originally published in *Liberation News Service,* February 26, 1972.)

Torpy, Sally. "Endangered Species: Native American Women's Struggle for Their Reproductive Rights and Racial Identity 1970–1990." Master's thesis, University of Nebraska, 1998.

Vaid, Jyotsna. "Seeking a Voice: South Asian Women's Groups in North America." In *Making Waves: An Anthology of Writings by and About Asian American Women,* edited by Asian Women United of California. Boston: Beacon Press, 1989.

Vargas, Roberto, and Samuel Martinez. *Razalogia: Community Learning for a New Society.* Oakland, CA: Razagente Associates, 1985.

Vaz, Kim Marie, ed. *Black Women in America.* Thousand Oaks, CA: SAGE Publications, 1995.

Velez-Ibañez, Carlos G. "Se Me Acabó La Canción: An Ethnography of Non-consenting Sterilizations Among Mexican Women in Los Angeles." In *Mexican Women in the US: Struggles Past and Present,* edited by Magdalena Mora and Adelaida Del Castillo, 71–91. Los Angeles: UCLA Chicano Studies Research Center, UCLA, 1980.

Vernon, Irene S. "Violence, HIV/AIDS, and Native American Women in the Twenty-First Century." *American Indian Culture and Research Journal* 26, no. 2 (2002): 115–133.

Villarosa, Linda. *The Black Women's Guide to Physical Health and Emotional Well-Being.* New York: Harper Collins, 1994.

Walters, Karina L., and Jane M. Simoni. "Reconceptualizing Native Women's Health: An 'Indigenist' Stress-Coping Model." *American Journal of Public Health* 92, no. 4 (2002): 520–524.

Walters, Karina L., Jane M. Simoni and Curtis Harris. Patterns and Predictors of HIV Risk among Urban American Indians. *American Indian and Alaska Native Mental Health Research: The Journal of the National Center* 9, no. 2 (2000): 1–21.

Wandersee, Winifred D. *American Women in the 1970s: On the Move.* Boston: Twayne Publishers, 1988.

Ward, Martha C. *Poor Women, Powerful Men: America's Great Experiment in Family Planning.* Boulder, CO: Westview Press, 1986.

Watson, Lilla. "Black Is the Colour of My Soul." In *Different Lives: Reflections on the Women's Movement and Visions of Its Future,* edited by Jocelynne A. Scutt. Victoria, Australia: Penguin Books, 1987.

Wattleton, Faye. *Life on the Line.* New York: Ballantine Books, 1996.

White, Deborah Gray. *Ar'nt I a Woman? Female Slaves in the Plantation South.* New York: W.W. Norton, 1985.

———. *Too Heavy a Load: Black Women in Defense of Themselves, 1894–1994.* New York, W.W. Norton, 1999.

White, Evelyn C. *The Black Women's Health Book: Speaking for Ourselves.* Rev. ed. Seattle: Seal Press, 1994.

Wies, Jennifer, and Charon Asteoyer. *Wakanhejah (They Too Are Sacred): Federal Funding, the Current Education State and Achieving Academic Excellence for All Children in Lake Andes.* Lake Andes, SD: NAWHERC, 2000.

Wilder, Marcy J. "Law, Violence and Morality." In *Abortion Wars: A Half Century of Struggle 1950–2000,* edited by Rickie Solinger. Berkeley: University of California Press, 1998.

Wing, Adrien Katherine, ed. *Global Critical Race Feminism: An International Reader.* New York: NYU Press, 2000.

Witt, Shirley Hill. "Native Women Today: Sexism and the Indian Woman." *Civil Rights Digest* 6 (Spring 1974): 29.

Women and Pharmaceuticals Project, Women's Health Action Foundation, and WEMOS. *Norplant: Under Her Skin.* Delft, The Netherlands: Eburon Press, 1993.

Yu, Connie Yung. "The World of Our Grandmothers." In *Making Waves: An Anthology of Writings by and About Asian American Women,* edited by Asian Women United of California. Boston: Beacon Press, 1989.

INDEX

About the Authors

 **Marlene Gerber Fried** (PhD, Brown) is known nationally and internationally as a writer, lecturer, and advocate for reproductive justice. She was founding president of the National Network of Abortion Funds, served on the board of the Women's Global Network for Reproductive Rights, and was Interim President of Hampshire College in 2010–2011. She is currently Faculty Director of CLPP (Civil Liberties and Public Policy Program). She edited *From Abortion to Reproductive Freedom: Transforming a Movement* and is a co-author of *Undivided Rights: Women of Color Organize for Reproductive Justice*. She received the first Marlene Gerber Fried Abortion Access Vanguard Award (NNAF, 2015), the Felicia Stewart Advocacy Award (APHA, 2014), and a Warrior Woman Award from SisterSong (2014).

 **Elena R. Gutiérrez** is an associate professor of Gender and Women's Studies and Latin American and Latino Studies at the University of Illinois–Chicago. She is author of *Fertile Matters: The Politics of Mexican-Origin Women's Reproduction* and curator of the Reproductive Justice Virtual Library. She is committed to reproductive justice advocacy and documenting the activism of women of color.

 **Jael Silliman** was a tenured associate professor of Women Studies at the University of Iowa from 1996 to 2002, where she worked on issues of race, reproductive rights and health, and gender and the environment in the United States and South Asia. She has published widely on these issues. Jael served as Program Officer for Reproductive Rights and Women's Rights at the Ford Foundation in New York (2003–2009). She has been an activist in the transnational women's

movement for four decades and served on the boards of many women's organizations. She is currently an independent scholar and writer documenting her community, the Bagdadi Jews of Calcutta, and has curated http://www.jewishcalcutta.in.

 **Loretta J. Ross** was the National Coordinator of the SisterSong Women of Color Reproductive Justice Collective from 2005 to 2012. She has appeared on CNN, BET, *Lead Story*, *Good Morning America*, *The Donahue Show*, the National Geographic Channel, and *Charlie Rose*. She has been interviewed in the *New York Times*, *Time*, the *Los Angeles Times*, and the *Washington Post*, among others. She helped create the theory of reproductive justice in 1994 and led a rape crisis center in the 1970s. She co-authored *Undivided Rights: Women of Color Organize for Reproductive Justice* in 2004.

About Haymarket Books

Haymarket Books is a nonprofit, progressive book distributor and publisher, a project of the Center for Economic Research and Social Change. We believe that activists need to take ideas, history, and politics into the many struggles for social justice today. Learning the lessons of past victories, as well as defeats, can arm a new generation of fighters for a better world. As Karl Marx said, "The philosophers have merely interpreted the world; the point, however, is to change it."

We take inspiration and courage from our namesakes, the Haymarket Martyrs, who gave their lives fighting for a better world. Their 1886 struggle for the eight-hour day reminds workers around the world that ordinary people can organize and struggle for their own liberation.

For more information and to shop our complete catalog of titles, visit us online at www.haymarketbooks.org.

Also Available from Haymarket Books